Mickey Mouse History and Other Essays on American Memory

In the series

Critical Perspectives on the Past

edited by Susan Porter Benson, Stephen Brier, and Roy Rosenzweig

Mike Wallace

Mickey Mouse History and Other Essays on American Memory

Temple University Press
Philadelphia

Temple University Press, Philadelphia 19122

Published 1996
Printed in the United States of America

♾ The paper used in this publication meets the requirements of the American National Standard for Information Sciences—Permanence of Paper for Printed Library Materials, ANSI Z39.48-1984

Text design by Anne O'Donnell

Library of Congress Cataloging-in-Publication Data

Wallace, Mike, 1942–
Mickey Mouse history and other essays on American memory / Mike Wallace.
p. cm.—(Critical perspectives on the past series)
Includes bibliographical references.
ISBN 1-56639-444-9 (cloth : alk. paper).—ISBN 1-56639-445-7 (pbk. : alk. paper)
1. Historical museums—United States. 2. Historic sites—Interpretive programs—United States. 3. Historical preservation—United States I. Title.
E172.W35 1996
973'.075—dc20 96-3555

Contents

Contents

Section III

Section IV

Introduction

Battlefields of Memory

Memory Unearthed: The milk can, discovered on December 1, 1950, beneath Nowolipki Street in Warsaw, contained documentation of life and death in the wartime Jewish ghetto. It was gathered secretly by the *Oneg Shabbos* (Joy of the Sabbath) group of historians led by Dr. Emmanuel Ringelblum. (Courtesy of the United States Holocaust Memorial Museum.)

In the early 1990s, Serbian troops besieging cities in Croatia and Bosnia-Herzegovina set their artillery to blowing up museums, monuments, libraries, archives, mosques, and churches. At times the occupying forces dynamited what remained of such structures, then bulldozed the rubble. Not content to evict or eradicate their enemies, Serbian hyper-nationalists scoured away evidence of long-standing Croat or Muslim occupation of coveted territories—an effort at historic cleansing.

Fifty years earlier, when the Nazis had also tried to erase a people and their past, a group of guerilla scholars managed to save memories, if not lives. In the doomed Warsaw Ghetto, historian Emmanuel Ringelblum led an underground effort to document life in the Jewish quarter. Several dozen writers, teachers, rabbis, and historians maintained a chronicle, recorded deportations, commissioned papers (one on the effects of starvation), and collected posters, decrees, and copies of underground newspapers. On the eve of destruction they placed this archive in milk cans and metal boxes and buried them deep beneath the city streets. In a posthumous triumph for these historians, one milk can was unearthed in 1946 and another surfaced in 1950; the exhumed work went on to inform the vast enterprise of Holocaust commemoration that blossomed in Israel, the United States and Germany itself.

These two instances—the first a ferocious attempt to eradicate memory, the second an implacable determination to preserve it—are extreme examples of the interplay between power and memory, one of the major themes in this volume. Yet they are so extreme they might seem extraneous to a book that explores the place of history in contemporary American culture and politics. Fervent arguments over collective memory puzzle most Americans, who find it hard to get passionate about the past, to take it so *seriously*.

The past is not our favorite tense. It seems dead and done with. History is a repository of names and dates school children memorize, regurgitate, and forget. Or it is a listing of prior achievements that, like those in the *Guinness Book of Records*, are certain to be soon surpassed. To cuttingly dismiss someone, we say: "He's history."

We prefer the present. We want to "be here now." Or to focus on the future, and make today "the first day of the rest of our lives."

Ironically, the ahistorical strain that runs through our culture is deeply rooted in our history and economy. Our Revolutionary forebears believed they had broken free both of England and the past's dead hand. Shattering tradition's chains became the young nation's go-ahead mantra. In succeeding centuries, millions of immigrants shed their pasts and moved to America, land of the future. Capitalist entrepreneurs repeatedly dismantled customary constraints on profitable investment, demolishing the old to make way for the new. Few Americans, even the elite, had a stake in the past; where European aristocrats justified their position through pedigree, U.S. millionaires proclaimed their self-made status.

This impatience with the past had its attractive qualities. It fostered innovation (U.S. economist Joseph Schumpeter hailed capitalism's capacity for "creative destruction"). It gave Americans an exhilarating feeling of freedom, a sense they were exempt from the crushing weight of history under which places like the Balkans seemed buried. Yet ultimately this feeling was and is illusory. It is not, in fact, possible to step outside of time. A culture that generates such fantasies might fairly be called "historicidal," not for murdering some objective body of history, but for promoting an ahistorical temper, for obscuring the ways the past continues to shape the present, and for leaving us marooned in the now, adrift on the temporal surface of things.

Yet ahistoricism is only one way Americans relate to the past. It is a powerful tendency, but by no means all-embracing or determinative. Many people are deeply interested in specific histories—their own biographies (and the story of their generation), the lives of family forebears, the lore of their local communities, particular chapters from the national saga (notably the Civil War).

Attitudes toward the past vary from place to place. Residents of some regions have strong historical sensibilities, closely attuned to vernacular traditions. I have met Massachusetts farmers who trace their forebears back two centuries and for whom rebel Daniel Shays remains a living presence. The past is equally alive in the South, where the Lost Cause, or the legacy of slavery, continues to burden or inflame the citizenry. Nor did all immigrants check their pasts at the nation's door. Many wanted to build improved versions of their former habitats (an endeavor nicely captured in place names like New York, New Amsterdam, New Orleans, and New Berlin), and numerous ethnic communities nourish Old Country memories to this day.

Attitudes also varied from time to time. Scholars like Michael Kammen have analyzed the historicity of historical consciousness, watching the relative strength of tradition and futurism shift from era to era (colonial revival uppermost in the 1890s, art deco modernism ascendant in the 1920s). Almost always, however, there were some Americans who envisioned history as an inexorable wave, of which they were the breaking edge. Their wave's trajectory and certain triumph were predestined by God, by Manifest Destiny, by the invisible hands of the Market, by implacable social forces such as "modernization," or by the iron laws of something called History. Such philosophies gave believers a potent sense of righteousness and inevitability: History was on *their* side.

And what of our era? How stands the balance between memory and forgetting? Arguably, we have been on a heritage binge and remain thoroughly obsessed with the past. We have preserved and restored old urban centers and historic landscapes. We have constructed vast numbers of museums (and halls of fame) that explore an astonishing range of subjects and localities. Retrofashion in clothing is big; so is golden oldyism in music (recycled rock bands, revived Broadway musicals); and postmodern architects assiduously deploy historic flourishes. Family reunions are popular. Genealogical investigations are booming—some spilling over into the parapsychological, with new age channelers offering contact with forebears or former incarnations. Monuments and memorials have made a comeback. Civil War battle reenactors take on the identities of particular soldiers, falling where they fell, reproducing their wounds when possible. Americans crowd into historic sites, collect antiques, consume historical novels, take in costume epics and movies about time travel, and devour innumerable docudramas and documentaries on television.

Much of this interest, to be sure, is quite compatible with an ahistorical bent. These various pasts may be interesting places to visit and explore, they may be sources of artistic inspiration or cool commodities, but they are often imagined as unproblematic givens—an inert bundle of things that happened, dead events. These pasts remain segregated from the present. We rummage around in them for pleasure or profit, we appropriate them, we consume them, but we do not think it crucial to understand them in order to understand ourselves. We do not focus on the ligaments connecting then and now, nor acknowledge the past's ongoing constitutive power in the present.

Not all our absorption with days gone by can be characterized in this fashion, however. Hot heritage skirmishes have broken out all along the history front that has opened up since the country's culture war erupted.

Some conflicts over collective memory have been fought in the educational arena. Recent firefights include disputes over grade school curricula, polemics over university canon, faceoffs between creationists and evolutionists, censorship of CD's treating gay history, attacks on the *National Standards for United States History*, and efforts to dismantle the National Endowment for the Humanities. But much of the combat has taken place outside academia, on the terrain now known as Public History.

Museum exhibitions have aroused stormy reactions, notably *The West as America* show in 1991 at the National Museum of American Art; and the National Air and Space Museum's proposed *Enola Gay* exhibit in 1994–95 generated such a uproar it was canceled before it opened. Plans for *Disney's America*, a theme park devoted to U.S. history, came under fierce fire and were set aside. Property rights activists have taken aim at historic preservation programs in Washington and state capitols around the country, imperiling landmark and historic district legislation. And cinematic presentations ranging from *Mississippi Burning* to *JFK* to *Forrest Gump* have evoked rancorous controversy.

African Americans have challenged southern states for flying the Confederate flag or maintaining memorials to Klansmen; called for commemorating Malcolm X and saving the African Burial Ground in New York City; fought with the National Park Service over who is to present the civil rights movement story (and how) at Martin Luther King's house; and critiqued Colonial Williamsburg's use of dramatic recreations to evoke slave life. Acrimonious (but instructive) debates engulfed the Columbus quincentennial. And African American, Hispanic, and Native American residents of San Antonio have sought to wrest control of the Alamo—and the power to interpret it—from the Daughters of the Republic of Texas.

None of these quarrels over what pasts should be preserved, or how they should be presented, match the murderous confrontations in Bosnia or Warsaw. Dictatorships deal ruthlessly with historical issues. They police the past as well as the present, suppressing some memories, embellishing others. Stalin's Russia notoriously promulgated an official historiography; those who fell from favor were stricken from the *Soviet Historical Encyclopedia*, rendered nonpersons. When such official grips falter, abrupt revisions of the past ensue. The end of Russian hegemony transformed the history museums of Eastern Europe overnight.

If America's conflicts over history have been less blunt and brutal than in many other societies—in large measure because the state was seldom heavily involved here—they have not been less consequential. And although our interpretations have rarely issued from the barrel of a gun, they have not been unaffected by considerations of power.

The essays in this book examine the way Americans have grappled with the preservation and presentation of history in public settings. While occasionally dropping back to the earliest days of the republic, they deal mainly with recent decades.

In most cases, the base period is the postwar era of the 1940s and 1950s, when our attention was fixed firmly on the looming American Century, and we avidly tore down the past to make way for the future. Yet we also spent a lot of time in the past, venerating the ancestors whose wisdom and virtue had shepherded us to what seemed our prevailing state of grace. Our national historical narrative, with all its assumptions and its silences, was not an official imposition (although its borders were patrolled by McCarthyite vigilantes who branded alternative readings "un-American"). Yet it blanketed the country, dominating both the academy and sites like Colonial Williamsburg and Disneyland, despite the almost total segregation of the professoriate from popular historical culture.

In the 1960s and 1970s this narrative crumbled. Dissenters from the present—civil rights activists, Vietnam War protestors, gender-based dissidents—contested the quasiofficial past. They rejected the exclusion or marginalization of the majority of the population, challenged interpretations they believed reflected and reinforced agendas of established power, and cracked open the informal but potent constraints on what had been permissible to think about the past. Historical reassessments ensued—not imposed by fiat, but worked out by scholars asking new questions, finding new evidence, adopting new values.

New interpretations flowered as well in popular historical culture, partly in tandem with local community and social movements, partly in interaction with social historians. Museums, archives, and historical societies became more "professional," hiring more credentialed staffs, a move midwived by the funding policies of the National Endowment for the Humanities and state cultural agencies. At the same time, the pool of available academics on which these public institutions could draw grew steadily larger. In part this was a function of the 1970s recession and a depressed university job market, but it also reflected the principled desire of many new historians to work with wider constituencies. The result was a collaborative revamping of public history.

My first set of essays explores how this transformation played out in history museums. Some of these pieces, written over the last fifteen years, are scholarly efforts that set the movement in historical context; others are dispatches from the front, mixing reportage with unsolicited advice. A full-time history professor in the City University of New York, I have never actually labored in the curatorial trenches, but served instead as commentator, consultant, cheerleader, and critic. I have taken the liberty of offering suggestions and encouragement from the sidelines, but I have not had responsibility for *doing* anything. Only the encouragement of the real professionals, who have professed to find these interventions useful, has kept me at it this long.

The second group looks at how Walt Disney and his corporate progeny negotiated the same sea change in attitudes about the past. Though not conventionally considered sites of historic interpretation, Disney's theme parks are in fact drenched with strongly held and presented perspectives about the past, which I have collectively labeled "Mickey Mouse History," the rubric that provides this book its title. The first essay looks at how those perspectives changed between the 1950s and the 1980s; the second updates the story with a look at the aborted Disney's America.

Next, a duet of articles treats the historic preservation movement, concentrating on the same years of transformation, but focusing on the struggle to preserve the built environment. The first piece, a brief history of the movement, looks at the battles fought over whether or not to save the past, and if so, which pasts were worth saving. It runs the story down to the mid–1980s, a moment of seeming triumph. The second updates the narrative, looking particularly at the emergence/revival of a property rights movement determined to restore the unbridled days of the postwar era, when futurists were in the saddle, and demolition of the historic (and natural) environment proceeded essentially unchecked.

Historical revanchism dominates the last two essays as well. In the 1980s and 1990s, I argue, a backlash emerged against the interpretive transformations wrought in the previous two decades. Powerful figures, garbed as populists, claimed that historians and curators (even theme park operators) had imposed their "politically correct" views on an unwilling populace. They called for a return to old-time narratives, rather as their counterparts in the property rights movement called for a return to older patterns of land development. The first piece here looks at Ronald Reagan's largely ineffective efforts at rollback. The second, using the battle over the *Enola Gay* as a fulcrum, explores the more determined efforts of nineties-era revisionists to bring back an older past. The Newt Gingrich phalanx, despite its professed anti-government principles, has not hesitated to deploy state power to censor perspectives with which it disagrees.

America's history wars are not likely to be settled with shot and shell—though some of Gingrich's more bombastic denunciations of his opponents carry a whiff of grapeshot. It is, however, quite possible that future encounters over the nature of the past will partake more of the deadly seriousness with which they are customarily fought elsewhere on the planet. If so, perhaps these essays may serve as premonition, and assist in preparation for combat to come.

Readers will note minor differences of tone and style in these pieces, which were presented in a variety of venues and formats. Some were talks, some were reviews, others were scholarly articles. Some I have left intact, some I have lightly retouched, some I have vigorously revised or amalgamated with kindred works, and some are newly minted for this book. A paragraph at the end of each essay recounts its particular trajectory. E-mail comments are welcome (MAWJJ@CUNYVM.CUNY.EDU).

Over fifteen years, debts pile up. I am enormously grateful to the scores of public historians who have provided me with information and inspiration, counsel and critiques. Those who labor in the public history vineyards are a dedicated and talented group of people; it has been a delight to make their acquaintance and, in many cases, to gain their friendship. Essay-specific thanks will be found at the end of each article, but here let me acknowledge some who have been vital to the project as a whole.

Ted Burrows, my comrade and collaborator in our mammoth, still-in-progress *History of New York City*, offered shrewd readings of many of these pieces as they came along. Dan Bluestone commented on the entire manuscript, and his penetrating assessment resulted in innumerable improvements. The editorial collective of the *Radical History Review*, where several of these essays first appeared, provided a nurturing and committed context for exploring public history concerns. Anne Leiner's supportive counsel helped bring the project to fruition. Richard West Sellars of the National Park Service offered the opportunity to test fly the introduction in a keynote talk at Harper's Ferry. Janet Francendese, my editor at Temple, shepherded me expeditiously through the process of production.

Roy Rosenzweig, my long time friend and *RHR* colleague, has been indispensable to this enterprise. A pioneering and prolific historian in many media, Roy was indefatigably generous with his time and his insights. He read draft after draft of virtually every essay, shared the fruits of his own investigations, helped me think through difficult problems of analysis and presentation, urged me to gather my scattered essays into one accessible volume, and then helped fashion them into a coherent whole. This book would be much the poorer, perhaps nonexistent, without his help.

Doing public history has been a labor of joy, most particularly in providing the opportunity to meet and marry my lady love Hope Cooke. In 1984, with Jo Blatti, Eliot Willensky, and others, I organized "Presenting the Past," a three-day conclave in New York City that attracted historians, writers, curators, and filmmakers. There, across a crowded conference room, was Hope, who had already begun work on her superb *Seeing New York*, published by Temple University Press in 1994, a pioneering piece of public history. Ever since, Hope has been my co-practitioner, counselor, companion, and playmate. Her wisdom has enriched this book, her being has transformed my life.

Mickey Mouse History and Other Essays on American Memory

Section I

Visiting the Past:

History Museums

in the United States

(Top) Hostess and Visitors at Governors Palace, Williamsburg, 1967. (Bottom) Black History Program at Williamsburg, 1990. (Colonial Williamsburg Foundation.)

On any given summer afternoon, a considerable number of Americans visit the past. They drive to Greenfield Village, or Colonial Williamsburg, or Old Sturbridge. They stroll through old houses, admire antique cars, or watch colonial farmers and shoemakers at work. Perhaps they also see a movie, read a guidebook, or listen to costumed interpreters explain the way things used to be. Hundreds of these history museums dot the U.S. landscape, and it seems reasonable to suppose that they help shape popular perspectives about the past.

In this essay I intend to discuss the kinds of perspectives the museums promote. By looking at their history, I will try to demonstrate that from the mid-nineteenth century on, most history museums were constructed by members of dominant classes and embodied interpretations that supported their sponsors' privileged positions. I do not contend that those who established museums were Machiavellian plotters; the museum builders simply embedded in their efforts versions of history that were commonplaces of their class's culture. From the 1930s onward, elite control of these markers of the public memory came under increasing challenge. My survey examines how the museums responded and concludes with some speculations on their future.

Pioneering the Past

Antebellum Americans were not sentimental about saving old buildings. In the midst of the War of 1812, the State of Pennsylvania tried to tear down Independence Hall and sell the land to commercial developers.

Protests saved the building, but not before two wings had been demolished and the woodwork stripped from the room in which the Declaration of Independence had been signed. Most other venerable buildings situated on valuable real estate fared less well. This exuberant and cavalier demolition of the remains of the past reflected partly a booming land market and partly the antihistorical bent captured in Thoreau's contemptuous dismissal of England as "an old gentleman who is travelling with a great deal of baggage, trumpery which accumulated from long housekeeping, which he has not had the courage to burn."[1] It was not until the approach of Civil War in the 1850s that a small segment of the patriciate, frightened that the Republic was coming apart and persuaded that a memorial to the nation's founders might serve as an antidote, began to reconsider this position. In 1850 Governor Hamilton Fish asked the New York State Legislature to save George Washington's revolutionary headquarters in Newburgh from impending demolition. The legislators agreed, noting, "It will be good for our citizens in these days when we hear the sound of disunion reiterated from every part of the country . . . to chasten their minds by reviewing the history of our revolutionary struggle." On 4 July 1850 the flag was raised over the first historic house in the United States—as much a shrine as a museum.[2]

Three years later a group of businessmen tried to buy Mount Vernon and turn it into a hotel. This provoked another and far more significant preservation effort. The governor of Virginia asked John Washington, the current occupant, to sell it to the state. Washington agreed, but asked a stiff two hundred thousand dollars. The price, he noted somewhat defensively, "may appear to be extravagant, yet I have good reason to believe it is not more than could be readily obtained for the property were it in the Public Market." The governor asked the Virginia legislature to appropriate the funds, arguing that although the figure might be "exorbitant," if considered as an "ordinary transaction of business, . . . dollars become as dust when compared with the inestimable patriotism inspired by a visit to the tomb." The outraged legislators balked, and the movement to preserve Mount Vernon shifted to private hands.[3]

Ann Pamela Cunningham, daughter of a wealthy South Carolina planter, announced a crusade to save the homesite. She, too, wanted to create a rallying point for nationalist forces, but was perhaps even more worried by the disintegrating effect of a commercial and capitalist political economy, of which the attempt by "soulless speculators" to disturb "the shades of the dead," was yet another symptom. Because it was thought to be woman's special role to preserve the frail bonds of social solidarity against threatening commerce, she turned for help to wealthy, socially prominent women who had family connections to the Revolutionary generation. Cunningham and her new colleagues formed the Mount Vernon Ladies' Association (MVLA) and set out to create a "shrine where at least the mothers of the land and their innocent children might make their offering in the cause of the greatness, goodness and prosperity of their country." The MVLA campaign soon attracted members of the middle and upper classes, North and South, who were working to preserve the Union. Edward Everett, a former Massachusetts senator and secretary of state, gave an immensely popular oration on the life of Washington to 139 gatherings across the country and contributed the proceeds to the MVLA. He hoped that Mount Vernon would offer "a common heritage for the estranged children of a common father, the spell of whose memory will yet have the power to reunite them around his hallowed sepulchre."[4]

Mount Vernon was saved in 1859, but the Washington cult failed to spark a pro-Union revival. Nor did it inaugurate a widespread change in attitude to the past. John Hancock's house was demolished during the Civil War: He had been an exemplary revolutionary hero, but when the market value of the land reached one hundred and twenty thousand dollars his birthplace was turned over to the wreckers. In the postwar Gilded Age, it was definitely business as usual, and even the centennial celebrations of 1876 looked more to the dynamos of the future than the inheritance of the past.[5] Still, the crusaders of the 1850s had blazed a trail to the past. Their legacy included an insistence that private gain be subordinated to larger concerns; a demonstration that it was possible to appropriate the aura that Washington's presence had invested in particular buildings and put it to work; and a certification that it was proper for upper-class women to preserve and present history to the public.

In the 1880s the dominant classes' attitude toward history began to change. By the 1890s it had undergone a remarkable transformation. Upper and middle-class men and women established great numbers of ancestral societies and historical associations. They also set about rescuing old buildings and displaying them to the public, preserving battlefield sites, and erecting shrines and monuments. By 1895 there were twenty house museums; by 1910 there were one hundred.[6] How are we to account for this?

These were, of course, years of triumph and consolidation for corporate capitalism in the United States. But the masters of the new order—the industrial magnates, the financiers, the old patrician families, and the powerful middle class of managers and professionals—found their position contested by social classes who had also been summoned into being by the new order of things. The battles with discontented workers, discontented artisans, and disgruntled small farmers were often brutal and direct trials of military, political, and economic strength. But the combat had cultural dimensions as well, and it was in this area that new attitudes toward history were generated.

The Haymarket affair and the great strikes of the 1880s appear to have galvanized the bourgeoisie into reconsidering its disregard for tradition. Convinced that immigrant aliens with subversive ideologies were destroying the Republic, elites fashioned a new collective identity for themselves. They believed that there was such a thing as the American inheritance and that they were its legitimate custodians. Class struggle was transmuted into defense of "American values" against outside agitators.[7]

The progenitors of this class culture were chiefly the older patrician elite—those who had inherited landed, mercantile, or early industrial wealth. They found longstanding cultural and political authority suddenly being challenged; the Adams family's turn to the past accelerated markedly after the Knights of Labor captured the Quincy town meeting in 1887. Nor were they pleased with the rough-hewn plutocrats whose command of immense concentrations of capital had catapulted them to political prominence. Patricians discovered in their historical pedigrees a source of cultural and psychic self-confidence and took the lead in forming a host of new institutions. Some were exclusive ancestral societies like the Sons of the American Revolution (1889), the Daughters of the American Revolution (DAR) (1890), and the Mayflower Descendants (1897). They also took part in establishing historical societies and preservation groups, like the Association for the Preservation of Virginia Antiquities (1888), the Native Sons of the Golden West (1888), the American Scenic and Historic Preservation Society (1895), and the Society for the Preservation of New England Antiquities (1910).[8]

Patricians formed the vanguard of these groups, but the rank and file often included middle-class professionals, small business owners, and civic and political leaders. Some big capitalists followed their lead, either as members (John D. Rockefeller joined the SAR) or as fiscal underwriters (Jay Gould supported the still-flourishing MVLA and C.F. Crocker, California's first millionaire, aided the Golden Sons), but the center of gravity of the movement lay in the ranks of the old monied.[9]

A central and enthusiastically pursued activity of these groups was the construction of shrines and memorials, including finding and marking the graves of old soldiers.[10] The MVLA was the model; many leaders of the new organizations were daughters of MVLA members. They sought out, bought up, restored, and displayed the houses in which famous persons had lived. These projects enabled the elite to associate themselves and their class with the virtuous and glorious dead. In the process they also constructed and cultivated a class aesthetic: seventeenth and eighteenth century architecture became something of a cultural emblem. Some groups (like the Society for the Preservation of New England Antiquities, founded by William Sumner Appleton, grandson of Nathan Appleton, one of the first textile magnates) were consequently willing to preserve buildings hallowed by association with the entire pre-immigrant social order, even if not connected with any particularly distinguished patriot. This class aesthetic tastefully demarcated them from both immigrants and vulgar nouveaux riches—the railroad barons, mine owners, and streetcar magnates, who were then transporting dismantled European castles to the United States in order to live in "simulated feudal grandeur."[11]

The Americanization Campaign

The house museums also served a didactic function in the patricians' cultural offensive. Along with campaigns for patriotic and military education and drives to foster a cult of flag and Constitution, the museums sought to "Americanize" the immigrant working class. The shrines were thought magically to transform aliens brought within their walls. Mrs. J. V. R. Townsend, Colonial Dame, vice-regent of the MVLA, and chairwoman of the Van Cortlandt House Committee in New York City, explained in 1900 that the "Americanizing of the children—by enlisting their interest in historical sites and characters has a great significance to any thinking mind—the making of good citizens of these many foreign youths." Good citizenship meant accepting bourgeois rules of political action and abandoning radicalism. The working classes, one speaker told the Sons of the American Revolution, "must be educated out of all these crass and crazy notions of popular rights . . . into a true understanding of American liberty as handed down by our Fathers." The past, including the revolutionary tradition, had been transformed into an abstract symbol of order.[12]

It is difficult to assess the impact of this Americanizing campaign. A rich literature shows that working-class communities fought to preserve their various national customs, traditions, and communal cultures. Sometimes their efforts took defensive, conservative, and ethnocentric forms; at other times they offered a base for revolutionary fervor. But always the community provided a self-identity that aided resistance.[13]

It seems likely that the Americanization campaigns had the greatest impact on those who organized them. The bourgeoisie buckled History around themselves like moral armor. The more they felt threatened, the more they grew convinced of their inherent, because inherited, legitimacy. Finally, what had been a relatively benevolent, if patronizing and provincial, mentality turned nasty and belligerent. Groups like the Immigration Restriction League (IRL)—bankers and professors driven to the point of hysteria by strikers and socialists—began to argue, with ever-greater racism and religious bigotry, that, in the words of IRL member John Fiske (the ancestral societies' favorite historian), "the antidote to the bane of foreign immigration" was "the enforcement of those American ideas inherited from the Revolution."[14] This tendency reached its peak in 1917–19 when the U.S. bourgeoisie, terrified first by the Bolshevik victory and then by the postwar strike wave, transmuted Americanization into a xenophobic and anti-left demand for 100 percent Americanism. The viciousness of the time—the crushing of strikes, the raids on radical parties, the incarceration or deportation of critics, the support for lynch mobs and vigilantism—was fueled in large measure by the bourgeoisie's self-righteous conviction that it was defending not simply class privilege but a historic legacy.

The Corporate Past

After World War I corporate capital led a return to the past.[15] With labor and the Left set back severely, business leaders began to exude a smug assurance that they were the sole and legitimate heirs of the American tradition. The president of the National Association of Manufacturers was sure that the citizens were "tired of chasing the will-o-wisps of radicalism in government, in religion, in art, and in social life, and are about ready to return to the God, the Bible, and the fundamental principles of their forefathers."[16]

Increasingly in the 1920s, business leaders became involved in bringing history to the masses. Some of these interventions into public history followed the patterns developed earlier. In 1923, for example, a group of New York lawyers and financiers directed a drive to save Thomas Jefferson's Monticello. But though Wall Streeters, not patrician women, were in charge, the outcome was the same: another traditional shrine.[17] The really decisive transformations in the history museum genre came at the hands of Henry Ford and John D. Rockefeller Jr.

Before the war Henry Ford had been the very model of the ebullient, go-ahead capitalist; the mood of the 1880s and 1890s barely touched him. He had dabbled in Americanism, albeit of a forward-looking sort. At the Ford Company's English School (compulsory for all non-English-speaking employees), students acted out a pantomime in which some, dressed in national costume and carrying signs denoting their country of origin, entered a giant "melting pot"; simultaneously, prosperous-looking students streamed out of the pot dressed in business suits and waving little U.S. flags. In 1916, convinced that he and his class were revolutionizing the world, Ford made his most famous pronouncement: "History is more or less bunk. It's tradition. We don't want tradition. We want to live in the present and the only history that is worth a tinker's dam is the history we make today." Lampooned as an ignoramus, he stuck to his guns. "I don't want to live in the past," he told journalist John Reed. "I want to live in the Now."[18]

The war years badly shook Ford, a committed pacifist, and the postwar labor upheavals unsettled his conviction that American capitalism could transcend class struggle via such devices as the five-dollar day. By 1919 he had discovered a new respect for the past.[19] In that year Ford began excavating and restoring his own history. He fixed up the old family farm, a schoolhouse he had attended, an inn he had once danced in. He and his friends dressed up in old costumes and held nostalgic parties.[20]

In 1923 he intervened in a more traditional preservation effort. A drive was on to save the Wayside Inn, a Sudbury, Massachusetts, hostelry built in 1702 and celebrated in a Longfellow poem. Ford bought the place outright and single-handedly restored it, added on a new wing and a ballroom, purchased 2,667 surrounding acres, built a special highway to detour auto traffic away from it, and transported there a gristmill, sawmill, blacksmith's shop, and little red schoolhouse allegedly once attended by the Mary of "Mary Had a Little Lamb." When he had finished, he had created one of the first museum villages in the United States at a cost of somewhere between three and five million dollars. "I'm trying," he said, "in a small way to help America take a step, even if it is a little one, toward the saner and sweeter idea of life that prevailed in prewar days."[21]

Little steps soon grew to giant strides. Ford reformulated his position on history: Only history as traditionally taught in schools was bunk. It concentrated too much on wars, politics, and great persons (perhaps he had the ancestral societies in mind) and not enough on the material reality of everyday life for common folk. It also relied too heavily on book learning. Ford thought, "The only way to show how our forefathers lived and to bring to mind what kind of people they were is to reconstruct, as nearly as possible, the exact conditions under which they lived." This required assembling "the things that people used." "Get everything you can find!" he ordered the thirty-five thousand Ford dealers across the United States. He wanted "a complete series of every article ever used or made in America from the days of the first settlers down to the present time." As Ford was the richest man in the world, offers to sell poured in, and in short order he had become the world's greatest collector of Americana.

Carloads of relics were dumped into the tractor plant warehouse in Dearborn. In 1927 Ford announced that he would open an Industrial Museum to display his now immense horde of objects. By 1929 he had constructed a fourteen-acre building (with a replica of Independence Hall for an entrance facade) that housed exhibits recording the mechanization of agriculture and industry, the evolution of lighting, communications, and transportation, and the development of objects used in domestic life.[22]

In 1928 Ford announced that he would construct an Early American Village next to the museum and had trucked in a windmill from Cape Cod, the courthouse where Lincoln practiced law, two slave cabins, which went behind the Lincoln courthouse, a country store, an old inn, a New Hampshire firehouse, a Massachusetts shoeshop, several assorted buildings associated with his own youth, and the entire Menlo Park "invention factory" in which his good friend Thomas Edison had invented the light bulb.[23]

Ford's museum village—popularly known as Greenfield Village—was inaugurated in 1929 in the grandest possible manner. The Ford Motor Company teamed up with General Electric to reenact Edison's discovery of the electric light bulb in a ceremony presided over by President Hoover and attended by such titans as Charles M. Schwab, Gerard Swope, Otto H. Kahn, Owen D. Young, Henry Morgenthau, and John D. Rockefeller Jr. History had arrived. Greenfield Village also became a popular success, with attendance figures dwarfing those compiled at the shrines. In 1934, the first year records were kept, 243,000 visited; in 1940, 633,000 stopped by.[24]

Most historians of the Ford phenomenon believe that Greenfield Village lacks any "clear central idea." Keith Sward, for instance, finds it a "hodgepodge, despite its core of excellent restorations. It has the appearance of an Old Curiosity Shop, magnified 10,000 fold." But there are, I believe, some clear messages embedded in Ford's construction.[25]

The first is that life was better in the "saner and sweeter" Good Old Days of the rural republic. The vehicle to prove this assertion was Ford's Early American Village. Perhaps unwittingly, the village drew upon a well-established European genre—the open-air museum. A brief sketch of that earlier movement will help illuminate Ford's vision.

Back in 1891 Dr. Artur Hazelius had opened Skansen, a seventy-five-acre outdoor museum on a site overlooking Stockholm Harbor. There he assembled farm buildings from various parts of Sweden and soon added an ironmaster's house, a manor house, a log church, windmills, stocks and whipping posts, and a series of craft shops. He staffed the museum with guides dressed in folk costumes, stocked it with farm animals, and threw in strolling musicians and folk dancers. It became quite popular, and similar enterprises soon opened in Norway, Finland, Russia, Germany, Belgium, Wales, and the Netherlands. The Skansen movement blended romantic nostalgia with dismay at the emergence of capitalist social relations. As the new order had introduced mechanized mass production, a burgeoning working class, and class conflict, these museums, often organized by aristocrats and professionals, set out to preserve and celebrate fast-disappearing craft and rural traditions. What they commemorated, and to some degree fabricated, was the life of "the folk," visualized as a harmonious population of peasants and craft workers.[26]

Ford's Greenfield Village can best be understood as an Americanized Skansen. Ford celebrated not "the folk" but the Common Man. He rejected the DAR's approach of exalting famous patriots and patrician elites. Indeed, he banished upper class homes, lawyers' offices, and banks from his village. This museum-hamlet paid homage to blacksmiths, machinists, and frontier farmers, celebrated craft skills and domestic labor, recalled old social customs like square dancing and folk fiddling, and praised the "timeless and dateless" pioneer virtues of hard work, discipline, frugality, and self-reliance. It was a precapitalist Eden immune to modern ills, peopled with men and women of character. As Ford's friend and collaborator William Symonds wrote during the Depression, a "significant lesson of the Village" was that in the old days, when Americans "looked to themselves for a means of livelihood rather than to an employer," there had been "no destitution such as is seen today in large industrial centers during slack periods."[27]

Ford's village was a static utopia. There was no conflict, no trouble within its grounds. Ford had banished war and politics. He had also—by excluding banks, lawyers, and the upper classes—precluded discussions of foreclosures, depressions, and unemployment. That, in turn, obviated the need to refer to farmers' movements, strikes, and radical political parties. Ford's thrifty and self-reliant common folk (if only his assembly-line workers had been half so virtuous!) acted as individuals; square dancing was about as close as they got to collective action. There was no hint that nineteenth-century shoemakers and blacksmiths had possessed a vibrant alternative, and often anticapitalist, culture.

Ford did not leave Greenfield Village trapped in an idyllic past. In the Industrial Museum he supplied the motor force of history. The serried ranks of machines, arranged in developmental order, and the tributes to inventors and entrepreneurs like Edison (and himself) conveyed the other unmistakable message of Greenfield Village: life had been getting better and better since the good old days. Progress—as evidenced by ever-improved machines and commodities—had been made not by the farmers and craft workers, but by the mental labor of men of genius and rare vision.

The two messages together—life had been better in the old days and it had been getting better ever since—added up to a corporate employer's vision of history. From the vantage point of the village a gentle criticism of the current order was permitted; the declension in virtue from the times when men were men (and women were women) could be bemoaned. Still, one would not really want to turn the clock back to those primitive times, so it was best to get on with life, perhaps inspired to emulate not George Washington but the sturdy pioneers. Greenfield Village distorted the past, mystified the way the present had emerged, and thus helped to inhibit effective political action in the future.

But why would the billionaire master of mass production indulge in a vision that contained even a smidgeon of anticapitalist nostalgia? Why would the man who presided in the 1920s over a plant regarded as one of the worst sweatshops in Detroit, laud even a fictionalized and gutted old order of farmers and artisans? Part of the answer is that by the 1920s Ford had become a most atypical capitalist. Ford Motor, though gigantic, was still a family firm. He hated the newer forms of organization and the initiation of competition through models and colors instituted by Alfred P. Sloan at General Motors. He also despised financiers and considered Chrysler a plot by Wall Street bankers to destroy him. It was precisely when Ford began to lose out to these new forces, as his biographer, James Brough, notes, that he sought to underline the connections between his business approaches and traditional ways. Greenfield Village took shape at just the time that the Model T was forced into retirement. More broadly, Ford was something of a utopian and really believed that mass production/mass consumption capitalism could be made to work. The upheavals of 1919 had disturbed him, and he spent the 1920s oscillating between past and future. When it all collapsed in 1929, he turned sour and ugly, bitter toward the bankers he held responsible, and vicious toward his protesting employees. In the 1930s he spent more and more time at Greenfield Village, which became a retreat for him. Here he could criticize contemporary society without having to examine too closely the part he had played in creating it.[28]

Colonial Wiliamsburg

Greenfield Village departed dramatically from the DAR formula. The other great enterprise of the twenties, John D. Rockefeller Jr.'s Colonial Williamsburg, was more like the traditional house museum but in the end proved equally revolutionary. Unlike Ford, Rockefeller Jr. was quite comfortable with the new world of corporate capitalism; he had, after all, been born into it. But what really engaged his mind and spirit was not business, but buildings.[29] In 1923 he embarked on his long career in historic restoration. Attending a June fete at Versailles, he was disturbed to find the walls crumbling and water coming through the roof. He discovered to his dismay that Fontainebleu and Rheims were in a similarly deplorable condition. He immediately sent off a check for one million dollars to the French government to help repair the structures; he added another $1.85 million in 1927. His donations enabled the French to replace acres of roof. Rockefeller was particularly pleased that workers had also been able to revive the thatched houses and hedged lawns of Marie Antoinette's play peasant village and to restore her marble-walled dairy to working order. It was, he thought, a "perfect dream of beauty and delight."[30]

After repairing the abodes of French monarchs, Rockefeller turned next to the planter elite of eighteenth-century colonial Virginia. The original idea of resurrecting Williamsburg belonged to W. A. R. Goodwin, a local minister. He had first written to Henry Ford, heatedly insisting that the Motor King underwrite the cost of restoring the town the automobile culture was destroying, the town where Washington, Jefferson, and Patrick Henry had once walked. Ford never answered. But Rockefeller, to whom Goodwin next broached the idea, was hooked. He authorized Goodwin to purchase property in the town anonymously, sending him money under the name of "David's Father." When, in 1928, Goodwin disclosed who was behind the massive purchases, some old southern families were outraged at this intrusion of Yankee gold (as of 1980 a Mrs. Armistead was still refusing to sell). But the majority waved such reservations aside, and restoration began.

Rockefeller and a host of supporting experts selected the 1790s as a cutoff decade and proceeded to demolish all 720 buildings constructed after that and to remove as many traces of modernity as possible, even rerouting the Chesapeake and Ohio railroad. Then they restored eighty-two surviving eighteenth-century buildings and, after meticulous research, reconstructed 341 buildings of which only the foundations remained. Rockefeller took to spending two months each year in Williamsburg. Ruler in hand, he was all over the site, insisting on scrupulous accuracy regardless of cost. When architects discovered that they had reconstructed a house six feet from where new research showed it had actually stood, he immediately provided the money to move it. "No scholar," he said, "must ever be able to come to us and say we have made a mistake."[31]

When the bulk of the work had been completed by the mid-1930s, Rockefeller, at a cost of $79 million, had built an exquisite little eighteenth-century town, clean, tidy, and tasteful. He was delighted. So was Virginia. In 1942 the commonwealth made him an honorary citizen, the first person so honored since the Marquis de Lafayette in 1785.[32]

Williamsburg, however, was far more than simply a personal indulgence à la Antoinette. Nor was it a Greenfield Village. Perhaps Ford's project had whetted Rockefeller's competitive appetite a little. But though there would be craft shops and costumed guides at Colonial Williamsburg, Rockefeller was not the least bit interested in recapturing the culture of "the folk." There were precious few "folk" in evidence, and absolutely no reference to the fact that half of eighteenth-century Williamsburg's population had been black slaves. This town commemorated the planter elite, presented as the progenitors of timeless ideals and values, the cradle of the Americanism that Rockefeller and the corporate elite inherited and guarded. Rockefeller had suggested such a connection as early as 1914. When a member of a congressional committee investigating the Ludlow Massacre, perpetrated by the Rockefeller family's Colorado Fuel and Iron Company, asked whether Rockefeller would continue to fight unionization "if that costs all your property and kills all your employees?" Rockefeller responded that he would do whatever was necessary to defend the "great principle" of the open shop: "It was upon a similar principle that the War of the Revolution was carried on."[33]

But Colonial Williamsburg was more than simply the DAR approach writ large. While the ancestral societies had saved isolated houses, Williamsburg "offered an opportunity to restore a complete area and free it entirely from alien or inharmonious surroundings." In a 1937 statement about his motives in building Williamsburg, Rockefeller wrote that "to undertake to preserve a single building when its environment has changed and is no longer in keeping, has always seemed to me unsatisfactory—much less worthwhile."

A similar concern for an all-encompassing approach characterized his other projects in the 1920s and 1930s. While staking his claim to the past at Williamsburg, he was building Rockefeller Center, his notion of the future, in midtown Manhattan. Tearing down 228 brownstones and stores, he raised in their stead a mammoth entertainment-business complex in which, for the first time, skyscrapers became constituent parts of an integral order. He applied a similar logic and practice to land conservation. Touring western national parks in the mid-twenties, he was appalled to find that Jackson Hole, a valley in the Grand Tetons, was being developed in a hodge-podge, piecemeal fashion. His response was to buy out every single private owner in a 33,000-acre area—ranchers, farmers, lumbering industries, everybody—and deed the land to the U.S. government as a park. Like his father, who had made his fortune by overcoming the anarchy of production by a multitude of individual entrepreneurs in the Pennsylvania oil fields, Rockefeller Jr. was interested in totalities.[34]

Colonial Williamsburg flows from this perspective. It does not simply borrow and display a historical aura, it embodies a vision of a total social order. Unlike Greenfield Village, Williamsburg's order flows from the top down. It is a corporate world: Planned, orderly, tidy, with no dirt, no smell, no visible signs of exploitation. Intelligent and genteel patrician elites preside over it; respectable artisans run production paternalistically and harmoniously; ladies run well-ordered households with well-ordered families in homes filled with tasteful precious objects. The rest of the population—the 90 percent who create the wealth—are nowhere to be seen. The only whiff of conflict appears in recollections of the stirring anti-British speeches in which the founders enunciated the timeless principles since passed down, like heirlooms, to the Rockefellers and their kind. Colonial Williamsburg was the appropriate past for the desired future; in this sense, Williamsburg and Rockefeller Center formed a matching set. Ford, at least, had grappled with history in the course of mystifying it; Rockefeller denied that history had ever happened.

Whose History?

The crash, Depression, and revival of working-class movements brought the decade of complacent capitalist supremacy to a sudden end. The great corporate and genealogical museum projects continued through the thirties, but as the balance of class forces shifted, so did the nature of public history.

Franklin Roosevelt's administration supported new approaches to the past, partly as a matter of symbolic politics. Roosevelt attacked—by mocking—the DAR, reminding them that they were descendants of immigrants and revolutionaries; when they denied black singer Marian Anderson access to Constitution Hall, he supported his wife Eleanor's arrangment of the famous concert at the Lincoln Memorial.[35] Apart from such cultural signals that elite claims to exclusive possession of the past were now open to question, Roosevelt and his advisors embedded within the federal government an approach to public history that expanded the definition of the historic.

Several bureaucratic agencies demonstrated that the state could compete with private capital as guardian of the public memory. In 1933 a National Park Service architect proposed to Secretary of the Interior Harold Ickes that unemployed architects be set to work surveying and recording all "historic" buildings in the United States. Within two weeks twelve hundred were employed by the Historic American Building Survey (HABS); by 1938, they had produced twenty-four thousand measured drawings and twenty-six thousand photographs of 6,389 historical structures.

This campaign was remarkable in that many of the buildings surveyed had no connection whatever to famous people. The HABS architects preserved evidence of a wide variety of buildings: pueblo churches, taverns, smokehouses, forts, barns, toll houses and jails—"structures of all types, from the smallest utilitarian structures to the largest and most monumental," in the words of the Washington office's 1933 instructions to field workers. Alabamian surveyors photographed and measured slave quarters and log outbuildings, not just the great mansions to which they were attached. Such attention to the architectural qualities of vernacular buildings had little precedent. Yet this was, in the end, an architectural project and historical research was kept to a minimum. And while the focus (at least outside Virginia) shifted away from great persons, it gravitated less to local memories and traditions than to formal questions of design and technology—to buildings, rather than the people who lived in them.

Similarly, the Works Progress Administration (WPA) set writers and historians to work in the Federal Writers' Project. The WPA state guidebooks and collections of local lore reflected a populist shift away from the approach fostered by the traditional and corporate elite, uncovering legacies of struggle and redefining American history as something that included common people as historical actors.

In 1933 the Civilian Conservation Corps began actual restoration projects, and in 1935 the Historical Records Survey hired thousands to inventory public records in every U.S. county.[36] In the same year the Historic Sites Act authorized the Department of the Interior, acting through the National Park Service, to undertake an extraordinary range of preservation activities, including the actual acquisition of property, the preservation and operation of privately-owned historic sites, the construction of museums, the development of educational programs, the placement of commemorative tablets, and the perpetuation of survey programs similar to HABS. Almost overnight, a massive federal presence had been authorized. It was not, however, exercised. In a few years the forces of reaction and the onset of war put an end to the New Deal and its public history initiatives.[37]

In the postwar period labor gains were rolled back, left movements were suppressed, and multinationals and the military moved internationally to establish what they hoped would be the American Century. The cultural concomitant of capital's renewed supremacy was the thorough suffusion of cold war ideology, with stultifying effects on public presentations of history. The appropriators of past labor reappropriated labor's past. The populist openings of the thirties were checked and reversed, and the meaning of "historical" was narrowed once again, as the bourgeoisie set out to uproot "un-Americanism" and celebrate, with renewed complacency, "the American Way of Life." This revanchist movement took a variety of forms.

First, there was what might be called the corporate roots movement. Boeing invested heavily in the new Museum of History and Industry in Seattle in 1952. The American Iron and Steel Institute spent $2.35 million in 1954 to restore the seventeenth-century ironworks at Saugus, Massachusetts. R. J. Reynolds, Inc., donated substantial funds to restore the Miksch Tobacco Shop in Old Salem in 1957 and went on to pour large amounts into the restoration and "interpretation" of the old Moravian community. The Stevens family and others in the textile industry sponsored the construction of the Merrimack Valley Textile Museum (in North Andover, Massachusetts) in the late fifties and early sixties. Most of these enterprises focused on technological developments and ignored social relations of production, to say nothing of class struggle. Visitors to Boeing's museum were not introduced to the Wobblies or the 1919 Seattle General Strike.[38]

Second, several Skansen-type villages were established. The Farmers' Museum at Cooperstown, New York, composed of buildings transported from nearby sites, was dedicated to chronicling the everyday life of pioneer farmers and artisans. The museum focused relentlessly on objects and work processes rather than social relations or politics (visitors learning nothing, for example, about the antirent wars in New York State). In the Ford manner, the Farmers' Museum projected a sentimentalized portrait of the past and celebrated the transcendence of primitive living conditions. It romanticized the drudgery of women's domestic labor—"here was a sense of contentment, and satisfaction with a long day's work well done, which we might well envy"—yet also praised the new textile mills as labor-saving devices without asking who worked in those mills or what crises in the countryside had forced women into them.[39]

Another example of this genre was Old Sturbridge Village, which opened in 1946 in Sturbridge, Massachusetts after a long oscillation between the Ford and Rockefeller approaches. Albert B. Wells, a wealthy businessman, had begun collecting à la Ford in 1926. In 1936 Wells decided to build a museum village and called on the Williamsburg architectural firm of Perry, Shaw, and Hepburn. He soon fired them, believing that they had no feel for the locality and were overly influenced by their collaboration with Rockefeller in a project where they "had all the money in the world." After a visit to the Scandinavian open-air museums in 1938, Wells settled on a plan of bringing together a few local buildings and adding local artisans plying the old trades. He wanted to demonstrate both the early New Englanders' "ingenuity and thrift" and the way that "modern industry assures a life far more abundant than existed under a handicraft system."[40]

The third kind of postwar enterprise was the traditional patriotic shrine, now converted to cold war purposes. One million people visited Mount Vernon in 1948, and in the 1950s new shrines, like Philadelphia's Independence National Historical Park, were opened. But the flagship of the fifties fleet remained Colonial Williamsburg.[41]

In 1939 John D. Rockefeller III became the chairman of the board of Colonial Williamsburg and called for an aggressive educational and public relations campaign. During the war he arranged a liaison program with the armed forces, and troops were brought to Williamsburg for inspirational purposes.[42] The wartime effort proved to be the prelude to a massive cold war enterprise. Rockefeller III, Williamsburg President Kenneth Chorley, and Educational Director Edward P. Alexander set out to make Colonial Williamsburg "a shrine of the American faith," a source of "spiritual strength and understanding" at a "historic time of trial, questioning and danger." Thomas J. Wertenbaker, a Princeton historian who retired from teaching to work at Williamsburg, stressed in 1949 the political importance of the museum's mission:

> It would be difficult to exaggerate the educational value of historical restorations. At a time when the foundations of our country are under attack, when foreign nations are assailing our free institutions with all the misrepresentations which malice can suggest, when they are seconded by a powerful Fifth Column within our borders, when it has become a frequent

> practice to attribute selfish motives to Washington and Jefferson and Hancock and Samuel and John Adams . . . it is of prime importance that we live over again the glorious days which gave us our liberty.[43]

Chorley hoped that millions would come to Williamsburg and be reminded of the ancient heritage of contemporary ideals. John Edwin Pomfret, president of neighboring William and Mary College, suggested that such visits would help Americans "overlook those real or illusory differences of political or economic interest which ordinarily divide us. The flame of the patriots' passion welds us as nothing else can into a spiritual whole."[44]

Alexander, in his capacity as Williamsburg educational director, drew on the latest techniques to "create a historic mood through sensory perception." He wanted to generate a "moving inspiration of the American heritage" for visitors and to use guidebooks to inform them precisely what that heritage was. He taught that "eighteenth-century Williamsburg embodied concepts of lasting importance to all men everywhere." There were five such concepts: opportunity, individual liberties, self government, the integrity of the individual, and responsible leadership. There was no mention of the concept—much less the reality—of slavery, nor of equally plausible revolutionary legacies like equality, the right of revolution, or anticolonialism. Williamsburg's concepts, though certainly capable of being invested with democratic meaning, were more often drafted into the service of the status quo. In the 1950s Chorley counseled the nation to follow its leaders as the young nation had harkened to the counsel of the founding fathers ("responsible leadership"), arguing that contemporary Americans should recognize that this "is becoming such a world as the Common Man cannot operate."[45]

Alexander's "concepts" could be bent to almost any purpose because they had been detached from the realities of eighteenth-century life. In the 1950s, as in the 1930s, Williamsburg was profoundly ahistorical. Fittingly, it received an accolade from the scholar most committed to the consensus history of the period, Daniel Boorstin. He applauded, as democratic and un-European, Williamsburg's attempt "to reconstruct the way of life of a whole past community." "Williamsburg," Boorstin said, was "an American kind of sacred document." It asserted a "continuity of past and present" and reminded us that "the past," rather than any "political ideology," was the living wellspring of contemporary ideals.[46]

Williamsburg launched aggressive programs to attract visitors. The Williamsburg staff initiated the Student Burgesses program, which brought together student leaders to discuss the nature of freedom; international assemblies for foreign students, at which they could learn about American ideals; and democracy workshops (co-sponsored by the U.S. Junior Chamber of Commerce and the Radio-Electronic-Television Manufacturers Association) on freedom of expression. At the 1955 democracy workshop—co-moderated by the president of the American Committee for Liberation from Bolshevism—Vannevar Bush explained that preservation of the Bill of Rights would depend on a "natural aristocracy."[47]

With the arrival of the Eisenhower administration in 1953, Williamsburg became a semiofficial auxiliary of the state, a site of great bourgeois rituals and political ceremonies. Williamsburg served as the customary arrival point for heads of state on their way to Washington. Winthrop Rockefeller would greet the arriving dignitaries and ride them down Duke of Gloucester Street in an eighteenth-century carriage; the guests would make brief remarks and might attend an evening's ball at the governor's palace; and the next day they would proceed to Washington. Over one hundred heads of state went through this Rockefeller rite. Nor were lesser luminaries ignored. Together with the Department of State and the United States Information Agency, Williamsburg worked out a foreign visit program for political and professional leaders, and hundreds came to town each year. (The trustees also made foreign visits themselves, as when they presented the Williamsburg Award to Winston Churchill at a glittering gathering at Drapers' Hall, London, in 1955. Churchill fondly recalled, in mellow after-dinner remarks, that his 1946 Williamsburg visit had helped him recapture "the grace and the ease, and the charm of by-gone colonial days.") By the late 1950s, Williamsburg required a staff of over 1,900 people to manage its booming affairs.[48]

Turning Point

In the 1960s another transformation occurred in the museum field. Again it was closely connected to larger social and political developments. Since the late 1940s the highway and housing industries had been tearing up the material, cultural, and historical fabric of the country. State-backed developers rammed roads through cities, demolishing whole areas; urban renewal then devastated much of the remaining urban landscape. By 1966 fully one half of the properties recorded by HABS in the 1930s had been torn down.[49]

By the early sixties the people most threatened with urban dislocation and disruption had begun to protest. Amid this ferment, a small band of social scientists, architectural critics, psychologists, and journalists began critiquing the social and psychological consequences of the urban renewal and highway programs. People like Jane Jacobs, Herbert Gans, Edward Hall, and Ada Louise Huxtable argued that the demolition shattered social networks and healthy urban communities, replacing them with bleak new high-rise projects and sterile suburbs. The new housing forms, they argued, denied human needs for historical connectedness: Suburbs and projects alike undermined individual and social identities by ripping people out of history.[50]

These social critics and others involved with the historic preservation movement noted that the history museums exhibited a similar temporal one-dimensionality and historical disconnectedness. And so, in the course of criticizing the American present, they leveled their guns at the American past. Colonial Williamsburg, Huxtable thought, "pickled the past." It lacked "any sense of reality, vitality or historic continuity." David Lowenthal found this to be true of most of the museums: "The American past is not permitted to coexist with the present. It is always in quotation marks and fancy dress . . . an isolated object of reverence and pleasure . . . detached, remote, and essentially lifeless."

The sterility of the museums now came under scrutiny. "Williamsburg," Walter Muir Whitehill thought, is a "fantasy in which the more pleasing aspects of colonial life are meticulously evoked, with the omission of smells, flies, pigs, dirt and slave quarters." It was "history homogenized, cleaned up, and expurgated . . . an entirely artificial recreation of an imaginary past."[51]

"Williamsburg," another critic noted, "has the flavor of a well-kept contemporary suburb." Others pointed out that the reverse was also true: Postwar suburbs looked like Colonial Williamsburg. This was not mere coincidence. Banks and insurance companies had accepted "false colonial" as a sound style on which to base their lending programs, and so vast areas of the East and Midwest modeled themselves on the restoration. During the fifties the United States was "Williamsburgered": There were Williamsburg drive-ins, Williamsburg hotels, Williamsburg gas stations, Williamsburg A&Ps. Small wonder that Daniel Boorstin saw past and present as continuous: Past and present looked remarkably alike.[52]

Added to this set of criticisms, rooted in resistance to the devastation of historic properties and urban neighborhoods, was another critique created by the political upheavals of the decade. Black, feminist, Native American, and antiwar (hence anti-national-chauvinist) activists began producing history in order to grasp the deep-rooted nature of the processes they were protesting against and to dismantle those readings of the past that provided powerful justifications for the status quo. In this climate of increasingly widespread awareness of the selective and distorted character of official history, the history museums' celebratory certainties became harder to sustain.

These various streams of thought and action produced a great ferment in the history museum field in the 1960s and 1970s. Grassroots museums sprang up around the country to preserve and commemorate local heritages. Many were amateur enterprises with an anticommercial ethic. "We are not out for the almighty buck," wrote one of the citizens of Russell Springs, Kansas, who saved their old courthouse and used it to display antiques, diaries, manuscripts, and memorabilia contributed by town residents. "We simply want to show people our past, of which we are rightly proud." Black residents in Bedford-Stuyvesant, New York City, rallied in 1969 to block the demolition of four farmhouses that had been the nucleus of a nineteenth-century free black community and converted them into a black history museum. "One does not have to be a member of the Daughters of the American Revolution to be interested and concerned about their roots," insisted a black Kansas City preservationist. "It was good that we saved, and now maintain, Williamsburg, Virginia. And for the same reasons, we must save and maintain the slave cabins and some of the shotgun houses, little frame churches, jails and one-room school houses around the country that tell the story of black people in America."[53]

There were also fruitful collaborations between community groups and younger historians whose work reflected a critical approach to the past. At Lowell, Massachusetts, community and university people produced a museum—housed in a still-working textile mill—that examined the history of the town from a perspective sensitive to working-class history and diverse ethnic cultures, and attuned as well to the nature of capitalist development in the nineteenth century.[54]

Many of the professional history museums changed with the times as well.[55] Some abandoned the filiopietistic approach (in some cases only after considerable internal conflict), and insisted on rigorous standards of historical accuracy, adopting the premises of the social historians then practicing in the academy. Many developed imaginative strategies for creating a more comprehensive portrait of past communities.

In the middle and late 1960s museologists unhappy with static reconstructions launched the Living Historical Farm movement. They sought to create a dynamic picture of farm life by organizing working farms that employed old agricultural processes. At some of these, like in Plymouth, Massachusetts, interpreters lived in the old houses to accustom themselves to the furnishings and work practices. Structures developed a lived-in look; chickens and sheep wandered in and out of the buildings, which consequently became (as they once had been) fly-ridden and smelly. Abandoning Howard Johnson standards of cleanliness allowed a marked gain in historical accuracy. Even where simulations were not taken so far, as at Old Sturbridge Village, the museums reflected the influence of a new generation of historians and educators concerned with exploring work and family life with ever-higher standards of accuracy and, in some cases, with an eye to modern parallels.[56]

The waves of change even beat against the walls of Williamsburg. Winthrop Rockefeller stayed at the helm until his death in 1973, when Supreme Court Justice Lewis Powell took over, and Rockefeller money continued to flow; so did the stream of domestic and foreign dignitaries (the

Shah of Iran stopped by three times). Still, the pressures were intense. A series of blistering critiques lambasted Williamsburg's focus on elites, its pinched definition of the revolutionary legacy, its stopped-time quality, its genteel banishment of din, disarray, and disorder.[57] One of the few people who had anything good to say about Williamsburg during this period was Alvin Toffler, and he liked it precisely because it was so unreal. A future-shocked society, he argued, will "need enclaves of the past—communities in which turnover, novelty and choice are deliberately limited. These may be communities in which history is partially frozen. . . Unlike Williamsburg, . . . however, . . . tomorrow's enclaves of the past must be places where people faced with future shock can escape the pressures of overstimulation for weeks, months, even years, if they choose."[58]

Finally, in the 1970s, slavery was discovered at Williamsburg. The 1972 edition of the guidebook maintained Alexander's interpretive framework of the five concepts (he retired that year), but noted that, for example, the concept of individual integrity had been conspicuously limited in reality for slaves, women, debtors, and others. This trend was continued during that decade as a new, "modernizing" management team brought in a staff of young social historians who felt ill at ease with the traditional approach and who worked to transform the interpretive program. They consulted local black community groups and black historians on how to include the slave experience at Williamsburg and employed some imaginative street theater as a beginning. Alexander himself came to agree that the museums had been "too neat and clean, and [did] not pay enough attention to the darker side of human existence—to poverty, disease, ignorance and slavery," and he called for interpretations that would appeal "not only to the affluent and the elite, but also to the underprivileged and the discontented."[59]

But if the limits of the acceptable had been pushed back, limits remained nonetheless. Many museums abandoned "the American heritage" notion for a more pluralistic conception of the U.S. past: Williamsburg was now willing to set the story of the black slaves alongside the story of the planters. What they were less willing to tackle were the relations between those classes. Much in the manner of some of the "new social history," they shied away from politics and struggle: Slave culture was one thing, slave revolts were another. Nor did the museums often explore how the present evolved out of the past. Williamsburg did not, for example, explain the economic connections between eighteenth-century slavery and twentieth-century sharecropping and debt peonage, or slavery's cultural legacies of racism and black nationalism. Admitting that the reality of exploitation contradicted the ideal of liberty was only a first step.

These limits were interconnected, and they reinforced each other. The refusal to confront internal conflict lent a static and falsely harmonious quality to the projects, which in turn diminished their capacity to explain historical movement and relate their stories to the present. Many farm museums concentrated on sowing and reaping; they balked at examining tenantry, foreclosures, world markets, commodity exchanges—the processes of capitalist development at work in the countryside—and the agrarian movements that responded to these processes. They were therefore unlikely to help visitors understand how family farms (whose values many of the living museums enshrined) had succumbed to the corporate agri-businesses that today dominate American agriculture. Some industrial museums could now explore, often quite critically, the unfortunate living conditions of textile workers in the 1850s; the most advanced could even admit to historical memory the legacy of strikes. But it proved more difficult to locate the source of these problems in the dynamics of a capitalist political economy, dynamics that are still at work.

Alexander pointed to one crucial reason for the museums' reluctance to press beyond these limits when he noted, in his 1979 retrospective, that the museums were not interested in "securing social change." The disconnection of past from present and the separation of culture from politics was itself a political act. History was to be confined to providing entertainment, nostalgia, or interesting insights into vanished ways of life. It was not to be freed to become a powerful agent for understanding—and changing—the present.[60]

The Uses of History

J. H. Plumb has noted that the "acquisition of the past by ruling and possessing classes and the exclusion of the mass of the peasantry and laboring class is a widespread phenomenon through recorded time."[61] I have argued that history museums were one way the dominant classes in the United States—wittingly or unwittingly—appropriated the past.

They did so, first, by presenting particular interpretations. Of course the museums cannot be faulted for having read the past selectively. There is, after all, no such thing as "the past." All history is a production—a deliberate selection, ordering, and evaluation of past events, experiences, and processes. The objection is rather that the museums incorporated selections and silences on such an order that they falsified reality and became instruments of class dominance.[62] The museums generated conventional ways of seeing history that justified the mission of capitalists and lent a naturalism and inevitability to their authority. And, perhaps more importantly, they generated ways of not seeing. By obscuring the origins and development of capitalist society, by eradicating exploitation, racism, sexism, and class struggle from the historical record, by covering up the existence of broad-based oppositional traditions and popular cultures, and by rendering the majority of the population invisible as shapers of history, the museums inhibited the capacity of visitors to imagine alternative social orders—past or future.

The museums served established power indirectly as well. Quite apart from any particular message a museum suggested, its very structure promulgated a deeper one: History was irrelevant to present-day concerns. Recall here that the museums emerged in an inhospitable culture, one marked by a profound contempt for encrusted tradition. Business leaders had few qualms about demolishing the past in the interest of profit, and ruling groups took much longer to become attentive to the uses of the past than did their European counterparts. When patrician women and mugwumps turned to the past to legitimate their social order, their interventions necessarily took the form of rescuing isolated bits of the old order from the juggernaut of progress. The museums became preserves where the past, an endangered species, might be kept alive for visitors to see. The museums and other "genuine historical places" thus conveyed, by their very form, the idea that the past was something sharply separated from the present. History became antiquarianism—pleasant but irrelevant to present concerns. The museums did nothing to help visitors understand that a critical awareness of history, although not a sufficient guide to effective action in the present, was an indispensable precondition for it, and a potentially powerful tool for liberation.

If we now know a little about the museums' messages, we know a great deal less about how they are (and have been) received. Reception, in part, depends on who is listening, and we do not know who visits the museums. It is clear that there has been a steady increase in their popularity.[63] There is some evidence that current museum-goers are better-off and better educated than the average American; almost certainly they are overwhelmingly white, although schoolchildren are transported in from inner-city ghettos in large numbers.[64]

Nor do we know why people go. One hypothesis often advanced is that increased attendance is simply a function of the spread of automobile culture and the increase in leisure time. There is clearly some truth to this, but vacationers could motor elsewhere. The museums have some obvious appeal: many are charming places that demonstrate interesting old craft techniques and exhibit quaint antique objects; there are, after all, real pleasures in antiquarianism. The museums are also safe, well promoted, and one of the few available "family" experiences. Probing a bit deeper, some analysts suggest that the sterility of suburban life generates an attraction to places embodying a sense of authenticity and human scale.[65]

Perhaps advanced capitalism itself has fostered a desire to visit these mythic precapitalist enclaves. If there is indeed a human need for temporal connectedness, then capitalism's ruthless destruction of the old—its severing of people from one another across time as well as in space—may have created a desire to reestablish linkages to the past. The postwar years, after all, witnessed the breakup of tight local, ethnic, and regional communities, the fragmentation of families, the increasing segregation of the population into age ghettos, the devitalization of folk traditions, and the rise of corporate-dominated mass communications. It is conceivable that these concomitants of capitalist development made it more difficult for people to hand down their history to the next generation, and that citizens have been, as in other areas, partially transformed into consumers. Were tradition alive and vibrant, people might not be so willing to pay to visit these embalmed remnants of the past: Zoos did not become popular until everyday familiarity with animals had become a thing of the past.[66]

Nor do we know what visitors come away with. Perhaps the affluent find their world ratified. Perhaps those not so well served by the status quo nevertheless prove susceptible to the museums' messages. But maybe they invest the messages with different meanings. There are, after all, truly radical dimensions to the U.S. tradition, and the shrines may serve to celebrate democratic as well as capitalist values.

Scholars have only just begun to investigate popular attitudes toward the past, so we are in no position to render definitive judgments. There are some heartening signs that popular memories of radical traditions are still intact, and we would do well to explore that possibility. Most Americans, however, know relatively little about their past and have an underdeveloped sense of how history happens. This is not a reflection on popular intelligence, but an estimate of the strength of our historicidal culture. People are clearly interested in the past, but when they seek understanding they are confronted with institutions (of which the museums are only one) that tend to diminish their capacity to situate themselves in time. The political consequences of this impoverished historical consciousness are profound, and it is critical that historians contest those institutions that promote it.

If we are to take part in the history museum movement, it is important to assess what lies ahead for it. The burden of my argument has been that this question cannot be answered without considering the social and political state of the nation. The 1980s and 1990s are a period of right-wing offensives. Those who seek to repeal the gains of the working class, women, and African Americans in the present are also working to reverse their gains in the field of history. It is necessary to resist these moves to reappropriate the past.[67]

One avenue is to work with the local museums created in recent years, many of which might survive because they are community supported and not critically dependent on state funds. We should also support the more established museums in what I think will be their spirited resistance to any attempts to reimpose right-wing nostalgia. The social history movement, despite its limitations, was a decided advance, and should be defended. Critics have been too quick to dismiss the Williamsburgs, which, despite their origins, contain splendid possibilities for popularizing a meaningful and critical history.

More generally, as participants in the work, or as supportive critics, we should urge the museums to press ahead beyond social history to become places that deal with politics as well as culture; that reconstruct processes as well as events; that explain the social relations as well as the forces of production at work in the societies whose stories they seek to tell. The museums should give credit to historical actors where due, but stop short of inculcating an incapacitating awe. If their subjects were critics of their society, the museums should not blunt the jagged edges of the original message. The museums should work to break down the distinctions between amateur and professional that stultify both. They should walk that difficult line between fostering a definition of the present solely in terms of the past and disconnecting the past so thoroughly from the present that we forget that people in the past produced the matrix of constraints and possibilities within which we act in the present. Above all, the museums should consider it their fundamental mission to assist people to become historically-informed makers of history.

Notes

This essay appeared in the *Radical History Review* 25 (1981). Thanks to Sue Benson, Steve Brier, Ted Burrows, Janet Corpus, Vicki de Grazia, Susan Henderson, Mike Merrill, Roy Rosenzweig, Alan Wolfe, and the New York Mid-Atlantic Radical Historians Organization Collective.

There has been a phenomenal growth in museum studies over the last decade and a half. I have not, however, attempted substantial revision of this essay, much as it might benefit from the new scholarship, partly because it has an integrity of its own that seems worth preserving, and partly because I still find its central arguments persuasive.

1. Cited in David Lowenthal, "The American Way of History," *Columbia University Forum* 9, no. 3 (summer 1966), 28.
2. Charles B. Hosmer Jr., *Presence of the Past: A History of the Preservation Movement in the United States before Williamsburg* (New York, 1965), 35–37; Richard Caldwell, *A True History of the Acquisition of Washington's Headquarters at Newburgh by the State of New York* (Salisbury Mills, N.Y., 1887), 21.
3. Hosmer, *Presence*, 42–43.
4. Grace King, *Mount Vernon on the Potomac: History of the Mount Vernon Ladies' Association of the Union* (New York, 1919), 22; Mount Vernon Ladies' Association, Historical Sketch of Ann Pamela Cunningham, "The Southern Matron," Founder of the "Mount Vernon Ladies' Association" (Jamaica, N.Y., 1903), 20. On the Washington cult see Hos-

mer, *Presence*, 44–46; George B. Forgie, *Patricide in the House Divided: A Psychological Interpretation of Lincoln and His Age* (New York, 1979), 168–99; Michael Kammen, *A Season of Youth: The American Revolution and the Historical Imagination* (New York, 1978), 252, passim.

5. Hosmer, *Presence*, 39; Kammen, *A Season of Youth*, 59–60.
6. Laurence Vail Coleman, *Historic House Museums* (Washington, D.C., 1933), 20.
7. John Higham, *Strangers in the Land: Patterns of American Nativism, 1860–1920* (New Brunswick, N.J., 1955), 45–63; Wallace Evans Davies, *Patriotism on Parade* (Cambridge, Mass., 1955), 46.
8. Barbara Miller Solomon, *Ancestors and Immigrants: A Changing New England Tradition* (New York, 1956), 29–30; Hosmer, *Presence*, 55, 66–70, 73, 88–89,122, 126–27; Davies, *Patriotism*, 44–73; Margaret Gibbs, *The DAR* (New York, 1969), 32–76.
9. Hosmer, *Presence*, 55; Davies, *Patriotism*, 79–82.
10. Lewis Mumford, *Sticks and Stones: A Study of American Architecture and Civilization* (New York, 1924), 123–54.
11. Hosmer, *Presence*, 237–59; Matthew Josephson, *The Robber Barons: The Great American Capitalists*, 1861–1901 (New York, 1934), 332–46.
12. Hosmer, *Presence*, 138–39; Kammen, *A Season of Youth*, 219.
13. See, for example, Herbert Gutman, *Work, Culture, and Society in Industrializing America* (New York, 1977).
14. Solomon, *Ancestors and Immigrants*, 87.
15. The ancestral societies continued their efforts, however. By 1930 there were over four hundred house museums, the bulk of them patriotic enterprises of the older sort. Coleman, *House Museums*, 20.
16. James Warren Prothro, *The Dollar Decade: Business Ideas in the 1920s* (Baton Rouge, 1954), 4, 191.
17. Hosmer, *Presence*, 153–93.
18. Higham, *Strangers*, 248; John B. Rae, ed., *Henry Ford* (Englewood Cliffs, N.J., 1969), 5; William Greenleaf, *From These Beginnings: The Early Philanthropies of Henry and Edsel Ford*, 1911–1936 (Detroit, 1964), 96.
19. Walter Karp, "Greenfield Village," *American Heritage*, 32 (December 1980), 101–2.
20. Ibid., 102–3; Geoffrey C. Upward, *A Home for Our Heritage: The Building and Growth of Greenfield Village and Henry Ford Museum, 1929–1979* (Dearborn, Mich., 1979), 1–21.
21. Roger Butterfield, "Henry Ford, the Wayside Inn, and the Problem of 'History is Bunk,' " *Proceedings of the Massachusetts Historical Society* 76 (1965), 57–66; David L. Lewis, *The Public Image of Henry Ford: An American Folk Hero and His Company* (Detroit, 1976), 225–26; James Brough, *The Ford Dynasty: An American Story* (New York, 1977), 161; Karp, "Greenfield Village," 102.
22. Walter Muir Whitehill, *Independent Historical Societies* (Boston, 1962), 466; Greenleaf, *From These Beginnings*, 71–112; Karp, "Greenfield Village," 104.

23. Upward, *Home*, 21–58.
24. Lewis, *Public Image*, 278–81.
25. Keith Sward, *The Legend of Henry Ford* (New York, 1948), 259–75; Allan Nevins and Frank Ernest Hill, *Ford: Expansion and Challenge, 1915–1933* (New York, 1957), 504–5.
26. R. Douglas Hurt, "Agricultural Museums: A New Frontier for the Social Sciences," *History Teacher* 11, no. 3 (May 1978), 368–69; Nathan Weinberg, *Preservation in American Towns and Cities* (Boulder, Colo., 1979), 18–19; Edward P. Alexander, *Museums in Motion: An Introduction to the History and Functions of Museums* (Nashville, 1979), 10.
27. William Adams Symonds, *Henry Ford and Greenfield Village* (New York, 1938), 183.
28. See Karp, "Greenfield Village," for an alternative interpretation.
29. Raymond B. Fosdick, *John D. Rockefeller, Jr.: A Portrait* (New York, 1956); Alvin Moscow, *The Rockefeller Inheritance* (Garden City, N.Y., 1977).
30. Fosdick, *Rockefeller*, 356–57.
31. Cabell Phillips, "The Town That Stopped the Clock," *American Heritage* 11 (February 1960), 22–25; Fosdick, *Rockefeller*, 282–300; Rutherford Goodwin, *A Brief and True Report Concerning Williamsburg in Virginia* (Williamsburg, 1936); *Colonial Williamsburg: The First Twenty-five Years, A Report by the President* (Williamsburg, 1951), 7–18.
32. Colonial Williamsburg, *The President's Report* (Williamsburg, 1962), 32. Hereinafter cited as PR.
33. Testimony before the House Committee on Mines and Mining, in *New York Times*, 7 April 1914, 2; Graham Adams, *The Age of Industrial Violence, 1910–1915* (New York, 1966).
34. John D. Rockefeller Jr., "The Genesis of the Williamsburg Restoration," *National Geographic Magazine*, April 1937, 401; Moscow, *Rockefeller*, 104–6; Manfredo Tafuri and Francesco Dal Co, *Modern Architecture* (New York, 1979), 232. See E. R. Chamberlin, *Preserving the Past* (London, 1979), 43–50.
35. *The Public Papers and Addresses of Franklin D. Roosevelt*, 1938 vol. (New York, 1941), 158–61; On the HABS survey see C. Ford Peatross, *Historic America: Buildings, Structures, and Sites* (Washington 1983), especially Charles Peterson, "The Historic American Buildings Survey: Its Beginnings" and Carl Loundsbury, "Vernacular Construction in the Survey."
36. Thomas F. King, Patricia Parker Hickman, and Gary Berg, *Anthropology in Historic Preservation: Caring for Culture's Clutter* (New York, 1977), 22; Wolf Von Eckardt, "Federal Follies: The Mismanaging of Historic Preservation," *Historic Preservation* (January–February 1980), 2 (hereinafter cited as HP); Weinberg, *Preservation*, 24; Edward Francis Barrese, "The Historical Records Survey: A Nation Acts to Save Its Memory" (Ph.D. diss., George Washington University, 1980).
37. King, Hickman, and Berg, *Anthropology*, 23, 202–4; Ronald F. Lee,

"The Preservation of Historic and Architectural Monuments in the United States," *National Council for Historic Sites and Buildings Newsletter*, 1 (December 1949), 2; hereinafter cited as NCHSB Newsletter.

38. Whitehill, *Independent Historical Societies*, 386–90, 469–70; Frank Stella et. al., *New Profits from Old Buildings: Private Enterprise Approaches to Making Preservation Pay* (New York, 1979), 247–48; Merrimack Valley Textile Museum, *The Housing of a Textile Collection*, Occasional Report no. 1 (North Andover, Mass., 1968), 7–12.
39. My interpretation is based on a 1980 visit and an examination of old exhibits.
40. Richard M. Candee, "Old Sturbridge Village: From Model Village to Village Model," paper presented to Society of Architectural Historians, April 1975; A. B. Wells, *Old Quinabaug Village* (Sturbridge, Mass., 1941), 4.
41. Lee, "Preservation," 8.
42. *CW [Colonial Williamsburg] News*, Fiftieth Anniversary Issue (27 November 1976), 4.
43. *Colonial Williamsburg: The First Twenty-five Years*, 10, 12, 18; Thomas Wertenbaker, "Historic Restorations in the United States," NCHSB Newsletter, 1 (September 1949), 9.
44. Kenneth Chorley, "Historical Preservation—Issues and Problems, 1948," NCHSB Quarterly Report 1 (March 1949), 2; Colonial Williamsburg and the College of William and Mary, *They Gave Us Freedom* (Williamsburg, 1951), 5.
45. Daniel J. Boorstin, "Past and Present in America: A Historian Visits Colonial Williamsburg," *Commentary*, January 1958, 4; Edward P. Alexander, "Historical Restorations," in *In Support of Clio: Essays in Memory of Herbert A. Kellar*, ed. William B. Hesseltine and Donald R. McNeil, (Madison, 1958), 195; Edward P. Alexander, *The Museum: A Living Book of History* (Detroit, 1959), 13; Kenneth Chorley, *The New Commonwealth of the Intellect* (London, 1958), 23–24.
46. Boorstin, "Past and Present," 3, 5–6. In 1969 Boorstin was appointed to the board of Colonial Williamsburg.
47. These developments are discussed in the presidents' reports of the 1950s. Bush is quoted in PR (1955), 14.
48. PR (1959), 37; PR (1955), 13; *CW News*, Fiftieth Anniversary, 10; CW, *Proceedings of the Presentation of the Williamsburg Award by the Trustees of Colonial Williamsburg to the Rt. Hon. Sir Winston S. Churchill at Drapers' Hall, London, December 7, 1955* (Williamsburg, 1957).
49. Weinberg, *Preservation*, 30.
50. Peirce F. Lewis, "The Future of the Past: Our Clouded Vision of Historic Preservation," *Pioneer America* 7 (July 1975), 1–20.
51. Ada Louise Huxtable, "Dissent at Colonial Williamsburg," *New York Times*, 22 September 1963; Huxtable, "Lively Original Versus Dead Copy," *New York Times* 9 May 1965; Lowenthal, "American Way," 31; Walter Muir Whitehill, "Promoted to Glory . . .: The Origin of Preser-

vation in the United States," in *With Heritage So Rich*, ed. Albert Rains et al (New York, 1966), 43.

52. Carl Feiss, "Preservation of Historic Areas in the United States," HP [*Historic Preservation*] 16, no. 4 (1964), 145; Lowenthal, "American Way," 31.

53. America the Beautiful Fund, *Old Glory: A Pictorial Report on the Grass Roots History Movement and the First Hometown History Primer* (New York, 1973), 63; on the Society for the Preservation of Weeksville and Bedford-Stuyvesant History, see HP 31 (March–April 1979), 23; Joe Louis Mattox, "Ghetto or Gold Mine—Hold On to That Old House," *American Preservationist* 1 (February–March 1978), 4.
54. Visit and interview with museum staff and university historians.
55. Not all did, however. See George L. Wrenn III, "What Is a Historic House Museum?" HP 23 (January–March 1971), 55–57.
56. Hurt, "Agricultural Museums," 367–75; James Deetz, "The Changing Historic House Museum—Can It Live?" HP 23 (January–March 1971), 51–54; Darwin P. Kelsey, "Old Sturbridge Village Today," *Antiques* (1979), 826–43; G. Terry Sharrer, "Hitching History to the Plow," HP 32 (November–December 1980), 42–49.
57. See, for example, Wrenn, "Historic House Museum," 55–56; David Lowenthal, "Past Time, Present Place: Landscape and Memory," *Geographical Review* 65 (January 1975), 1–36; Lewis, "Future of the Past," passim; Frank Barnes, "Living History: Clio—or Cliopatria," *History News* 29 (September 1974), 202. Thomas J. Schlereth's excellent survey presents the new consensus in summary form: "It Wasn't That Simple," *Museum News*, 56 (January–February 1978), 36–44.
58. Alvin Toffler, *Future Shock* (New York, 1970), 390–91.
59. CW, *Official Guidebook*, 7th ed. (Williamsburg, 1979), x–xi; Cary Carson, "From the Bottom Up," *History News* 35 (January 1980), 7–9; Shomer Zwelling, "Social History Hits the Streets: Williamsburg Characters Come to Life," *History News* 35 (January 1980), 10–12; James R. Short, "Black History at Colonial Williamsburg," *Colonial Williamsburg Today* 2 (winter 1980), 10–11; Alexander, *Museums in Motion*, 210–11.
60. Alexander, *Museums in Motion*, 222. The disconnection of past and present generated peculiar but instructive difficulties. At Williamsburg, Rockefeller had stopped time just before that junction at which artisanal production succumbed to capitalist social relations. Williamsburg craft workers went through actual apprentice programs and had to have a masterpiece approved by masters around the country and by Colonial Williamsburg, Inc. One problem with this system was that the craft workers could not, as the real ones did, develop their art; they had always to produce in the same style. This inhibition was enhanced by CW's desire to sell their pewter candlesticks and silver bowls. Indeed when the old methods failed to keep up with demand, a modern factory was set up (not, of course, in the historic area), which churned these products out. And when the master silversmiths said they wanted the

profits from such sales—their forebears, after all, had owned their finished products—CW briskly reminded them of the facts of capitalist life: Despite their wigs and shoppes, they were employees. The silversmiths departed from CW in a huff to set up their own company.
61. J. H. Plumb, *The Death of the Past* (Boston, 1970), 30.
62. See Raymond Williams's excellent discussion and deployment of this kind of analysis in *Politics and Letters* (London, 1979), 324–29, and *The Country and the City* (New York, 1973), 22–34, 120–26.
63. Attendance at CW went from 166,251 in 1947 to 708,974 in 1967 to over 1.2 million in 1976. Greenfield Village passed the 1 million mark in 1960 and hit 1.7 million in 1973; and Mount Vernon drew over 1 million visitors in 1975. William T. Alderson and Shirley Payne Low, *Interpretation of Historic Sites* (Nashville, 1976), 22; Tony P. Wren, "The Tourist Industry and Promotional Publications," HP 16 (May–June 1964), 111; Eleanor Thompson, "Mt. Vernon, America's Oldest Preservation Project: Past Accomplishments, Present Status, Future Prospects" (precis), *Journal of the Society of Architectural Historians* 35 (December 1976), 264; Lewis, *Public Image*, 280.
64. An unpublished 1979 Williamsburg survey found that 64 percent of their visitors had total family incomes over $25,000, and 17 percent had incomes over $50,000; 54 percent had some graduate credit or a graduate degree.
65. Wren, "Tourist Industry," 111, 112.
66. John Berger, *About Looking* (New York, 1980).
67. See Walter LaFeber, "The Last War, the Next War, and the New Revisionists," *democracy* 1 (January 1981), 93–103; and Paul Berman, "Gas Chamber Games: Crackpot History and the Right to Life," *Village Voice* (10–16 June 1981).

Razor Ribbons, History Museums, and Civic Salvation

¿Porque Brooklyn? Exhibition at the Brooklyn Historical Society. (The Brooklyn Historical Society.)

In the Tremont section of the Bronx, seventy-one-year-old Pedro Pagan has ringed his house with ribbons of razor wire to ward off thieves, vandals, and drug addicts. Even his front yard statue of the Virgin Mary is encased in plexiglass. Nearby Dominican nuns have also resorted to the coils, which now encircle the walls of their one-hundred-three-year old convent.

The razor ribbon business is booming; located in Queens, it is one of New York's growth industries. The lethal loops are especially popular in neighborhoods unable to afford doormen, sophisticated alarm systems, or private security patrols. In some beleaguered areas, residents (and institutions) hunker down behind bricked-in windows, caged-up entryways, bullet-proof glass, steel plates, and wrought iron bars. "When I come home," says Mr. Pagan, "I feel like I'm entering a jail."

While these fortifications and barricades might sooth individual anxieties, some suggest they perhaps worsen the overall situation. When people abandon the streets and retreat into hideyholes, their communities crumble, further shredding any sense of security. At least so say the people at the Project for Public Spaces, a group that counsels communal rather than individual solutions. Its members create miniparks and playgrounds, which bring people back to the streets, the better to reclaim their neighborhoods.

I applaud such efforts. They are, perhaps, a bit innocent, a bit naive. The crises of many American cities have profound roots and will not be solved by small-scale campaigns. But these folks—and countless other community organizations—are bravely doing their best to reknit America's tattered urban fabric. Over the past decade, Reaganites exalted self-seeking, revered "privatization," shirked civil responsibility, eroded public discourse, and decimated federal funding for cities. Razor wiring, in its way, is a logical consequence of such ideas and actions. Hence, any efforts at rehabilitating our civic sensibilities are to be hailed, even if they generate only modest returns.

I feel the same way about urban history museums. I believe they have a role to play in reconstituting civic comity and saving our cities. I think they can serve as public forums, as spaces where citizens can come together to consider common concerns. They can help restore severed chronological connections—reknit our temporal fabric.

I am going to discuss ways in which city museums do, or might, set contemporary problems in historical context. The exhibits I will describe, or propose, are by no means the only things urban museums are, or should, be doing. Great rewards can be reaped from presenting particular periods utterly on their own terms, and from exploring themes which have little or no bearing on present ills. But I think museums can also be important venues for interpreting, and transforming, their host cities. So I will try to suggest—drawing on work-in-place and work-in-progress in the United States—how historians might bring to bear, on the harrowing problems that vex our fellow citizens, such insights as we are capable of mustering.

A New York Story

Let me begin with a bit of history. That we can even consider the questions I am raising here is a measure of the extraordinary distance urban history museums have travelled since their inception.

Arguably the first U.S. institution devoted specifically to urbaniana was the Museum of the City of New York (henceforth MCNY). Interestingly, in light of current events, the MCNY was born of dissatisfaction with the NYHS—the New York Historical Society, founded in 1804. In 1917 Mrs. John King Van Rensselaer denounced the older body as "a deformed monstrosity filled with curiosities, ill-arranged and badly assorted." It was, she declared, an "old man's club"—"dead," "uninteresting," and "dull." She organized a Society of Patriotic New Yorkers and fought to have the then derelict East River mansion of Archibald Gracie (her great-grandfather) opened as a historical museum, "under the patronage of twenty society women, representatives of the oldest families in New York."

But custody of Gracie Mansion was awarded to a rival group, spearheaded by Henry Collins Brown, a zestful antiquarian. Brown had already produced *Old New-York* (1913), a book of antique prints interspersed with "Delightful

Memories of Bygone Days By Men Still Living." In 1916, he had revived the long defunct *Valentine's Manual* and begun issuing annual compendiums of miscellaneous lore "concerning the past of our glorious city." In 1920, he had produced a chatty guidebook (which eschewed the "sordid and squalid side of New York" in favor of "the beautiful.") In these, and a flood of successor titles, Brown mingled charming reminiscences of his boyhood New York with self-confessedly "romantic," "sentimental," and "nostalgic" (and occasionally penetrating) reflections on earlier eras. His books, wrote one reviewer, marshaled the memories of old New York "in the easiest of prose, for the pleasure of the City's best people."

In 1923, after years of feisty struggle, Brown incorporated the MCNY and became its first managing director. He assembled a stellar group of trustees (and a formidable ladies' auxiliary) drawn from the city's patriciate—scions of ancient Knickerbockers, Protestant millionaires of more recent vintage, and pillars of the wealthy German-Jewish community. (Family names on the roster included Belmont, Bleecker, Carnegie, Choate, Cutting, De Forest, Dodge, du Pont, Gould, Guggenheim, Lehman, Livingston, Morgan, Morris, Pratt, Vanderbilt, Van Rensselaer, and Warburg.)

Gracie Mansion drew few visitors, being difficult of access, and Brown turned to obtaining the old Vanderbilt mansion (on the Plaza just below Central Park) for the MCNY's permanent home, on the grounds that a "high-class" house "was the proper place for it." On the verge of realizing his dreams, the sixty-five-year-old director was shunted aside in 1925 by his powerful trustees in favor of a young professional curator, who had never seen New York before being appointed. Brown promptly had a nervous breakdown and was committed to the Bloomingdale Asylum in White Plains, New York.

Under the leadership of Trustee J. W. Speyer, a highly assimilated German-Jewish financier, and Brown's replacement, Hardinge Scholle, the MCNY set out to transcend Brown's antiquarianism. The new goal, in the words of its 1927 annual report, was "to make visual in a comprehensive and arresting manner the story of the city's development," in order "to awaken in the schoolboy and immigrant an understanding and pride in his citizenship." This was a tutelary vision. The Museum would speak *to* these groups, reminding them exactly *whose* city they lived in. It would lay out "the city's development" as an historic fait accompli, a parade whose tail end newcomers were being invited to join, on the organizers' terms. As Trustee John V. Van Pelt made clear, this approach had political ramifications. Writing in 1932, amid proliferating challenges to the Depression-era status quo, Van Pelt argued that the "true mission of the Museum" was to teach children "who are the great men of the City, living as well as dead." This would ensure that, "not deceived by charlatans, they should become able to evaluate their fellow citizens and be filled with desire to emulate those of real worth."[1]

Abandoning the Vanderbilt site, the trustees asked the city to donate land for a permanent home in Washington Square. They were forced to settle for a site on upper Fifth Avenue, bordered to the south by affluent Carnegie Hill and luxury apartment houses, but to the north by the mixed racial and ethnic populace of East Harlem. There they constructed a neo-Georgian, colonial revival mansion, after a fund drive raised two million dollars (half from just two men—Speyer and John D. Rockefeller Jr.). It opened to the public in 1932.

Inside, innovative exhibits deployed state-of-the-art museology as practiced at the Musée de Carnavalet and the London Museum. Miniature models and dioramas—historical tableaux—depicted events and scenes deemed significant, such as the purchase of Manhattan Island and the trial of Nathan Hale. Temporary exhibitions provided good government lessons on the workings of civic agencies (schools, subways, firefighters, hospitals); portraits of the worlds of retailing, communications, and the stock exchange, sponsored by the depicted industries; and explorations of commercial culture—baseball, boxing, and the Broadway stage.

For all this, the museum's heart lay in the procession of period parlors, paintings, and domestic possessions donated by wealthy and genteel Manhattanites—old ball gowns, family portraits, silver services, maps, ship models, military uniforms, mementos, and urban scene paintings. Some of the items were surrendered enthusiastically with a sense of participation in a historic enterprise. Others were let go for more mundane reasons: they no longer fit in with "modern" decor or regnant fashion, or there was less space in which to store them (even the wealthy were being squeezed out of townhouses into apartments). (When John D. Rockefeller Sr.'s town house was demolished to make way for Rockefeller Center, several of its rooms were carted off and reassembled at the museum.) Sometimes, in fact, the museum served as a literal, not just metaphorical, attic: Donors temporarily reclaimed dresses, say for use at a costume pageant, and returned them after the ball was over.

For the next three decades, the bulk of the exhibitions were drawn from the silver, ship's models, paintings, and toys donated by wealthy well-wishers. Year after year witnessed shows like *Costumes Worn at the Prince of Wales Ball, 1860* (1933), *Dining in Old New York* (1937), *Dressing for the Ball* (1946), and *Jeweled Heirlooms of New Yorkers Past* (1951). The museum's notion of a "comprehensive" treatment of city life never managed to embrace the varied urban worlds constructed by nineteenth-century immigrants. Its exhibits and collections policy elided the historical experience of the vast majority of the city's populace. Apart from its photographic and theatrical collections, MCNY artifacts and exhibits had little or nothing to say about Italians, Hispanics, African Americans or Russian Jews. For all its interest in outreach, the MCNY remained an elite aide-mémoire, a fitting memorial to Founder Brown.

New Departures

New York's genteel bastion, with its narrow definitions of city and citizenry, drowsed along for decades, its version of municipal museology uncontested. In the absence of a strong working class movement, nothing like Glasgow's People's Palace emerged to collect the material culture of the laboring classes, or to address city life in more critical ways.

Slowly, however, the happy complementarity between trustees, curators, audiences, collection policies, interpretive strategies, and the architecture of the building itself began to fracture. One problem was the MCNY's address. In the early 1930s, its location was mildly daring—the right numbered avenue (Fifth) but too highly numbered a street (103rd)—although it was assumed that the northward expansion of the monied precincts, a process already a half century old, would continue. But Ninety-Sixth Street proved to be fashion's cutoff point. The institution was left marooned, just to the north of its primary constituency, and just to the south of Hispanic and African American Harlem. In this its fate was analogous to that of many downtown Manhattan churches, originally ensconced amid wealthy parishioners but then left high and dry—islands of gentility in an immigrant sea—when their pewholders fled uptown.

Slowly, the institution began altering its traditional approach. In 1944, noting it was on "the fringe of possibly the largest colony of Spanish speaking people in the city," the MCNY inaugurated a lecture series in Spanish. In 1945 came a show on the Union Settlement House and, in 1947, a presentation of its Jacob Riis photographs. In 1951 the Museum acquired and displayed Bojangles Robinson's dance shoes (preserved in bronze); in 1957 it presented *The Art of the Negro in Dance, Music and Drama.* In 1955, three years after Mayor Vincent Impellitteri visited the institution, the MCNY offered *Four Centuries of Italian Influences in New York.*

In 1963 the trustees announced they had discovered a distinct imbalance in their collections—on the side of decorative arts, to the neglect of political and economic history. They declared their readiness to transcend their "curio cabinet of pleasantly arranged objects" approach. They would open a sequence of galleries that used artifacts to tell the city's history from the early days down to the present. Two years later they opened a Dutch gallery, embodying a "total museology" approach: objects were displayed in the context of their original use, and models of the seventeenth-century fort and windmills were installed. The installation was indeed a step forward, though it managed to bypass such matters as the centrality of slavery and the polyglot nature of the town's population. Nor did the promised sequence ever get beyond the Dutch.

During the museological revolution of the 1960s and 1970s, when, across the country, those left out of history demanded entry, the museum made an effort to reach out to its *de facto* neighbors (as some downtown churches reached out to their *de facto* parishioners). A temporary exhibit on East Harlem in 1973 (that included parties for local children), one on Puerto Rican New York in 1978, and three exhibits on drug addiction, alcoholism, and venereal disease brought great attention and a wider audience. In 1979 a technically innovative (though vaguely boosterish) multi-media show was inaugurated.

In the early 1980s, however, the museum seemed to run out of steam, as well as money, as the city cut back its contributions. Exhibitions reverted to type (*Elegant Eighties: New York Clothing of the 1880s; The House of Worth: The Gilded Age in New York City, 1860–1918*). For a time, the primary audience remained faithful, drawn by the certainty, the comfort, even the charm of an institution that managed to portray New York as an overgrown small town. Parents brought their children to view the old exhibits in part to relive their own childhood visits to the old fire engines and Peter Stuyvesant's fort.

But it was not enough. Grants withered, attendance tapered down, and an air of genteel mustiness suffused the place. Another generation of neighbors grew up convinced that whatever was going on inside the imposing Georgian walls had nothing to do with them.

In the face of this crisis, the MCNY did not—could not—flee to the suburbs, as had other inner city institutions. Instead, in the mid-1980s, a team of curators with a social history orientation and a desire to reach a broader populace was brought on board to turn the ship around. A pioneering exhibition on the history of homelessness, modest in materials but ambitious in goals, set contemporary reality in historical context. Drawing on a team of scholars (itself a novel development), the institution issued an attractive and substantial catalog that served as a manifesto, a declaration of new intentions.

It soon became apparent, however, that museums, like ships in motion, have an immense inertia. The past loomed up to hamper new plans and bold initiatives. Above all, perhaps, there were the artifacts amassed by their predecessors. The new curators wanted to tell the city's story in a *truly* "comprehensive" fashion, but owned little that dealt with the vast majority of New York's population. In addition, the collections represented an obdurate mass of things to be cared for as a financially stricken city continued to hack at the museum's budget, forcing sizable layoffs of staff. Some trustees cautiously supported change, others grumbled at plans to seek "relevance" or wider audiences. Some in the old audience applauded new departures, others considered them an affront. There was the vexing locational problem: Downtowners did not flock north, and locals remained alienated.

Despite the odds, the MCNY has produced some excellent temporary exhibitions[2], opened the New York City Community Gallery (a space given over to cultural groups for mounting their own shows), and collaborated with outside organizations on exhibit design (a folklorist association, City Lore, produced shows on childrens' play and ethnic social clubs). The permanent installation, to be sure, looks remarkably the way it did decades ago, but overall MCNY has done better than its predecessor across Central Park.

For seven decades after Mrs. Van Rensselaer's blast, the New York Historical Society's old line trustees largely ignored urban life outside their walls. When people outside ignored them back, they made up for minuscule attendance (and income) by nibbling at, then gobbling down, their endowment. In 1988 they discovered their ship was taking on water (quite literally—the roof leaked). A new board undertook some structural and intellectual renovations, but their efforts were insufficient. By early 1993, the NYHS had arrived at death's door. And when it turned to the larger community for support, it heard only the sound of no hands clapping.

Fortunately for the NYHS, their world class library, if not their galleries, *did* have a constituency. Scholars, librarians, architects, and publishers rallied to its defense. We even mounted a demonstration in front of the closed bronze doors, which CNN transmitted worldwide. We created enough of a ruckus that local political leaders stepped in with a temporary rescue. A new management team has declared a commitment to bold new initiatives, but it remains to be seen if the nearly two-century-old institution can be rescued.

New Directions

While Manhattan's institutions work to regain momentum, elsewhere in New York and in cities across the country—notably Chicago, Washington, San Diego, Richmond, Philadelphia, Pittsburgh, and Atlanta—urban history museums are making tremendous strides. They have expanded the range of subjects they cover and have widened their audience—two developments that have proceeded in tandem.

The most obvious signs of change are the arrival of African Americans, workers, ethnics, and women inside the museums—as objects of attention, as audiences, and, increasingly, as partners in production.

Perhaps the most startling changes have occurred in the South. The Valentine Museum has produced a brilliant series of shows on African American life in Richmond, Virginia, from the eighteenth through the twentieth century. The same city's Museum of the Confederacy (no less!) has tackled the story of urban slavery. And the Atlanta Historical Society is planning a major exhibition on middle and upper-class black life at the turn of the last century, a story the Historical Society of Washington has also touched upon.

Other exhibitions around the country have further pried open a once clenched definition of the urban citizen by mounting shows that deal with workers, women, and immigrants. The new programming has drawn new audiences and garnered new funding. The Valentine's annual visitation in 1991 exceeded one hundred thousand, up 400 percent since 1984.

Even more striking is the way museums are involving urban communities in fashioning exhibitions. Curators determined to transcend the limitations of collections gleaned from upper class attics now routinely seek help from those they want to chronicle.

When the Brooklyn Historical Society decided to present the history of the borough's Hispanics—recognizing that immigrants from a dozen different Latin American countries now constitute over 20 percent of the population—they undertook extensive oral histories, photographed people and places, and collected artifacts of everyday life. In response to appeals, the Latino community contributed passports, airline and boat tickets, cigar making tools, cooking utensils, political posters, family photographs, *santos*, and costumes from religious street processions. Similar solicitations to Afro-Caribbeans, Italian Americans, and former workers at the Brooklyn Navy Yard reaped analogous bounties. Indeed, one half of the one-thousand artifacts used in their permanent exhibition on Brooklyn history were collected in the preceding *three* years of the Society's one-hundred thirty-year existence. The outreach, in turn, generated publicity—such as coverage on Spanish-language TV—and multiplied attendance fifteen fold in eight years.

Currently, the Brooklyn Historical Society is venturing into the borough's Sunset Park—New York's third Chinatown—in conjunction with the Chinatown History Museum (CHM), another venturesome urban institution. In the absence of any collections of Asian New Yorkers' material culture, the CHM posed historical questions and sought community participation in providing answers and artifacts. It sponsored reunions, held town meetings, set up booths at celebrations, street fairs, and subway stations. It collected material documenting community activities ranging from laundry work to Cantonese opera, and gave back exhibitions, slide shows, movie series, and other public programming.

Where Brooklyn has adopted a seriatim approach to multiple urban constituencies, others emphasize simultaneity. Providence, for instance, is bringing together a constellation of nine historical groups and housing them in the Rhode Island Heritage Center, a converted downtown department store equipped with a joint exhibition space.

Another approach is that of the San Diego Historical Society, whose inherited collections also primarily reflect the lives of well-off white donors. While it, too, is engaged in proactive collecting and in working with more focused organizations (like the youthful and gallery-less African American Museum), it interprets multiple cultures not in rotation but in every exhibition. An example is *War Comes To San Diego*, which explored the impact of the 1940s conflagration on women, blacks and Japanese-Americans.

The Chicago Historical Society (CHS) did much the same in *Chicago Goes to War*, creating video installations that mixed historic images, period film clips, and oral history interviews to portray what it was to like to be a child, a worker, a black, or a Japanese American in wartime. For *A City Comes of Age: Chicago in the 1890s* they turned to Polish, German, Irish, and Swedish communities for help in assembling objects. The CHS plans to expand its work with Chicago neighborhoods by identifying local memory-keepers and having them participate in exhibit formation. They hope, for example, to provide a Puerto Rican gang, now turned community-organizing group, with the tools to collect, document, and interpret its own history.

In addition to inviting new people in, urban history museums are trying to break out of their marble mausoleums. Though few have gone as far as the Community Museum Program in Sheffield, England, which used a mobile museum to ferry exhibitions to housing estates, several now maintain a variety of sites around their cities. The Valentine mounted its *Working People of Richmond* show away from its own base and hopes eventually to have a series of minimuseums around town that will encourage people to consider their whole city a historic site.

A logical extrapolation of this trend might be a "museum without walls." In New York, for instance, a guerilla group of past-minded artists recently affixed streetsigns, recalling darker moments of municipal history, to downtown lampposts. And a citizens' action group in Los Angeles, called the Power of Place, takes artifacts out to street corners, parks, markets, subway stations, and public housing projects. Museums could consider undertaking similar initiatives.

Baltimore's City Life Museums [*sic*], another multisite institution, is doing something equally innovative: blurring the line between history museum and settlement house. Their core operations are in a poor black neighborhood, near the center of a former riot area. Rather than walling themselves in with razor ribbon, they are talking and meeting with local residents; providing after-school programs; hiring local teens to landscape an historic park; and acquainting youngsters in nearby projects with the microhistory of their area.

One novel Baltimore exhibit—called *Heroes, Just Like You: Choosing a Career*—re-creates three workspaces: an 1890s domestic parlor, a 1940s corporate office, and a 1990s microbiology lab. Using black actors, it examines the opportunities and barriers African Americans confronted in each period and compares the lives of earlier eras' servants, laundresses, and secretaries with those of today's lab technicians and research scientists. At exhibit's end a computer station describes local career options, suggests courses needed in high school, and dispenses information on college scholarships.

The San Diego Historical Society, another multilocational institution, is doing comparable things at its Villa Montezuma, a historic house in a low-income area plagued by crime, drugs, gangs, and absentee landlordism. Confronting declining attendance, and income, the society set out to help solve neighborhood problems. In addition to historic programming focusing on black and Chicano subjects, it acts as a community center, offering after-school programs, repainting campaigns, and a little league team. Neighbors have become protectors: the museum is among the few un-vandalized buildings in the area.

Ongoing Problems

I hope it is clear that I applaud these initiatives and would like to see more of them. But I also have some reservations about the current enthusiasm for "sharing authority" with local communities, for example:

- It is not always easy, as many community activists discovered in the 1960s and 1970s, to define exactly *who* the "neighborhood" is.
- Community affirmation can too easily tumble over into uncritical celebration.
- Too relentless a focus on ethnicity can overlook internal divisions—along lines of class, gender, age, or micro-culture—and even veer off towards an essentialist nationalism.
- Too resolute a concentration on "culture," narrowly defined, can deflect attention from considerations of power—rather as academic social history has sometimes shortweighted political and economic factors.
- Too determined an emphasis on history from the bottom up can neglect the top-down doings of the rich and powerful.

What concerns me most, however, is that localism can lead to provincialism. It can slight big picture developments that transcend particular neighborhoods while impacting them profoundly.

This is not an inevitable or inherent danger. Particularist digging can unearth fundamental matters. When Liverpool's Museum of Labour History produced a show on blacks in the city, done in close collaboration with the black community, it forced a confrontation with the slave trade—a central facet of Liverpool's history that other institutions had played down or shied away from.

Still, I am concerned about those aspects of city life that might escape too finely meshed a net, and therefore want to underscore some urban issues to which museums are perhaps devoting insufficient attention. I will suggest specific exhibit topics. Some will present special challenges to curators who seek, quite properly, to avoid books-on-walls, but I am convinced that innovative design solutions can be fashioned for most of what follows.

New Possibilities

Let us go back to Mr. Pagan's razor wire and talk about crime. This is something most museums don't do—which is amazing, given the phenomenal popularity of places like Les Martyrs de Paris, or the London Dungeon. These places draw 650,000 a year by recounting criminality through the ages, admittedly in Grand Guignol style. Urban crime is both an indisputably sexy subject and a matter of immense contemporary concern.

So why the museological silence? Here is a place where a community approach can limit possibilities. The Chicago Historical Society has encountered resistance to raking up Capone-era muck. And New York's Ellis Island Museum, while presenting a rich canvas of turn-of-the-century working-class life, nevertheless whited out any references to the immigrant underworld—no Italian mafiosi or Jewish prostitutes mar its galleries.

It is easy, however, to allay fears of ethnic stereotyping by painting the story of city criminality with a sufficiently broad brush. Why not a mammoth show on the history of crime in, say, New York City? It could explore the way criminal entrepreneurs seized the possibilities of their particular historical moment. It could *include* the doings of the rich and infamous, while also probing fundamental issues. Such as, in the seventeenth and eighteenth centuries: piracy (Captain Kidd); smuggling (in an imperial context); and slave revolts (attempts to steal property in oneself). In the early republic it could treat the harbor and railyard thieves who preyed on the city's emerging transport grid; the reformers' war on gambling, drinking, and prostitution; and the rise of Anglo and Irish-American gangs. In the post–Civil War era, it could address: white collar crimes like counterfeiting, stock swindling, and shoplifting, facilitated by new developments in finance and retailing; political plundering by Tammany Hall; new immigrant criminality (the Black Hand and various Jewish gangs); the moral panic over "white slavery," birth control, and pornography; and the repression of so-called political criminals: union organizers, anarchists, and socialists. A twentieth-century section could track prohibition and the rise of organized crime; the movement of ex-bootleggers into gambling, loansharking, drug pushing, and labor racketeering; the grip of organized parasites on docks, markets, airports, unions, and small businesses; the explosion of the drug trade and the arrival of a new crop of immigrant entrepreneurs; the continuing criminalization of certain kinds of sexual behavior, notably that of gays and lesbians; and the increasing spread of white collar criminality, from insurance fraud (including arson for profit), to computer theft, to the savings and loan and junk bond scandals.

In truth any one of these would make an interesting show—tracking the sex trades alone could illuminate a host of urban issues—but an overarching exhibition would focus attention on comparative issues visitors find appealing: were cities safer in the old days? Why are activities legal at some times and not others? Is there a relation between crime and poverty?

One reason museums speak of poverty so sporadically is that the poor leave the least detritus, which in turn has implications for contemporary collecting policy. Museologist Andrew West has suggested gathering the material culture of welfare recipients, including the official forms which so govern the lives of the poor, and the cardboard boxes, blankets, sleeping bags, and makeshift shelters in which homeless people sleep on the streets of London.

But there are other ways to explore the history of urban poverty. Museums could examine the institutions that cities past and present have created to deal (or not deal) with poverty, including poorhouses, charity wards, and jails. They could compare Victorian discussions of the deserving and undeserving poor with their eerie echoes in contemporary debates on the so-called underclass. They could survey efforts by the poor themselves to organize and demand assistance or social transformation. They could explore the history of unemployment—towards which end Glasgow has collected redundancy notices from railway workers, doo-huts from out-of-work pigeon keepers, and ephemera from the Miners' Strike.

Or museums could raise still deeper questions about the production of poverty. Perhaps by tracking the macroeconomic shifts in urban economies that periodically rendered entire job categories redundant, or by examining how the rhythms of urban life were influenced by oscillations in the world economy. It might be valuable to have a show on the way capitalist cities characteristically lurched from eras of surging, even feverish prosperity, into periods of deep depression, which, among other things, drove the marginally employed below the poverty line. This could provide an antidote to the contingent and particularist ways in which contemporary hard times are often addressed.

How about transport? True, lots of places assemble cars or amass old trolleys. But often these embody the worst kind of consumerist collectorism—history as the display of beautiful, uncontextualized, objects. Or the autos are used to demonstrate that history is progress, by marching us past ranks of ever-improving models. It is true that social and cultural historians have taken over some of these institutions. The Henry Ford Museum now deals with advertising, popular culture, the symbolic dimensions of auto ownership, the transformation of roads, roadsides, and leisure time. What still seems to be missing are assessments of the social consequences—particularly for cities—of organizing a nation's transport system around the private automobile. What are the costs in pollution, in traffic, in living arrangements? What political initiatives, such as highway acts and urban renewal, facilitated the triumph of the auto and the demise of mass transit? The London Transport Museum does an excellent job on some of these issues—in particular the way transport decisions shaped city growth and promoted class-specific neighborhoods—but why (apart from the obvious bulkiness of relevant artifacts) must such matters be left to specialized institutions?

Public health seems another underaddressed topic, though AIDS, and the revival of ancient killers like tuberculosis, has remobilized attention in New York. The Museum of the City of New York is planning a major exhibition on the history of epidemics. It will (I hope) set contemporary scourges in a solid historical context, illuminating the way diseases are in part social, political and cultural creations, not merely artifacts of microbes run amuck. The Brooklyn Historical Society has collected oral histories and the grim material culture of the AIDS epidemic—photographs, medical records, t-shirts, phone bills, herbalist bottles, workshop pamphlets, and the sickroom contents of a man felled by the disease.

We could do with more treatments of these matters and others that deal more generally with what we might call urban ecology. The New York Public Library recently did a show called "Garbage!," which dealt with the political, economic, and cultural dimensions of the way cities dispose of their wastes. More broadly still, we need treatments that bring home to urban visitors the complex interactions between cities and their hinterlands. San Diego's permanent exhibit, for example, plans to remind viewers they live in a desert-at-bay, and thus will confront the politics of water.

How about shopping? Consumerism and consumer culture are hot topics in academic circles. Some of the fruits of recent research might make rewarding exhibitry. One approach might trace transformations in retailing—from off-the-ship wholesaling, to specialty stores, to the rise of department stores and downtown retail complexes, to the competition from chain stores, to the flight to suburban malls (which in turn raises issues about markets and public space and the collapse of inner cities).

Shopping for entertainment could provide another avenue into consumer culture. The trajectory of a survey of the rise and fall of public amusements might ascend from street buskers through dime museums, theaters, and vaudeville houses, to an apogee in the early twentieth century's giant pleasure arenas: sports stadiums, dance halls, picture palaces, and amusement parks. It might then trace the decline of these peculiarly urban spaces under the combined impact of privatized entertainment (radio, television, and video cassette recorder) and the flight of many arenas to the suburbs, with devastating consequences for public life in the contemporary city.

Let's talk about housing. Museums do deal with housing. Many are actually located in historic houses. And while most of these tend to be gentry domiciles, breakthrough operations like the Tenement Museum on New York's Lower East Side or Baltimore's 1840 House, now portray middle and working-class domestic lives. What I miss, however, are broader assessments of the history of urban housing that go beyond architectural assessments to get at issues like the emergence of rental markets and multiunit housing; changes in building technology and the organization of the construction trades; the politics of mortgage financing; the relative importance of speculative developers versus urban planners in shaping cityscapes; the impact of zoning laws; the variety of ways the poor are wretchedly housed; the attempts by reformers, unionists, and radicals to constrain or transcend the market; the story of gentrification and historic districts, the struggle for public housing and the contours of contemporary homelessness.

Pieces of this story have been told here and there. Washington's National Building Museum investigated tensions between the capitol's symbolic core of monuments and the indigenous (predominantly black) metropolis. The Museum of the City of New York offered a pioneering exhibition on the history of homelessness. And the Old Grammar School in Hull, England, produced a candid video on the history of local housing.

Still, how about the mega-developments that have profoundly altered U.S. cities. Who has tackled urban renewal? Who has discussed suburbanization? Who has taken on deindustrialization?

The Bostonian Society partially addressed the first of these with its West End show on the demolition in the 1950s, under federal slum clearance legislation, of a poor, working class, multiethnic community, and its replacement by high-rise luxury apartments and office complexes. The show examined the assumptions of the city fathers, urban planners, middle-class commuters, and financiers who considered the West End a slum whose demolition would revitalize the city. It looked at the devastating impact on displacees of losing their support network of family and friends, and recounted the subsequent reassessment of bulldozerism by municipal and federal authorities.

But for the most part the big issues remain untouched. For example, where can U.S. city dwellers learn about the federal government's role—through mortgage guarantees and highway construction—in underwriting the suburbanization that depleted tax revenues, altered racial demographics, and sapped the political and cultural strength of older metropolitan areas?

Where can they find explorations of the devastating consequences of capital flight as corporations sidestepped organized labor and pressures to pay their fair share of social costs by moving to quiescent pastures in the South and abroad, in a restless search for areas willing to provide tax breaks, cheap land, or the muscle needed to repress labor? We have lots of industrial museums, housed in defunct factories in devastated cities. But although they recreate bygone work relations, how many explain why the industries decamped, tell where they went, or describe the impact of their departure?

Which urban history museums examine the governmental and military role in bleeding northeastern and midwestern cities to build up sunbelt/gunbelt metropolises? Which trace the urban impact of swapping unionized blue collar jobs for "service sector" positions that are usually unorganized and relatively poorly paid? Which consider the looming departure of even these jobs, as financial back offices take flight, and computers make it increasingly possible to disaggregate financial services altogether?

And where do we examine the relation between capital flight and the newest urban immigration? Scholars have studied the cascading impact of the multinational corporate export platforms established in Latin America and Southeast Asia: Peasants are displaced to urban factories and relocate from Third World shantytowns to U.S. cities where their labor is exploited to help "reindustrialize" America by reviving sweatshops. Could not a show bring such a trajectory to life by tracing the story of a young woman or an entire family as they moved, say, from the Malaysian countryside to an electronics assembly plant in Penang's free trade zone, to an apartment in Asian Flushing or Los Angeles? Recent museological concentration on new immigrant neighborhoods is admirable, but it tends to treat the global context which engenders them as a given.

Or how about examining the phenomenon of "guest workers"—Mexicans in the United States, Africans in France, Turks in Germany? Such a topic cries out for comparative analysis. Could not urban history museums collaborate internationally on presentations that trace historical commonalities and divergences and relationships between their various metropolises? (In this regard, parenthetically, I urge a policy of videotaping exhibitions, appending comments from curators and visitors, and placing them in a lending videolibrary from which other institutions can draw ideas and inspirations).

Have we traveled too far from city streets? Become too embroiled in global economic considerations? How about something at once rooted in urban material culture and intriguingly postmodern? Why not a show that tracks the production, transformation, and exploitation of representations of the city. An exhibition on urban images might analyze the changing vocabularies artists have used to capture the urban experience and to shape urban consiousness. Such a show could draw on readily available materials—prints, paintings, theatrical sets, silverware, literary texts, photographs, tourist paraphernalia—to establish a typology of a city's images. It could compare attempts made at different times, and in different media, to grasp similar urban phenomena—Walt Whitman, say, with King Vidor on crowds. It could look at the way images of city sinfulness were wielded as bludgeons by rural antagonists or watch urbanites attain the cultural wherewithal to sneer at hayseeds.

Or how about a survey of the way images of a single city, in a single medium, changed over time. I would love to see a "New York City in Cinema" show that used media not as an adjunct to artifacts, but as itself an artifact. It could display short clips from movies and television portraying the city as a criminal-ridden danger zone; executive suite for the power elite; nest of aliens; hub of glamour; pit of decadence, and on and on. It could explore the way the city's changing fortunes get depicted cinematically, moving from *On the Town* to *Escape from New York*. It could contrast commercial portraits like *Fort Apache* with documentary images on the South Bronx. It could track the relation between cultural production and changing demographics. In the 1920s, 1930s and 1940s, many radio and television shows were set in New York's ethnic neighborhoods; in the 1950s and 1960s sitcom families motored to the suburbs as advertisers followed their prime markets to whitebread land (the Ricardos and Mertzes bundled off to Connecticut in their '55 Pontiac); then, in the 1970s and 1980s, the television metropolis underwent a revival, of sorts, with the emergence of Archie Bunker's Queens and Bill Cosby's St. Luke's Place.

Or how about a show on "Tourism over Time?" Some years ago my wife and I visited Sicilian cities with three different guidebooks in hand—a 1908 Baedeker, a post World War II traveller's account, and a recent Frommer's. Reading them added a fascinating comparative dimension, underscoring the change both in conditions and in ways of seeing. A similarly multipart exhibition could deploy collections in parallel tourist itineraries, accompanied by excerpts from contemporary guides and promotions, to show the changing ways a city was portrayed (or sold) over the years.

Despite this plethora of suggestions for particular shows, what I really want to see are more general exhibitions that combine these disparate elements into grand narratives that sweep boldly through a city's entire history. I believe we need not simply social history sagas but an overarching interpretive perspective that gets at a city's deepest dynamics and allows us to reflect on where it (and we) might, or should, be going.

Razor Ribbons, History Museums, and Civic Salvation

Several years ago I proposed a permanent exhibition to the Museum of the City of New York. It emphasized the way the city's history was crucially shaped by its evolving relationship with a developing world and national capitalist order. Since its inception, I argued, New York has been a strategic nodal point on a global grid—a vital conduit for the flow of cultures, commodities, capital, labor, and ideas. It has been, successively: a trading post perched on the periphery of a Dutch mercantile empire; a vital seaport link in a flourishing English imperial network; the mercantile, financial, and cultural interface between European industrialism and a burgeoning American agricultural hinterland; the facilitator of the continental development of United States industrialism (and a manufacturing center in its own right); and the headquarters of an American-based multinational economy. I proposed organizing the collections around this periodization, using segments that took their internal coherence chiefly from the city's relation to the wider world. I then proposed presenting the nature of life for the range of class, gender, ethnic, and racial groups in each period, concentrating on the uses they made—at work, at home, at play—of the possibilities the city presented at that moment.

I went so far as to suggest an exhibit design modeled on those science fiction movie orbiting space stations—the ones with a hub in the center from which corridor spokes radiate out to pods arranged around the circle. In the center was to be a grand central time terminal—a cross between a bustling depot for temporal travelers and a cosmic tourist agency. Here, at four different booths, costumed interpreters/barkers would hawk the virtues of traveling to four points in New York's past. Visitors would choose a portal, get their time passports stamped, and then head down one of the four corridors to nodes that presented particular periods in depth. (This, went my logic, would ease the straightjacket coerciveness of the march-through-time approach, allowing those who sought conventional chronology to swing round the circle, while affording others the opportunity of making random forays.)

Although the MCNY passed this proposal by, happily such overviews are now breaking out all over. The Atlanta Historical Society's permanent exhibit will contain a central gallery surrounded by a ring of four historical environments. Visitors can "time travel" directly to the rural frontier, the late nineteenth-century transportation center, the early twentieth-century commercial city, or the suburban metropolis. The Historical Society of Western Pennsylvania, where I am a consultant, is creating a similar format for their permanent exhibit on the history of Pittsburgh. Baltimore plans a variant of the same strategy. And San Diego is also constructing an overview exhibition, which divides its narrative into chronological segments while arranging its material in broad thematic packages.

The last item in my MCNY scheme was a device for travelling ahead in time. I suggested an area whose exhibits would explore the city's future.

Here would be a place to raise questions about what might happen next. Will New York retain its global position? Will manufacturing and finance continue to move out? What do changing immigrant demographics portend?

This is perhaps the hardest kind of proposal to swallow, as it goes against the grain of what it is that history museums *do*. The Museum of London has opted for the more usual approach. At least for the moment, its permanent exhibition comes to an abrupt halt with the Battle of Britain—though if New York had a "finest hour," I might be tempted to stop there, too. Similarly, the Historical Society of Pennsylvania's new overview boldly casts Philadelphia's growth as a series of struggles over urban space between contending groups, but fails to carry the story on down to the recent past, much less speculate on possible futures.

I think we should invite visitor participation in debates about where the city should be going. If our exhibits have made clear, as I believe they should, that cities have been shaped by conscious (and contested) decisions, rather than molded by blind impersonal forces, then it follows that people today also have the power to reshape their environment. At a time when the public sphere is so impoverished, museums can provide safe places for a heterogeneous citizenry to reflect on issues that affect them all.

I see three general ways museums can accomplish this: by intervening directly in inter-community conflicts; by presenting alternatives on issues of public policy; and by promoting historically informed planning initiatives.

As an example of the first, consider the Jewish Museum of New York's recent collaboration with the National Association for the Advancement of Colored People in mounting *Bridges & Boundaries: African Americans and American Jews*. This assemblage of photographs, artifacts, film clips, and other memorabilia surveyed the history of alliances and conflicts between the two groups. It was not a perfect presentation; it muted certain tensions, shied away from certain issues, overstated certain commonalities. Still, it was an ambitious effort to foster "meaningful dialogue" in a dangerously frayed city.

Also in New York, a trio of Brooklyn institutions—the Brooklyn Historical Society, the Brooklyn Children's Museum and, the Society for the Preservation of Weeksville and Bedford-Stuyvesant History—produced a show called *Bridging Eastern Parkway*. (Bridging is again the apt and operative metaphor). With the full participation of the affected communities, it recounted the history of Crown Heights and its peoples—notably the African Americans, Caribbean Americans, and Lubavitch Jews who have recently been at each other's throats. The hope is that the process of collaboration will help focus attention on common problems and solutions.

The second approach would set current urban issues in historical perspective. Such shows could take a minimalist (and inexpensive) form. The

Chicago Historical Society (CHS) is thinking about producing video responses to current events that draw on the museum's collections and expertise. If the mayor talked about, for example, legalizing gambling casinos, the Society could produce a mock news show—CHS Cable News—that interviewed historians and made use of artifacts relating to the history of gambling in the city.

Alternatively, a museum could present a full-rigged exhibition on a controversial subject, and conclude by presenting various proposed solutions, perhaps screening short video presentations by spokespersons for alternative approaches. Visitors could then vote, and a computer terminal would tally and present updated results.

Rochester's Strong Museum offered *Altered States*, an exhibit that surveyed the use and abuse of drugs, from the colonial era's rum, coffee, and tobacco to present-day cocaine. Artifacts ranged from Prohibition-era alcohol flasks and Tommy Guns, to 1960s dope paraphernalia, to a door battered down in a police raid on a crack house. The show explored issues of discriminatory law enforcement in an assortment of cities. It examined the relationship between crime and drug policy, considered the possibility of the former being an artifact of the latter. It ran excerpts from a video on legalization that compared the experiences of Amsterdam and New York City. It presented graphic testimonies from local Phoenix House residents about the horrors of their own addiction and screened a video sequence on needle exchange. After all this, it offered visitors the opportunity of voting on: drug testing in the workplace, legalizing marijuana, banning cigarette advertisements, and other issues. (Parenthetically, in the aftermath of a string of dynamic shows, annual attendance more than doubled to over 140,000.)

If we can raise questions about drug use, why not on housing policy (should rent control be eliminated?), on deindustrialization (is the North American Free Trade Association good or bad for United States cities? For Mexican cities?), on urban ecology (should garbage disposal be by big-burn incinerators or recycling?), on immigration (should resident aliens be given the right to vote?). The possibilities are endless.

Thirdly, just as we might have exhibitions that treat urban development past, we could have forums on urban development future. The San Diego Historical Society is working with the city's planning agency to develop computer simulation games that will let visitors act as the highway commissioner, who plots out future roadways, or the water commissioner, who decides how to allocate aqueous supplies when they run low.

The Chicago Historical Society's 1890s show concluded by asking visitors to write out "*Your* vision of a better Chicago, today and for the future." Many did, and the walls were soon festooned with statements about crime, racism, and assorted urban ills. Now the CHS hopes to get even more directly involved in city planning. It is working to establish a program called *Vision 2020: Preparing for the 21st Century, Lessons from the Past.* Its mission would be to catalyze, in conjunction with civic and community leaders, the crafting of a new, historically informed, strategic plan for the city.

Richmond, Virginia's Valentine Museum is proposing the city and state undertake planning and transport initiatives that strengthen the locale's appeal to conventions and visitors, enabling it to better compete with Orlando's Disney World, the five-hundred-pound guerilla of American tourism. There are perils, perhaps, in getting so deeply involved with one's host city's development—nouveau-boosterism might conceivably blunt one's critical historical sensibilities—but it is intriguing to find a museum that can afford such worries.[3]

I conclude, then, by urging municipal museums to strengthen the democratic process by enhancing visitors' ability to make historically informed decisions. These urban establishments have always had civic functions, but they used to be relatively narrow and self-interested. Today's institutions can adopt a broader vision. No doubt only the most modest expectations of what such enterprises can accomplish are warranted. That does not mean we should not try.

Notes

This paper is a slightly revised version of a keynote address presented on 19 April 1993 at "Reflecting Cities: An International Symposium on City Museums," sponsored by the Museum of London. The gathering, after hearing presentations on remarkable work being done in—among many other places—Belfast, Amsterdam, Zagreb, Montreal, Birmingham, Jerusalem, Lagos, Paris, Melbourne, and St. Petersburg, established an International Forum of Museums of Cities, which met again in Barcelona in 1995. My thanks to Nichola Johnson, currently director of museology at the University of East Anglia, for inviting me and for offering helpful commentary.

This essay also incorporates some material from my "History Museums and the Prison of the Past," *Culturefront* 1; no. 1 (May 1992), and a detail or two from Max Page's excellent dissertation-in-progress, "The Creative Destruction of New York: Landscape, Memory, and the Politics of Place, 1890–1930." My thanks to MCNY Director Robert R. Macdonald for making the museum's archives available, and to the many curators across the country who discussed their exhibitions with me.

1. Here the MCNY echoed the Metropolitan Museum of Art's American Wing, which had opened in 1924, twenty blocks farther down Fifth Avenue. The curator, a wealthy stockbroker who traced his lineage to the 1630s, aided by similarly wealthy and pedigreed benefactors, assembled period rooms and high-style furnishings that celebrated the aesthetic

taste and sensibility of the old elite. The wing was seen, quite explicitly, as an antidote to the "influx of foreign ideas utterly at variance with those held by the men who gave us the Republic." A journey through the American wing, it was felt, would be "invaluable to the Americanization of so many of our people to whom much of our history has been hidden in a fog of unenlightenment."

2. I assess these in "History Museums and the Prison of the Past," *Culturefront* 1; no. 1 (May 1992).
3. As it turned out—from a vantage point two years further on—the chief "peril" from the Valentine's developmental thrust was not the blunting of its interpretive edge, but rather a near-bankruptcy, brought on, in part, by overexpansion. The museum built an extraordinarily ambitious "interactive history park" on the site of Richmond's old Tredegar Iron Works. The eight acre edu-tainment complex included an on-site archeological dig, raft rides, tours of historical sites, an African American monument, a million-dollar outdoor sound and light show, and a super high-tech multimedia program tracing the development of Richmond. Opened before fully completed, attendance was good, but not quite good enough to handle the payments on an $8.6 million bank loan. Massive staff layoffs and the resignations of Director Frank Jewell and other top administrators ensued, but the museum is still operating, and hopes to continue its innovative urban history programming. A thorough airing of this affair is needed, especially to determine if a sharp drop off in promised corporate contributions—which helped precipitate the crisis—reflected a delayed backlash against the politics of the museum's programming.

Boat People: Immigration History at the Statue of Liberty and Ellis Island

Baggage Exhibit at Ellis Island Immigration Museum. (© Norman McGrath. All Rights Reserved.)

Despite the general outrage at the commercialized way financing for the Statue of Liberty and Ellis Island restorations was obtained, I confess I felt somewhat ambivalent about it. On the one hand, the hawking of "commemorative Ellis Island urinals" was a bit much. Even more annoying, the hucksterism was unnecessary; it was made inevitable by the failure of the Reagan administration (for all its patriotic fervor) to insist that Congress allocate sufficient public funds to pay for the rehabilitation.

That failure stemmed as much from ideology as parsimony. Richard Rovsek, the marketing impresario (and administrator of the Reagan White House Easter egg rolls), originated the campaign for corporate sponsorships and product tie-ins. He saw the restoration of the statue and Ellis as being "the ultimate statement that the private sector could accomplish work that the Government had traditionally done and that it could accomplish it better." Rovsek was later bounced from the commission he initiated, accused of conflict of interest practices, but his approach governed the ensuing fund raising drive. Still, we should be grateful the money was raised, admit that it is embarrassing it had to be raised in this manner, and be thankful that the Reaganauts, in a burst of privatizing frenzy, did not sell off the statue altogether.

Yet for all the tawdriness, I found it hard to work up an appropriate degree of indignation. The franchising of national symbols (especially the statue, which was used in marketing even before it was built), and, more generally, the commercialization of civic culture, is such an old American story that it has lost its power to shock. This is particularly true these days, when our society appears barely aware that a distinctly public sphere does or even should exist. Moreover, there is something oddly comforting in the use of the statue to proclaim the virtues of beer, flour, and soapsuds. The ability of commerce to desacralize, to deflate pomposity, is one of the more appealing aspects of American culture. When we recall the way the statue was deployed in World War I to whip up a self-righteous, murderously repressive, anti-immigrant 100 percent Americanism, we might well be thankful for Madison Avenue's gentler approach.

The really disturbing thing about Liberty Weekend, 1986, was the revival, amidst the genial fireworks and show business glitz, of the older, more menacing modes of "statuolatry." At the rededication ceremony Reagan advanced three pseudohistorical arguments. First, he equated the Nicaraguan contras with the founding fathers, hailing recent congressional funding as having "put a smile on the face of our Statue of Liberty." Second, he sought to reawaken a millenarian vision of America's manifest destiny, a rough beast that had been slumbering of late, through a perverse reading of John Winthrop's "Model of Christian Charity." And third—our primary concern here—he tried to define the historical "immigrant experience" in a way that facilitated contemporary anti-immigrant politics.

In various Liberty Weekend addresses, Reagan argued that the "secret of our progress, our power, and our prosperity" is that we were a "striving, God-fearing, self-reliant people." "In this era of big government," he added, "we sometimes forget that many of our proudest achievements as a nation came not through government, but through private citizens, individuals whose genius and generosity flourished in this climate of freedom." Lee Iacocca, fundraiser for and major domo of the restoration, argued similarly that refurbishing the statue and Ellis Island "gives us a chance to honor those who came before us and the values they cherished: individual enterprise, hard work, and voluntary sacrifice."

At the heart of the Reagan/Iacocca reading of the history of immigration was the "up-from-poverty" saga of the model white ethnics. They, the story went, escaped squalor and repression and came to the land of opportunity, where American freedom made it possible for them to climb the ladder of success through their own individual, family, and community efforts, without help from big government or the taxpayer. This antigovernment scree suited Reagan but ill befitted Lee Iacocca, a man who had supped well at the taxpayer's table.

This version of the immigrant experience simultaneously flattered now comfortable ethnics by lionizing their ancestors as rugged and successful individualists, and legitimated the right wing's dismantling of the New Deal. It also suggested that contemporary immigrants and African Americans should rely on themselves, and implied their depressed situation was a temporary phenomenon. In time, blacks, Asians, and Hispanics, too, would move to the suburbs. And if they did not, the record of prior immigrant success would prove their failure to be a matter of insufficient grit and determination. This approach appropriately acknowledged the very real braveries of individual immigrants. But it obscured the fact that older ethnics and African Americans were instrumental in creating precisely the institutions and practices currently despised by the Right—labor unions, the New Deal, unemployment insurance, social security, old age pensions, civil rights, GI benefits, and health care—all the things, that is, that provided the collective underpinning for individual efforts and successes.

Certainly there is truth in the traditional story. Tens of millions of people from around the globe have voted with their feet for the United States. Often what attracted them, in addition to the jobs produced by the industrialization of a continent, was a culture markedly freer than the one they left behind. But it is worth noting that for all Reagan's celebration of the Statue as the "mother of exiles," he was then doing his best to slam the open door shut. Hundreds who fled the war in El Salvador were incarcerated in detention centers, even without the suggestion of criminality on their part, and required to petition for asylum from jail. The Immigration and Naturalization Service had just opened a six thousand-person capacity camp in Louisiana. Church groups and local political leaders who offered sanctuary to Central American refugees, though arguably the inheritors of Emma Lazarus' mantle, found their efforts opposed, indeed vigorously prosecuted, by the administration.

The American Museum of Immigration

Although Reagan and Iacocca used their command over the commemoration ceremony to promulgate a distorted historical interpretation of the immigrant experience, their media-amplified kickoff was, essentially, a one shot deal. But Liberty Weekend also saw the inauguration of a museum, installed in the base of the statue itself, which will be a more permanent memory marker. What kinds of historical messages will it promote over the long haul? Between 1986 and 1991 that depended on which floor visitors went to, for there were two, quite different museums inside the statue, a fact that requires some explanation.

As part of the larger project of overhauling the Statue of Liberty and Ellis Island, the National Park Service, together with an advisory committee of historians, issued a prospectus, in 1984 that called for an interpretative approach dramatically different from Reagan's and Iacocca's. The historians proposed that the American Museum of Immigration (AMI), then ensconced in the base of the Statue of Liberty, be ousted from its quarters, relocated to Ellis Island, and incorporated into an entirely new museum of immigration. In a word, killed. To replace it in the monument, they proposed a new museum focused on the history of the statue itself.

The historians and the Park Service disliked the AMI's interpretive approach. The AMI had been conceived in the 1950s and had been dedicated by its founders (headed by Pierre S. du Pont III) to promoting a cold war perspective on immigration. At its heart was the proposition that various immigrant groups had fled misery abroad, triumphed over adversity here, and gone on to make distinctive "contributions" to American life. Life in the "teeming tenements," its text said, was hard, but "at least there was hope and always the inspiring example of those who had succeeded by self-sacrifice and hard work."

The exhibit admitted some darker aspects of American life, but drew relentlessly upbeat conclusions. The Chinese, it noted, had faced discrimination, violence, and exclusion, but "nevertheless many rose to prominence in the sciences and professions." True enough. But the subtextual message was that the overcoming of adversity was always an *individual* triumph; apart from soldiers in wartime, the heroes of the AMI exhibit tended to be business persons, inventors, and artists.[1] Amidst all the Horatio Algerism, there was no mention of collective activities and achievements by organized immigrants—of bunds, churches, or nationality groups, much less unions or radical political parties. Nor, despite mentions of various movements for immigration restriction, was sufficient attention paid to the realities of differential exclusion. Despite the imposition of quotas in the 1920s, the AMI exhibit stated, "when the need has been urgent, America has re-opened her doors to the distressed," a generosity perhaps less than self-evident to the Jews who, fleeing Hitler in the 1930s and 1940s, found themselves turned away lest they (in the words of a 1939 *Christian Century* editorial) "exacerbate America's Jewish problem." Finally, the nationality-by-nationality approach, although appealing to many visitors, underscored the absence of those left out, most particularly Asians and South Americans, and triggered occasionally violent animosities, as when a Croatian group, objecting to the classification of their forebears as Yugoslavs, attempted to blow up the statue.

The AMI was intended to be a private sector effort. But fundraising flopped, and the museum had to be bailed out by the federal government, which paid almost all the five million dollar cost. By the time the design was announced, the 1960s had rolled around, and the AMI approach met with a great uproar from African Americans, various ethnic groups, and many historians. Critics charged that the exhibits embodied a nationalistic perspective, stressed the contributions of great men (with emphasis on "men"), propounded a discredited "melting pot" thesis, focused excessively on European immigrants, and had a distinctly martial tone. As one reviewer wrote, "the overall impression you get there is that there are two ways to prove yourself as an American—one is to become rich and famous and the other—not as good—is to die in a war." Protests got some minimal changes made before its grand opening in 1972—an event presided over by Richard Nixon, who used the occasion to make political hay and ideological points—but its essential approach remained intact. Hence the 1984 demand for its removal was, in part, the insistence by a new generation of social historians that a crucial public memory marker reflect contemporary scholarship.

The AMI-Park Service bout ended with a split decision. On their key goal of dismantling the AMI, the Park Service lost. DuPont and other powerful board members got the Reagan administration to order the Park Service to leave the museum in place. Only one major change was made—the excision of a section called "And Still They Come" that had been tacked on in response to protests about the invisibility of the newest immigrants. Invisible once again, they were replaced by two corporate exhibits that trumpeted their institutions' support for the statue's renovation, one by AT&T, the other by "the 55,000 representatives, employees, and suppliers of Avon Corporation (and their families)." Early on in the fundraising effort, rumor had it, a proposal was floated to sell space along the staircase going up to the crown of the statue to corporate advertisers, rather as is done in subways. (Remember the campaign to turn postage stamps into mini-ads?) This seems to have struck even the Rovsek marketeers as transgressing some faint but still discernible line of decency. In the end, only Avon and AT&T managed to get their own little chapel in the shrine.

Presenting Miss Liberty

The Park Service failed to oust the AMI, but it was given a green light to build another museum, dealing strictly with the statue, on a separate floor in the monument's base. In September 1984, the National Park Service hired a consortium of designers to turn the ideas of their new prospectus into an exhibit. It opened on 4 July 1986.

It is an appealing and accessible installation. It does not address the immigration story, but instead concentrates narrowly on the statue's history, examining the impulse behind and the process of the monument's construction. The most popular parts are those that deal with engineering techniques. First-rate videos portray the original production process and depict the transportation of the statue from Paris and its reassembly in New York.

Another video presentation shows modern artisans building a full-scale copper replica of the statue's foot using the original repoussé technique; the replica is available for touching.

A good deal of information is of the *Guinness Book of Records* sort of history: how big, how heavy, how much, how many. Still, there is a fair amount of material that deals with the social and symbolic dimensions of the statue (although it appears to be less gripping to the bulk of the visitors). Much of this material is sensitive to the concerns of the new social history and shows an awareness that the monument had different meanings for different social groups at different times.

The section on the 1880s pedestal fundraising effort points out that early appeals for contributions fared badly because "ordinary citizens considered the colossus a rich man's folly; many rich felt it too much of a populist symbol." A contemporary cartoon, called "The Money Kings and the Statue of Liberty," which criticizes the tightfisted rich, is displayed.

A section explicating the statue's iconography gives some sense of the way symbols of liberty, originally rooted in popular political movements, were here tamed, even domesticated. Laboulaye, the statue's progenitor, is shown emphasizing the distinction between the American notion of liberty and that of the French Revolution or the Paris commune. He and Bartholdi, the sculptor, agreed it "should not be seen as leading an uprising, but rather as lighting the way, peacefully and lawfully." Skillful use is made of a backdrop of Delacroix's revolutionary heroine brandishing a musket and banner, in explaining that Laboulaye "shunned this violent image," arguing that "the American liberty . . . does not hold an incendiary torch, but a beacon which enlightens." The show takes no stance on this material, leaving it up to the visitor to decide if this was a good thing or not. It does not, however, provide enough information on the contemporary context—Laboulaye and his circle's suspicion of the French masses and horror at the commune, their use of the statue to create ties with an American industrial and political elite then confronting and repressing labor organizers and anarchist militants in the United States—to help those not already informed to make up their minds.

The show examines the way the statue has been used in political discourse, commercial exploitation, and popular culture. A presentation on political cartoons includes a reasonable range of opinions, showing the monument's use by jingoists, immigration restriction proponents, opponents of U.S. materialism, and black activists. It even displays a recent cartoon criticizing the activities of the Immigration and Naturalization Service, which depicts the statue as an agent raiding a factory barking: "OK you huddled masses, I know you're in there!"

More problematic is a video of old newsreel clips showing World War I troop ships departing and returning past the statue. This material, and an adjacent display of the statue's use as an advertising symbol for Liberty Bonds, passes silently over the way the ensuing fervor of 100 percent Americanism provided moral armament for those who, in liberty's name, trampled on rights of free speech, and incarcerated and deported dissenters.

The part on commercial exploitation assembles an awesome number of ads that have run over the past century; while the popular culture part makes imaginative use of immigrants' recollections, folk art, postcards, and replicas. A section on the "mother of exiles," tracing the iconographic shift from "enlightenment" to "welcome," makes good use of moving letters and audiotape voiceovers from individual contributors to the statue's renovation (mercifully eliding any corporate puffery, though, again, providing no hint that many immigrants sought social transformation as well as individual advancement).

On the whole I liked the show. Given its location in one of the central shrines of American culture, its ability to keep idolatry to the minimum is refreshing. On the other hand it took only the most minimal risks of interpretation. While the overall feel of the place differed markedly from the American Museum of Immigration upstairs, it did not, ultimately, promote a perspective on either the history of immigration or the nature of liberty that sharply contradicted Reaganesque pieties. Perhaps out of a realistic appreciation for the limits of the possible, the exhibit, while assembling material that provoked reflections on the complexities and contradictions of the American experience, seldom set the artifacts in the larger context that would illuminate them.

The objects, left to speak for themselves, tell an ambiguous story. The final section of the exhibit, for instance, consists entirely of "quotations about liberty." Fairly militant phrases from (among others) Marti, Tubman, Lafayette, Gandhi, and Sartre are set upon a wall. Martin Luther King Jr. is cited saying: "We knew through painful experience that freedom is never voluntarily given by the oppressor; it must be demanded by the oppressed." The problem, again, is with the level of abstraction: unless visitors already know the author, and the context within which she or he uttered the quoted words, implicitly inflammatory phrases lose their punch. Nor is there any exploration of the wide and often conflicting uses to which the term "liberty" has been—and is now being—put. It would have been interesting perhaps for the exhibit to have touched on current debates, in a way that would give the Reaganauts their due—for there is a case to be made that one traditionally American definition of freedom has been the right to private accumulation of capital—but which would also acknowledge other meanings and other traditions.

It must be kept in mind, however, that the Park Service and its designers knew that the statue museum would not be their last opportunity to comment on such matters, for just across the water, on an adjacent island, a truly mammoth enterprise of historic rehabilitation and interpretation was well under way.

Resurrecting Ellis

Renovating the Statue of Liberty was not cheap—it cost $87 million—but it took $161 million to restore Ellis Island. The bulk of the money went to physical reconstruction of the United States Immigration Station; roughly $12 million went to the interpretive program. The island and its structures were under the aegis of the National Park Service. The same private organization, the Statue of Liberty/Ellis Island Foundation, gathered the funds for both projects.

Corporations, ethnic associations, and wealthy individuals anted up much of the cash. The larger contributors are acknowledged in stainless steel panels in the lobby. (So is Dr. Peter Sammartino, the Fairleigh Dickinson University founder who was instrumental in launching the preservation drive.) The biggest donors could choose to have their commemorative plaques affixed in particular rooms but had no say whatever in exhibit design. These markers are fitting and discrete—with the exception of the tacky Kodak logos which emblazon the route to its "America's Family Album" (a video disk display of contributed immigrant photographs).[2]

Another piece of the funding pie was provided by almost two hundred thousand individuals or families. They gave one hundred dollars to have their ancestors' names engraved on one of the 470 copper panels which now line a 971-foot Wall of Honor outside the building along the sea front.

Getting Ellis up and running took more than just a big budget; it required an innovative interaction between its various creators. The National Park Service, in the person of project manager Gary Roth, directed the overall process. Roth went to great lengths to secure the involvement of professional historians. In part this was a reaction against the American Museum of Immigration approach, where the advice of historians had been ignored, with disastrous results. From the very beginning, in 1983, immigration scholars were consulted, first on an ad hoc basis, then through a formal advisory committee. Its members—including Rudolph Vecoli, Virginia Yans-McLaughlin, Louise Año-Nuevo Kerr, Victor Greene, Roger Daniels, Alan Kraut, Kathleen Conzen and Moses Rischin—served without pay. For some it proved an eight-year, *pro bono* part-time job. The historians were involved from initial conceptualization to final reading of exhibit copy. Not all their suggestions were taken up, but the degree of their participation was unprecedented.[3]

Actual design work was handled by MetaForm, Inc., under project manager Jack Masey.[4] MetaForm hired its own historical consultants (including Nathan Glazer, Neil Harris, John Higham, and Thomas Kessner). But the real spadework was done by their talented researchers Phyllis Montgomery, Mary-Angela Hardwick, and Fred Wasserman. The designers were at first leery of the historians' involvement—wary of the "books on walls" approach scholars often advance. By all accounts, however, the three sets of participants soon meshed into a truly collaborative working relationship. The strongest evidence of this are the absorbing, provocative, and richly nuanced exhibits themselves, which I explored a few months after the official reopening in September 1990.

A Walk Through Ellis

My shipmates on the boat to the island chatted excitedly in a dozen different languages as we pulled up to the dock and stepped ashore. Awed at the huge structure confronting us, its giant doorway decked with stone eagles, we entered timidly, bewildered by its size, unsure how to proceed. Then, dead ahead of us, we saw a massive assemblage of heaped-up trunks, wicker baskets, rope-bound suitcases, and baggage carts. Above this pile of antique luggage, plastered with faded ships' stickers, hung blown-up photos of earlier arrivals lugging and dragging similar objects. Their faces displayed a mixture of puzzlement and anticipation with which we could immediately identify. We had arrived, it was clear, at a museum that would use the immigrant processing station's original spaces to recreate, viscerally and intellectually, the experience of those who passed this way nearly a century ago.

Once visitors get their bearings, they can trace a variety of paths through the colossal building. One approach, beloved of tour guides (both in-house National Park Service rangers and outside professionals), is to recapitulate the route taken by the immigrants. We can clamber up the stairs to the Registry Room, where health inspectors once waited, watching our predecessors make the climb, chalking the coats of huffers and puffers, marking them off as potential rejectees.[5]

Some of my fellow pilgrims got no farther than the Great Hall. Those returning to a childhood scene (as many were) seemed transfixed by memories, overwhelmed by emotions. They buttonholed other visitors, poured out old stories, recalled old joys, rehearsed old grudges.[6] Ellis Island is not your ordinary history museum. Nor is it your typical restored house, haunted (at best) by a resident spirit or two. Here, undaunted by the renovations, armies of ghosts throng and jostle. The place is charged with massed significance.

From the Registry Room, the returnees, and those of us whose footsteps were less memory-driven, were free to wander the edifice at will. A host of exhibits awaited us, ready to evoke the old story and set it in a new and larger context. Surveying them thoroughly occupied the better part of a day, which ended definitively when the last boat left at 5:15 p.m. I had badly underestimated the time needed to grasp the place; it took another trip out to finish up.

To the west of the Registry Room lies *Through America's Gate*. Set (appropriately) in a warren of fourteen white-tiled rooms where officials once conducted inspections, this exhibit provides a step-by-step account of what immigrants experienced on the island. We flow from arrival, through medical and legal examinations, to final disposition with each room presenting a stage in the process. The displays deploy a deft mixture of photo-blowups, artifacts, videos of archival footage, and written and aural quotations recounting immigrant stories.[7] The texts are short, straightforward, never condescending, and often poignant. They deliver on the museum's promise to "portray and give voice to the immigrants themselves."

Many touches show how scary the process was. At a station displaying the required mental tests, few of us refrain from trying to solve the puzzles in the allotted few seconds. Seeing how rattled we get with nothing on the line—certainly not deportation—is illuminating. In general, one 1910 arrival recalls, the uniformed immigration officers "had a terrible effect on me"; they conjured up "the Russian uniforms that we were running away from."

In marked contrast to the Cold War pieties promulgated at the American Museum of Immigration, the museum refuses to sentimentalize the Golden Door. Ellis, it is made clear, was as much filter as portal. The island's function was to screen out "those considered undesirable—the incurably ill, the impoverished, the disabled, those who belonged to the criminal classes and all others barred by the immigration laws of the United States." "Criminality" was often defined politically. A depiction of the 1919 red scare raids discusses the deportation of Emma Goldman and her anarchist colleagues.[8] Other barriers were gendered in nature. Women unescorted by men were detained if unable to prove relatives awaited them. A fiance's arrival was not sufficient for white slave-wary officials: the couple was not allowed to leave unless they married on the spot. A last section of *America's Gate*—"Isle of Hope, Isle of Tears"—evokes the despair of those turned away; many people committed suicide on Ellis.

But the exhibit refuses to cast the immigrants as victims. The narrative sparkles with appealing glints of resistance to the bureaucratic flow. One young Macedonian Jewish girl with inoffensive hand warts was terrified at being chalked up for possible rejection; a kindly man explained she could beat the system simply by reversing her coat. A Swedish migrant, asked if he had twenty-five dollars, said he did when he did not. "That's one thing I put over on them," he chortles. Another young woman testee, asked "How do you wash stairs, from the top or from the bottom?" replied tartly: "I don't go to America to wash stairs."

Why she and others *did* come to America is dealt with at the opposite end of the building in *Peak Immigration Years: Immigration to U.S. 1880–1924*. This exhibit is also arranged as a flow chart but its focus is the movement of people to and through Ellis into America.

The initial sections—"Paths of Migration" and "Leaving the Homeland"—portray the events that jolted people into flight. Though primarily treating eastern and southern European conditions, they also deal with the pressures on Norwegians, Mexicans, Canadians, Jamaicans, and the Irish. Jumbo photo-blowups are prominent. Some, like photographer Lewis Hine's, we have seen often. Others—images taken by sympathetic Ellis-based officials—offer fresh perspectives. Audiotapes (voices counterpointed by folk music), videotapes, artifacts, and text complete the package.

Next, "Passage to America" presents appealing wall displays of massed objects: ships manifests, postcards, passports, steamship tickets, boat models, railroad route maps, and timetables. "Ports of Entry" gives a capsule reprise of the Ellis story and, by including a condensed treatment of Angel Island, attends to Asian immigration. (The limited attention to late nineteenth, early twentieth-century African Americans in motion is understandable, since few came through Ellis. Still, might it not have been possible to devote a section to the phenomenon of internal migration? The vast movements from the southern countryside to northern cities could have provided a point of comparison with the international developments.)

Peak Years goes on to present a superb analysis of what immigrants did when they left Ellis—offering, in effect, a panoramic perspective on the remaking of the American working class.

An "At Work in America" section ranges broadly over the continent. It discusses those who labored in mills, mines, and factories, at sea, in small businesses, on construction sites, in sweatshops, and households. "At Work" directly addresses the realities of low wages, child labor, and "inhuman working conditions." It pays particular attention to the varieties of women's work. It also addresses the uneasy and conflict-ridden convergence of American craft unions with immigrant industrial workers to fight what the exhibit is candid enough to call "exploitation by employers." These immigrants were not uprooted singlets, moving from time-frozen villages to America where one-by-one they climb the ladder of opportunity.

Nor were they deracinated by transplantation. "Between Two Worlds" explores their rich and self-sufficient cultures. It dramatically delineates immigrant neighborhoods, churches, families, fraternal groups, newspapers, theaters, and political associations. "Go Betweens" evaluates how immigrant children walked a fine line between two opposing cultures.

Just how opposing the "native" culture could be is interpreted strikingly in "The Closing Door" and "Fear of Outsiders." Huge posters (Restrict All Immigration!) and Klan cartoons complement texts that discuss the social, political, cultural, and economic sources of antiforeign hysteria. The exhibit relates how those who fought to keep the door open were beaten back, and quotas were imposed. A "New Americans" section (its entryway emblazoned with a BE LOYAL poster blowup) reviews the efforts of employers, teachers, bureaucrats, and social workers to submerge newcomers in the melting pot, especially during World War I. And it describes the way hyphenated-Americans negotiated their way to striking a balance between the Old World and the New.

My only reservation about this material is that it never quite conveys the degree to which each immigrant community was divided internally along class lines. In part this follows, justifiably, from the focus on Ellis itself. Here and elsewhere, visitors are reminded that those who passed through the island were a preselected lot. First and second-class passengers were examined at sea and most got permission to land as soon as their ship docked at Manhattan. So it is fair enough that better-off entrants are not scrutinized here. But not emphasizing more strongly that there were *prominenti* as well as *contadini* misses some of the dynamics of the immigrant experience.

At the other end of the social spectrum, the exhibit portrays an immigrant community shorn of its underworld. Perhaps the designers (and donors?) sought to break with unfortunate stereotypes, but prostitutes and gangsters were part of the story, too. Given the exhibit's inclusiveness, they warranted a nod.

On leaving *Peak Years*, the hardy tourist can travel upstairs for greater specificity or downstairs for a global perspective.

The third floor houses *Treasures from Home*, a spinoff exhibit from *Peak Years* emerging as the most popular destination in the museum. In response to a general call, Americans lent or donated cherished items carried from the Old Country. Some were snatched up in flight, others packed with leisurely care. All evoke the difficult decisions confronting people cutting loose from their moorings. The cornucopia of artifacts—mangle boards and prayer books, pillowcases and featherbeds, ouds and clogs—are arrayed by type (clothing and ornament, personal papers) or grouped in shrine-like clusters by donor family (the Semerdjians from Turkey, the Lipovacs from Croatia). Audiotapes, broken when I visited, provide context: Owners describe the objects' provenance.

Also on this top floor are three site-specific exhibits. *Ellis Island Chronicles* covers the history of the island itself, from Native American days to the closing of the station in 1954. Then *Silent Voices* artfully captures the eerie glory of the era of abandonment. Here glassed-in cases of dusty clerical detritus (signs, cash machines, typewriters, file cabinets) complement photographs of deserted spaces, peeling walls, and fallen ceilings. Together they provide a satisfyingly Ruskinian portrait of a weather-lashed crumbling complex; no need for audioghosts here. (Throughout the building, portions of graffiti-covered wall are preserved in place. One area proudly displays entire chunks, as if they were the Elgin Marbles.) *Restoring a Landmark* completes the trilogy with a detailed accounting of the salvage story. This Homeric enterprise involved archaeologists, architects, an expeditionary force of construction workers, and materiel large enough to warrant creation of a temporary bridge to New Jersey.

Two flights below, in the old Railroad Ticket Office (next to the Baggage Room point-of-entry) lies *The Peopling of America.* Here we are reminded that those who passed through Ellis constituted only one segment of a lengthy chain. *Peopling* sets the southern and eastern European influx in a larger temporal context. It recalls those who came earlier—many in shackles—and those who followed later and who continue to come today. It suggests the nature of these global population flows over four centuries not with artifacts or representations but through a statistical survey, with the numbers flourished in cleverly graphic ways.[9]

A fiber-optic display on a globe six feet in diameter traces in flashing lights the major migration pathways of key periods since 1700. Shifting points of embarkation and destination and changing volumes in emigrant flows are presented in an easy-to-comprehend way. The consequences for the United States are tallied at a nearby station. Multicolored three-dimensional piles starkly illustrate the shift in origins from northern European to Asian and Latin American locales. The gender characteristics of succeeding waves is swiftly apparent from a glance at the paired green and orange cardboard-cutout figurines whose size is correlated to male/female demographics. A slew of other charts-made-easy convey information in an almost cartoon-like form (and with cartoon-like accessibility) about the first Americans, the Atlantic slave trade, and the westward expansion.

Peopling emphasizes the multicultural consequences of this rich variety of population sourcing. A word tree reveals the other-language roots of idioms now presumed peculiarly American; a flag of faces portrays a multihued quiltwork; and video monitors (broken during my visits) present interviews with contemporary immigrants. Jamaicans, Salvadorians, Vietnamese, and Ethiopians talk frankly (I am told) about their varied experiences since arriving. The overall thrust pushes hard against the notion that the only "true immigrants" were those who passed through Ellis.

All in all, the contrast between this gargantuan banquet and the thin gruel available at the American Museum of Immigration would have been startling, even jarring, were it not that in January 1991 the Park Service shut the old show forever. The AMI board, so vocal and powerful back in 1985, had virtually faded away by the time their giant new rival opened for business; several members had died, including du Pont. So when Statue of Liberty National Monument Superintendent Ann Belkov moved decisively, dismantling AMI's dioramas and packing them off to NPS headquarters in Harper's Ferry, there were only a few small squeaks of protest, which quickly subsided.

Future Prospects

My one overarching reservation about the museum, aside from the difficulty of grasping it in one visit, is that it is relatively easy to divide context from content. The designers and historians clearly intended the manifold offerings to be a single package. Most expected that visitors—who are left completely to their own devices—would go first to the Registry Room, then up to the various site- and period-specific exhibits, and finally down to *Peopling* for the broader view. In practice, museum guests, like the original processees, are bucking the intended flow. Most head first to the introductory film, Charles Guggenheim's twenty-seven minute long "Island of Hope, Island of Tears."[10] Then, after the Registry Room, they make a beeline for the "Treasures" show, the least contextualized in the building, drawn by the power of its authentic objects. From there, they take in one or more of the upstairs shows, depending on the time available. (Many stay only an hour or two, combining their Ellis trip with one to the Statue of Liberty.) Most never do get down to the contextual discussion in *Peopling*. This set of choices, which seems to be informally encouraged by Park Service personnel, is reinforced by the sharp disjuncture between the intensely human exhibits above and the number-crunching perspectives below.

This is a pity. What gets lost is precisely what the historians struggled to get included, a sense that the "immigration" experience transcends Ellis. I believe *Peopling* might have been more appealing and more able to compete with the photos and artifacts upstairs, if at least some humanizing elements had been provided along with the numbers (some leg irons and photoblowups along with slave trade statistics). Since they were not, wouldn't it still be worth nudging visitors, perhaps via appropriate signage, toward spending at least a few moments in *Peopling* rather than scooting them off in other directions? Even the briefest visit would provide a broadening counterthrust to the narrower material upstairs.

Yet even an extended session in *Peopling* would do little to remind visitors that immigration remains an explosive political subject. There is nothing there that helps citizens sort through contemporary debates over national legislation, nothing that examines in detail the situation of today's illegal aliens, nothing that explores current animosities toward recent arrivals. It would be perfectly possible to leave Ellis with warm feelings toward old migrants, and preexisting resentments of gooks, spics, and towel-heads left intact.

The Park Service suggested in 1991 that such issues would be handled by ongoing temporary exhibits—and indeed one of the earliest such shows presented photographic images of modern sweatshops—but in the years since the opening, there has been little attempt to grapple with contemporary issues. With no ongoing funding base, the staff depends on outside sponsors, and most of these have been ethnic associations, interested in treatments of Italians or Germans, Irish or Swedes. It is a pity because Ellis would be a splendid venue for imaginative exhibitions.

How about a show that, for instance, set current debates about immigration policy in historical and international perspective? Major controversy is now underway, as it has been for decades, over the continuing influx of Mexican workers into the Southwest, and of undocumented immigrants into the country in general. Might not public understanding of the issues at stake be illuminated by an exhibit that set national policies on labor migration in historical and international perspective, perhaps by comparing the experience of various countries with "guest workers"—exploring the role of Mexicans in the United States, Turks in Germany, North Africans in France, Chinese in Africa? Such a show, which might be constructed with cooperation from curators from all those countries, could perhaps overcome some of the temporal and cultural provincialism that marks much of the conventional discourse.

Another exhibit could discuss the pros and cons of current and proposed immigration policies, such as California's Proposition 187. (I myself would love to see submitted to public scrutiny the recent suggestion of a Heritage Foundation fellow that immigration rights be auctioned off, in effect admitting only the highest bidders. This would, its sponsor admits, discriminate among applicants, but only "according to the standard of a market-oriented society: ability and willingness to pay.")

Still another exhibit might examine the effect of national foreign policies in engendering mass demographic movements. It might be intriguing to compare the role of English imperialism in launching the mass Irish migration of the nineteenth century, with the impact of contemporary U.S. and European corporate expansion on Third World peasantries who first moved to urban shantytowns in their home countries, and eventually to United States and European cities. Perhaps if visitors to Ellis Island were aware of the effect on immigration flows of actions taken by the International Monetary Fund, major multinationals, and the Central Intelligence Agency, it might generate some fresh thinking on the subject. Despite its complexity, by the way, such an exhibit, like any of the shows I am proposing, need not be dry or dull. One could, for example, track and compare the migratory experience of two families; one, composed of 1850s Irish refugees; the second a contemporary Dominican family, displaced from the island's countryside to an ITT-leased free trade zone where they do industrial assembly work at twenty-seven cents per hour, who then, after the U.S. invasion in 1965, move to Washington Heights in New York City.

In a related vein, why not a comparative show on America as a haven for political exiles—assessing the varying welcomes accorded Germans in 1848, Russians in 1905, European Jews in the 1930s and 1940s, Hungarians in 1956, Cubans in 1959, Chileans in 1973, and Haitians, Vietnamese, Cubans, and Salvadoreans in the 1980s and 1990s. It would be interesting to examine who America has refused (and is refusing) entry, on political and "moral" grounds. Again, this might provide a context within which to evaluate our contemporary policies on, say, Caribbean and Central American immigration.[11]

Still another show might treat the intersecting histories of gender and immigration. An entire exhibit could fruitfully be devoted to the special meanings of migration—and of "liberty," for that matter—for immigrant wives. There has been much interesting work done recently on tensions within immigrant families, especially between mothers and daughters, the incorporation of which into public presentations might move us past the patriarchal cinematic images that still dominate much thinking on the subject.

There are many other potentially interesting and germane history presentations Ellis might house, and one day perhaps will. But for the moment there is plenty to occupy visitors, who are unusually reflective, spending much more time lingering over artifacts, examining texts, and commenting to one another than is customary at museums. They appear moved and challenged, not only by material that affirms prior convictions, but by warts-and-all sections like the antiimmigrant material that challenges conventional understandings. Some exemplary public history is being shown on those islands; it is well worth taking the boat over to check them out.

Notes

This is a combination of three pieces: "Ronald Reagan, Ellis Island, and Popular History," *Newsletter of the Organization of American Historians* (1987); "Hijacking History: Ronald Reagan and the Statue of Liberty," *Radical History Review*, 36 (1987); "Boat People: A Review of the Ellis Island Museum," *Journal of American History* (December 1991).

Boat People: Immigration History at the Statue of Liberty and Ellis Island

Thanks to Diana Pardue and Gary Roth for their interviews and to Fred Wasserman for rounding up the graphic.

1. Only African Americans somehow failed this test of individual initiative. Although the exhibit noted the handicaps under which they labored, and profiled the "significant contributions" of some black inventors, preachers, and soldiers, one caption stated somewhat apologetically that although "relatively few outstanding black immigrants have been identified and their contributions confirmed, many more are sure to come to light as our research continues." Among the many social contributions that get lost by searching for celebrities is the fact that slave labor constructed much of the foundation of this country.

   It is also worth noting that this classic theme of individualism permeated the Liberty Weekend festivities. Reagan and Iacocca were not voices in the wilderness. The mass media, especially the weeklies like *Time* and *Newsweek*, were full of success sagas about recent immigrants who had "made it."
2. The NYNEX learning center is less self-promotional. Planned to mesh with Ellis exhibits, it offers a sixteen-screen interactive video wall for use by school and other groups. Monumentally successful, it draws two hundred school groups a month.
3. Despite differences in perspective and approach among the scholars, on the whole they were agreed in contesting the uses to which the immigration saga was then being put by the Reagan Administration.
4. Exhibit designers included John Grady, Tom Geismar, and Ivan Chermayeff. Exhibit construction was handled by Rathe Productions, Inc., and Design and Production, Inc. For more on the design process, see Robert A. Parker, "The Ellis Island Immigration Museum," *Communication Arts* (January/February 1991), 82–93.
5. Some preservationists in the Park Service opposed reconstructing the demolished stairway, but the exhibit designers and the historians committee wanted visitors to be able to re-create the experience. The latter group prevailed, though in all other respects the Great Hall has been restored to its 1918–24 incarnation and left intact and uncluttered. Photo exhibits on the east and west balconies portray its appearance during other periods.
6. The Park Service continues to collect oral histories from selected visitors.
7. Audiotaped reflections, gathered in 1985, provide the bulk of these. In theory the background murmur of ex-immigrant voices peoples the rooms with ghosts. A wonderful idea, it is not bug-free in practice; sometimes they are too low to hear, othertimes so noisy as to be intrusive. Like many other aspects of the exhibits, the taping system is slated for adjustment.
8. Political "criminals" of the 1950s, also detained on Ellis, are mentioned elsewhere, though all too briefly.

9. The sophisticated exhibit cautions that "statistics" must be read in a critical light. They are, it explains, not "factual" measures but themselves historical artifacts reflecting changing attitudes about race, ethnicity and national identity.
10. The film is a good introduction to the temporally specific exhibits, though its vision of a benighted Europe and benign America is somewhat out of sync with the more sophisticated and nuanced material presented upstairs. Too uncritical an acceptance of its images and interviews could render inexplicable such exhibits as those that treat the millions of "birds of passage" who after tasting life in the land of freedom and opportunity went back home. On the other hand the film's recognition of the "tears" aspect of the immigration process was strong enough to rouse the ire of at least one Reagan official.
11. A coda to such a show might treat the history of the inclusion/exclusion of ideas. It might examine the kinds of ideas that have historically been deemed too dangerous to admit to the free marketplace, and the individuals who have been, and are currently, considered too dangerous to be allowed even temporary access to willing American audiences. This could have a popular dimension—an audio-exhibit featuring taped segments of banned speeches—and a more scholarly component, depicting the way the history of censorship illuminates our changing and shifting political and sexual culture.

Progress Talk: Museums of Science, Technology, and Industry

History of Water Transportation exhibit, Smithsonian Institution, Arts and Industries Building, circa 1885. (Smithsonian Institution Archives Record Unit 95, Box 43, Folder 10, Negative #2964.)

When I lived in Baltimore, my next door neighbor was an engineer who worked at a big steel company. Most weekends he would, as it were, duck into a phone booth, doff his civvies and mild mannered demeanor, don overalls and a striped cap, and emerge in his vigorous alternate persona as President of the Steam Historical Society. And off he would go to play with giant locomotives and assorted engines. He took me along a few times. I had great fun strolling amid the huffing-puffing machines. But I was more fascinated by my neighbor's fascination with technology. I never quite understood it. Despite my own childhood love affair with electric trains and erector sets, I felt something was eluding me. After reading and reflecting upon recent work on science and technology museums, I think I have come somewhat closer to understanding my old neighbor.

It has always seemed to me that while museums serve many purposes, perhaps their progenitors' highest priority has been promoting particular views of whichever aspect of reality their institution focuses upon. I also think that, as Donald Horne puts it in *The Great Museum*, these versions of reality "tend to suit dominant groups and to uphold a certain social order," but I am less interested for the moment in the effectiveness of museum messages than in what they tell us about the convictions of those who assemble, finance, and direct them.

If museums can provide clues as to how their designers saw themselves (or how they wanted themselves to appear), then studying the history of technology museums might (among other things) help us to understand the formation of the engineering community, in particular, and, more broadly, what has been called by some the professional-managerial class. More to the point, the reverse might also be true: Perhaps the development of technology museums can be illuminated by considering them as aspects of a developing class culture.

Engineering the Past

Engineers emerged in the course of the nineteenth century out of the wider world of mechanics and skilled workers, by abandoning tradition and empiricism in favor of the application of science. Slowly at first, then picking up speed during and after the Civil War, the process of invention and technological change passed into the hands of university-trained engineers. Knowledge was transmitted not by masters to apprentices but through colleges, professional organizations, and technical literature; the old trial and error approach was replaced by a disciplined, systematic, and administrative outlook. This transformation, which took place in canals and rails, bridge building and mining, and then, most dramatically, in the chemical and electrical industries, was part of a larger phenomenon, the development of science-based capitalism.

Statistics tell part of the story: There were 5,600 engineers in 1870, 38,000 in 1900, and 217,000 in 1930. (The number of managers went from 57,000 to 313,000 in the same 60 year period.) But we are dealing with more than the growth of an occupational category here; we are watching the development of a substantial fragment of a new class, replete with its own culture.

Like other new classes summoned into being by larger ecodynamics, engineers had to sort out their status. This was difficult, as they did not quite fit. For all their training, they were not independent professionals, as they swiftly became corporate employees. But they were hardly to be classed with blue or white-collar workers; indeed, many became corporate managers. In universities they were looked down on by classicists; in the culture at large, they felt they lacked a status commensurate with their centrality to the economy.

Not surprisingly they were drawn to a constellation of ideas that lauded precisely the movement from empiricism to science that had constituted their own field. To positivists, science was the really potent force, more so than class, race, or economic interest, in shaping the direction of cultural change. In their schema, the emergence of the scientific-industrial system was the most significant development in modern history. The syncretic progressive thought of the era was a historicist creed—historicization was easy to come by in an era of such overwhelming change. Here was the Victorian bourgeois creed at its most buoyant and optimistic, brimming with belief in progress, reason, the arts and sciences, education, and emancipation. Self-confident natural and social scientists were convinced they had uncovered the invariant general laws which, if left to themselves, would transform the world.

But how to spread the gospel? Industrialists had been proclaiming the good news at industrial expositions; in the late nineteenth and early twentieth century a new site of cultural assertion emerged, the technology museum.

At the Smithsonian Institution museum director and scientist George Brown Goode provided the theory for dealing with technological artifacts—situating them on a progressive continuum from rude to complex, savage to civilized—and John Elfreth Watkins, a civil engineer, started collecting, drawing upon his contacts in the railroad industry. Their sustaining year round audience was the high-density scientific community of Washington, composed of thousands of professional, technical, and scientific workers who operated the government's network of research bureaus.

Watkins was followed by George C. Maynard, an electrical engineer with contacts at Bell and elsewhere. And he was followed by Carl W. Mitman, the mining engineer who in 1920, in collaboration with the mechanical engineer Holbrook Fitz-John Porter, suggested creating a full-blown museum. The proposed institution's promotion of professional pride and prestige, its ratification of engineering as an "applied science" (i.e., not what workers do), and its call for a hall of fame, all attracted the enthusiastic support of the engineering societies.

While it is important to connect the emergence of technological history to the ideological interests of American engineers, and to link the new museology to the intellectual universe of the community of scientific and technical workers in Washington, it is also important to note the degree to which both the ideological interests and the intellectual constructs were themselves shaped in the process of conflict with rival (indeed antagonistic) ways of perceiving and interpreting contemporary reality. And this, in turn, might make it worth our while to dig a bit more deeply into the process of class formation.

For one thing, the sunny side up assessments of the progressives and the engineers clashed with other accounts, which dwelt upon other aspects of reality. There were, for example, contemporaries who argued that technological development in capitalist society had a serious down side. At one end of the social scale, the American antimodernist followers of Ruskin and Morris in the arts and crafts movement thought the machine less promethean than demonic. At the other end, the followers of Henry George noted that progress seemed all too consistent with poverty.

George, in 1883, wondered aloud if labor-saving inventions and the greater division of labor had not in fact produced "positive evils" for the working classes by "degrading men into the position of mere feeders of machines." Engineers considered the factory system an advance but industrial laborers were less convinced, and their explosive protests provided a dark and bloody counterpoint to the optimistic conclaves of industrialists and engineers. One year after the centennial celebration of 1876, parts of Pittsburgh went up in the flames of the Great Railroad Strike, and twenty carloads of hi-tech equipment turned scrap iron, were carted off to Altoona. The Columbian Exposition festivities of 1893 were swiftly followed by the massive street shootouts of the Pullman Strike of 1894. Nor did theories of steady incremental progress mesh neatly with the wrenching ups and downs of the boom-bust cycle.

The problem was that progressive theory had reversed reality: Science, in fact, was the servant, not the master, of the capitalist order, and the imperatives of profit, not abstract reason, ruled the economic jungle.

It might, therefore, be worth considering the degree to which the positivists' ideology (soon to be embedded in museum exhibits) contained significant elements of wishful thinking or denial—making the irrational seem rational, making the exploitative seem emancipatory. It might be worth exploring the way it developed, not in immaculate isolation but in dialectical and adversarial relationship to other ideologies, advanced by other interests. Eric Hobsbawm, among others, has suggested that the emphasis on the uniform, continuous, and non-revolutionary operations of natural laws beyond query or wilful modification, rather as the laws of laissez-faire political economy were held to be, might have stemmed from a distrust of social revolutions, from a desire to reduce change in human society to the rules of biological evolution. (This was, we must recall, a position that could be remarkably radical in the context of Victorian times, when it also led to a distrust of traditional religion with its discontinuous miracles and creationism.)

If this is the case, it renders another aspect of the emerging technology museum more comprehensible—the tight narrowing of its focus to machines. Partly, of course, this is an variant of a standard museum problem, the tyranny of objects, the lure of the authentic, the tendency to venerate things as sacred in themselves. Partly it is a case of what David Lowenthal, citing Baudrillard and Clifford, who in turn draw upon Marx, calls the tendency of museums to foster "the illusion of a relationship between things [in] place of a social relation." But partly it is specific to a particular period and problematic: by paying homage to machines and products, by presenting machines as the movers of the Industrial Revolution, by ignoring the fact that machines were central to the invention of the factory system and formation of the working class, by encouraging reverence towards machines for their own sake as if all machines were self-evidently good and their results progressive, by making human progress seem to depend on machines begetting machines in a process midwived by genius inventors—all this tended to imply that machines, not capitalists, were in charge. This further implied that the motives for change lay in the machines rather than the economic necessities perceived by their owners and that the social processes of factory production or the negative aspects of technology's effects on peoples lives were not worthy of consideration.

But why, to return to our class protagonist, would engineers be drawn to such a rendering of reality? Pride in their status and their science need not inherently have led to such a political stance. Indeed there had long been a radical strain amongst engineers, professionals, and managers in general. Veblen, for one, thought engineers might be the new revolutionaries. He saw that their ideals might lead them to denounce what Veblen saw as the inevitable conflict between rationality and profit. And some engineers, who believed their allegiance lay with civilization, not capital, did enlist in the ranks of progressive reform; some even became socialists. Why, then, did the engineers line up behind the new museology?

Industrial Museums and the New Corporate Order

The answer, I suspect, is tied up with the answer to another question: Why did the industrial museums suddenly flourish in the 1920s? For if Mitman and Porter's 1922 public sector effort came a cropper, the private sector stepped in with vigor and resources.

Henry Towne, an engineer and president of a manufacturing company, endowed the New York Museum of Science and Industry in 1926, and opened it in 1930. Henry Ford worked on Dearborn through the late 1920s until it was ready in 1930. The Franklin Institute opened its science museum in 1934 (with aid from industrialist Samuel Fels). Amateur historical societies of technology and engineering like the Railway and Locomotive Historical Society sprouted. And Julius Rosenwald started promoting the Chicago Museum of Science and Industry in 1921 and got it established in 1926.

Why then? Why the 1920s? Some have noted that wealthy industrialists, who had been funding art museums, now shifted their patronage stream, but not why they did so. Could part of the story be that the 1920s marked the (admittedly temporary—but they did not know that) end of a long and difficult period of industrial warfare, of a roller coaster economy, of foreign war? In the 1920s American capitalists triumphed over a host of foreign and domestic opponents, and were ready to celebrate their newfound stability, and provide themselves with a pedigree. They were also flush with the funds to make it all happen.

The twenties were also the time when engineers (and most of the professional-managerial class) got absorbed thoroughly into the corporate structure. Through control over the educational process and licensing, professional engineers gained a monopoly over scientific technology. And by hiring them in massive numbers, industrial corporations gained a monopoly over professional engineers, a process probably speeded up by World War I and professional-managerial recoil from the Russian revolution and domestic radicalism. From 1900 to 1920 many engineering societies witnessed struggles between engineer-professionals and business-oriented engineers loyal to employers. By the 1920s, what Edwin T. Layton calls the "revolt of the engineers" was over. They had been absorbed into the corporate-industrial order as a subaltern class.

This need not be construed as a sell-out. The engineers could well have believed that progressive, science-based capitalism was being changed, humanized, in part by their own entry into the corporate world. Mumford was not alone in projecting a change from a sordid paleotechnic to a cleaner, neotechnic era. It was correspondingly easy for engineers to convince themselves that scientific management was not about exploiting or controlling the workforce, but about producing as efficiently as possible. Henry Towne had long been a promoter, in the engineering world, of making "shop management . . . of equal importance with that of engineering." It was easy not to discern the ways their language was packed with capitalist imperatives. A similar blindness would afflict the new museums.

It was also the case that, in the 1920s, the legitimacy of the corporate order, for all its new solidity, continued to be challenged and thus required defense. Abroad, there were rival national capitalisms (economic and military). (They had museums: indeed the Deutsches Museum celebrated Germany's attainment of ascendancy over Britain as the leading scientific-industrial society.) At home, many objected to the role of technology in perpetrating the phenomenal slaughter (and profit) levels of World War I. (It is interesting, in this regard, that Towne first called his museum "peaceful" and that Ford had been a pacifist.) It should not be surprising to find some industrialists being drawn to a museum movement that promised to project a good image, especially in a decade that thrived on salesmanship, advertising, and public relations. (It is perhaps not irrelevant that Rosenwald was a master not of production but of consumer sales.)

Perhaps the industrial museum flourished in the twenties because it could now draw upon the resources of corporations, and of engineers who had made their peace with the corporate world. But there was a price to be paid. The broadness of vision of the earlier engineers and curators went out the window. The wide-angle story of the growth of science-based capitalism (with its pluses and minuses) turned into a narrow-gauge story about the growth of technology in the abstract. Industry donated carloads of objects but they came prelabelled, enmeshed in assumptions. The packaging could be challenged but that would render future deliveries less likely.

The development of the Chicago Museum was symptomatic. Waldemar Kaempffert, made director in 1928, was an evolutionist alive to the connections of technology to social and cultural life, aware of such "ironies" as the relationship between the cotton gin and the perpetuation of slavery (even though he remained basically optimistic about the capitalist order). Kaempffert was apparently ousted in 1931 by "forceful business executives" who did not appreciate complex messages. Their distaste for ambiguity was perhaps heightened by the Depression, in that the system's collapse, and the mounting attacks on it, made its justification all the more important. The 1933 Century of Progress Fair set out to defend industrial corporations, then being criticized for their size and private power, by "domesticat[ing] science and identify[ing] decisively its contributions to the public welfare with the industrial corporation." Lenox R. Lohr, one of the fair's organizers and one of the new breed of engineers thoroughly integrated into corporate management, was brought in to redo the Chicago Museum. That was the end of any efforts to address the negative social effects of capitalism.

This process accelerated in the 1940s, against the backdrop of the Cold War and a commercial boom. Lohr took the logical next step and invited the corporations themselves to design and build the exhibits. They were delighted at the opportunity to build public good will in a "noncommercial" setting.

A similar process went on in the public sector. At the Smithsonian, Mitman's protégé Frank Taylor, yet another curator-engineer, got the Museum of History and Technology established in 1964. But the new museum retreated from the earlier broad vision. It presented sanitized versions of technological history bereft of human agency, assembled artifacts in evolutionary array, and pronounced progress inevitable.

Which brings me to the subject of hegemony. Anthropologist Richard Handler has warned museum historians not to "buy into" revisionists' "simplistic theories of cultural hegemony"; given the solitary nature of his citation, "revisionists" apparently means me. Perhaps my own imprecision is to blame, for Mr. Handler suggests that I see museums purveying ideologies "that can be used to dominate and control the mass public," and I don't quite recognize myself in that categorization. So perhaps I can fold a clarification of my position into these concluding reflections on science and technology museums.

In several essays on cultural institutions that promote historical consciousness (or unconsciousness), I have tried to explore several issues. First there is the matter of the motivation of those who construct the institutions.

On one hand, there is no need to assume simple-minded conspiracies to fleece mass flocks; more often than not what museum progenitors do is to embed in their institutions the commonplace ideas of their class's culture. Science museum founders were often didactic. They had a point of view and intended, often quite consciously, to get it across. But this did not seem "biased" or self-interested to them for they knew they spoke the truth. When Lenox Lohr wrote that "we [at the Chicago Museum] have no political bias, we are proving merely the truth" he was simply formulating, in rather a bald way, the manner in which intellectual constructs common to the scientific and professional community informed museum exhibitry.

On the other hand, a proper predilection for subtlety does not require that we overlook more straightforward self-promoting motives, especially when they are boldly proclaimed as such. Lohr was quite explicit in saying there was "no reason that the Rosenwald Museum should not be the largest factor in the country to make good public relations for industry." (The imagineers at Disney World were similarly upfront in selling the services of Mickey Mouse to the corporate world.) Museums also pushed a particular line when they saw themselves in combat with alternative perspectives. The Commercial Club of Chicago was eminently aware that, in their words, "old standards are falling," "traditions are being looked at askance," and "new ideologies are creeping in." In response, it set out to show that "the American way of life" was a product of "free enterprise" and the "profit motive." One cannot get much more straightforward than that.

It is true, of course, that matters are seldom so black and white. I have tried to suggest that even where there is a crude owner intent, actual museum messages do not simply reflect it, for they are the outcome of negotiation among various players within the cultural institution itself, and of an implicit dialogue held with the potential audiences who must be attracted. Still, not all parties at a bargaining table are equally powerful. Those who command financial or political resources may not make intrusive use of their power, but power remains a reality, and he who pays the piper may indirectly call the tunes that are not to be sung. Remember Chicago's "forceful business executives."

From the question of motivation, let's move to the question of content. Mr. Handler says I focus on the "purveying of patriotism." While that can be part of the picture, I think of hegemony in broader terms: as promoting ways of seeing, or of not seeing, the nature of the social order. Mr. Horne refers to it as "a culture shared by rulers and ruled, ways of doing things and seeing the world so ingrained as to have become 'common sense.' " These unexamined assumptions undergird the legitimacy of a social system, so Gramsci argued, far more effectively than crude ideological cudgeling.

At technology museums, we are given carefully edited stories of mining or industry that leave out labor relations, pollution, foreign competition, credit arrangements, labor and radical movements—the list of omissions is endless. Going deeper still, we find in what is referred to as "hardware history," a set of assumptions about technology embedded in the very nomenclenture, assumptions that finesse all the interesting questions about the formation and social consequences of technology, and have the effect of depowering those who accept them.

But even if the motivation is conscious and the message is well crafted, the most difficult aspect of the problem of hegemony concerns effectiveness. And here the short answer is that we do not know if the messages projected by science and technology museums are the messages received. I certainly do not assume people are blank cassettes waiting to be magnetized. But the problem is even more complicated when "consumers as co-producers" are factored in. In the case of the hugely popular science museums, I am willing to guess that many in the audience—perhaps especially engineers like my former neighbor—already share the assumptions the museums embed, and that they go to have a world view ratified. I also believe that the technological determinist perspective of "progress talk" works against the long-term interests of many museum spectators.

Which brings me to my last point, the question of change. I have long argued that museum messages reflect not just internal institutional negotiation, but also a larger balance of social forces. My general theoretical perspective, and my empirical work on places like Williamsburg and Disney World, suggests that changing political and ecological consciousness in the 1960s and 1970s had a tremendous impact on prevailing interpretations. Those institutions could no longer get away with approaches that worked in the 1950s. Nor did the social historians of technology who began working in those decades want to purvey the old messages any longer.

Since the founding of the journal *Technology and Culture* in 1959, a considerable amount of work has broken with the myths of autonomous and progressive technological development. The new studies demonstrate that technical designs can not be abstracted from their social, indeed political contexts. They show the malleability of inventions, their susceptibility to other than technical influences—such as capital's desire to control labor. They explore the way cultural preferences speed, slow, or shape technological development, how technical designs are cultural value-laden artifacts.

A whole new field has opened up that examines the relations between technology and gender, focusing on such topics as the way labor-saving machines make home management more burdensome, or how word processors, with the capability of eliminating secretarial drudgery, are in fact used to extort greater output and monitor employee activities.

Can technology museums better reflect this new work? Can such institutions be reconceived—as Patrick Geddes and Lewis Mumford proposed long ago—as civic galleries that aim to enhance citizen understanding of, and power over, the politics of technology? Could we have museums that explored the social and political basis of the production of technology, the nature of the use and misuse of technology in the workplace, the social consequences of particular technologies?

Once we deconstruct the notion that technological development is a blind and automatic process that moves according to its own inner imperatives, we can begin to debate different possible technological directions from the standpoint of their social implications. We need to regain social control over technological policy. Museums can help.

Note

This previously unpublished paper was originally given as a comment on two papers presented at a conference, "Collections and Culture: Museums and the Development of American Life and Thought," held at the Wilson Center on 15–16 October 1987. The papers were Arthur P. Molella, "The Museum That Never Was: Anticipations of the Smithsonian's Museum of History and Technology," and James Mann, "The Chicago Museum of Science and Industry." It has been revised to stand on its own. Molella's piece has since appeared as "The Museum That Might Have Been: the Smithsonian's National Museum of Engineering and Industry," in *Technology and Culture*, 32, no. 1 (April 1991), 237–63. Mann's Rutgers doctoral dissertation (1988) is: "Engineer of Mass Education: Lenox R. Lohr and the Celebration of American Science and Industry."

Industrial Museums and the History of Deindustrialization

Blast Furnaces being demolished, Youngstown, Ohio. (© Copyright 1982, *The Vindicator*, Youngstown, Ohio. All Rights Reserved.)

The 1970s and 1980s ushered in dramatic changes in the world of industrial museums. The focus of attention shifted from industrial objects, processes, and entrepreneurs, to the universe of the working class: its experience, its culture and cultural creativity, its forms of economic and, to a lesser degree, political organization. In North Carolina, many public historians now tell the story of the region's mill towns largely from the point of view of the workers. They examine the experience of paternalism, the nature of textile workers' culture, and the story of the populist movement, recalling especially its attempts to transcend racism in the south. In New Jersey, Paterson's Botto House chronicles silk workers' lives in the mills, in their homes, and on the picket lines. In Massachusetts, Lowell's National Historical Park chronicles the world of labor from the mill girls through the ethnic workers of the twentieth century. South Bend Indiana's Discovery Hall, a city-sponsored museum of industry, presents reminiscences of Polish and Hungarian autoworkers and recalls the sitdown strikes. Some years ago I decried the thinness of museums' attention to working class life and their tendency to avoid conflict in the past. Times have changed. This is clearly due to the efforts and the struggles and the courage of public historians, and I think it is a splendid development.

For all the progress, possibilities for creative new approaches still exist. I would like to suggest some pathways that public historians might consider worthy of exploration. Let me first state them abstractly, and then give an example of a specific interpretive project that might both serve as a vehicle for the theoretical propositions and yet be of practical interest to industrial museum designers.

First, I think we need to strive for a still better connection of past, present, and future in our exhibitry, to overcome the tendency many Americans have of seeing the past as something that is over and done with, and of merely nostalgic, academic, or entertainment value. This has, of course, become something of a ritual piety in our profession. The difficult question, really, is how to accomplish this?

One clue might lie in my second abstract point: I think we need to stress that our museums treat moments in larger processes, processes that are still in operation. Exhibits should be analogous not to snapshots, but to frames from an ongoing movie.

Third, I'd like to see our presentations set in a larger spatial as well as temporal context: I think even the most "local" of exhibits would benefit from a more global perspective. Fourth, I believe we would benefit from paying considerably greater attention to the role of the state in the histories we are relating. We need to recall, for example, that industrial workers and, for that matter, industrial capitalists, were citizens, and still are.

As a way of illustrating how these concerns might be brought to bear on a particular historical problem, I'm going to focus on "deindustrialization," a contemporary issue of enormous relevance to museums that treat the history of industrialization. Indeed, the very creation of an industrial museum is often a response by a community to the collapse of its manufacturing base, part of an attempt to transform defunct plants into marketable historical commodities and thus generate jobs. But the value to museums of telling the story of "deindustrialization" goes deeper than institutional self-reflection: the issue is a matter of considerable public concern and an accessible treatment of it might attract visitors. Tour guides at industrial museums tell me people repeatedly ask them: "Why did the factories leave?" and "Where did they go?" Yet most industrial museums deal with this matter at best tangentially. An opportunity is being lost to inform visitors about great historical processes that have drastically affected their lives, and thus to empower them by enhancing their capacity to understand, and perhaps change, their world.

Industrialization

Before we can tackle the matter of "deindustrialization," we have to talk about "industrialization"—the concept around which most industrial museums organize their interpretive structure. I have problems with the word as it is commonly used to describe the course of American economic history. It sidesteps the fact that industrialization in the United States was of a particular variety: it was carried out under capitalist auspices. And capitalism is only one of a variety of possible roads a society may travel down if it chooses or feels itself impelled to embark on industrialization.

Adding the word "capitalist" is not a nominal quibble. It alters interpretive strategies. It forces a shift of attention from technology to the social relations of production, and then beyond (and to some degree behind) those relations. It highlights the way members of all classes find their actions constrained, though not determined, by the rules of the capitalist game and the logic of the capitalist system.

Take Lowell, Massachusetts. Nineteenth-century Boston capitalists dreamed they could avoid the European experience and build capitalism without class conflict. They thought they could step outside of history (in this, of course, they were typical Americans). But they found soon enough that competition, in a context of unequal class power, led to old world results. The Lowell museum's introductory slide show demonstrates this quite nicely. It notes that "ironically, success led to competition"; that competition forced employers to push wages down in order to keep profits up; and that this engendered working-class resistance, which shattered the utopian vision of harmony. What happened, in other words, was a textbook case of the increasing exploitation of labor (at least if Volume 1 of *Capital* is the text), not because the mill owners were bad guys, but because the nature of the capitalist game circumscribed the choices individual entrepreneurs faced. Rationality at the level of the firm led to a larger social irrationality. This was not the first time such a thing happened. Nor would it be the last. I think museum goers benefit from Lowell's pointing out, with inventiveness and economy, that large systemic issues were at stake in the mill girls' story.

A quick caution here: Obviously, telling the full story of a local situation requires close attention to the specific historical context. One cannot deduce the nature of particular events from an abstract analysis of capital-labor relations. A full presentation of the Lowell case, for instance, would have to consider the crucial role of gender, the existence of a regional and international labor mobility, the role of the state, the nature of capitalist development elsewhere on the planet—and many other matters. But keeping the more abstract issues in the front of our minds reminds us of several things.

First, before capitalism could be fully constituted in this country (as elsewhere), it required not just factories and workplaces, but an entire support structure of laws, spatial reorganizations, and political and cultural transformations. Second, capitalism did not come over on the first ships nor grow spontaneously out of American soil. It was, rather, merely one of a variety of contending modes of organizing an economy and society. It was resisted by artisans, small farmers, and slave planters as well as native and immigrant laborers. Most of these people, who together constituted the overwhelming majority of Americans, rejected capitalism. They saw the industrialists and "moneyed aristocrats" it engendered as potential usurpers of the republic. They believed the spread of wage labor, and the growth of the urban poor, to be degrading and dangerous reversals of the gains achieved for working people by the American Revolution. The nineteenth century was marked by clashes not only over wages and hours, but over tariffs, immigration policy, slavery, the gender order, the judicial and financial systems, and the overall future course of the United States—a future that, at the time, seemed very much up for grabs. Capitalism's opponents would repeatedly propose a variety of other systemic paths for the United States to follow—a slave republic, an agrarian freeholders democracy, a cooperative commonwealth, a socialist society.

A third and closely related point: Workers were citizens, not just workers. This is an area museums have not sufficiently explored, either at the grand level of systemic social choices, or in recounting local situations. It is splendid that attention is now paid to social and labor history, but the old tyrannies of artifact and place may have been replaced by the new tyrannies of shop floor and boarding house. To thicken the Lowell story, for instance, it would be good to know: Who ran the town, who ran the state? What was the impact of the emerging Irish machine on the nature of work life? How did the struggle over social welfare and labor reforms affect workplace matters? Where did working-class voters stand on issues of labor or capital mobility, in the debates, for instance, over immigration restriction? What stance did workers and businessmen take on federal politics and the battles over the banking system? Most broadly, what difference did the possession of political liberty and the exercise of political power make to the people whose lives museums have taken to chronicling?

Fourth, paying attention to capital-labor relations in the sphere of politics as well as production might draw our attention to the complexity of those relations, forcing us to note that, despite their enmity in the factory, they were often allies in the legislature. One issue that occasionally brought them together was foreign affairs. Where workers accepted capitalist rules of the game they could be persuaded that improving their own position required them to support their employers' attempts to obtain tariffs (and stand with them against free trade opponents). Or that workers' self interest (or cultural identity) might incline them to backing the nationalist or imperialist policies that might win access to raw materials or new markets. Even if they rejected capitalism, they might be led to form political alliances with it against still less acceptable socio-political economies, such as those based on slavery. All these issues might create cross-cutting pressures that could weaken workplace solidarities. Attending to these complexities would help us avoid romanticized images of working people.

Fifth, museums should make clear to visitors that these capitalist rules of the game are in fact still operative, that the system that was instituted in the nineteenth century is fundamentally intact. To be sure capitalism has survived only by making major adjustments. Over the intervening century, capitalism came to terms with changing local, national, and international conditions; with new technologies of production, distribution, and communication; with the legacy of struggles over the rules of the games themselves by contestants whose relative balance of power fluctuated over the years; and with the far greater centrality of the state to the workings of the economy. For all that, the fundamental imperatives and tendencies of the "free enterprise" system continue to profoundly affect life in the United States, and its impact on American industry over the last fifty years has been decisive and devastating.

Deindustrialization

As I object to industrialization, so I object to deindustrialization as a concept. It obfuscates what is happening in the United States today. As usually deployed, the word implies within a stages-of-development theory. Pre-industrial gives way to industrial, which then moves on to a service (or, as it is often called, a post-industrial) economy. There are several difficulties here. For one thing this approach generates banal and vacuous categories. Such terms as "pre-industrial" or "post-industrial" self-evidently fail to illuminate the key characteristics of the epochs they seek to describe, other than by reference to a different period.

Secondly, the implied notion of historical process is teleological: The movement from "pre" to "post" has no subject, it just happens, presumably the result of imminent tendencies working themselves out. In this it resembles that other triumph of tautology, modernization theory, which tracks a similarly inevitable and unidirectional march from pre-modern through modern to post-modern society. In neither theory are we drawn toward considering human agency (much less human conflict) a crucial variable.

Thirdly, as historical development is imminent, so too it is ineluctable. To some this inevitability is sad, a Spenglerian saga of decline. To others it is a source of Spencerian self-satisfaction: Despite the anguish and cost, it is all a manifestation of "progress."

A fourth, and more particular reason to balk at the concept of deindustrialization is that to the degree we accept it, we automatically relegate "industrial" museums to the dustbin of history. Their object, by definition, is a superseded historical period. Studying the industrial era becomes a perhaps interesting but essentially antiquarian exercise. Certainly the experiences of the women and men who labored in sooty or linty nineteenth-century factories can tell us little about life in the new tertiary economy. The definition dooms the industrial museum to being, willy nilly, a purveyor of nostalgia.

But see how different matters become if we think not about deindustrialization but about the global reorganization of capitalism in the twentieth century. Industry, after all, has not been surpassed, it has just moved. Why not re-conceptualize our subject not as deindustrialization but as capital flight—the story of how corporations have sidestepped organized labor, and pressures to pay their share of social costs, by moving to more quiescent pastures, first to the southern United States and then abroad, in a restless search for areas willing to provide tax breaks, cheap land, or the muscle needed to repress the economic and political organization of labor. What has emerged—seen in a planetary perspective—is not a deindustrialized society, but a global redivision of labor.

Such an approach situates deindustrialization not in some mystical urge toward a service economy inherent in the industrial order, but in the recent history and current logic of contemporary capitalism. It helps us see capital flight as yet another instance of short-term private rationality producing long-term social insanity. The point of industrial production under capitalism is to make a profit for the firm, not simply to produce socially useful items. It would be absurd for managers to pass up the opportunity to make higher profits through relocation, or shifting out of production altogether into financial speculation, simply because doing so would wreck communities and lives in the towns, cities, or regions being deserted. Indeed, to the extent that global mobility allows managers to play off regional or national workforces one against the other (the way they once played off ethnic, gender, and racial groups within communities) it would be a virtual dereliction of duty for them not to do so.

Corporate directors, after all, when they act in their corporate capacity, see the country, indeed the planet, not as a society or a human community, but as an economy, a grid of opportunities. Nor, according to capitalist ethics, is capital flight immoral, much less illegal. The factories—the means of production—are, after all, privately owned. Their proprietors can do with them as they wish. Understanding this explodes in a flash the illusions generated by the massive structures of the industrial plants themselves. What is remarkable about capitalism is that behind the facade of solidity lies the quicksilver reality of mobility and relentless transformation, a phenomenon Marshall Berman brilliantly explored in his book, *All That Is Solid Melts into Air*, the title of which is a quotation from Marx.

Finally, attributing deindustrialization not to the working of invisible hands, but to the very visible decisions made by governments and businesses, prompts the realization that it is possible to contest the social irrationality of capital flight—though only by shifting to a different (i.e., social) system of cost accounting and ethical standards. Museums cannot facilitate this realization if their attention is restricted to the tactical considerations that govern activities of workers and businessmen at the point of production, or even in the surrounding social community.

New Approaches

Assuming for the moment the validity of this analysis, let me return to my original concern with how industrial museums might incorporate new perspectives, and sketch out what an exhibit on deindustrialization might look like. As I am not a practitioner, but merely a critic, of public history presentations, I am all too aware of the insufficiencies of what follows as a guide to practical action. Hopefully, professionals may find these suggestions useful as they go about the difficult task of making economic history accessible to popular audiences.

One way to confront the central issues involved in deindustrialization might be to approach them head on. When I attended a conference at Paterson, New Jersey, some time ago, I was told that the designers who put the museum together faced a fundamental problem. Many in the community believed that the great strike of 1913 had caused the collapse of Paterson, that the worker demands for higher wages led the silk mills to depart to more exploitable climes, thus bringing on the deindustrialization process. Given these bitter memories of the strike, the museum avoided confronting the question, and dealt instead with the social history of the contemporary working class communities. An alternate approach would be to mount a special exhibition devoted precisely to the central question: Did labor militancy drive the silk industry out of Paterson? I would not want to prejudge the findings, but it is certainly conceivable that the answer would be, yes. This in turn might force visitors to confront not just the limitations of struggles at the workplace, which today's workers confront every day of their lives, but also help them to imagine alternative political and economic strategies.

This approach need not be restricted to towns like Paterson. Any museum that focuses on industrial history has a great opportunity to connect past and present, to demonstrate the lines running from the institution of capitalist industrial relations in the nineteenth century to the condition of the host town in the twentieth century. An exhibit that boldly focused on the history of capital mobility and its consequences would not be easy to put together. To present the complex story in all its richness might require demonstrating, for instance, how the process was aided mightily by the state. In the United States, for example, the decline of the frostbelt was related to the construction of the sunbelt. That enterprise, in turn, depended in large measure on federal fiscal transfers of money from the North to the South, spurred by the disproportionate power of southern and western congressmen, by military sponsorship of the textile industry in the South during World War II, and by postwar federal support for the aerospace and electronic complexes. In addition, governmental underwriting of the cost of constructing highways, water projects, and natural gas pipelines laid the basis of sunbelt metropolitan development. This made it easy and feasible for northern capital to flee to antiunion climates.

Deindustrialization was also rooted in the formation of a growth coalition—Alan Wolfe and John Mollenkopf have written most illuminatingly on this—that promoted both urban renewal and suburbanization, processes that eroded industrial cities.

Deindustrialization had a foreign policy dimension, too. Staunchly (if shortsightedly) supported by the AFL-CIO, the United States installed or propped up regimes that maintained low-waged export platforms to which multinational capital could move. An exhibit investigating the emergence of industrial competitors in the American, Mediterranean, and East Asian borderlands might examine the role played by U.S. investment capital (and union pension funds), the World Bank, the International Monetary Fund, the Central Intelligence Agency, and the U.S. Marines—in short, the nature of contemporary imperialism.

This would in turn provide a chance to inject the global dimension I referred to earlier. It might, for example, be interesting to trace where local factories went when they left, either in the United States or abroad. It would be illuminating to examine the conditions under which their new employees work—in Taiwan, Korea, the Dominican Republic, and Singapore. An innovative exhibit might explore parallels between nineteenth-century American conditions and those prevailing in the new sweatshops of New York City and Hong Kong. As we now have sister cities, so we might have sister museums. Why not a comparative exhibit examining the move from farm to factory in Puerto Rico and Massachusetts?

A capital flight exhibit might also attempt to connect the collapse of the productive sector with the shift of capital into financial circuits—with the consequent spectacular rise in levels of debt, of currency and stock speculations and manipulations, of takeovers and mergers, of assorted swindles and scams all too reminiscent of the late 1920s.

Finally, it would be helpful to present the current debates over the responses which have been proposed to deindustrialization, ranging from accelerating it via deregulation (the Reagan plan), to hindering it by erecting tariff walls (the AFL-CIO plan), or reversing it through federal investment support (the Rohatyn/Iacocca plan). Our hypothetical exhibit might analyze these options—discussing critically, for example, such conventional axioms as "high-tech jobs can replace departed manufacturing ones," a notion I find largely illusory. It might be interesting for such a solutions section to assess whether worker-ownership takeovers of ailing plants is a way to move forward or a device that leaves workers holding the unprofitable bag; to debate the feasibility of municipal or state ownership; to debate the desirability of altering U.S. foreign and interregional policies; to ponder placing legal constraints on the mobility of capital. Involving museum-goers as citizens might enhance their capacity to make historically informed decisions and thus strengthen the democratic process.

Here again, visual presentations of such complex matters might seem beyond a museum's capabilities, but short video presentations, perhaps in a debate format of the sort popular on television, might be one way. Or we could (had we the money) draw upon immensely successful practices developed at Disney World. One exhibit there brilliantly presents a discussion between animated cartoon spokespeople for and against various *Alternative Energy Sources for Tomorrow's Automobiles*. One after another speaker presents, in remarkably few words, their preferred choice—a Yuppie woman promotes nuclear power, a hard-hatted miner pushes coal, a mad dwarf Japanese scientist with a Peter Lorre accent suggests inventing a water engine—and each is in turn ridiculed or dismissed (this is, after all, a General Motors presentation) until the field is left to "Tex," the lanky GM persona whose drawling conclusion favors the "good 'ole reliable internal combustion engine." I raise this not to promote either gasoline, GM stock, or the hard sell approach, but to note that in the business and commercial world, extremely complex matters are routinely made accessible to audiences numbering in the millions. Surely there are some pointers to be picked up there as well as a compendium of things to be avoided.

But even if we were to design a presentation that treated these difficult matters in a popularly appealing way, a host of obstacles would remain to obstruct our presenting such an interpretation of deindustrialization. The most obvious one stems from the likely resistance of conventional sponsors: who would fund such a show? (Animation is not inexpensive, although video is much more affordable). This sober question brings us to the realities of power, something I have avoided so far, and to the very real constraints imposed upon public history producers. Asking the question, in fact, should be an integral part of exhibit designing. It might be a salutary exercise for all public history programmers to prepare, as a matter of course, a "political impact statement." Doing so would direct attention to the necessity of lining up political support for any given interpretative strategy.

In this case, a plausible first assumption might be that business funders would not be interested in helping explicate the "downside" of a capitalist economy. But the experience of a South Bend, Indiana, museum suggests that even businesspersons might not be quite as antagonistic to such an exhibit as might be thought. There were certainly some entrepreneur-funders who wanted Discovery Hall Museum to avoid even the mention of the strikes during the 1930s. They feared discouraging outside investors thinking of bringing in new businesses to South Bend by making them aware of a history of unionism. They proposed instead a celebratory saga centered on the history of the largest auto firm, the Studebaker Corporation. But other business professionals in South Bend rejected a narrow-gauged focus on antique cars in large part because they were enraged at Studebaker, a capital-flight company perceived as having left the city in the lurch.

Despite the Indiana case, it is probably more likely that support for a deindustrialization exhibit would be forthcoming from labor groups. Some unions are more open to such approaches in this time of crisis when old analyses and practices seem to be of little service. Conceivably there might also be sources of public funding in frostbelt states from outraged communities interested in understanding what has happened to them and where they might go from there. Working people and ordinary citizens might be drawn to supporting museums' work if they believed such institutions could help make sense of their world.

Supporters might be more readily attracted to a deindustrialization show if they were persuaded that a range of analytic points of view would be presented. Perhaps the videotaped debates mentioned above could be a way to integrate multiple perspectives. It would, for instance, be most illuminating to let a spokesperson from the Heritage Foundation try to convince working class and small business audiences in shattered "rustbelt" towns that deindustrialization and the workings of the free market, by increasing productivity, are in their long run interest.

Whether or not such an exhibit ever gets mounted, thinking about its merits and demerits may be of use to industrial museum designers. Deindustrialization is only one topic they might consider—the history of depressions and the story of automation are others that come to mind. And the larger principles—that public historians can situate today's world in a temporal continuum, locate their subjects within still evolving processes, set their local stories in a global context, and emphasize that historical actors and contemporary visitors were and are political actors—might be helpful for continuing the exciting transformations of the past decade.

Postscript (1995)

In the 1850s the Mahoning Valley in northeastern Ohio was one of the nation's leading centers of iron production. By the 1920s it was lined with steel mills; those of Youngstown, Ohio outdid even Pittsburgh in pig iron production. In 1977 Youngstown Sheet and Tube's flagship, Campbell Works, shut suddenly. This triggered four years of mill closings, the loss of twenty-five thousand jobs in steel alone, and a fierce grass-roots campaign to restart the idled plants, which failed. By the late 1980s, the area's steel industry was, as they say, history.

Enter the Youngstown Historical Center of Industry and Labor. At the behest of an influential state senator, the state of Ohio appropriated the funds for, and the Ohio Historical Society undertook to create, a museum that chronicled the rise, and addressed the fall of steel. In 1989, the Center's $4.5 million building was completed—a postindustrial monument from postmodern architect Michael Graves. In 1992, the center inaugurated its permanent exhibition, *By the Sweat of Their Brow: The Forging of the Steel Valley*.[1]

The show concentrates on shop floor experiences, working class culture, and labor and business history. It uses videotaped oral history interviews with retired steelworkers, blown-up photomurals and historic film footage, telling artifacts like wooden shoes (furnace heat would have set leather ablaze), reconstructed physical environments (a plant locker room, a company house), mill models from the 1930s, and imposing industrial artifacts like an enormous blooming mill pulpit.

Most of the exhibition is devoted to the growth years of this century, but a final section addresses the era of decline. Visitors approach a steel mill guard house, from which issues the recorded voice of a laid-off worker now turned security man. "Steel mills been in the Valley for a long time," he muses. "Most people thought they'd be here forever. [PAUSE] I don't know who's responsible for what's happened, everything closing. Some people blame the companies, some blame the workers, some even blame the government. All I know is a lot of people lost their jobs." He also knows, and goes on to mention, that downtown businesses were devastated, and he worries about his generation's children and grandchildren. Visitors then pass through a gate where they confront an immense photo mural depicting a simultaneous demolition of several blast furnaces—the image with which this chapter begins. They also find a video monitor displaying a film featuring excerpts from "Shout Youngstown," a moving 1983 documentary chronicling the city's desperate efforts to save the mills.

It is good to see a museum finally grappling with the issue of deindustrialization, even if this exhibit does not cut terribly deeply. Educational handouts go somewhat farther, making reference to the substitution by auto and other manufacturers of plastic for steel, and the rise of competition from newly industrialized countries using the latest technology. But this hardly exhausts the issue.

Local memories are still as "raw and poignant as a vat of molten metal," the *Youngstown Vindicator* observed in 1990, which may explain the cautious approach to the question. But given the considerable residual anger in the valley, I wonder if a more forthright approach might not help lift the dismal attendance figures—a scant seven thousand came by in 1994, though visitation has since increased substantially in response to outreach efforts. Youngstown is not a major tourist destination, so the numbers will never be astronomical, and some local pundits put the low regional turnout down to people's reluctance to be reminded of the debacle. But others, attentive to ex-millworker buzz, report a feeling that the museum is somehow slanted toward management. Perhaps an analysis that included a more thoroughgoing investigation of corporate culpability—why, for instance, they failed to modernize plant and machinery—would help rectify that image.

A more ambitious effort to tackle deindustrialization is in the works in Pittsburgh, where the Historical Society of Western Pennsylvania is completing a core exhibit for its new Pittsburgh Regional History Center. The show, for which I served as consultant, surveys two hundred years of urban and regional history. It will include a vivid treatment of the steel industry at full blast, followed by a starker segment treating the subsequent collapse. Artifacts from abandoned mills will evoke feelings of desolation, and local newscast video footage will trace the devastating local impact. The curators plan to document the parades and protests by activist steelworkers who fought the loss of their jobs, and to explain how geography, changing technology, labor and management relations, and the globalization of capitalism all contributed to the loss of steel in western Pennsylvania. A concluding section will carry the story on into the present and future, examining the changing identity of the region, and the steps Pittsburgh has taken to remain viable in the new economic climate.

These two enterprises suggest that history museums are taking up the challenge of contextualizing one of the country's most vexing problems.

Notes

Apart from the postscript, which was written for this book, this chapter is the unrevised text of "Industrial Museums and the History of Deindustrialization," which appeared in *The Public Historian* (1987). That paper in turn grew out of a comment I gave at the "Sixth Annual Lowell Conference on Industrial History" in 1985. The papers I reviewed there were the sources of information about the museums discussed here. They include: Brent Glass, "Making Sense of Textile History: Public Humanities Programs in North Carolina"; Marsha A. Mullin, "Discovery Hall Museum: A Museum of Industrial History"; Loretta A. Ryan, "The Remaking of Lowell and Its

Histories: 1965–1982"; and John A. Herbst, "The 'Life and Times in Silk City' Exhibit".

My thanks to Robert Weible, the conference organizer, for his helpful comments. Thanks also to Mark Twyford and Laura Tellman of the Youngstown Historical Center of Industry and Labor, and to David T. Wilson, its former curator. I also thank John Herbst and Greg Smith of the Historical Society of Western Pennsylvania, and Bart Roselli, formerly at Pittsburgh, now at the Adirondack Museum.

1. See reviews by Curtis Miner in the *Journal of American History* 80, no. 3 (December 1993), 1019–24; and by Chris Dawson on H-Net.

The Virtual Past: Media and History Museums

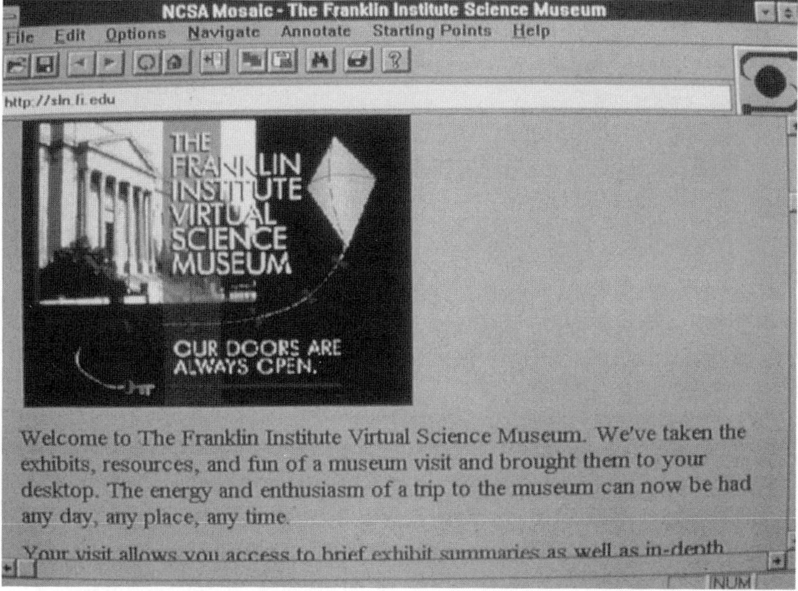

Franklin Institute Web Site. (© The Franklin Institute Science Museum. Photographer: Jim Abbott.)

How will history museums adjust to the cyberculture of the twenty-first century? Will today's children—coming of age in a computerizing era—visit tomorrow's institutions? What will be the impact on historical sensibilities of growing up in a media-drenched environment? It is hard to consider such questions in the abstract, as electronic literacy varies so markedly by country, class, and culture, so I will begin my exploration of these issues with an example close to home.

My granddaughter Khendum experienced her first postmodern confusion the other day. Her father had videotaped her and her mother exchanging coos. When my wife and I came to visit, he played back the tape for the assembled family. Six-month-old Khendum's eyes shuttled back and forth in puzzlement between her real and her simulated mother. She also contemplated her instant replay self with intermittent fascination. The stack of videotapes chronicling her life will no doubt grow as tall as she does (as once my parents inserted countless brownie shots of me into leatherette black-paper albums). Should Khendum later edit her tapes into a video diary, or incorporate them into an autobiographical school "paper" (perhaps using software already available for helping write personal histories), will such electronic aide-mémoires give her a different understanding of her own transformation than my fragmentary snapshots gave me? Will our understanding of change over time change?

In a few years Khendum and her peers will likely be playing with computer history games (at home for those whose families can afford the hardware; at arcades for those who can not). There is already a bumper crop to choose from. One is Merchant Colony, a "fun-packed, high resolution video game that the whole family will enjoy!" You begin in London during the eighteenth century (the time "when Britain became Great.") Picking up an electronic ship, you proceed to "hire troops and tradesmen to protect and maintain your fleet, establish colonies, develop industries and battle native uprisings while you import and export products to exotic destinations, selling your goods for profits that you reinvest back into your empire." (You can also stock up on teachers, who "build schools adjacent to native huts, helping to prevent uprisings there.") I hope Khendum will prefer more benign games, like Where in America's Past Is Carmen Sandiego? in which players chase bandits back in time, with the computer disbursing clues as to their current "whenabouts," and providing lifts to various eras via chronoscanner. This game is wildly popular with ten-year-olds (interestingly, girls as much as boys).

In her teens, Khendum will perhaps be reading (viewing?) electronic history books. Friends of mine at the American Social History Project just finished reformatting their textbook on U.S. history from 1876 to 1914 into hypermedia. Lying in bed with their Powerbook or seated in a school computer lab, readers—viewers?—can branch off from conventional text and swing from media-to-media, summoning up film snippets of factory sites in the 1910s, or listening to reminiscences by Triangle Fire survivors.[1] Khendum and her classmates will be able to write papers (construct presentations?) on compact disk, assembling bits of film, sound, narrative, and document to bolster their arguments. As a writer and teacher I remain committed to books. Will the next generation or two be? At the end of 1994, there were fifteen million CD-ROM drives in active use in the United States (a figure expected to jump dramatically in the next few years) and eight thousand CD-ROM titles available for purchase.[2]

For after-school entertainment, Khendum might go to an Interfilm. One played recently in New York. It was a thriller in which characters got into conundrums and turned to the audience for advice; we all pushed buttons, our votes were tallied, and in seconds the character (and plot line) responded to the will of the majority. Will we become accustomed to rewriting the script of history films, sending Wellington down to defeat at Waterloo, granting Lee victory at Gettysburg?

Such pastimes are likely to pall with the advent of virtual reality. I recently went to a virtual reality (VR) gallery. Popping on my helmet I was launched into a three-dimensional world of enemies-behind-pillars with whom I exchanged electronic rifle fire. As I moved my head, my angle of vision moved—360 degrees; as my real hands moved, so did my simulated ones; as my feet paced, I seemed to race through hyperspace. The possibilities of this technology for the historically inclined are extraordinary, although for now innovators mainly seem to be working feverishly towards building better war games and achieving breakthroughs in "teledildonics," the science of simulated sex.

Electronic Galleries

With such delights to occupy her, will Khendum be likely to visit a history museum (apart from being shepherded through on obligatory school field trips)? Yes, says one curatorial camp, but only if institutions reorient themselves around the technology her generation will find familiar and be expert at using. If history museums are to have a future, according to this argument, they must fully plunge into this new world.

Many institutions have ventured part way down this road by deploying devices that allow them to interpret their artifacts more effectively. Particularly popular are techniques that evoke an object's temporal quality, or illuminate the social context within which it was created and used.

The Smithsonian's *Engines of Change* exhibition brings machine tools back to working life, setting static objects into absorbing motion, as does the Strong Museum, which animates its Jacquard looms and automatic toys. The same museum's *More Perfect Union* show has soldiers on tape explaining how they used tools of war. Videotaped actor-workers at the Valentine's *Working People of Richmond* demonstrate the use of rolling mills and talk heatedly about factory life. At the Lowell Mills, voiceovers simulate dinner table talk among laborer mannequins. The J. Paul Getty Museum in Malibu, California, offers mini-movies on the techniques of medieval scribes. And an interactive video produced by a consortium of American art museums allows users to explore four Impressionist artists: Clicking on icons brings up details of paintings, biographies of the painters, and commentators who offer points of view and interrogate one another.

The possibilities of this bring-it-back-to-life approach are endless. Think how many inert period rooms could be vividly animated by an adjacent video of, say, a maid discussing what it takes to keep the parlor clean, or describing how the mistress orchestrates a parlor visit. The maid could be shown walking into the parlor (as visitors are barred from doing), picking up objects, talking about them, forcing the visitor's eye to shift from screen to exhibit and back again.

Technology also aids museums in deploying memories as artifacts. At Ellis Island, donor audiotapes explain the provenance of mangle boards and prayer books, ouds and clogs. In the *More Perfect Union* show, a mockup of a Japanese internee room is enhanced by a full-size video projection of a survivor—glimpsed as if through a door, with a sage strewn mountain scene in the background—explaining the site to his daughter. Nearby, using now commonplace touch screens, visitors can "ask questions" of five internees; the testimony of Mary Sukamoto and her peers complements the show's "material" artifacts.

Some computer devices stray a bit farther from objects. At Boston's Museum of Science interactives put visitors in the shoes of a mayor confronting a water shortage; the Smithsonian's *Tropical Rain Forest* show allows interactive strategizing about preservation versus development issues. The new technology permits more "personalized" encounters. The South Australian Maritime Museum affords computer access to passenger lists, letting visitors track ancestral arrivals and take away a printout record. The National Museum of American History's *Information Age: People, Information and Technology* offers participants a bar code they can use to input and retrieve personalized data at various scanner stations. The Holocaust Museum in Washington matches each visitor with a victim of the same age and sex, letting one follow the fate of a temporary twin.

Virtual Museums

"Virtual museums" provide a still more mediated relationship between users and objects by presenting information, in varying formats, on the World Wide Web portion of the Internet.

Many institutions simply advertise their collections or offer multimedia representations of their objects. Summoning up, say, the Dallas Museum of Art's available images provides potential travellers a glimpse of what is available, helping them sort out what they want to see in person. Such digitzed information can also offer an armchair alternative to those who, by virtue of distance or disability, would never manage an on-site trip. Small, hitherto obscure institutions have blossomed on the Internet. The University of California's Museum of Paleontology gets only about fifteen visitors a day, but its virtual counterpart receives roughly one thousand daily drop-ins. (It also allows for feedback: Users can post comments in a "guestbook," which is made immediately available to all other browsers, or they can send e-mail directly to curators.)

Some web sites attempt to re-create the museum setting, electronically reproducing its physical layout. One group—the JASON project at the National Museums and Galleries on Merseyside in Liverpool—is attempting a mechanical/electronic version of this. It plans to mount video and sound devices on lunar-lander-type vehicles, which can be activated by satellite, allowing remote "visitors" to cruise around a museum after it is closed for the night.

Others are working to design "virtual exhibits" specifically for electronic viewers. In theory such presentations can convey experiences not available to visitors in the museum—changing an object's scale, juxtaposing it with nonadjacent artifacts (even items in other museums), linking it with contextualizing documents that can be downloaded and perused at leisure.

All these techniques remain in some way linked to actual artifacts in actual museums. But the technology offers the possibility of breaking these bonds altogether, and creating totally artificial museums, which exist nowhere but in hyperspace.

Columbia University is developing a computerized Networked Virtual Reality Museum. Multiple users can visit it simultaneously—each "virtually" represented as a graphical figure to others using the system—and either explore an Egyptian temple or test glide Leonardo da Vinci's human-powered flying machine.

One designer is attempting to fashion a cyberspace museum that "virtually preserves" Birkenau, the Auschwitz camp that is being left to disintegrate. Electronic visitors would move from one chamber to another, listening to or reading recollections of events that occurred there, while being able to interact with other viewers on real-time chat lines and bulletin boards.

An Austrian museum (Castle Tollet) has embarked on an Interactive People's Museum project. Anyone with access to the Internet is invited to deposit text, pictures, or sound describing their *heimat,* or homeland. These will then be "placed" in virtual exhibition rooms organized around such themes as childhood, food, language, and living space that are available for virtual viewing on the web. At some point the "objects" will be rematerialized and put on more tangible display in their own institution.

More dramatic still is the full-fledged virtual reality technology of the helmet and body sensor variety that creates the illusion of being in a three-dimensional, 360 degrees situation, in which one can move about and interact with computerized characters. Though still in its infancy, VR is already capable of amazing feats. Experts recently "reconstructed" the original eleventh-century Cluny Abbey—which had been destroyed after the French Revolution—and allowed viewers to wander about inside its hallways.[3]

It may well also be possible in the not too distant future to install these machines in one's own museum, and use them to project users into various historical epochs. Imagine the possibilities: Donning a helmet and seeing oneself in the Acropolis listening to a Platonic dialogue; or being seated behind Orville Wright as he skims over Kitty Hawk; or being trapped inside the flaming Triangle Shirtwaist Factory; or being a Vietcong guerilla under fire from an American helicopter gunship; or being a slave and having the option of talking back to an overseer and discovering the consequences (having your electronic hide whipped).

Not everyone is delighted by these developments and possibilities. While there is widespread agreement on the benefits of object-associated technology, some worry that Internet museums and virtual reality machines pose threats to the ways of knowing that history museums facilitate, and perhaps their very existence.

Advocates of web sites insist that remote access is not meant to replace museum going, that it does not and can not provide an alternative to the unmediated experience of real objects. But we live in a convenience culture. Might not the ease of summoning up a museum's offerings on one's home computer—via the Internet or CD-ROM—outweigh the desire for an authentic encounter, rather as harried families opt for microwaved TV dinners or Big Macs over the pleasures of home-cooked meals? Could devices intended to tap new users have the unintended consequence of depleting the pool of older ones?

There are, after all, appealingly democratic possibilities in direct access. If an institution's entire collection is on line, browsers could access discrete items, in a non-linear way, and construct their own interpretations. Curators might object that this admittedly desirable option would probably be of value (and interest) mainly to already knowledgeable researchers and students, and that museums have educational responsibilities they should not abdicate. But even traditional exhibits—especially those that feature flatware like prints, photos, paintings, text, and video, though three dimensional objects are also digitizable—can be dispatched into cyberspace in the sequence designers want them viewed.

So why go to museums at all? Would it not it be tempting just to stay at home and plug into the information grid? Couch-potato museumgoers would forgo the social pleasure of an outing, to be sure, though such journeys can be arduous as well as entertaining, and families so inclined could do their virtual visiting together. The societal consequences might be unfortunate. It would mean an erosion of public space. But that is an old story by now. Crowds used to assemble in front of the great newspapers' bulletin boards on election night, or during war time; now they are home, tuned to CNN. Why expect museums to be exempt from this privatizing trajectory? The arrival of full-blown virtual reality technology of the helmet and body sensor variety might delay this for a time. Many people will use VR machines, as they once used phones (and now faxes), in centralized settings. Their presence in a museum might well be a potent drawing card. But when prices tumble far enough, they too will become available to the upscale home market.

Internet-style virtualization, far more affordable, still restricts museum access to the more affluent. There are the hardware and software costs of setting up a home computer station. There are also accessing expenses. At the moment, the subsidized Internet keeps these low, or even free, for those with the right institutional affiliations. But efforts are underway to privatize the net. They may well succeed. It is only too customary in the United States. that the public pays for development costs and private interests reap the subsequent profits. If privatization comes to pass, gaining entrance to virtual museums will become considerably more costly, creating differential categories of users. Museum going is already largely a class-bound phenomenon, however, so perhaps the net effect would be minimal. Or maybe inexpensive compact disks—museums-on-a-disk are already being mass-marketed—will provide an off-setting democratization.

There is, however, a more fundamental problem. If museums melt into air, who will collect and care for the objects to be beamed into cyberspace? Bucks must start as well as stop somewhere. Are we headed toward a time when artifacts are pooled in warehouses—under the care of curators turned custodians—and only made available to production teams on a need-to-transmit basis?

Or will virtual reality eliminate the need for objects altogether? If, eventually, reproductive technology becomes capable of producing perfect simulacra, and future generations come to consider the line between original and copy both hard to discern and of less philosophical moment, perhaps virtual museum designers of the future will draw not from a warehouse of objects, but a storehouse of images.

These hypothetical possibilities give some museologists the horrors, and impel them to resist further technology. They argue that only holding the line, insisting on an absolute primacy of objects will allow museums to survive. They think that in an era of infinite reproducibility Khendum and her counterparts will become repulsed by inauthenticity, wary of endless fraud, that they will be drawn inexorably to the artifacts that provide historical links to actual human actors, that they will thirst for old objects which, blessedly, were not made and "patinaed" last week.

Critics of virtual history reject as absurd the notion that different eras can be "virtually" re-created. Even if it became possible to create a plausible simulacrum into which visitors could be virtually transported, only those who have capitulated to cinematic ways of knowing would believe that experiencing something is the same as understanding it, that sensation is equivalent to analysis. Indeed virtual presentations might undercut Khendum's historical capacity by engendering the kind of passive receptivity characteristic of the media world. This de-skilling could become self-sustaining: The less one grows accustomed to considering material culture as evidence that historical narratives must take into account, the more vulnerable one becomes to epics constructed out of whole cloth. The border between truth and fiction, ambiguous at best, might dissolve altogether, leaving listeners vulnerable to whomever spins the most compelling story.

But there are also problems with the artifactual alternative of having museums become shrines—tranquil, sacred spaces for the savoring of relics. Speaking Latin when all about are into the vernacular invites disaster. A heightened exclusivity might well widen the existing gulf between those who feel comfortable with museum culture codes and those who—failing to crack them—opt to stay away. Public authorities out to downsize or close institutions might strike a pseudo-populist stance. They could denounce curators as latter-day medieval scribes, fearfully warding off the electronic equivalent of movable type, seeking to preserve elitist mausoleums out of sheer self interest.

Further epistemological and political dilemmas would attend any cult of pure objects. Relics only have meaning if invested with it by the host culture; artifacts are, to a degree, constituted by narratives in which they are embedded. I find London's low-technology Churchill War Rooms, frozen from V-E Day, enormously evocative; but will they resonate equally with generations for whom the Battle of Britain is as temporally remote as the Punic Wars?

And how to present subjects for which you do not have objects? The poor, notoriously, leave little detritus behind. Nor have museums collected history's leftovers with an even hand: Until quite recently the Smithsonian's National Museum of American History had forty silk top hats but not a single snap-brim cap.

Romancing the "real" can foster empiricism, forget that artifacts do not speak loudly to untutored ears, and lead to the fetishization of things: industrial machines become lovely *objéts* when presented in gleaming isolation from their original man-eating context.

Media as History

In the end, however, I find the notion of a looming and inevitable Armageddon between object and image unconvincing. For most museums, the outline of a coming detente with media seems clear enough. Most institutions will (to the extent of their resources) want to use the new hardware and software to elucidate objects, explain contexts, and involve visitors, especially youthful ones. Novel exhibition forms will continue to evolve as imaginative curators get ever more conversant with the possibilities of the new technologies. Nor will the emergence of new capabilities require the shedding of old ones. Museum makers need not automatically opt for a high-tech solution when, as is often the case, a low-tech and cheaper approach will do just as well, if not better. At a glitzy science museum in New Jersey schoolchildren routinely scoot by interactive computer modules and scurry instead to tunnels they can crawl through, or rock faces they can climb.

Some institutions will no doubt decide to let go of objects altogether and evolve into multimedia hybrids, combining aspects of theme park, movie studio, and learning center. These will certainly appeal to many of Khendum's generation, and add to the mix of competing cultural attractions with which museums already contend. This does not foredoom object-based operations—any more than the arrival of hi-fi and CD wiped out live music, or television and video cassette recorders obliterated movies—but it will require some innovative museological responses to the changed environment.

One such approach might be for museums to go beyond borrowing media tools and techniques and begin interpreting the world of media itself. This can be done in two different ways. First, by examining the history of that world, exhibits could explain developments in image and information production. They could lay out the political, cultural, and social contexts, and their transformations, within which such production occurs. Secondly, by assessing the impact of media on society through investigations of how historical consciousness gets constructed in a media-enmeshed world.

Forays have been made on both fronts. In the first category, London's Museum of the Moving Image [MOMI] presents a social history of the film and television industries, offering visitors a look behind the screens. Portions of the Smithsonian's *Information Age* raised critical questions about the context and impact of older technologies like the telegraph and telephone (though the latter half fades into a celebratory display of products offered by the computer and communications industries—not coincidentally, the show's sponsors). The Strong Museum's *Selling the Goods: Origins of American Advertising* and the Valentine's *Smoke Signals: Cigarettes, Advertising and the American Way of Life* both examined the cultural impact of the persuasion industry, though they shied away from tackling some of the tougher questions, such as the influence of sponsors on content.

Shows in the second, deconstructionist category begin with the recognition that visitors now enter museums with well-stocked mental film banks. A vast amount of media history is being produced and consumed. People carry in their heads both raw footage (video clips culled from endless replays on television) and narrative sequences (recalled from movies, docudramas and documentaries).

Students in my history of the 1960s class have a host of moving images tucked away: the assassination of John F. Kennedy, astronauts bouncing around the moon, the shooting of a bound Vietcong, American helicopters lifting off from the Saigon embassy, King orating on the steps of the Lincoln Memorial, the Beatles performing on Ed Sullivan, police dogs savaging southern demonstrators, and on and on, a virtual film library. They don't know quite what to *do* with these images, having little or no sense how they connect one with the other, but narratives are provided them by Hollywood and television movies. Films like *Rambo*, *Apocalypse Now*, *Deer Hunter*, *Platoon*, *Full Metal Jacket* and a host of made-for-TV documentaries and docudramas constitute a strong component of their historical reality.

This media history world has its own history. There is quite a distance between *Gone with the Wind* and *Roots*, between the treatments of General Custer in the 1940s and those of the 1960s. Indeed, there is such a bewildering array of different interpretations available that it is conceivable that the plethora of media narratives has fostered a peculiarly malleable sense of the past. Critical iconic images were once graven in stone on church walls; now they are subject to instant revision as we flip from channel to channel. Or—and here is a question for historians of our historical sensibilities in the media age—do some images gain an indelible primacy of place? Will Wallace Beery forever be Pancho Villa despite Telly Savalas' best efforts? Will the encircled wagon train revolve forever in our cinematic brain, protecting the women and children as their menfolk fend off the howling redskins while awaiting the Seventh Cavalry, despite the valiant revisionism of Arthur Penn and many others?

The mass media is perhaps the single most critical source of popular historical imagination. For many, because cinematic modes of perception seem so real, moviepast *is* the past. When curators at the Alamo erected a mural depicting their site's historic events they used the faces of Hollywood actors from a 1960 movie as visual stand-ins for the original heroes: Davy Crockett *became* John Wayne. Certainly for Ronald Reagan, who portrayed General Custer in the *Santa Fe Trail*, the line between movie America and historical reality was notoriously blurred.

As images and narratives together constitute a goodly (and growing) portion of most people's historical capital why shouldn't museums turn media itself into an artifact? Why not mount shows that deconstruct for visitors the kinds of historical messages embedded in Hollywood movies or television docudramas? How about exhibits that use snippets of film, along with other objects, to demonstrate that film, like written history, conveys not an unequivocal "truth" but a narrative interpretation?

Again, some pioneers have pointed the way forward. The exhibit "Tropical Rainforests: A Disappearing Treasure," organized by the Smithsonian Institution Traveling Exhibition Service in 1988, had a nice example of what is possible in its "Reel Jungle" video. It displays the way Hollywood has distorted the jungle, by stringing together excerpts from Tarzan movies, scenes of drunken natives cooking missionaries, safari expeditions seeking King Solomon's mines. The exhibit confronts our cliches, not by attacking us for having them, but by reminding us of how we came by them.

England's National Maritime Museum mounted a show on pirates that began not with historical "reality" but historical fiction. The exhibition moved from literary images (Byron and Stevenson), to stage portraits (*Pirates of Penzance*, Peter Pan's Captain Hook), and then to clips from cinematic treatments like Errol Flynn's swashbuckler *Captain Blood*. Only then, when people had a better sense of how the stereotypes in their heads got there, were they ushered towards a historical recounting. By making it plain to people that their misconceptions were the result of media-promulgated myths, not personal stupidity, the process defused resistance to reconsideration.

A National Museum of American History exhibit, *American Encounters*, examined the roots of stereotypes that linger in the minds of visitors to the Southwest. It did so by analyzing how the nineteenth-century tourist industry manufactured and marketed exotic and romanticized images of Indian and Hispanic cultures.

London's Museum of the Moving Image has a penetrating corner where it runs, on adjacent monitors, two news accounts covering the same antiwar demonstration. One is a snide putdown. The other is earnest and empathetic. It is a quick and compelling lesson in the way putatively objective accounts are heavily value-laden in their selection, emphasis and explication of images.

The Gene Autry Western Heritage Museum has created an exhibition entitled *Imaging the West* that uses books, photographs, videos, music, advertisements, and tourist ephemera to examine the production and consumption of popular western imagery. In the wrong hands, of course, such an approach can easily tumble into uncritical celebration. At the Disney-MGM Studio's *Great Movie Ride*, display cases house objects from movies featured during the presentation—the piano from Rick's American Bar in *Casablanca*, Dorothy's ruby slippers from *The Wizard of Oz*. In this weird inversion of the virtualization process, images are transformed into artifacts.

The format has other potential perils. Media images are so powerful, they can overwhelm analysis. When I teach my Hollywood and history course, it is not easy to break the spell cast by a film such as *The Birth of a Nation*, and present alternative narratives of Reconstruction history. One response to this dilemma is to pit memory-as-artifact against media-as-artifact. As many museums have taken up oral and video history work, it might be interesting to juxtapose these different kinds of media. Imagine an exhibit that contrasted clips from *Rambo* and *Apocalypse Now* with filmed interviews with veterans and antiwar activists. Or exhibits could play off popular movies and television series, like Oliver Stone's *JFK* or Ken Burns' *Civil War*, with videotaped assessments by a variety of informed commentators.

This approach is available to even the smallest of local house museums. Video histories of community residents, produced in collaboration with oral historians, could bring out oldtimers' reflections on local history, and events (like Vietnam) that played out on larger stages. Costs are not negligible, but numerous opportunities exist for collaborative state-local efforts, of the sort pioneered by the Texas, Ohio, and Wisconsin state historical societies. Group purchase or leasing of equipment, together with cost sharing of editing and mounting time, is one route. Alliances with the telecommunications departments of universities and community colleges is a second. The recycling by small institutions of shows (like *Engines of Change*) produced by large ones is a third route to explore.

Museums can also deconstruct media constructions that are much closer to home. They can, and increasingly do start with themselves. *Gallery 33* at the Birmingham Museum is one such self-reflexive show. It examines the lives and motives of its founding collectors, and situates the institution in the context of British colonialism. An interactive video underscores this for visitors, demonstrating that who you are helps shape how you see, and that a single object can mean different things in different surroundings. In the United States, artist Fred Wilson's *Mining the Museum* presentation at the Maryland Historical Society illuminated the subversive meanings that can be extracted from artifacts originally accumulated to bolster dominant historical narratives. It might also be fun to examine the images of museums themselves that crop up in contemporary popular culture, such as the portrayals in *Batman*, *Ghostbusters II*, and *When Harry Met Sally*.

More generally, there seems to be a trend toward acknowledging publicly that exhibitions are particular interpretations rather than universal truths. Here again technology can be helpful. At the Smithsonian's *Information Age*, the curator offers videotaped comments on the background and intentions of the show. It is worth noting, however, that interactive displays can also undercut this promulgation of authorial responsibility. They can foster the illusion that a machine is providing value-free interpretations when of course it presents pre-programmed perspectives. This might be offset by building a critical component into the system; touch-screen users could select a box labeled A Different View to bring up a short commentary from someone outside the museum (or from recent visitors) who argues against the exhibition's central premises.

It is certainly possible, when pondering the future relationship between media and museums, to leap into techno-utopianism, or fall into apocalyptic gloom. It seems more likely, however, that the new technologies, judiciously employed, will enhance the possibilities for learning history in an enlightening and entertaining way. Indeed, Khendum and I are looking forward to seeing what the new century will have to offer.

Notes

Parts of this essay were presented as a keynote address for Museum, Media, Message: The Third International Conference in Museum Studies, University of Leicester, April 4th–7th 1993. It has been substantially revised and updated for this book.

My thanks to Gaynor Kavanagh and Eilean Hooper-Greenhill of the University of Leicester.

For additional (and extremely astute) commentary on these issues, see Andreas Huyssen, "Monument and Memory in a Postmodern Age," *The Yale Journal of Criticism* 6, no. 2 (1993), 249–61; and Robert Baron, "Why People Go to Museums," an 11 April 1995 post to the MUSEUM-L network (LISTSERV@UNMVMA.UNM.EDU).

1. Roy Rosenzweig, Steve Brier and Josh Brown, *Who Built America?*, CD-Rom (The Voyager Company, 578 Broadway, Suite 460, New York, New York 10027).
2. Roy Rosenzweig, " 'So, What's Next for Clio?': CD-ROM and Historians," *Journal of American History* 81, no. 4 (March 1995), 1623.
3. Smithsonian Institution Secretary I. Michael Heyman reports plans to open a trial three-dimensional digitizing lab to test the emerging technology that might soon allow on-line visitors to look at 3-D images, and to "hold" an item in their hands, turning it through all its dimensions. [Smithsonian Press Release: Testimony of I. Michael Heyman before the House Appropriations Subcommittee on Interior and Related Agencies (10 March 1995)]

Museums and Controversy

"Becoming Visible: The Legacy of Stonewall." Exhibition at New York Public Library, 1994. (Photographer: Mimi Bowling, 1994.)

Museum Metamorphosis

In the 1940s, 1950s, and 1960s, America's history museums drowsed happily on the margins of a go-ahead culture, tending their genteel artifacts, perpetuating regnant myths in which African Americans, women, immigrants, and workers figured as supporting actors or not at all.

But then came rude poundings at the door. In the 1970s and 1980s a new generation of curators—inspired by movements in the streets and leagued with youthful colleagues in the academy—entered these institutions and began to revamp their agendas. Museums shifted from enshrining objects toward using them to explain social relations. Novel exhibits tackled issues of race, gender, class, imperialism, and ecology.

The results can be read in the current museum landscape. A quick survey of work displayed in recent years suggests the scope of the transformation.

Consider race. Colonial Williamsburg, which long elided even the existence of black slaves, now has African American guides interpreting the lives of the once thousand-strong slave labor force at Carter's Grove plantation. In the old capitol building in Jackson, where 1950s lawmakers once yahooed segregation bills into law, the Mississippi State Historical Museum displayed Klan paraphernalia of intimidation in telling the story of *Reconstruction and Its Aftermath*. In Richmond, former capital of the Confederacy, the Valentine Museum has produced a series of shows like *Jim Crow: Racism and Reaction in the New South* and *Race Relations in Richmond, 1945–85*. And the same city's Museum of the Confederacy, long a sanctum of the Lost Cause, mounted *Before Freedom Come: African-American Life in the Antebellum South*.

Explorations of America's racial experience have become almost routine, from the Chicago Historical Society's *A House Divided: America in the Age of Lincoln*, featuring living history performances about black abolitionist Frederick Douglass, to such Smithsonian shows as *Field to Factory: Black Migration 1915–1940* and *A More Perfect Union: Japanese Americans and World War II*, which recounted the story of the internment camps.

Turning to imperial expansion, which in the United States took the form of conquering the continent, the National Museum of American Art (in *The West As America*) examined how painters of iconic frontier scenes wittingly or unwittingly contributed to the process of appropriation. At historic sites (like the former Custer battlefield, now renamed Little Bighorn), and at institutions like the National Museum of the American Indian in New York, indigenous peoples contribute to their own representation. Hidatsa Indians helped create the Minnesota Historical Society's complex portrait of their forebears' response to invasion, *The Way to Independence;* Cherokees welcomed a Trail of Tears Commemorative Park, recalling the forced deportation march in which four thousand died. The National Museum of American History's [NMAH] *American Encounters* presented a complex story of conflict and compromise between Native Americans, Africans, Asians, and Europeans, showing how these interactions changed each of the participants and constituted the region's identity.

Perhaps most amazing is the way the Columbus myth—a stunningly obdurate fairy tale of flat earth, hocked jewels, and benign "discovery"—was vanquished. Museum shows like the National Museum of Natural History's *Seeds of Change* included the perspective of those for whom his advent prefigured pestilence, servitude, and death. Some exhibits, like *First Encounters: Spanish Explorations in the Caribbean and the United States* at the Florida Museum of Natural History, faced protests from American Indian activists; when *First Encounters* traveled to the Albuquerque Museum, its host offered a handout embodying alternative points of view. Such U.S. protests were only a faint echo of those in South America, where indigenous peoples demonstrated from Mexico to Peru. Even at the Seville World's Fair and the Barcelona Olympic Games, Columbus proved an embarrassment. As the *New York Times* noted, Christopher Columbus' fall from grace in 1992 was even steeper than that of George Bush.

Consider museological treatments of class. In sites across the country, often housed in abandoned factories, museums address the lives of vanished laborers, recall their skills and sacrifices, and confront management-labor conflicts. A Valentine exploration of the history of Richmond's tobacco and iron workers treated issues of race and ethnicity, examined Knights of Labor organizing, and connected home life with work life. At Homestead, the Historical Society of Western Pennsylvania laid out the context of the great

1892 strike. The Essex Institute presented *Life and Times in Shoe City*. The South Street Seaport looked at urban craftworkers. Ellis Island surveyed the movement of immigrants into the national workplace. The National Museum of American History's *Symbols and Images of American Labor* compared worker self-representations with public perceptions. And a Smithsonian Traveling Exhibition Service (SITES) show, *Who's In Charge*, examined management-labor relations past and present.

Class analysis has not been limited to workers—Rochester's Strong Museum put on *Neither Rich Nor Poor: Searching for the American Middle Class*—though unfortunately, after being the primary focus of attention for so many years, upper-class lives are now scanted.

Consider gender issues. The National Women's Hall of Fame, which opened in Seneca Falls in 1968, has been joined by the National Park Service's Women's Rights National Historical Park in chronicling feminist history. Though institutions devoted specifically to women's history are still rare, museums like the Mark Twain house, Lindenwald, and Greenfield Village have reinserted domestic servants into their settings, and major institutions have produced substantial exhibits incorporating new historiography. Curators at NMAH put up *Men and Women: A History of Costume, Gender, and Power*, and *Parlor to Politics: Women and Reform, 1890–1925*, but perhaps most remarkable was their redoing of the First Ladies' gowns exhibit. This long-time semisacred site, to which Hillary Clinton's violet confection was quickly whisked, was completely remodeled. Now the dress graveyard is preceded by rooms that present the women as political and cultural actors, and interpret presidential couples as emblematic of the gender relations of their era. It is hugely popular. I heard one woman remarking to her twelve-year-old daughter: "You know, dear, the last time I was here they only had the gowns. They said nothing about the First Ladies themselves. It was so insulting."

On the ecological front, recent exhibits have admitted the ambiguous impact of progress on human and natural ecology. *Engines of Change* at NMAH salted its portrayal of an essentially beneficial industrialization with accounts of worker setbacks and environmental destruction. The Grand Rapids Public Museum provided insights into the impact of technology and industry on the local ecosystem. The State Historical Society of Iowa explored the impact of expanded agricultural productivity on forest, wetlands, and prairie. *Seeds of Change*, the Smithsonian's National Museum of Natural History show, compared the 1492 and 1992 ecoscapes, brought the Mexico City story down to its festering present, and argued for renewable resources.

Tropical Rainforests: A Disappearing Treasure, an exhibit organized by the Smithsonian's Traveling Exhibition Service, not only described the forests' decimation over the past century, but ascribed responsibility to specific agents—developers, loggers, ranchers, agribusiness, international banks, and consumers of rainforest commodities. It also provided visitors with names of organizations working to solve the problem. The design was the product of a collaboration between a politically committed academic—a tropical ornithologist/conservationist—and professional curators.

Museums have also taken up issues of recent history rather than restricting themselves to a more safely distant past. In Memphis' former Lorraine Motel, the National Civil Rights Museum places Martin Luther King's assassination in broader context, setting portions of a charred freedom rider bus and a replica of King's Birmingham jail cell right next to the balcony where he was felled. Interactively inclined visitors can board a 1950s era segregated bus, and get told by a driver-mannequin to "Go to the back"; or sit down next to sculpted protestors at a lunch counter sit-in. The Birmingham Civil Rights Institute displays King's actual cell along with segregation artifacts like separate water fountains against an audio backdrop of gospel and crowd sounds, sirens, and speeches. And a civil rights memorial in Montgomery, Alabama, honors victims of the movement. Malcolm X's legacy has proved tougher to museographize, with major battles being fought over the preservation and interpretation of his assassination site, New York's Audubon Ballroom.

In the former Texas State schoolbook depository, the Dallas County Historical Foundation offers *The Sixth Floor: John F. Kennedy and the Memory of a Nation*. It introduces the various assassination theories and commission reports, as well as audioaccounts by witnesses. Kent State University plans a memorial to the students shot there. More official versions of recent events can be found at presidential mausoleums, including those of Eisenhower, Nixon, Kennedy, and Johnson (the Lyndon Baines Johnson Library and Museum is the second most popular tourist attraction in Texas after the Alamo). George Bush was hard at work on his the first day out of office.

Some exhibits have provided historical perspective on contemporary issues. The National Park Service's bicentennial show at Philadelphia, *The Promise of Permanency*, explained how the Constitution's development was shaped over centuries as much by citizen action as judicial decision. Using touchscreen and video techniques it invited reflection on the document's applicability to aid to parochial schools, birth control, compulsory flag salutes, gay rights in the classroom, and other controversial questions. It presented exponents on different sides of these issues and allowed visitors to vote for the arguments they found most compelling. By jettisoning the conventional omniscient narrator stance, the exhibit also helped teach that historical perspectives—like court cases and current politics—are open to various interpretations.

Taboo Topics

If history museums have embraced a far wider range of subjects, objects, and issues than ever before, distinct limits remain on what can be said. Some politically volatile topics—delicately referred to as "controversial"—can be addressed only if the discussion is not brought down to the present; others are entirely taboo. Let us look at exhibits that can not yet or are just beginning to be mounted.

Although it has been decades since America first intervened in Indochina and the last helicopters lifted off from the roof of the Saigon Embassy, there has not been a single substantial museum exhibition on the causes, course, or consequences of the war in Vietnam. To say nothing, literally, of the antiwar movement. Despite a huge and burgeoning body of reflection by participants, historians, novelists, moviemakers, and playwrights, and the erection of hundreds of memorials, the closest we have come was the Smithsonian's Vietnam Veterans Memorial Collection. This was a fascinating collection of objects left at Washington's Vietnam Memorial, ranging from personal memorabilia of the fallen, through tributes to gay soldiers, to rejected Congressional Medals of Honor accompanied by letters protesting Reagan's support for the contras. It was poignant, and powerful, but it eschewed any commentary whatever.

Exhibitions dealing with issues of sexuality and gender remain problematic. There have been some recent shows that treated the household as a workplace, in a way that broke with the seemingly ingrained nostalgia of historic house museums, with their butter churns and home-baked cookies for visitors. But topics like divorce, prostitution, birth control, abortion, and domestic violence—though abundantly written about and highly salient to people's lives—linger in the realm of the undoable.

So, until quite recently, did homosexuality. Though the subject had spawned a vast historical literature, and been represented publicly in institutions created by the gay and lesbian community, it seemed impossible to treat in mainstream museums. A group of major institutions (the Museum of the City of New York, the Brooklyn Historical Society, the New York Public Library, and the New York Historical Society) launched an ambitious attempt to treat the history of homosexuals in New York City, but potential funders in the corporate and public sectors shied away. Finally, in the summer of 1994, the New York Public Library went ahead on its own with a major exhibition, *Becoming Visible: The Legacy of Stonewall*. After a section devoted to the 1969 riots at Stonewall Inn, visitors found imaginative and provocative treatments of the history that led up to it. Supported entirely from private foundations and contributions—the National Endowment for the Humanities refused to back it—the excellent show broke all first week attendance records for the library, pulling 17,258 visitors, and an average of one thousand per day thereafter from June through September.[1]

In the arena of labor and the economy, for all the particular exhibits about nineteenth-century artisanal and industrial workers, no major museum treats twentieth-century white collar or public employees. Nor has there been a show—much less an independent museum—that covers the history of organized labor. A few pioneering exhibits have tackled homelessness in historical perspective, but for all the fierce debates over welfare recipients and the "underclass," who has examined such populations historically in a museum setting? And what museums discuss the production of poverty and unemployment? Most Americans are well aware of the current hard times, the crises of the 1970s, and perhaps the Great Depression of the 1930s, but few realize that busts have alternated with booms on virtually a clockwork basis since the early 1800s.

Nor, for all the defunct mines and mills recycled into museums, is much attention paid to what most visitors want to know when they enter these spaces: Why did the jobs leave town and where did they go? An exhibit presenting a global perspective on deindustrialization, perhaps arranged by a multinational museum collaboration, might track the flight of factories from New England to North Carolina to Singapore and China—noting the simultaneous impact on American cities and Asian countrysides. Indeed, the connections between "deindustrialization" and "immigration" demand exploration in their own right. Ellis Island does a wonderful job on the earlier twentieth century but, despite some nods towards recent arrivals, it fails to remind us that "immigration" is hardly finished business, and that the political battles that animated earlier Americans continue today.

Ecological concerns have made great strides in museums, but institutions have been more comfortable talking about tropical rain forests in Brazil than toxic dumpsites in their own back yard. In 1994 a New York Public Library exhibition—*Garbage!: The History and Politics of Trash in New York City*—made an important breakthrough on this front. It explored the sanitary conditions of urban life in the nineteenth and early twentieth centuries, the work of public health reformers, the contemporary debates over the dumping of oil and chemical wastes, and suggested ecologically responsible ways of restructuring production and consumption.

A green perspective might illuminate other historical issues. At Henry Ford Museum and Greenfield Village, the *Automobile in American Life* exhibition examines the social historical aspects of our car culture, a great improvement over earlier installations. But it avoids exploring the decision to opt for gasoline-based private autos over mass transit, or reckoning with the social and ecological consequences of that decision, or tracing contemporary contests over auto-based pollution. Nor are there shows on the history of the energy industry that discuss issues of public versus private ownership, or that delve critically into the debates on nuclear power.

Our living history farms might profitably concentrate a bit less on sowing and reaping and a bit more on those developments—tenantry, migrant labor, foreclosures, agrarian movements, commodity exchanges, and world markets—that help explain how the old farms, whose values they celebrate, succumbed to the corporate agri-businesses that dominate American agriculture and account for much of the damage done to the countryside.

I could go on. Indeed it is disconcerting to contemplate how numerous and varied are the contemporary issues, routinely given historical attention in the academy, the media, and in politics, that history museums simply do not touch at all.

I am not saying—let me be clear—that "controversial" or presentist subjects are the only ones worth talking about. But I do think they should be strongly represented in an institution's mix of presentations over time. Studies show that people who do not go to museums believe them to be irrelevant as well as intimidating; dealing with issues germane to people's lives might help overcome their resistance.

Objections

Some people oppose this approach on principled—or definitional—grounds. Museums don't do these kinds of things, they say; they never did before, and they should not start now. Museums have gone too far in exploring controversial matters; certainly they should not, or cannot, press on farther in that direction. Such exhibits are in the domain of politics not history.

My rejoinder is that history, and history museums, are inescapably political, and always have been. In the old days, people were a good deal more explicit about it. The museological giants and house museum pioneers all presented narratives linking the past with present-day concerns and prescriptions for the future. Usually museums were handmaidens of power, and they set the present in a continuum in such a way as to ratify present arrangements. But the (Carl) Beckerite and (Dixon Ryan) Foxite progressives who contested traditional establishments in the name of a people's history were equally straightforward. They wanted citizens to grasp where they had been so they could better assess where they might go. Only relatively recently did museums and scholars profess to be "objective," or apolitical; such preachments seldom governed museological practice.

Other criticisms are more pragmatic than principled. They note that controversial exhibits are less likely to find sponsors to fund them. That is true. Sponsors usually represent established power; they tend to balk at presentations that contest the way things are. They also dislike being associated with any controversy, whatever its content. Cities, unions, corporations, or local townsfolk tend to favor uplifting optimism or blandly judicious balance—exhibits fit for prime time, family viewing.

Gerald George, former director of the American Association for State and Local History, offered an allegory about a would-be reforming curator, Eddie Gibbon, who tried to turn the Hickory City Historical Society upside down. Dismissing the museum's filiopietistic inspirational approach, young Gibbon scrapped the Hall of Pioneers, the Victorian Period Gallery, and the Civil War cannon, and sold off George Washington's wig at Sothebys to fund social history exhibits on Chinese restaurant operators, baseball games, Baptist conventions, slavic miners, and analyses of urbanization and industrialization. For his pains he got himself blown away by a pioneer rifle in the hands of the society's outraged president.

An apt parable, but perhaps too intimidating. It can lead to overhasty self-censorship. Museums sometimes adhere to an unwritten understanding that there are limits on what can be said, even if they have not been laid down explicitly. Often prudence is justified. But sometimes it is not. Recent experience suggests that determined pushing can be rewarded. If the Mississippi State Museum can interpret the Ku Klux Klan, it is conceivable that institutions can garner more support from properly cultivated patrons than they might expect.

One way to make critical material more palatable to powers-that-be, and to audiences as well, is to present different interpretive points of view. Running two alternative approaches to the same material, side by side, would reveal that historians differ amongst themselves, and teach museum visitors not to accept any presentation as the gospel truth.

Another point. Gerald George's slaughtered curator was acting on his own. There are now signs that a critical professional community is emerging, one that includes academics, which can be mobilized to provide support to beleaguered colleagues. Academic historians used to get hired and fired by railroad magnates until the establishment one hundred years ago of the American Historical Association, which set limits on the power of autocratic university managements. Historian Al Young's proposal of a Museum Bill of Rights that would put "curatorial freedom" on a par with "academic freedom" merits further discussion.[2]

Professional collaboration can also take the form of an alliance (perhaps with academics and librarians) to increase the amount of government funding available for public education outside the school systems. If the sources of funding can be diversified, the influence of individual donors can be reduced.

It is also important to identify new sources of support, groups that might be interested in more critical presentations—labor unions, socially responsible businesses, women's clubs and groups, and environmentalists. The Macarthur Foundation contributed one-half of a million dollars to the rain forest show.

In the end, however, the power of donors is a fact of life. They will continue to shape and alter agendas. This is true both for house museums in tiny towns and for giant technology museums dependent on aerospace corporations for costly machinery. The best one can do is to keep pushing at the boundaries of the possible.

Demand Dilemmas

A different reservation concerns potential visitors, not potential funders. People want to be entertained, goes this objection. They do not want to be lectured, upset, or offended, nor do they want to hear about conflict. They do not want to think, they want to have fun. Museums have many competitors in the cultural marketplace; if their offerings are unattractive, shoppers will go elsewhere.

And even if people can be enticed to critical exhibits, museums (it is said) are not an appropriate venue in which to raise difficult and substantial issues. Few visitors track through a show from beginning to end; most race past expository prose. Besides, who can think about anything serious when they are standing on their feet, especially with two kids asking for hamburgers or the nearest bathroom.

These are strong arguments, based on hard-won experience, but perhaps a little too dismissive of actual and potential audiences. It may be that most visitors are uninterested in controversial issues. But a contradiction lurks in this assessment. If people are drawn to history museums by a nostalgic urge to escape the present, perhaps they are not utterly enamored of their contemporary situation. If so, might they not be receptive to presentations that explain how the glorious past (which, alas, was probably not quite so wonderful on close inspection) evolved into the wretched present (which, in fact, turns out to have redeeming qualities)?

More often than not, I suspect, audience conservatism is pre-presumed. The cry that something "won't sell" is often used as an excuse by those who want to kill a program on other grounds. Conventional wisdoms are fluid things. Audiences change with the times; when challenged, they often respond favorably. Like all producers for the cultural marketplace, museums must listen to their customers. But I also think they have a responsibility, as educators and professionals, to propose new ways of seeing things. They must both listen and lead—admittedly not an easy balance to sustain.

And why assume that controversial presentations can not be done in entertaining ways? Especially as such subjects are usually far more dramatic and gripping than many of the issues museums usually deal with? As I have suggested, a fair number of such shows have received notices that are overwhelmingly (and unexpectedly) favorable. The Holocaust Museum's spectacular drawing power is only the latest evidence that even the most difficult and disturbing material does not automatically alienate potential visitors.[3]

Certainly we should not overestimate what museums can do. There are limits on how much information and analysis people can absorb on their feet. But modest goals are surely attainable. Curators can raise issues and perspectives for people's consideration so the next time they confront the topic they have the gist of the presentation in mind (along with the experience of the exhibit). Museums can enhance visitors' skill at historical analysis—probably of more lasting value than imparting specific information about any particular issue. Nor does an exhibit have to be the last stop: It can be supplemented with take-home videos or publications that allow for more leisurely (and child friendly) reflections.

Broadening Constituencies

A more profound version of the audience-objection suggests that museums are akin to religious institutions, with curators as keepers of the nation's relics. Museums nurture the myths that provide a culture's moral scaffolding, so this argument goes; people attend them as they might a church service—to nourish and undergird their spiritual identity. The last thing such congregants want are exhibits that dismantle the mythic dramas that give meaning and value to their lives.

I have problems with this definition of museums. I prefer Robert A. Baron's careful distinction between theme parks like Disney World, where visitors are encouraged to live inside mythic metaphors, indeed to reenact in a ritual way the (putatively) essential events in American history; and history museums, where visitors are asked to stand outside these metaphors and to reflect on them both as participants and disengaged critics.[4]

But even if we accept the notion of museums as temples of myth, I would say that there are myths and myths, congregations and congregations. If curators are priests and priestesses they have to decide whether or not they approve of the spiritual values they have been promulgating. If they do, and their visitors do, there is not much motivation for change. If, however, they or their visitors do not so approve—and this, I submit, has been the case at many institutions over the last generation—then it behooves them to submit other historical narratives for popular consideration. They do not have to smash old ones—mere iconoclasm—but can affirm values they think merit retention, while presenting new alternatives, with all the power of their craft, thus turning temples into public forums.

There is another way to come at the issue. If traditional audiences will not support innovative programming, perhaps new ones will. Recent experience suggests that bold approaches to unusual subjects attract new audiences and increase revenues. The Smithsonian's *More Perfect Union* show brought in over five thousand Japanese Americans in the first week, some all the way from the west coast; that group's ongoing attendance has increased. The Valentine Museum was at the point of going under in the early 1980s, but when its shows reached out to new audiences, it tripled overall attendance. African American walk-in attendance went from less than one to more than fifteen percent, which in turn helped garner funding from the black city council and the black mayor.[5] In Wilberforce, Ohio, the National Afro-American Museum's treatment of black history has been facilitated by the involvement of AME bishops and black Ohio legislators; in turn, its pioneering show on the civil rights movement, *From Victory to Freedom*, has generated new involvement in the African American community. The Plains Indian Museum has established a similarly strong and organic relationship with its constituency. People, it seems, are willing to attend museums if institutions speak to their experience.

Reaching out to new audiences can also help museums overcome the limitations of previous collections policies. For the *More Perfect Union* show, the Smithsonian worked with the Japanese American Citizens League to solicit the loan or donation of objects needed to tell the story. Advertisements in newspapers brought hundreds of people, bearing artifacts, to temporary offices set up in malls and civic centers. The Baltimore Museum's Rowhouse exhibit generated the same kind of grass roots support, and the Brooklyn Historical Society established strong connections with the borough's Afro-Caribbean, Chinese, Italian, and Hispanic communities through similar campaigns.

Institutions that embrace community outreach programming are quite different from those that see themselves as purveyors of historical commodities, seeking to expand "market share." The former will often respond to issues of popular concern, while the latter, less driven by principle or passion, are no more likely than corporate sponsors to tackle difficult but interesting issues. The post-sixties transformations in museums were not "market-driven" but political phenomena. Black (and many white) parents wanted representations in schools and museums that broke with racist stereotypes; committed curators pushed for these transformations and, in turn, the new exhibits attracted new audiences and generated political support from elected officials. The show on Japanese internment was defended against attack by powerful senators responding to new constituencies.

There are, of course, dangers in targeting new audiences—of provincialism, or particularism, or ghettoization. Museums can fall prey to the fragmentation of the magazine racks, where specialty journals, one for every conceivable taste and interest, allow readers to immerse themselves in their chosen world to the exclusion of others. But this is a potential, not an inherent drawback.

There are also efforts underway to demystify and democratize museums by sharing authority with communities. I applaud efforts to involve formerly passive audiences in planning, collecting for, and evaluating exhibits. Exemplary work includes the Brooklyn Historical Society projects with AIDs victims; the Chinatown History Museum's neighborhood collaborations; the Valentine's assembling of advisory groups to help plan public programming, and its holding of "public editing sessions" with community spokespeople to critique completed shows; and the extensive consultations with local reminiscence groups and the incorporation of oral histories into work at the Springburn Museum in Glasgow, the Museum of London's *Peopling of London*, and *The People's Story* in Edinburgh.

I also applaud barefoot-historian projects whose members facilitate local communities in collecting, preserving, presenting, and interpreting their own past, producing exhibits that could have not have been generated by either the professionals or the community acting on their own.

But I part company from those who propose that curators de-professionalize themselves altogether and transfer power to "the community." Aside from being utopian, the historical record suggests that abuse of power is not inevitable. In the United States, activist curators, linked to committed scholars, were vital agents of change. And the strong professional communities they forged have been crucial in raising issues that transcend (but involve) particular communities, and in establishing an apparatus of critical commentary (notably the many journals that now review exhibits) that is indispensable to future progress.[6]

A strong public historical community will also be crucial in defending and sustaining recent gains. Some have wondered what difference these changes have made. Advancing a Marxist analysis—Groucho Marxist that is—they suggest that if African Americans and others have gotten into museums, museums can not be much worth getting into. The even more cynical say that museological alterations are sops—substitutes for changes in power relations; that blacks, women, and Indians have fared far better in exhibits than at workplaces, in homes, or on the streets. While the new historians were restocking museums and colleges, Reagan and Bush were restocking the judiciary and bureaucracy.

I disagree. While it is true that transformations in representation have outstripped those in reality, curators and scholars have made real contributions to shifting the terms of America's public discourse. And language counts. Proof comes from opponents. The *West as America* show's challenge to mythic pieties provoked a furor of complaints from conservatives incensed at its deconstruction of fables. The *Wall Street Journal* called it "an entirely hostile ideological assault on the nation's founding and history." To be sure, some of the exhibit's captions, humorless and bludgeoning, afforded tempting targets. But the real objections were to its having advanced critical theses amidst the yellow-ribboned frenzy of Operation Desert Storm, an exercise President Bush had explicitly cast as an opportunity to get beyond the historical self-doubts engendered by Vietnam. Critics had already attacked schools and universities that revised the traditional canon and fashioned multicultural curricula. Now museums, too, were accused of imposing stifling standards of "political correctness." These outcries serve as reminders of the fragility of recent gains, of their potential reversibility.

I urge history museums to press on in the direction they have been going, seeking not simply customers but constituents; becoming partners with communities in effecting change; serving as centers of civic debate and organization (with modest expectations about how much such forums can achieve); helping visitors develop their historical sensibilities, strengthening their ability to locate themselves in time, and enhancing their capacity as citizens to be historically informed makers of history. If museums continue to think imaginatively about new ways of saying things, and boldly about new things that are worth saying, I think they will find that their greatest contributions to the American past still lie in the future.

Notes

This is an amalgam of a keynote address, "The Future of the Past," presented to the Annual Meeting of the American Association for State and Local History on September 17, 1988; and a second keynote address, "Changing Media, Changing Messages," for Museum, Media, Message: The Third International Conference in Museum Studies at the University of Leicester in 1993.

1. For a review, see Lisa Duggan, " 'Becoming Visible: The Legacy of Stonewall,' " New York Public Library, June 18–September 24, 1994," *Radical History Review* 62 (spring 1995), 188–94. The Oakland Museum of California, it should be noted, had already included, in its permanent exhibit, information about a legendary local drag queen.
2. Alfred F. Young, "A Modest Proposal: A Bill of Rights For American Museums," *Public Historian* 14 (1992), 67–72. See also Young, "S.O.S.: Storm Warning for American Museums," *OAH Newsletter* 22 (November 1994), 1, 6–8.

3. See Edward T. Linenthal, *Preserving Memory: the Struggle to Create America's Holocaust Museum* (New York, 1995); and James Edward Young, *The Texture of Memory: Holocaust Memorials and Meaning* (New Haven, 1993).
4. Robert A. Baron, "Why People Go To Museums," a posting on the MUSEUM-L email bulletin board, 11 April 1995, accessible through LISTSERV@UNMVMA.UNM.EDU
5. The Valentine may have been too successful. See note 3 to "Razor Ribbons" in this volume, 54.
6. I would like to see more institutions taping their presentations and pooling them in a videolibrary, available to the curatorial community.

Section II

Mickey Mouse History: Portraying the Past at Disney World

Mick•ey Finn (mĭk′ē fĭn′) *n. Slang.* An alcoholic beverage that is surreptitiously altered to induce diarrhea or stupefy, render unconscious, or otherwise incapacitate the person who drinks it. [Origin unknown.]

Mickey Mouse *adj.* **1.a.** *Slang.* Unimportant; trivial: *"It's a Mickey Mouse operation compared to what goes on in Lyons or Paris"* (Jack Higgins). **b.** *Slang.* Irritatingly petty: *the school's Mickey Mouse requirements for graduation.* **2.** *Slang.* Intellectually unchallenging; simple: *His Mickey Mouse assignments soon bored the students.* **3.** *Music.* **a.** Blandly sentimental. Used of popular compositions and performers. **b.** Relating to a soundtrack that accompanies the action in an unsubtle, melodramatic way suggestive of music written for animated films. [After the cartoon character *Mickey Mouse*, created by Walt Disney.]

mick•le (mĭk′əl) *Scots. adj.* Great. **—mickle** *adv.* Greatly. [Middle English *mikel,* from Old English *micel* and from Old Norse *mikill;* see **meg-** in Appendix.]

"Industry has lost credibility with the public, the government has lost credibility, but people still have faith in Mickey Mouse and Donald Duck." [Marty Sklar, vice-president, WED Enterprises, Inc.]

Walt Disney never got a Ph.D., but he was, nevertheless, a passionate historian. At Disneyland in California and Disney World in Florida, the past is powerfully evoked for visitors with music, movies, robots, and the latest in special effects. As tens of millions of people visit these attractions each year, one might fairly say that Walt Disney has taught people more history, in a more memorable way, than they ever learned in school.

But a closer inspection of the theme parks raises questions as to who should properly get credit for their creation. There are, it turns out, *two* Walt Disneys. First, there was the familiar mustachioed fellow we all know, the man we might call "Original Walt." It was Original Walt who built the Magic Kingdom in Disneyland in the 1950s. Later, the Magic Kingdom was cloned and transported to Disney World in Florida. Today both Kingdoms remain essentially intact, frozen in time, their presentations of "Main Street," "Frontierland," "Adventureland," and the "Hall of Presidents" reflecting Original Walt's 1950s-style approach to history.

Original Walt died in 1966—despite persistent rumors that he had himself frozen, and may yet be back. But in a way he *did* live on. As WED (Walter Elias Disney) Enterprises, Inc., he was reincarnated as a corporation.

In the 1970s, this "Corporate Walt," claiming it was carrying out Original Walt's wishes, forged an alliance with other corporations (the crème de la crème of U.S. multinationals). Together they built EPCOT—the Experimental Prototype Community of Tomorrow—and housed it in Disney World, next door to the Magic Kingdom. EPCOT, too, is saturated with history, but of a remarkably different kind from Original Walt's 1950s version. It is these two historical perspectives, side by side in Orlando, that I want to explore and juxtapose.

Scrutinizing the Disney parks, in addition to being intrinsically interesting, affords some insights into the growing world of commercialized history. Nowadays it often seems as if the past gets presented to popular audiences more by commercial operators pursuing profit than by museums bent on education. Vacationers can now motor to dozens of historic theme parks: Knotts Berry Farm, Busch Gardens, Six Flags Over Texas, Dodge City, Railroads USA, Indian Village, and Safari World are only a few of the places that are blurring the line between entertainment center and "actual" museum. It well behooves historians and museum professionals to assess these competitors for public attention. What effect, if any, does corporate sponsorship have on the historical information presented? What is audience response to (and impact on) mass-marketed history? Tracking the transformation of Original Walt into Corporate Walt provides a case study that begins to provide answers to these questions.

Main Street and Its Enemies

In the early 1950s Walt Disney set out to build an amusement park that was clean, wholesome, and altogether different from the seedy carnivals he remembered from his youth. Against great odds (bankers frowned on the project and he had to borrow on his insurance policy to do the initial planning), he created Disneyland in 1955. At the heart of the project, right along with his fantasy characters, Disney placed a series of history-flavored entertainments.

This was new for Walt. Aside from the spectacularly successful *Davy Crockett: King of the Wild Frontier*, a few costume dramas like *Rob Roy, the Highland Rogue*, and *Song of the South* (whose idyllic depiction of master/slave relationships drew National Association for the Advancement of Colored People fire), Walt had shied away from history. Perhaps his turnaround was influenced by the crowds flocking to John D. Rockefeller, Jr.'s Colonial Williamsburg and Henry Ford's Greenfield Village as 1950s Americans took to the highways in search of their roots. Certainly his technique resembled that used at Williamsburg—he transported visitors back in time.

The minute you stroll through the turnstiles into the Magic Kingdom you "turn back the clock," as your guidebook tells you, "to the turn-of-the-century."[1] Your first steps take you to Main Street, the heart of a small American town. It is a happy street, clean and tidy, filled with prancing Disney characters. It has a toylike quality, perhaps because it is built five-eights true size ("people like to think their world is somehow more grown up than Papa's was").[2] It is like playing in a walk-in doll's house that is simultaneously a shopper's paradise, equipped with dozens of little old-time shops with corporate logos tastefully affixed.

But Main Street, ostensibly, is grounded in historic reality. It was fashioned, we are told, out of Disney's recollections of his turn of the century boyhood in Marceline, Missouri, a small town one hundred miles northeast of Kansas City. The intent, Walt said, was to "bring back happy memories for those who remember the carefree times it recreates."[3] This is puzzling to those familiar with Disney's own story, which was rather grimmer.

Disney's father Elias, a hardscrabble small operator, drifted back and forth between country and city in an unsuccessful attempt to establish himself and his family. After failing at citrus growing in Florida, he moved to Chicago, where he worked as a carpenter on the Columbian Exposition of 1893 before establishing a hand-to-mouth small contracting business. Walt was born in 1901, just before the business failed, and the family moved again, this time to a forty-eight-acre farm near Marceline, on which Elias entered into the precarious and indebted life of the American small farmer. (Perhaps the then pervasive agrarian resentment of bankers was a source of the elder Disney's socialism—he voted consistently for Eugene Debs and subscribed to the *Appeal to Reason*.) Walt was set to hard farm labor (which his two elder brothers escaped by running off) and a diet of stern patriarchal beatings. In 1910, Elias failed again. Forced to sell the farm and auction off the livestock, he moved to Kansas City, Missouri, bought a newspaper route, and set Walt and his remaining brother Roy to work as newsboys; Roy ran away the following year. After living meanly in Missouri a few more years, Elias drifted back to Chicago, where he became chief of construction and maintenance in a jelly factory, and put Walt to work washing bottles. Finally, in 1919, Walt made his own break. He spent the early 1920s in Kansas City as a commercial artist, hustling hard to stay alive and ahead of the bill collectors. In 1923 he moved to Hollywood, where his career began to click.[4]

The confectionery quality of Magic Kingdom's Main Street thus bears little resemblance to Disney's real childhood home. And indeed a Disney official history confesses that "historically speaking, this Main Street was quite unlike the real Main Streets of yesteryear. Here, everything would always remain fresh and new. And the rows of old-time shops and the traffic vehicles and all the other elements would function together in harmony and unison unlike anything grandfather ever experienced."[5]

Original Walt's approach to the past was thus not to reproduce it, but to *improve* it. A Disney "imagineer" (as the designers style themselves) explains how the process works: "What we create is a 'Disney Realism,' sort of utopian in nature, where we carefully program out all the negative, unwanted elements and program in the positive elements."[6] (This vacuum-cleaning of the past is reminiscent of Walt's film work in which he transformed Grimm's gothic horror tales into cute and cheery cartoons.) As another Disney planner puts it: "This is what the real Main Street should have been like."[7]

The Disney people do not consider this retrospective tidying up an abuse of the past—they freely and disarmingly admit its falsification, pointing out that this is, after all, just entertainment. But they also insist they are bringing out deeper truths. John Hench, a leading member of the organization, expanded on this in an interview, explaining that Disney sought to recapture the *essence* of a period. "You take a certain style, and take out the contradictions that have crept in there through people that never understood it or by accident or by some kind of emergency that happened once and found itself being repeated—you leave those things out, purify the style, and it comes back to its old form again."[8] Like the French architect Viollet-le-Duc, who, in the 1860s and 1870s, strove to restore churches to imagined Gothic purity, Original Walt aimed to strip away the accretions of time. In the case of Main Street, Hench explains, he was striving to re-create the Victorian era, "which is probably one of the great optimistic periods of the world, where we thought progress was great and we all knew where we were going. [Main Street] reflects that prosperity, that enthusiasm."[9]

The decades before and after the turn of the century had their decidedly prosperous moments. But they also included depressions, strikes on the railroads, warfare in the minefields, squalor in the immigrant communities, lynching, imperial wars, and the emergence of mass protests by populists and socialists. *This* history has been whited out, presumably because it would have distressed and repelled visitors. As Hench noted, "Walt wanted to reassure people."[10]

Walt's approach, though it had its roots in Hollywood, was emblematic of larger developments in 1950s America. The dominant culture, seemingly determined to come up with a happy past to match its own contented present, contracted a selective amnesia. Leading academic historians downplayed past conflicts and painted optimistic, even uplifting pictures of the American past. Colonial Williamsburg's recollection of olden times conspicuously excised the presence of black slaves, 50 percent of its eighteenth-century inhabitants. Greenfield Village—another conflict-free small town—overlooked such realities of rural life as foreclosures and farmers' movements. Walt's Main Street, therefore, can perhaps best be understood as part of a larger trend. As a stage set that cultivated nostalgia for a fabricated past, it contributed its bit toward fashioning an image—now deeply etched into popular memory—of the Gay

Nineties as a world without classes, conflict, or crime, a world of continuous consumption, a supermarket of fun. At the same time, it fastened this image on the future. Just as Colonial Williamsburg provided the model for thousands of "colonial" suburbs, Disneyland's Main Street became a model for the developing American shopping mall and the "ye olde" entertainment centers beginning to festoon the American landscape. On the face of it, Eisenhower-era citizens could assume that America's present had evolved gently, naturally, and inevitably out of its past.

There are places in Disney Land that recall the bumpier patches of the good old days. At Frontierland and Adventureland, contradictions are not deleted but dwelt upon. Here we go on rides that travel to the distant and benighted places that once threatened Civilization. In the Wild West, Darkest Africa, and the Caribbean, we are in the domain of dangerous opponents—Indians, pygmy headhunters, pirates. But there is no real danger in these realms. As Hench explains: "What we do here is to throw a challenge at you—not a real menace, but a pseudo-menace, a theatricalized menace—and we allow you to win."[11]

Scary but harmless images are a stock-in-trade of amusement parks. But it is striking that Disney's "pseudo-menaces" are all historical ones—the ghosts of once vigorous, now defeated enemies of Main Street—transformed into fun-filled characters. On the ride up the Congo River, your affable host regales you with such witticisms as "These natives have one thing in mind; they just want to get ahead." The robot pirates are agreeably wicked and the robot women seem to enjoy being ravished. In Frontierland you can hole up in an old fort and shoot Indians, with a barrage of canned gunfire as an accompaniment (this was Walt's favorite part of the park).

For all the whizzing bullets, the experience of reliving ancient passions is a soothing one. For one thing, as Hench comments shrewdly, these are "old-fashioned weapons. They're part of the safe past. Nobody worries about the past."[12] For another, cowboys-and-Indians is a well-established and conventional game, and historical conflict is thus shuttled into a regressive world of childhood fantasy. Frontierland and Adventureland brush up against some realities of the past, but in the end they serve as ritual reassurance of Main Street's triumph over its opponents.

Abe and Audioanimatronics

The Magic Kingdom includes a direct portrayal of American history at the Hall of Presidents. The hall has a peculiar history of its own. Designed in 1957 and 1958, it was put on the shelf because Disney imagineers lacked the technology to produce it. Breakthroughs in "audioanimatronics" (robot building) came in the early 1960s; at the 1964 World's Fair Disney tried out the new engineering. In collaboration with the State of Illinois, he built the "Visit with Mr. Lincoln" pavilion, starring an artificial Abe. In the 1970s, the original Hall of Presidents show was dusted off, and the Lincoln robot became its centerpiece.

The Hall of Presidents is housed at Liberty Square in a mockup of an eighteenth-century Philadelphia mansion. Visitors wait for the next show in the rotunda, where paintings of the founding fathers establish respectful atmospherics. Then they are ushered into a theater (and told that no eating is allowed—"to maintain the dignity of the presentation"). A film begins. It shows the founding fathers making the Constitution. We learn that the new document was soon challenged by the Whiskey Rebels, a churlish mob, and that George Washington crushed them. Then slaveholders, an aristocratic mob, threatened it again. Andrew Jackson threatened to hang them from the nearest tree. Lastly, the Confederates launched the greatest challenge to date, and Lincoln took up the burden of defense. The movie implies that internal disorder remains the chief threat to America's survival.

The film ends. With great fanfare the screen goes up, revealing a stage full of robots representing U.S. presidents. All of them, from Washington to Reagan, are in motion, nodding or solemnly (if somewhat arthritically) gesticulating. They are done up with scrupulous attention to detail. George Washington's chair is a precise reproduction of the one in which he sat at the 1787 Constitutional Convention. Their costumes are authentic down to the last stitch. Wig-makers in Guatemala reproduced their hair strand for strand. (The attention to detail, characteristic of Hollywood costume dramas, again reminds us of Disney's cinematic roots.)

A sepulchral voice-over calls the roll of these men "who have defended the Constitution." The audience is hushed—perhaps in awe at the solemnity of the occasion, perhaps in amazement at the spectacle of thirty-odd robots twitching about on stage. When the roll call gets to Franklin D. Roosevelt and the more recent presidents there is a whisper here and there. But when it gets to Nixon, chortles and guffaws break out. The contrast between the official history and living memories is too great (Nixon as defender of the Constitution?) and the spell snaps under the strain. I asked later if this was simply a bad day for Mr. Nixon, and was told that no, the crowd always rumbles when RN takes his bow.

The Nixon disturbance is symptomatic of a larger problem with the Hall of Presidents. By the 1970s, for all its technical sophistication, its ideology was old-fashioned, less believable than it was in the heyday of McCarthyism. The Disney people deny any dissatisfaction with it, but in retrospect we can see that in the 1960s they began exploring alternatives to the nationalistic approach. The transition to the eventual solution (EPCOT) was provided by another Disney 1964 World's Fair exhibit, the Carousel of Progress, created in collaboration with General Electric.

Progress is Our Most Important Product

At the Carousel of Progress, Disney takes visitors on a ride through time. After they settle down in the Carousel's small theater, the curtain rises on a robot middle-class family at home in 1900. Mom, Dad, and the kids are chatting about housework. They have the latest in labor-saving devices—gas lights, telephones, iceboxes—and think that life could not be any easier, but we see that poor Mom is still subject to all kinds of drudgery. Luckily, as Dad reads in the paper, some smart fellers down at General Electric are cooking up new gadgets. At this point the theater begins to revolve around the stage (accompanied by a cheery ditty whose refrain is "Now is the best time, now is the best time, now is the best time of your life") until it reaches a new stage, this one set with 1920-style robots. Mom and Dad enthuse about their new machines—percolators, refrigerators, electric irons—but note that those research people at General Electric are still at it. And on we go to 1940, and finally to 1960. Things have really progressed now. Dad is cooking dinner (though somewhat clumsily) and Mom is celebrating passage of a bond issue (on which she had time to work thanks to her GE dishwasher and dryer). At ride's end a hearty voice-over concludes that we live in "the best time" ("one of the reasons is that electricity has improved our lives"), and that things will get even better ("each new year and each new day will bring a better way of life"). Finally we are shuttled toward the Kitchen of Tomorrow to see what General Electric has dreamed up for us next.

The Carousel of Progress is more than simply an extended commercial break. It is a paean to Progress—defined as the availability of emancipatory consumer goods. This was new for Disney. He had tended to political rather than commercial themes. But it was an old line of argument for industrial corporations. Even the pseudofeminist claim that household commodities liberated women had been advanced by advertisers since the 1920s and had been a staple at the 1939 World's Fair. I would like to suggest that the Disney/GE collaboration represents an important merging of several longstanding traditions of American culture.

Consider first the roots of Disney's Magic Kingdom shows. They descend, in part, from the patriotic dioramas, *tableaux vivants*, and waxworks of the nineteenth century. Disney upgraded the technology—viewers were hauled into the dioramas and robots replaced live actors or wax representations—but the red, white, and blue spirit remained much the same.

In the 1950s, Disney married this tradition to the amusement park—a form that beer magnates, real estate developers, and transportation kings had fashioned for the urban working classes in the 1880s and 1890s, and whose culmination was Coney Island. Disney's park was a cleaned-up version, aimed at a middle-class "family" audience. He quite consciously stripped away the honky-tonk legacies of the carnival. It might be said that Disneyland represented another skirmish in a centuries-old struggle by the middle classes against popular culture's dangerous tendency to "turn the world upside down." By customary right, medieval carnivals—Twelfth Night, the Ship of Fools, Bartholomew Fair—allowed the dispossessed to ridicule the high and mighty and even (symbolically) to seize power for a day. Disney's park erased any lingering traces of rituals of revolt and substituted highly organized, commodified fun. In this the Magic Kingdom shows were like Rockefeller Jr.'s Williamsburg and Ford's Greenfield Village, which eliminated from "history" what their sponsors found inconvenient and unwelcome. But the essence of the form, selective reconstruction of the past, goes back to late nineteenth-century Scandinavian open air museums; to such eighteenth-century aristocratic productions as Marie Antoinette's play peasant village (complete with marble-walled dairy); French *folies* such as Parc Monceau; and the great landscape parks of the English gentry, which excised all signs of daily peasant activity and eradicated any sense of time other than the artificially constructed "natural."

In the 1960s, Disney took the Magic Kingdom approach and merged it with a favorite form of the entrepreneurial bourgeoisie—the industrial exposition. These expositions go back to London's 1851 Crystal Palace (and New York City's 1853 copy). They afforded places to show off and sell new inventions. They were also sites of ideological production, of boasting about how technology and business would transform the future.

From the perspective of its sponsors, the exposition form had long been riven by an annoying inner tension between commercial exhortation and crowd-pleasing carnival elements. The 1893 Columbian Exposition had huge buildings devoted to transportation, manufacture, and electricity presented in historical perspective; it also had seedier entertainment pavilions, located outside the White City, including "a real Dahomey village of genuine savages."[13]

The 1939 World's Fair overcame this dichotomy to a degree by subordinating celebration of production to fascination with consumption. Rather than the traditional presentation of awesome machinery, the fair showcased consumer goods: Companies displayed their commodities in dazzling and fun-filled surroundings. General Motors' Futurama shuttled visitors along in comfortable moving chairs; AT&T fostered audience interaction with a talking machine; and General Electric offered a House of Magic ("the packed audiences," it was noted, "came away thrilled, mystified, and soundly sold on the company"). Another GE show contrasted the lives of Mrs. Drudge and Mrs. Modern, anticipating the Carousel of Progress's argument of gender emancipation through household appliances. For all this, the fair's first year was a financial failure, partly because of the high admission price, partly because of the heaviness of the social message.

The financial and corporate sponsors presented the "world of tomorrow" as the product of a rejuvenated capitalism, a decade of depression and state intervention behind it. Entrepreneurs and technocrats would promote a rich future of mass plenty if given the opportunity, and public funds. At Futurama, as Walter Lippmann noted, General Motors "spent a small fortune to convince the American public that if it wishes to enjoy the full benefit of private enterprise in motor manufacturing, it will have to rebuild its cities and its highways by public enterprise."[14] The agitprop turned many off, critics and visitors skirted the educational and cultural theme exhibits, and even the *New York Times* called the fair a laboratory for "Tomorrow's propaganda." In its second year, the fair brought back sideshows and hootchy-kootchy girls.

Twenty-five years later, the 1964 Disney-GE collaboration put sanitized entertainment at the service of business boosterism, and pointed the way to EPCOT, which would brilliantly and successfully merge all these techniques and traditions, retaining the advantages and shedding the liabilities of fairs, waxworks, museums, and carnivals. One of the keys to the breakthrough was the Disney ability, adroitly displayed at the carousel, to construct highly selective versions of the past.

Free Enterprise Forever

Walt's original vision of EPCOT had nothing to do with history. The Experimental Prototype Community of Tomorrow was to be a laboratory city in which twenty thousand people would live. Disney dreamed of "a planned, controlled community, a showcase for American industry and research," a permanent testing ground for new ideas in urban planning. Under its gigantic bubble dome, American know-how, ingenuity, and enterprise would overcome the ills of urban life. ("In EPCOT there will be no slum areas because we won't let them develop".[15])

This extraordinary project might seem quite a jump from an amusement park, but the overheated reaction Disneyland evoked may have been instrumental in EPCOT's creation. Walt had been praised extravagantly as an urban planner. James Rouse, master builder of new towns and historical shopping malls modeled on Main Street (Boston's Faneuil Hall, Baltimore's

Harborplace, New York's South Street Seaport) told a 1963 Harvard conference that Disneyland was the "greatest piece of urban design in the United States today."[16] Architectural critic Peter Blake called the Anaheim park the only significant new town built in the United States since World War II—"staggeringly successful"—and suggested, only half-humorously, turning Manhattan over to Disney to fix up.[17]

All this went to Walt's head, and he flowered into a utopian capitalist. This was partly a family legacy: As Michael Harrington has perceptively noted, Disney's father had been an admirer of Edward Bellamy's "warm-hearted, futuristic authoritarianism."[18] Partly, perhaps, Walt had been inspired by the 1939 World's Fair's Democracity, a scale model of a perfectly planned "world of tomorrow"—a "vast, Utopian stage set" housed inside the great globe of the Perisphere. Whatever its roots, the hothouse atmosphere of the Kennedy-Johnson years speeded the process. Gigantic projects of social reconstruction seemed plausible in those boom years and though Walt was a Goldwater Republican (and an early financial supporter of Ronald Reagan), he too dreamed of creating a Great Society.

Like Johnson, Disney acted boldly. By 1965 he had bought up, secretly, forty square miles (twice the size of Manhattan) in central Florida. The state, anticipating mammoth tourist revenues, granted him virtually feudal powers. Democracy for the residents of the community of tomorrow would have been a nuisance. ("There will be no landowners and therefore no voting control.")[19] To ensure that EPCOT ran smoothly, Walt would be king.

But in 1966, in the midst of planning the new society, Walt died. WED Enterprises considered going ahead with his prototype city, but the company was nervous; it could see lawsuits in its future from disgruntled and disfranchised residents. So it scrapped the notion of a living city and went with a safer version, an extension of Disney's collaboration with General Electric. WED proposed to some of the biggest corporations in the United States a joint project, the construction of a permanent world's fair. There the companies, with the help of Disney imagineers, would display evolving technologies and promote their visions of the future. EPCOT was thus transformed from utopian community to sound business proposition.

By targeting grown-up Mouseketeers instead of their offspring, WED got itself out of an impending crisis—a looming baby bust that promised to shrivel its traditional prime market of five to nine-year-olds. (A similar marketing strategy dictated scrapping Dick Van Dyke movies for PG films like *Splash*: Pre-teens no longer flocked to traditional Disney fare and the studio was forced to respond to this cultural shift.) The participating companies would also profit: They could advertise new product lines and drape themselves in the mantle of Disney respectability, no small matter in the anticorporate atmosphere of the 1970s.

The corporate giants agreed. Kraft declared that sponsorship of a land pavilion was "the most effective way we can enhance our corporate identity." General Electric explained that "the Disney organization is absolutely superb in interpreting our company dramatically, memorably, and favorably to the public." Kodak observed, somewhat baldly, that "you might entrance a teenager today, but tomorrow he's going to invest his money in Kodak stock." General Motors took a broader view, noting not only that EPCOT would give them the chance "to make contact with millions of motorists," but that "it will be a good opportunity to point out how technological progress has contributed to the world and the free enterprise system."[20]

In the end, major multinationals—notably those who had been most successful at the 1939 Fair—signed on to tell Americans what life would be like in the twenty-first century. At EPCOT, Exxon explains energy and AT&T does communications. Transportation is presented by General Motors, the land by Kraft, the home by GE, "Imagination" is explained by Kodak. Each corporation has a high-tech pavilion, the heart of which is a ride. Seated passengers are conveyed through tunnels, which open out into drive-through dioramas—stage sets crammed with robots, videos, and holograms. Supplementing each ride are exhibits, films, and hands-on demonstrations. The pavilions are grouped into an area of the park called Future World.

Nation-states were also invited to EPCOT. England, France, Germany, Italy, Japan, China, Mexico, Canada—usually in conjunction with national businesses (Japan Airlines, British Railways, Labatt Beer)—exhibit their wares and promote travel to their shores. Disney imagineers helped them design terrains that portray the "essence" of their culture. Presiding over the World of Nations is the host pavilion, the American Adventure (presented jointly by American Express and Coca-Cola), which is devoted entirely to presenting the history of the United States.

In 1982 EPCOT opened. It billed itself as "a community of ideas and nations and a testing ground where free enterprise can explore and demonstrate and showcase new ideas that relate to man's hopes and dreams." In its first year, more than twenty-two million people visited. More businesses and countries signed on. By 1984, total investment had reached 1.75 billion dollars and was still climbing.

Tomorrow's Yesterdays

An amazing amount of EPCOT's Future World is devoted to remembering things past. Virtually all the rides are time travels. Passengers settle themselves into moving vehicles that carry them from the dim past to an imagined future. Voice-over narrators, like those on television commercials, explain the passing views and propound an interpretation of historical development.

Each multinational historian has its own style. GM's tends toward the relentlessly cheery; the past was endlessly droll, even "wacky" and "zany." AT&T's is more portentous: "Who Are We? Where Are We Going?" it asks in sepulchral tones as we climb aboard our time machines; we are informed that the answer must be sought in the "Dawn of Recorded Time." But it is the similarities that compel attention.

There is a discernible corporate vision of history. At first blush it appears merely that of the Carousel of Progress writ large: History is a record of the invention of commodities that allow humans to master their environment. But EPCOT goes beyond this. The temporal dimensions are far grander—from the cave men to outer space. And, significantly, each corporation admits there have been problems in the past.

Each journey begins in prehistoric times. GM's history of transportation has robot neanderthals "stumbling around" by footpower. Exxon's history of energy commences with robot dinosaurs (reminiscent of those in *Fantasia*) battling one another in a primeval swamp as fossil fuels cook beneath their feet. AT&T's history of communication starts with cavemen attacking mammoths and painting on walls.

Then Man climbs out of primitive times. GM's Man does this in an unrelievedly hearty way. As we ride along (accompanied by a background ditty proclaiming that "It's fun to be free, to go anywhere, with never a care"), we watch Man slowly produce improved forms of transport—canoes, horse-drawn vehicles—until we reach that favorite corporate period, the Renaissance. Here GM's robot Leonardo turns from culture to engineering: He is shown tinkering with a flying machine while a scowling robot Mona Lisa model taps her foot. Then it's on to the Era of Inventions and a cornucopia of improvements—bicycles, horseless carriages, trains, airplanes—that bring us to the present.

AT&T's trajectory is similar. It tracks the slow progress of communications—Egyptians invent scrolls (a robot pharoah gives dictation to a robot secretary), Greeks give birth to theater (robots declaim on stage), and monks illuminate manuscripts (one is shown cutely snoring at his desk). When AT&T hits the Renaissance, it tilts (unlike GM) toward the cultural dimension, featuring a robot Michelangelo, on its back, laboring at the Sistine ceiling. Then AT&T's Man also enters the jet stream of Progress, and inventions tumble out on what seems a self-sustaining basis.

But when the rides reach the near past, there is a sudden departure from triumphalism. Each corporation acknowledges some blemishes on the record. To be sure, many were inconsequential: One General Motors diorama jovially depicts the first traffic jam (which it blames on a horse). Other problems were serious. Kraft reminds us graphically of Dust Bowl days. Exxon reminds us that an energy crisis emerged. The past was *not* the best of all possible pasts.

The corporate histories are less than clear as to *why* problems emerged. Some seem facts of nature—dinosaur days bequeathed us limited quantities of fossil fuel. But people are responsible for others. Kraft tells us that "we" (or, occasionally, "technological man") made mistakes. "We" abused the environment. "We" polluted the air. There is a hint that "unplanned development" had something to do with it (a practice, presumably, in which multinationals do not engage).

Luckily, we are given to understand, people (or, more precisely, corporations) are working on these problems. The adjacent exhibits expand on this, and we shall return to them.

Each ride then breaks through the troubled recent past into the Future, which is always set in outer space. The narrative tapes and ditties shut off, *Close Encounters of the Third Kind* music comes on, laser beams flash, and we are launched into awesome starry expanses in which space stations and satellites hover. In the Future, problems have been eliminated, presumably by the corporations, whose logos are visible everywhere (as in the movie *2001*). Life in space looks remarkably like life on sitcom television. Mom back on earth communicates (via AT&T's Network) with Sis up on the space station, and they chat about homework and boyfriends. There is a sense of serene ordinariness about the Future, which is not accidental. Hench believes "nobody worries about the future, because that's going to be up in space, in the space colonies."[21] And Marty Sklar, WED vice president says: "We admit to being optimistic over man's future. You can call EPCOT our answer to the gloomy future predictions of the Club of Rome."[22]

Subsidiary exhibits explain the basis for this optimism—corporate problem solvers are at work. Kraft, in full environmentalist regalia, talks about the need for "symbiosis" with the land, shows films about replanting forests and reoxygenating rivers, and explains the artificial farms of the future. AT&T appropriates Bucky Fuller's environmentalist imagery—its geodesic dome pavilion is called Spaceship Earth—and shows how AT&T's Network will overcome communications bottlenecks on earth and in outer space. Exxon tells us it is working away at solar power (the roof of their pavilion is bejeweled with photoelectric panels). Solar, sadly, still seems far from practicable. So, Exxon explains, until the big breakthroughs come, we must rely on oil (videos sing the romance of off shore rigs and ecologically correct pipelines) and coal (films prove that strip mining can be beautiful). Exxon also wants us to keep the nuclear option open and visitors can play at running a nuclear plant. But the company is not heavy-handed about plumping for oil or atoms. All options must be kept open and in competition, including geothermal and biomass. Let the best one win.

GM, another corporate environmentalist, also believes in open options. In its Engine of the Future show, films project cartoon characters onto large overhead screens. Each promotes a different energy-conscious design. On the left, GM's own persona, a jolly cowboy, pitches for an improved internal combustion engine. Then alternatives are presented: an Archie Bunker sort favors coal, a Yuppie lady pushes solar, even the omnipresent Leonardo has a better idea. All these notions are shot down for one reason or another. Finally, on the extreme right, we meet a character who looks like a cross between mad scientist and Japanese dwarf, and sounds like Peter Lorre. He is working—fanatically—on a totally pollution-free and inexpensive water engine, using hydrogen. In the grand finale this crackpot blows everything up, and flames sweep across all the screens. Then cowboy Tex gets the floor back, applauds the others, says they have a ways to go before they beat out the "good ole reliable internal combustion engine," but assures them General Motors wants them all in competition, so the consumer will benefit in the end. (Consumers are indeed never far from GM's mind; the last exhibit is a showroom of current-model GM cars. GM is the most vulgar self-promoter—a hucksterism perhaps related to declining car sales?—but even the suavest of the multinationals have their tacky moments.)

From Leonardo to Exxon

The sensitivity of EPCOT to social and environmental problems is rooted in the 1970s corporate world's awareness of its image problems. Business wanted, with the aid of Disney publicists, to refurbish itself in the public mind. EPCOT designers knew Magic Kingdom boosterism would not suffice. So the imagineers admitted to problems in the past, but rejected corporate responsibility for them. More imaginatively still, they presented business as the cutting edge of the ecology movement. America's problems, Corporate Walt says, are technical ones; responsible corporations are the Mr. Goodwrenches who can fix them. A Kraft vice president summarized the strategy: "Hopefully [visitors to our pavilion will] be aware that major organizations are working at new ways of controlling the land—without disrupting the ecology—to ensure an adequate food supply. To our benefit will be the message that here is Kraft with that kind of concern."[23]

This is a difficult message to sell. Exxon championing alternative energy? General Motors promoting mass transit? Kraft and agribusiness practicing symbiosis with the land? AT&T acting as savior of Spaceship Earth? As with the Nixon robot, the discrepancy between claim and reality invites ridicule. Corporate Walt, a skillful communicator, tries to bridge the gap not only through bald assertion but in more indirect ways as well.

As in the Magic Kingdom sets, a "whiteout" approach is at work—silence blankets the sorry environmental record of the corporations. (This doesn't fool people who know better, but it doesn't enlighten those—particularly children—who do not.)

Another technique is EPCOT's bravura display of technological mastery and management capacity, which seems intent on inducing awe at the capabilities of the corporations, as machines in Greek temples once impressed the populace with the power of the gods. Imagine, the place implies, what business could do if let loose on America's ills (and never mind it created many of them in the first place, or that the cost of attaining EPCOT-level efficiency—one billion dollars per hundred acres—seems a mite high). EPCOT thus forms a chapter in capital's longstanding attempt to control social space as it controls production space; it echoes company-town experiments from Lowell to Pullman (all of which failed—but hope springs eternal).

But the most subtle and perhaps most powerful of the methods at work is the historical analysis that permeates the entire operation. Future World implies that capitalist development is natural and inevitable. It does so by riding visitors, literally on rails, from a bowdlerized presentation of the past to an impoverished vision of the future. The progression goes like this: History was made by inventors and businessmen; the corporations are the legatees of such a past (their slogan might be: "From Leonardo to Exxon"); this pedigree entitles them to run Tomorrow. Citizens can sit back and consume.

Disney did not invent this approach: It had respectable academic roots in "modernization theory." This analysis, fashionable during the 1950s and 1960s, updated the Victorian belief in a march of progress from "savagery" to "civilization," substituting a trajectory from "traditional" to "modern" society, with the latter-day terminus understood to be contemporary America. It is worth noting that EPCOT's popularization of modernization theory, reactionary though it is, was the product of a relatively liberal corporate culture. Had EPCOT been designed in the tooth-and-claw world of the 1980s it would probably have argued that the driving force of history was profit maximization, an approach that might make the actual version seem positively benign.

Corporate Walt's history is bad history. All historical interpretations are necessarily selective in their facts, but here the silences are profoundly distorting. Consider, for example, that in all EPCOT's depictions of the past as a continuous expansion of man's possibilities through technology, there is not a word about war. Nothing about the critical impetus it provided through the ages to scientific development, nor about the phenomenal destruction such "development" wrought. And nothing is said about the contemporary possibilities of planetary extermination. Perhaps the imagineers stuck their heads in the sand because they wanted us to think only the most positive thoughts. But the Magic Kingdom's justification for ostrichism ("this is only an entertainment park") doesn't wash here—EPCOT is explicitly devoted to enhancing understanding. Perhaps, as in Fantasyland, they think the wish is parent to the fact. Or perhaps the silences are related to the fact that many corporations are producing armaments as well as toasters, and that if they and Reagan had their way, the outer-space dioramas of the Future would have to be reconstructed to include killer satellites.

Corporate Walt's history, like modernization theory, is unidirectional. There were never any forks on the path of Progress, never any sharp political struggles over which way to go. EPCOT visitors would never guess that millions of Americans once objected to motoring down the capitalist road. The implication, moreover, is that there are no alternatives now. If there have been problems, they have been the price of progress. The only solution is full speed ahead on the corporate space shuttle; minor course corrections can be left to the pilot. Corporate Walt and the multinationals have produced a past that leads ineluctably toward their kind of future.

Corporate Walt's history is a top-down version. Popular political movements do not exist in this past. Rendering ordinary people invisible as makers of history hardly encourages visitors to believe they can make their own future. (And EPCOT's impact goes far beyond visitors: Its sponsors have launched a massive outreach program to the nation's classrooms; they are mass-marketing lesson plans and videos on land, energy, and communications.)

Corporate desire to fudge the past combined with Disney's ability to spruce it up promotes a sense of history as a pleasantly nostalgic memory, now so completely transcended by the modern corporate order as to be irrelevant to contemporary life. This diminishes our capacity to make sense of our world through understanding how it came to be. The Disney version of history thus creates a way of not seeing and—perhaps—a way of not acting.

Good historical analysis informs people about the matrix of constraints and possibilities they have inherited from the past and enhances their capacity for effective social action in the present. Future World does the opposite: It dulls historical sensibility and invites acquiescence to what is. It should, consequently, be regarded not as a historical, but as a historicidal enterprise.

Warts and All?

EPCOT'S American Adventure—American Express and Coca-Cola's direct exploration of U.S. history—is intriguingly different from the high-tech pavilions; it also marks a startling departure from Original Walt's 1950s approach to the subject. Like the Hall of Presidents, the American Adventure is housed in a simulated Georgian mansion, staffed by costumed hosts and hostesses. Again there is an inspirational antechamber, with quotes by authors ranging from Herman Melville to Ayn Rand. But here there are no films, no rides. The model is closer to a television variety show, with the presentation emceed by Ben Franklin and Mark Twain robots. The American Adventure consists of a series of turns by computer-operated robot ensembles, alternately raised and lowered by a 350,000-pound apparatus below the floor boards. The technology, as usual, is stunning. The robots are the latest in lifelike humanoids. The Franklin robot actually walks up stairs. The research into details (the size of Revolutionary War cannonballs, Alexander Graham Bell's diction) is scrupulous as ever. And this dazzling technology, when set in motion, proceeds to tell, in twenty-nine minutes flat, the entire history of the United States.

At first the show seems merely a spiffed up Hall of Presidents. It begins with an inspirational reading of the Pilgrims-to-Revolution period (robot Rebel soldiers chat at Valley Forge while a George Washington robot sits dolefully on a robot horse). But with independence won, and westward movement underway, the show departs dramatically from the expected. Emcee Twain tells us that "a whole bunch of folks found out 'we the people' didn't yet mean *all* the people," and a Frederick Douglass robot is hoisted up on stage. As he poles (somewhat improbably) down the Mississippi, Douglass speaks of the noise of chains, the crack of the whip, and his hope that "antislavery will unlock the slave prison." A subdued Civil War sequence follows, using Brady photographs to stress costs rather than glory.

The Civil War over, a new wave of immigrants pours in. This, Twain tells us, heralds "a new dawn to the American Adventure." But as we resign ourselves to melting-pot platitudes, a clap of thunder introduces a Chief Joseph robot. He notes that the "new dawn" means a "final sunset" for his people, who are being shot down like animals. He gives his famous "I will fight no more forever" speech, reminding us (as Twain says) of "our long painful journey to the frontiers of human liberty."

Then it is on to the 1876 Centennial. But before launching into a Carousel-of-Progress-type paean to inventions, a Susan B. Anthony robot surfaces. In ringing voice she says: "We ask justice, we ask equality be guaranteed to us and our daughters forever," and adds, quoting Edison (with whom she most improbably shares the stage), that "discontent is the first necessity of progress."

Edison, Carnegie, and the roll call of inventions then have their moment, but after hearing about zippers, trolley cars, vacuum cleaners, and airplanes, a robot naturalist John Muir reminds us that all this growth posed a threat to America the Beautiful, and urges a robot Teddy Roosevelt to build national parks. Next comes World War I—"ready or not, we were thrust into the role of world leader"—and Lindbergh's flight. But then comes the Crash of 1929, which "tarnished the golden dreams of millions," and we are into the Depression era. Here the set is a weatherbeaten southern post office-cum-gas station. Two black and two white robots sit on the front porch (there is a lot of implausible retrospective integration in the show). They strum "Brother, can you spare a dime," chuckle about ex-millionaires in New York, and listen to Franklin D. Roosevelt on the radio talking about "fear itself." (There is also a momentary descent into tacky self-promotion: The shack is plastered with contemporary Coca-Cola and American Express ads.) Then Will Rogers plumps for military preparedness, Roosevelt announces Pearl Harbor, and we are into World War II—which consists entirely of a stage set featuring Rosie the Riveter fixing a submarine.

The postwar material plays it safer. History becomes popular culture. A series of filmic images of personalities are projected—like *People* magazine covers—which then float up into clouds, to the accompaniment of ethereal music about America spreading its golden wings and flying high. It is an eclectic and distinctly integrated assortment, including Jackie Robinson, Marilyn Monroe, Jonas Salk, Satchmo, Elvis, Einstein, Walt Disney, Norman Rockwell, John Wayne, Lucy, Billie Jean King, John F. Kennedy (giving his "Ask not" speech), Martin Luther King (giving his "I have a dream" speech), Muhammad Ali, Arnold Palmer, the U.S. Olympic hockey team, and the men on the moon. We end with a blaze of traditional Disney patriotism, with Franklin and Twain perched atop the Statue of Liberty foreseeing a long run for the American Adventure.

The American Adventure is thus a dramatic departure from the Hall of Presidents (and the spirit of Future World). American history is no longer just about great white men; indeed it seems to be largely about African Americans, women, Indians, and ecologists. The show does not celebrate law and order; it recalls the words of critics. In some ways, the American Adventure represents an extraordinary step forward.

How do we account for it? One answer is the impact, by the mid-1970s, of the African American, women's, antiwar, and environmentalist movements that had heightened popular consciousness. After a generation of protest, 1950s celebrations would no longer do for public historical presentations; even Colonial Williamsburg had to restore blacks to its streets. As a Disney briefing pamphlet for hosts says: "we couldn't ignore certain major issues that questioned our nation's stand on human liberty and justice."[24] An American Adventure executive insisted that "the warts-and-all perspective is appreciated by most visitors because our country is not perfect and they know it."[25] In the last analysis, I believe, shifts in popular opinion forced the Disney people to update their ideology.

The writers, though not academics, were also influenced by the new social historians who reconstructed U.S. history in the 1960s and 1970s. Dr. Alan Yarnell, a University of California at Los Angeles historian consulted on the project, insisted that "the Jesse Lemisch approach—history from the bottom up" replace the great-white-men verities. The corporate sponsors went along with this approach—the heavy intervention of businessmen into Future World scripting was missing here, perhaps because it was an area of lesser political concern. Amex and Coke simply assumed from the Disney track record that nothing embarrassing would emerge from the design process.

In the end, they were right. Despite the trappings of the new social history, the American Adventure remains Disney history. The imagineers imposed a theme of "Dreamers and Doers" on the show: The past had to be portrayed in an upbeat manner. So Susan B. Anthony, Chief Joseph, and Frederick Douglass notwithstanding, American history is still a saga of progress. The dissatisfactions of African Americans, women, and ecologists are presented as having been opportunities in disguise. As Disney literature puts it: "Inevitably, Americans have overcome the tragedies of their controversies, which ultimately led to a better way of life."[26] In the American Adventure, social contradictions are transcended as easily as are natural ones at the Future World. The agents of change, moreover, were individual speakers and writers, not collective social movements. The spokespersons of the discontented knocked, and the door was opened.

Some "controversial" aspects of U.S. history remain completely unacknowledged—most notably, the history of labor. While the show embraces individuals associated in the public mind with the struggle for civil rights and civil liberties, i.e., the individual rights of particular groups, it finds itself unable to deal with a movement long founded on the principles of collective rights and collective action—namely unions. This reluctance, perhaps, is also rooted in the ongoing challenge labor represents to the capitalist system as well as to the particular corporations bankrolling the exhibits.

The silences get louder the closer the show gets to the present. There are no 1960s ghetto uprisings, no campus protests, no feminist or ecology movements, no Watergate. Most notoriously, there is nothing about Vietnam. One of the designers explained that he "searched for a long time for a photograph of an anti-war demonstration that would be optimistic, but I never found one." (A picture of a helicopter was recently added—a distinctly minimalist response to complaints.)

Although willing to accept that the past was made by the discontented, the show disconnects the present from that tradition. It abandons the narrative line on reaching the postwar period—King is there, but as an icon, not spokesman for a movement—and it implies our problems are things of the past. At show's end, Mark and Ben counsel Americans to worry only about the perils of plenty, the problem of how to use leisure time, and how each individual can fulfill his or her dreams. But because the show refuses to acknowledge the social constraints on individual actors—sexism and racism, poverty and unemployment remain obstinate components of contemporary U.S. culture—it peters out into complacent boosterism. Forced to confront a changed American popular historical consciousness and to incorporate the work of radical scholars, it opts for damage control. It defuses the danger inherent in the intrusion of "real" history by redeploying it within a vision of an imperfect but still inevitable progress.

Education and Entertainment

Does Corporate Walt's history have an impact? How does it affect the millions of people who visit? There is little direct evidence one way or the other. Only a few hundred have written letters, the largest single response coming from Vietnam veterans complaining about the obliteration of their experiences. But what do such cavils mean when set beside Disney World's status as the biggest single tourist destination on Earth? What accounts for this stupendous success?

Demographic statistics provide an avenue to an answer. The class spectrum of EPCOT visitors is dramatically narrow. They come from groups doing best in terms of pay and personal power on the job: The median income is $35,700, and fully three-quarters are professionals or managers. (Professional and technical personnel account for 48 percent of attendees; managers and administrators account for 26 percent.) This is not a working-class attraction. (Craftsmen makeup 4 percent; operatives makeup another 4 percent; sales persons makeup 8 percent; service personnel comprise 2 percent; laborers are another 2 percent.) Nor do African Americans (3 percent) or Hispanics (2 percent) come in large numbers. (To a degree these demographics simply reflect the cost of getting there: Only 22 percent of visitors come from Florida; 71 percent are from elsewhere in the United States, chiefly the Northeast and Midwest.)

A process of class self-affirmation seems to be at work. Certainly Disney World seems intent on reassuring this class and presenting it with its own pedigree. The seventies-style liberal corporatism of EPCOT seems tailor-made for professionals and technocrats. It is calibrated to their concerns—nothing on labor, heavy on ecology, clean, well-managed, emphasis on individual solutions, good restaurants—and it provides just the right kind of past for their hipper sensibilities. Perhaps, therefore, professionals and managers (many of whom, after all, function as subalterns of capital) flock there because it ratifies their world. Perhaps they do not *want* to know about reality—past or present—and prefer comforting (and plausible) stereotypes.

Yet many in this class are at least potentially antagonistic to the multinationals. Their members have spearheaded the ecology movement. It was

their growing sophistication that made it impossible for Disney to recycle 1950s approaches, either in films or theme parks (approaches now dismissed by a younger generation as "Mickey Mouse"). We must be suspicious of blaming messages on the receiving public, even one as affluent as this.

Would accurate history bore or repel them? Perhaps not. Audiences often respond favorably where conventional wisdom says they will not. (A dramatic and relevant comparison might be with the spectacularly successful *Roots*—which for all its Hollywood devices and elisions was a striking departure from *Gone with the Wind.*) Do Disney's sitcoms in space work because people want reassurance, or because that is all they are being given? Are visitors getting what they want, or what corporate publicists want them to want?

There is no simple answer to these questions. Some of EPCOT's consumers may be inclined to adopt the comfortable and convenient ideologies purveyed there. Others have no vested interest in or are profoundly disserved by doing so. Regardless of predisposition, however, EPCOT's casual subordination of truth to "entertainment" impairs visitors' ability to distinguish between reality and plausible fiction.

The consequences for museum curators are serious. Most museum visitors are probably alumni of Disney's parks (or of those established by competitors). Their prior encounters (I suspect) have helped shape their expectations, both of form and content. This is not all bad. There are a host of imaginative techniques the imagineers have invented to attract consumers; some of them (the more affordable ones) might well be deployed by heretofore staid institutions. But museums might also consider taking up the cudgels against the misinformation-purveyors (which include Hollywood movies, television docudramas, and mass market fiction as well as theme parks). An occasional exhibit devoted to decoding and critiquing the messages promulgated by such cultural institutions might be an enlightening and enlivening use of museum resources.

More broadly still, I think the country at large needs to reflect upon the consequences of the corporate commodification of history. George Kennan once noted that "when an individual is unable to face his own past and feels compelled to build his view of himself on a total denial of it and on the creation of myths to put in its place, this is normally regarded as a sign of extreme neurosis." A similar diagnosis, he argued, was warranted for a society "that is incapable of seeing itself realistically and can live only by the systematic distortion or repression of its memories about itself and its early behavior."[27] Kennan was referring to the Soviet Union. But the United States suffers from a similar malady. The past is too important to be left to the private sector. If we wish to restore our social health, we had better get beyond Mickey Mouse history.

Notes

This essay first appeared in *Radical History Review* 32 (1985), and then, in slightly revised form, in Warren Leon and Roy Rosenzweig, *History Museums in the United States: A Critical Assessment* (Urbana, 1989). I have used the latter version for this chapter.

My thanks to: Jean-Christophe Agnew, Jeanie Attie, Paul Berman, Ted Burrows, Jeanne Chase, Hope Cooke, Peter Dimock, Liz Fee, Brooks MacNamara, Ruth Misheloff, Bob Padgug, Roy Rosenzweig, Danny Walkowitz, Jon Wiener, the summer 1984 members of the Cummington Community of the Arts, and the staff at Walt Disney World.

A torrent of Disneyana has appeared in the last decade. Some of it I make use of in the next chapter, which carries the Disney saga on into the Eisner era, and explores the aborted Disney's America project. I have not recast the original piece, but had I done so, I would have particularly taken into account the following insightful contributions: Andrea Stulman Dennett, "A Postmodern Look at EPCOT's American Adventure," *Journal of American Culture*, 12, no. 1 (1989), 47–54; Stephen F. Mills, "Disney and the Promotions of Synthetic Worlds," *American Studies International* 28, no. 2 (1990), 66–79; Sharon Zukin, *Landscapes of Power: From Detroit to Disney World* (1991); Raymond M. Weinstein, "Disneyland and Coney Island: Reflections on the Evolution of the Modern Amusement Park," *Journal of Popular Culture* 26, no. 1 (summer 1992), 131–64; "The World According to Disney, a special issue of the *South Atlantic Quarterly*, 92, no. 1 (winter 1993), especially the excellent essays by Susan Willis and Jane Kuenz; Henry A. Giroux, "Beyond the Politics of Innocence: Memory and Pedagogy in the 'Wonderful World of Disney,'" *Socialist Review* 23; no. 2 (1993), 79–107; several of the essays in Eric Smoodin, ed., *Disney Discourse: Producing the Magic Kingdom* (1994); and Steven Watts, "Walt Disney: Art and Politics in the American Century," *Journal of American History* 82, no. 1 (June 1995), 84–110.

The most apposite text, however, is Stephen M. Fjellman's *Vinyl Leaves: Walt Disney World and America* (1992), a full dress anthropological analysis of my essay's primary subject. Fjellman's splendid book has many kind things to say about my original essay, but he also takes me to task for coining and using the term "historicide." As I have used it again in this book, some words of self-defense seem warranted.

"Wallace's accusation of 'historicide' invites some scrutiny," Fjellman writes, on the grounds that it seems to posit an essentialist body of history capable of being murdered. Yet I quite agree with Fjellman that "History of any sort is an imaginative discourse built out of some subset of available information, shaped by one or more available literary tropes, and presented as a gambit motivated by conditions contemporaneous to its invention. Thus, there is thus no essentialist history to be 'killed.'" Fjellman does admit that it is possible "to kill the *idea* of history", perhaps by presenting it, as Disney does, as an entertainment in which "the truth value of parts of the past is indistinguishable from the truth value of fantasy and futurology," thus transforming history into "crafted amusement." This is indeed closer to what I had and have in mind. "Historicide" admits of no corpus delicti, but that does not mean no crime has been committed. A historicidal culture is one that promotes an ahistorical way of seeing the world, that obscures or denies the links between past and present, that leaves us marooned in the now, adrift on the temporal surface of things.

1. *Walt Disney World: A Pictorial Souvenir* (Walt Disney Productions, 1977), 6.
2. Disney quoted in Richard Schickel, *The Disney Version: The Life, Times, Art and Commerce of Walt Disney* (New York, 1968), 316.
3. *Walt Disney World: A Pictorial Souvenir*, p. 6. For an insightful analysis of Main Street, see Richard V. Francaviglia, "Main Street USA: A Comparison/Contrast of Streetscapes in Disneyland and Walt Disney World," in the special issue of the *Journal of Popular Culture* on theme parks [15, no. 1 (summer 1981), 141–56]; other useful essays in that issue include David M Johnson, "Disney World as Structure and Symbol: Recreation of an American Experience," 157–65; Margaret J. King, "Disneyland and Walt Disney World: Traditional Values in Futuristic Form," 116–40; and Margaret J. King, "The New American Muse: Notes on the Amusement/Theme Park," 56–62.
4. For biographical information see Richard Schickel's excellent study, *The Disney Version* and Michael Harrington, "To the Disney Station," *Harper's* 258 (January 1979), 35–9.
5. *The Disney Theme Show: From Disneyland to Walt Disney World, A Pocket History of the First Twenty Years* (Walt Disney Productions, 1976), Volume I, 12.
6. *Ibid.*, I, 31
7. *Ibid.*, I, 12.
8. Charlie Haas, "Disneyland is Good for You," *New West* 3 (4 December 1978), 18.
9. *Ibid.*
10. *Ibid.*
11. Haas, "Disneyland," 16.
12. *Ibid.*
13. Elting E. Morison, "What Went Wrong with Disney's World's Fair," *American Heritage* 35, no. 1 (December 1983), 72.
14. Quoted in Warren I. Susman, "The People's Fair: Cultural Contradictions of a Consumer Society," reprinted in Susman, *Culture as History:*

The Transformation of American Society in the Twentieth Century (New York, 1985), 225.

15. Quoted in Harrington, "To the Disney Station," 38.
16. *Disney Theme Show*, I, 15.
17. Peter Blake, "Mickey Mouse for Mayor!," *New York Magazine* (April 1972), 41–2.
18. Harrington, "To the Disney Station," 39.
19. Disney quoted in Harrington, "To the Disney Station," 38.
20. Quotes from Earl, C. Gottschalk Jr., "Less Mickey Mouse," *Wall Street Journal* (26 January 1979), 27; "A Disneyland of Corporate Promotion," *Business Week* (26 March 1979), 114; and Harrington, "To the Disney Station," 86. Florida's Governor Reubin Askew was similarly taken with the plan: "this isn't just another undertaking of a private corporation," he enthused. "This is a stimulation and a recommitment to the entire system of private enterprise—without which whatever economy we may have in the industrialized West couldn't be what it is today." *Walt Disney Productions Annual Report 1978*, 6.
21. Haas, "Disneyland," 19.
22. Gottschalk, "Less Mickey Mouse," 27.
23. "Disneyland of Corporate Promotion," 114.
24. Epcot Center, *The American Adventure* (Walt Disney Productions, 1982), 5.
25. Letter from Frank R. Stansberry, 21 March 1984.
26. *The American Adventure*, 5.
27. George F. Kennan, "Two Letters," *The New Yorker* 60 (24 September 1984), 56.

Disney's America

Mouse amid Wolves

Mickey Mouse, that noted historian, has been extremely productive over the last decade. His passion for presenting the past seems to have been intensified by a near-death experience he and his parent company underwent ten years ago.

In the early 1980s Walt Disney Productions was languishing. Its films floundered at the box office as families seeking "family entertainment" turned to television, and movie-inclined teens turned to Spielberg and Lucas. Disney theme parks sagged as well. The 1982 opening surge of EPCOT proved unsustainable in the face of fierce competition. The name "Mickey Mouse" began to take on unflattering connotations.

The Disney firm seemed caught in a conundrum. It was legatee of the wholesome image that constituted its symbolic capital, its key to profitability. But to maintain or expand its markets Disney had to upgrade its cultural commodities, not stick too rigidly to Walt's original formulations. Tradition tugged in one direction, adjustment to changing times in another. The result was paralysis.

In 1984, with Disney stock trading at forty-five dollars per share (down thirty-nine points from the previous year's high), Wall Street wolves began circling the crippled company. In March, New York financier Saul P. Steinberg launched a takeover attempt. Disney managers, led by Walt's son-in-law Ronald W. Miller, scrambled to find a powerful outside protector—a white knight, in the era's parlance. They turned to the Bass brothers, billionaire Texas investors, and moved a block of stock into their friendly hands. Steinberg declared war, formally announcing his intention to buy control of the firm, oust the managers, and carve up the company, tossing its various parts (film library, Florida land holdings) to fellow wolves. Mickey Mouse seemed doomed.

In June, Disney managers bought Steinberg off. They repurchased his stock at above market value and tossed in twenty-eight million dollars for "expenses." Steinberg cleared sixty million dollars in "greenmail" simply for agreeing not to buy the company. The battle left the firm burdened with debt. Its stock plummeted more than 25 percent. A new group of raiders closed in, led by Minneapolis investor Irwin ("Irv the Liquidator") Jacobs. After another gunfight at the Disney corral, Jacobs departed (a tidy profit in hand), leaving the Bass brothers in control of a battered enterprise.

To offset multimillion dollar losses, the company put the screws to its workforce, ordering 16.1 percent pay cuts. At Disneyland 1900 employees took to the picket lines wearing "No Mickey" t-shirts. The company quickly crushed the strike, but such triumphs were hardly the route to corporate renewal. Other raiders were eyeing the firm. Only a decisive change in management and direction would fend them off.

Urged on by Walt's nephew Roy E. Disney, the board ousted Miller. On 22 September 1984 it brought in Michael Eisner and Frank Wells, two Hollywood heavyweights, as Chief Executive Officer and president respectively. Within a year they had pink-slipped over four hundred administrators, replacing many with Eisner's old colleagues at Paramount, most of whom had strikingly different cultural sensibilities than the old guard. Eisner himself was a Jewish New Yorker and Democrat (he would be a big backer of Bill Clinton in 1992), quite a departure from Uncle Walt, an anti-semitic Hoover ally and Goldwater supporter.

The new team went to work. thirty-one-year-old Jeffrey Katzenberg, former Paramount production head, revamped the Disney film studio and began churning out racy yet respectable blockbusters. At Roy Disney's urging, the company revived its animation heritage and, in collaboration with Steven Spielberg, produced *Who Framed Roger Rabbit*. By 1988 the studio had moved from last to first place in the Hollywood sweepstakes, and continued to generate hits.

Eisner opened up a second commercial front, recycling films into other commodity forms. Home videos sold phenomenally well: Baby-boomers who had grown up on Disneyana bought armloads of cassettes for their children. Movie characters were reformatted into toys and miscellaneous merchandise: five hundred licensed products were carved out of Roger Rabbit alone. By the early 1990s, Goofy neckties, Aladdin underwear, and Mermaid dolls were being purveyed directly from over three hundred Disney Store outlets. Also available, or in the offing, were video games, vacation clubs, a Broadway theater, a touring troupe, a publishing firm, a Disney Channel, a hockey team, and a cruise line—all products produced by the giant entertainment conglomerate now renamed the Walt Disney Company.

Of Mice and Theme Parks

What of theme parks, the company's former mainstay? Compared to the thriving film and consumer product divisions, their contribution to profits had fallen steadily. But Eisner was not about to abandon them. Lucrative in themselves, the parks were vital links in the corporation's hawking of a cross-referential chain of commodities. Film images became park rides, which in turn boosted video and souvenir sales. The parks also anchored mammoth real estate enterprises, the kind of hotel, condo, resort, and office construction that the Bass brothers had been pushing since their ascendancy.

Eisner announced that by 2000 he intended to "reinvent the Disney theme park experience." Turning to outside partnerships he broke with musty traditions without devaluing logo-capital. Michael Jackson, Francis Ford Coppola, and George Lucas collaborated in making the Captain E-O film. Lucas helped design rides as well. The Rouse Company and leading architects were brought in to revise hotel strategy. Rock groups pulled teens to Disneyland venues, while young adults flocked to Pleasure Island's video-festooned discos and themed nightclubs. By summer 1989, a three hundred million dollar Disney-MGM Studios Theme Park was up and running.

Competitors closed in fast, however. In June 1990 MCA opened its Universal Studios park, with impressive attractions. Conglomerate rival Time Warner launched a nationwide advertising blitz for its various Six Flags venues, promoting them as more affordable and closer to home. In Las Vegas, family-style casinos, complete with kiddie parks, raked in gambling revenues—too off-color a profit source for Disney to embrace.

One response was to go global. Eisner promised to "reinvent the Disney experience not just in California, but worldwide." Tokyo Disneyland, opened by the *ancien regime* in 1983, had done spectacularly well, but Disney's profits from the locally-run venture were limited to a percentage of the take. Euro-Disney, which opened in April 1992, thirty-two kilometers east of Paris, was meant to correct this error, with the parent company retaining just under 50 percent ownership. But turnout proved disappointing—a function of bad planning, bad weather, a European recession, French critiques of American cultural imperialism, labor troubles from workers resisting Disney regulations (female employees could wear only "appropriate undergarments")—and a sharp plunge in the French real estate market which hampered plans to build housing and offices on the five thousand acre site.

In November 1993 Euro-Disney announced first year losses of close to one billion dollars. The company arranged refinancing and prepared to stay the course, but competition loomed again, as Warner Brothers announced plans for a two-hundred million-dollar cartoon theme park in Rhine-Westphalia (featuring Bugs Bunny, Daffy Duck, and Tweety Bird).

That very month, however, the firm announced plans for a new theme park—Disney's America—which it hoped would solve its problems.

Serious Fun

Disney's America was to be situated on a three thousand-acre tract the company had optioned in Virginia's Prince William County. Located thirty-five miles west of the District of Columbia, the park would tap into Washington's thirty million annual day trippers, via a road network whose expansion would be subsidized by $163 million of public money.[1] The park itself would occupy only about one hundred acres, leaving lots of lebensraum for the hotels, residences, campgrounds, golf courses, and the nearly two million square feet of retail and commercial space the company admitted to be planning (with perhaps another fourteen million to follow).

The theme park core would evoke the history of the United States. This was a novel development. Heritage tourism and heritage development were well-established gambits. Enterprisers routinely promoted historic sites as vacation destinations or anchors for real estate projects. But in Virginia, Disney would use simulation not authenticity as the lure. The company insisted, however, that its park would impart substantial historical information, and here the company did have credentials none of its competitors could match.

Disney imagineers had drawn on contemporary scholarship in the seventies and eighties to update earlier historical narratives. Breaking with their tradition of wartless history, Disneyites cautiously admitted the existence of problems in the past and present—problems with which they knew their audiences were well familiar—while managing to keep their overall perspective cheerily upbeat.

Eisner's team was equally committed to updating the historical presentations. The Hall of Presidents—a cold war relic which enshrined a perfect Constitution, and the presidents who had defended it from assorted internal subversions—seemed particularly creaky alongside EPCOT's spiffy new productions. Its counterpart in California drew so few visitors that in 1990 the company had considered retiring Abe Lincoln and replacing him with Muppets.

So when Columbia University Professor Eric Foner wrote Disney criticizing their approach, the company was ready to listen. Working with Foner,

Disney's America

Disney revised the Hall of Presidents over the summer of 1993. The new version presented the Constitution as a democratic triumph, but also acknowledged that it legitimated slavery. United States history was then reconceptualized as a struggle to extend democratic rights to an ever-widening percentage of the population, with the founders' legacy no longer an heirloom but an unfinished agenda. Management and audiences alike applauded the new departure.

Disney's America was meant to be the next step—a "serious fun" celebration of U.S. history.

The park's "playlands" would include an Indian village and a Lewis and Clark raft ride; a Civil War fort with reenactments; an Ellis Island replica; a factory town with a ride through a blazing steel mill; a World War II airfield with flight simulators; a state fair with a ferris wheel; a family farm with country wedding and barn dance.

Few details were given—it is not clear that many existed—but the company insisted the playlands would be "serious" as well as "fun." Promotional literature vowed they would "examine the conflicts and struggles that have marked the nation's passage from colony to world power." No subject was too controversial, nothing taboo. "We will show the Civil War with all its racial conflict," said Eisner. "We want to make you feel what it was like to be a slave or what it was like to escape through the underground railroad," echoed Disney Vice President Robert Weis. The presentations would not take "a Pollyanna view" of American history; they would not be "propaganda"; they would be "painful, disturbing and agonizing."

"Serious fun" indeed! Disney appeared ready to follow history museums in their new willingness to tackle sensitive subjects. Indeed in claiming they would treat recent military events—"And, look, we'll be sensitive about the Vietnam war," Weis promised—they seemed prepared to go beyond current museology. Vietnam was a subject no full rigged exhibition had yet dared touch.

Mouse under Fire

If Disneyites had expected plaudits from scholars they were swiftly disabused. Some professors, to be sure signed on enthusiastically, if warily. James Oliver Horton said: "If Disney is going to do history, and they almost certainly will, somewhere, why not encourage them to use their considerable technology to do it well?" Horton found exciting and potentially fruitful possibilities for using, say, virtual reality technologies to help visitors "understand ecological change, migration patterns, the development of neighborhoods, and the growth and social impact of cities." Scholars would be unable to control the interpretations—piper-payers would ultimately call the tune—but "as historians we do have the power of our expertise."

Most historians, however, saw an irreconcilable tension between the subjects Disney planned to treat, and the way it planned to treat them. "Edutainment" seemed an oxymoron to William Styron, who doubted Disney's technical wizardry could "do anything but mock a theme as momentous as slavery." No "combination of branding irons, slave ships or slave cabins, shackles, chained black people in their wretched coffles, or treks through the Underground Railroad could begin to define such a stupendous experience," Styron claimed. "To present even the most squalid sights would be to cheaply romanticize suffering."

Civil war historian Shelby Foote suggested that "The Disney people will do to American history what they have already done to the animal kingdom—sentimentalize it out of recognition."

And *New York Times* columnist Frank Rich contrasted "real history, which requires education and reflection to be understood," with the kind of "socko virtual reality" that generates escapist fun.

Most such objections came from liberals. Some right wing commentators dismissed their concerns. Columnist Charles Krauthammer admitted that "Disney's America will idealize and sentimentalize history the way Disney's movies have idealized and sentimentalized nature," but added: "So what?" The "shamelessly sweet, hopelessly inauthentic" theme parks were, after all, mainly for children. Intellectuals need not worry "that a children's entertainment will destroy real history."

Republican apparatchik William Kristol was less inclined to slight the importance of messages aimed at children. "If you're going to have a schlocky version of American history," Kristol grumped, "it should at least be a schlocky, patriotic, and heroic version." The new park, he feared, would be "politically correct" and make "suitable bows to all oppressed groups."[2]

The strongest objections to Disney's America, however, mixed complaints about *what* it was with dismay at *where* it was. Opponents claimed that collateral damage—strip malls, traffic congestion, air pollution, urban sprawl—would devastate the surrounding historic environment of tiny towns and battlefields.

The planned theme park was a scant five miles west of Manassas National Battlefield Park. Twenty-seven thousand had died there in 1861 and 1862. In recent decades additional battles had been fought—and won—to preserve the site from commercial exploitation.

In the 1970s, the Marriott Corporation had purchased a tract of land (the staging area for Lee and Longstreet's victorious assault) that was adjacent to the battlefield. Marriott, too, planned a theme park, but lost interest in the face of citizen opposition.

In 1986 John "Til" Hazel, Northern Virginia's most powerful developer, optioned the Marriott site. The following year he announced plans to build a 1.2 million-square-foot shopping mall. A grass roots coalition of local farmers, civic activists, preservation lawyers, and Civil War reenactors collected eighty thousand signatures opposing the project. Raising funds at auctions and dinner dances, they took their protest to county fairs, garnered press attention and legislative support, and in 1989 prevailed on Congress to buy the 542-acre site for one hundred twenty million dollars and add it to the Battlefield Park.

Five years later these battle-tested activists took on Disney. Powerful new recruits signed up. These included environmentalists, rival tourist entrepreneurs, free market opponents of state handouts, and, most crucially, a nest of powerful local residents. These included Virginia gentry, suburban squires, and Washington power brokers—like James Carville and Mary Matalin, who feared Disney's America was "going to be incredibly disruptive" to their Front Royal hideaway. Affluent members of the Piedmont Environmental Council—Eisner later admitted he had not realized "so many wealthy people" lived out there—pledged six hundred thousand dollars and hired an aggressive Washington law firm (whose clients ranged from the Clintons to Ollie North) to drag out the regulatory process.

The struggle also attracted out-of-state combatants. National Trust for Historic Preservation president Richard Moe, calling the Disney battle "one of the most significant preservation issues to come along in many years," put northern Virginia's Piedmont at the top of the Trust's 1994 list of "America's 11 Most Endangered Historic Places."

In May two hundred scholars formed Protect Historic America. James McPherson, the group's president, argued that "Inevitably—tragically—urban sprawl will reach for miles in every direction, all along the key roads intersecting the region, destroying the character and cheapening the historical attractions." Positing a kind of Gresham's Law in which synthetic, inauthentic history (the Disney simulacrum) would drive out real, authentic history (the Manassas battlefield), Protect Historic America called on Eisner to "take your fantasy elsewhere and leave our national past alone."[3]

In the effort to establish even stronger moral grounds for resisting the intruders, some historians employed a quasi-religious imagery. "We have so little left that's authentic and real," said historian David McCullough, that "to replace what we have with plastic, contrived history, mechanical history is almost sacrilege." Scholar Roger Wilkins, a descendant of Virginia slaves, said the theme park and its attendant development would besmirch a "sacred ground where men fought and died for what this country is today."

Disney Backs Down

Disney fought back. Adopting a populist stance, company publicists attacked opponents as "landed gentry" foxhunters, or genteel "no-growth proponents" who would turn the piedmont into an economic no-man's land and deprive working people of jobs.

Academic opponents were lumped with the horsey Virginia set, as out of touch elitists.[4] Eisner also speculated that "historians are maybe overly threatened by the project." Was this because alongside Disney's presentations their work seemed arid? Eisner seemed to think so, declaring their work "boring." "I sat through many history classes where I read some of their stuff, and I didn't learn anything," he told *The Washington Post*. He extended this judgment to museum exhibitions, recalling that "I was dragged to Washington as a kid and it was the worst weekend of my life." (It was not clear if he had been back since).

Yet Eisner took care not to cut his ties to the professoriate. "Our debate is not with historians," he insisted; "we respect them and, more important, respect our history." He was simply seeking to perform a public service. Given that, "sadly, American students do not know enough about our history," Eisner would step in where academics had failed and help "educate through entertainment."

The CEO did, however, back away from initial claims that Disney's America would probe the darker regions of the nation's past. He now stressed the park's "celebratory" intentions. "The conclusion of this park is going to be [that America] is the best of all possible places, this is the best of all possible systems." The park's general manager insisted: "The idea is to walk out of Disney's America with a smile on your face. It is going to be fun with a capital 'F'."

For a time Disney hung tough. Then environmentalists and historians got a bipartisan group of sixteen House members to introduce a resolution opposing the park. They also urged federal agencies to meticulously check on Disney's compliance with all laws on air quality, transportation, and historic preservation. Eisner cooly praised their strategy: "To delay costs money," he admitted, but he insisted that while "many companies would throw in the towel" such tactics "will certainly not stop us."

But the firm was still absorbing Euro-Disney losses. It did not relish the costs (in money and negative publicity) of upcoming lawsuits. And the Disney machine had been thrown into disarray by the spring 1994 heli-skiing death of Frank Wells; the departure of movie chief Jeffrey Katzenberg, who was miffed that Eisner refused to give him Wells' slot; and by Eisner's summer heart attack and emergency quadruple bypass heart surgery. With the land options up for renewal or cancellation in early October, Disney announced on 28 September 1994 that it would "begin immediately to seek a less controversial site where we can concentrate on our creative vision."

Sacred Ground?

As a long time David-rooter, I would be tempted to cheer Goliath's fall unreservedly, if it were not that some of the stones that laid him low strike me as problematic. Given the certainty of similar combat in the future, it seems worthwhile to revisit the battlefield and reassess the campaign.

I'm particularly troubled by the "sacred soil" argument. It is wonderful to see that a sense of the sacred still exists; that Americans believe there are places where the writ of mammon should not run; that sites drenched in blood and history can serve as spiritual sanctuaries from a voracious market. But while it is tempting to use "hallowed ground" as a club to beat back developers—as the spotted owl and striped bass have been used to ward off loggers and polluters—I am concerned we might save some battlefields but lose the wider war.

For one thing, sacred soil is extremely site-specific, and while usually a source of strength, this can also be a point of vulnerability. As not many locations can claim consecrated status—it is hard to decree vast territories sacrosanct—rendering historic sites unto God allows Mammon to walk off with everything else. The market would eventually bypass, surround, and overwhelm the holdouts.

Another problem concerns the kind of sites that get sacralized. Historians John Bodnar and Linda Shopes have faulted the Protect Historic America (PHA) group for ignoring "the historic landscapes of, for instance, the Pennsylvania coal fields or South Chicago," places where battles were "fought to sustain American democracy and economic justice."[5] It is true that PHA launched no crusade to preserve abandoned steel works or inner cities, sites equally sanctified by suffering. A single issue organization, it effectively disbanded after Disney's retreat. Its members should not be faulted for this, but rather thanked for a successful effort. Still, the narrow focus of their campaign does suggest the need for broadening the grounds for resistance beyond a defense of "sacred soil."

I am also worried by the potential tension between the historical and sacerdotal projects. If historic remains are sacralized, and historians serve as relic-guarding priests, they become vulnerable to the pseudopopulist thrusts Disney delivered (just as timber companies pit unemployed lumberjacks against owl heads). More to the point, certifying a person or place as sacred tends to render it inviolable, beyond change, impervious to questioning.

Such permanence is precisely what is attractive to those combatting reckless transformation. But it can also work to paralyze the historical imagination, which is fundamentally concerned with asking questions and probing change.

Consider the consecrated Civil War battlefields themselves. Lincoln hallowed them for being milestones on the road to freedom and popular government. But in the 1890s most battlefields were rededicated in a very different way. Both armies were canonized, whether they fought for freedom or slavery, in the interests of a political rapprochement between the white north and white south, and at the expense of African Americans.

It is disturbingly easy for the sacred to be put to repressive ends. We are once again in mid debate over sanctioned narratives about American history. Putative conservatives like Congressman Newt Gingrich evoke a mythic, unchanging, quasi-sacred past and use it not to understand but to condemn contemporary cultural and political trends. A sacralized past, sealed off against critical analysis, can be readily deployed as a weapon of ideological war.

A final note about the drawbacks of using the sacred to resist the market. Historians seem to be taking this tactic up just as historic preservationists are dropping it. Preservationists once saved shrines associated with hallowed figures—"George Washington slept here"—but have long since shifted to a broader conservationist strategy.

Preservationists start from the well-established maxim that private property owners have no right to wring maximum profits from their holdings if doing so conflicts with the larger public good. One component of that larger good, they argue, is knowing one's place in time. Therefore just as one is not allowed to befoul a neighbor's property with pollutants, one should not be allowed to rent the temporal fabric by demolishing duly certified landmark structures—a designation now bestowed on a wide variety of heritages.

Historic environments should similarly be considered a part of the common cultural heritage, the national patrimony. Like natural resources, they should be held in trust for future generations. I agree with National Trust president Moe, that what was most heartening about Disney's initiative was that it "brought historians, conservationists, and preservationists together in a unified front that, I hope, will set a precedent for the future."[6]

Edu-tainment?

Turning to the debates over *how* rather than *where* Disney intended to present the past, I do not find compelling the claims that there is an inherent contradiction between education and entertainment. If entertainment is defined not merely as providing amusement, but as generating absorbing interest, it is perfectly consonant with what history museums have been doing—developing exhibitions that evoke experience as well as offer explanation.[7]

Historian Alon Confino properly insists that both must be present, and that Disney imagineers, extrapolating from cinematic or dramatic ways of knowing, assume one can "understand" the past by seeing it or by "experiencing" a recreation of it. Quite apart from their uninformed conviction that it is as easy to replicate past reality as it is to construct appealing fantasies, the great forces that sweep though every historical epoch—the social, economic, political, and cultural trends of an era—can not simply be translated into personal experience.[8] And Linda Shopes wonders reasonably if simulations might not "lead participants to a facile, if not arrogant, view that because they've experienced a re-created version of an event, they know it?"[9] Yet there is nothing inherent in the goal of crowd pleasing that precludes Disney from attending to larger issues of causation.

It is also true that there are distinct limits to what can and should be expected from a day's outing in a historical theme park. But Disney has demonstrated a formidable outreach capacity. It could in theory develop an education department to work out follow-up projects for home and classroom. One simple barometer of good intentions would be to include a book and video store, which sold popular and scholarly historical works, not just Disney products.[10]

Nor do I see an intrinsic moral incommensurability between Disney techniques and difficult historical topics. Similar complaints were raised about dramatic presentations of slave life at Colonial Williamsburg, only to be retracted when the performances proved compelling. And history museums have deployed Disneyesque devices in tackling subjects as tough as the Holocaust.

I do see more stubborn dilemmas inherent in Disney's purveying of historical information in commodity form. There is a tendency to fashion mass cultural artifacts into self-containable morsels, the idea being not to whet the consumer's appetite, but to sate it. If historical presentations had to be neatly packaged, with closed narratives and happy endings, it would conflict with the open-ended, question-raising nature of the historical enterprise. The Holocaust museum's spectacular success shows that the grimmest of stories, honestly confronted, can attract vast crowds. A museum that told the truth about slavery might do equally well. But would Disney be willing to fashion an environment that might make rides and souvenir sales unseemly, undercutting profits?

Then there is the worry that Disney might wind up stripmining the national past, as it has expropriated the world's stock of childrens' fantasies, in a restless quest for new cultural images to sell. Here we must remember the larger corporate story with which I started. Icon factories faced with vigorous competitors tend to run short of cultural capital. Sometimes (as with the Disney's dealings with MGM) they can buy out a competitor's stock. Sometimes (as with Roger Rabbit) they can work out passable variations on earlier themes.

But such enterprises are always on the lookout for new image-commodity sources; might not American history seem a tempting, near inexhaustible storehouse? Remember the craze for Crockett's coonskin cap? I am sure Disney has not forgotten. If the Underground Railroad ride were ever to get rolling, or the slave experience to get "reproduced," would Simon Legree whips start turning up in Disney stores worldwide?[11] Could we expect to see efforts made to trademark famous personages or events? It is now legally impermissable, of course, but Disney thrives on logos—virtually every square inch of Disney World is branded by one corporate entity or another (Michael Sorkin has called it the world's first copyrighted environment). Perhaps if we got a sufficiently business-minded administration—perhaps one run by former history professor and market ideologue Newt Gingrich—the legal system might be adjusted to facilitate merchandising the past.

More seriously, what is unnerving about commodifying history is that it further blurs an already all-too fuzzy line—not between sacred and secular, but between private and public. Disney's America promised to provide "a forum for symposia on public issues and the challenges of the future." But is a total corporate environment the proper setting for addressing issues whose resolution demand the exercise of civic agency? What are the implications for a civil society whose public and historical discourse gets confounded with entertainment?

Disney theme parks, moreover, are utopian spaces, where the social ills confronting Americans are held at bay, courtesy of corporate skillfulness. Here death, crime, war, dirt, and disorder have no dominion. It is not inherently impossible to use such a safe space as a base for confronting the issues from which it is theoretically providing a haven. But is it likely?

Remember how quickly Disney backed away from its vow to tackle difficult issues. Part of the company's problem, of course, was the need to protect symbolic capital from contamination by controversy—a timidity to which most mass market corporations are prey. But another reason for backpeddling, I suspect, was that Eisner and his colleagues had not quite grasped the contradictions involved. Not between education and entertainment, but between critical history and the interests of a multibillion dollar corporation with a considerable vested interest in the status quo. At EPCOT, Disney baldly allied itself with other major corporations, and presented narratives about the history of food, energy, and transportation, which were tailored to the needs of Kraft, Exxon, and General Motors. The exhibits promoted particular ways of seeing, and not seeing, contemporary realities. How likely is that things would have been (might yet be) different at Disney's America?

The proposed Disney's America ride that would have whisked guests through an synthetic steel mill might perhaps have given some idea of the thunderous drama of the process. But would it have had side exhibits that dealt in an arresting way with the life of steel workers and their families, with the nature of life in industrial cities, with the rise (and demise) of the union movement, with the environmental and social costs as well as the productive triumphs of capitalist industrialization, with the devastating results of deindustrialization?

They might yet have a mockup family farm, but will they probe the historical conflicts between small-scale farmers and the giant agribusinesses touted at EPCOT?

They might well have an ersatz Ellis Island, where multicultural tales are told. As museums have discovered, new audiences are unlikely to attend presentations at which they are invisible. But will they grapple with clashes between immigrants, with the intersections of ethnicity and economy, with issues of immigration restriction on down to and including Proposition 187 in California?

They may have a wartime airfield, but are they likely to explore the causes of wars—the fight against fascism, the war in Vietnam? And if they take on the latter, what interpretation will they opt for—well-intentioned mistake, noble crusade, defense of the empire? And will they move on to American-backed death squads in El Salvador and Guatemala, or cover Panama and the Gulf War?

It is not utterly impossible, if they thought these were saleable products. It is a matter of how they read the market, and how willing they are to expend capital in making markets which do not yet exist. In this sense the private and profit-making nature of the enterprise, and the culture of this particular company, do raise possibilities for doing critical history.

Indeed, it might be tempting to see commercial operations as being havens from the public storms. At Disney, after all, one only has to convince Michael Eisner of the worth of a historical product, and let him worry about selling it to consumers. But market researchers and politically savvy CEOs have to factor in the political climate as well; the current crop of culture warriors will have little compunction about attacking even so sacrosanct an entity as Disney should it stray from the fold.

It is not at all clear where Disney's America will go from here (assuming it goes anywhere at all). Or what its relations with historians will be should the enterprise proceed. The company claims that "We are starting afresh and are reaching out to historians to make sure our portrayal of the American experience is responsible." Public historian Otis Graham has urged meeting Disney halfway, with the aim of "maneuvering the Disney view of history away from fantasy and toward less pat, but more interesting and honest representations of the past." Many former critics have already signed on as consultants. One can imagine Eisner emerging a benefactor of the profession, rather as he has become a major patron of American architects.

Should historians work for Disney's America? Sure. But with their eyes wide open, aware of the constraints as well as the possibilities. Obviously, theme parks are not museums, and we should not expect anything like the coverage and complexity demanded of public historical sites. But Disney is claiming it wants to educate as well as entertain. Hiring historians to help them is a great idea. But the unleashed historical imagination is a powerful, potentially corrosive force, not always compatible with the myth-making dimensions of their project to date. In the aftermath of retreat at Manassas, the Disney people had best be honest with themselves and their advisors about which terrains of human experience, and what kinds of interpretation, they are determined to avoid. And then to live with the fact that a priori censorship is inherently antithetical to the historical project, and likely to produce only the most "Mickey Mouse" of narratives.

At the same time, with the public sphere in danger of being throttled, those inclined to work with the private sector might be well advised to concentrate on using their professional associations to underscore the enhanced civic obligations of commercial operations in a privatized era. If there is no ongoing political pressure on Eisner from the outside, if it is left to a few consultants to do the job, what we will likely get from his corporate theme park will be not America's America, but only *Disney's* America, a poor counterfeit indeed.

Notes

This essay was written specifically for this book. Another version appeared in a roundtable on Disney, published in the *Public Historian* (fall 1995). My thanks to my friend Eric Foner for his help on this piece, and for innumerable kindnesses over the years.

1. State legislators had been swayed by the carrot of 19,000 jobs [unaware that most would be seasonal and low paid] and the $47 million that Disney lawyers and publicists claimed would be pumped each year into the state's economy (or into a rival state if Virginia didn't come up with the cash).
2. Kristol was no doubt also displeased with the reconstructed Hall of Presidents, where a Clinton robot shared audioanimatronic honors with Honest Abe.
3. Ada Louise Huxtable sounded the alarm about a new "unreal America"

in her 1992 essay "Inventing American Reality" (in the *New York Review of Books* 39 (3 December 1992), 24–9). Huxtable feared that "themed entertainment" was driving out not just "actual deposits of history and humanity" but "our sense of reality or interest in it." "The big bad wolf is standing right outside the door, poised to devour our past."

4. Disney booster Governor George Allen argued similarly that "History is not just for historians" or for "smug, self-appointed arbiters of culture. . . ."
5. John Bodnar contribution to "A House Divided: Historians Confront Disney's America," *OAH Newsletter* 22, no. 3 (August 1994), 10–11; Linda Shopes, "Some Second Thoughts on Disney's America," *Perspectives: American Historical Association Newsletter*, 33, no. 3 (March 1995), 7–8.
6. Richard Moe contribution to "A House Divided: Historians Confront Disney's America," *OAH Newsletter* 22, no. 3 (August 1994), 9.
7. As Cindy S. Aron notes, there is a tradition of mixing entertainment and education: "The Education-Entertainment Continuum: A Historical Perspective," *Perspectives: American Historical Association Newsletter* 33, no. 3 (March 1995), 5–6.
8. "On Disney's America: Consumer Culture and Perceptions of the Past," *Perspectives: American Historical Association Newsletter* 33, no. 3 (March 1995), 8–10.
9. Shopes, "Some Second Thoughts on Disney's America," *Perspectives: American Historical Association Newsletter* 33, no. 3 (March 1995), 8.
10. Though in Anaheim, it is worth noting, a local school district sued Disney over its plans to build a new three-billion-dollar "WESTCOT" annex that would bring thousands of new workers, and their children, who would have to be educated. But Disney had no interest in coming up with money for new schools and teachers.
11. Roger Wilkins is right to note that the Holocaust Museum—dedicated to fostering remembrance—would have a different feel if it was essentially dedicated to making a profit (much less hawking concentration camp commodities).

Section III

Preserving the Past:

A History of

Historic Preservation

in the United States

Advertisement in *Historic Preservation,* 1985. (Sybedon Corporation.)

Ronald Reagan's efforts to dismantle the leading New Deal and Great Society reforms are well known. But Reagan and his team also wanted to scour away a host of secondary programs that were no less pernicious, in neo-conservative eyes, for being less familiar. One of these was historic preservation, whose sin, the right claimed, was that it constrained the "free market" from demolishing the nation's built inheritance whenever it was profitable to do so.

The charge was and is accurate. Indeed, the historic preservation movement was born, over a century ago, in opposition to a free wheeling, free market era, when profit-seeking Americans—as disrespectful of the past as of the environment—routinely demolished what prior generations had constructed. Historicide, like ecocide, had become embedded in the culture.

Slowly, some groups began to resist these attitudes and activities. Boston Brahmin anthropologists sought to rescue the remnants of Indian cultures. Old New England families preserved their homesteads. Descendents of southern planters fashioned legislation to prevent the marketplace from demolishing their homes. By the 1920s these genteel classes had carved out some historic enclaves and preserved them from the onrush of development.

The great boom of the late 1940s and 1950s threatened to reverse, even erase, these small victories, as a remorseless juggernaut of development crunched its way through the nation's heritage. The patricians broadened their movement, rallying a coalition of disparate social groups to contest this onslaught. Launching a brilliant counter-offensive against the bulldozers, this preservation coalition achieved passage of the Historic Preservation Act in 1966, a law which began to curb the rampage. In the next decade, the movement allied itself with a broad spectrum of anticorporate forces, ranging from populist neighborhood conservationists to environmentalists and won a further series of legislative and judicial triumphs.

For a time, in the 1970s, it seemed as if the entire culture had done an about-face. Community groups and corporations, banks and courts, state governments and private developers all supported "historic preservation." Thousands of organizations set about saving whole swatches of cities and countrysides from demolition, rehabilitating old houses, setting up historic districts, reusing old factories, conserving and preserving the past.

In the 1980s, however, this movement came under attack. The Reagan right considered protecting the past as objectionable as imposing health and safety rules on corporations. And the historic preservation movement discovered its considerable victories quite vulnerable to reversal. In no small part, I will argue, the movement's fragility stemmed from its latter-day tactics—an abandonment of militant allies, a concordance with traditional enemies. This essay will sort out the tangled history of the historic preservation movement in order to assess its critical contemporary situation and suggest an alternative strategy for the future.

Escaping the Past

In the colonial period and the seventy years of explosive growth following the Revolution, Americans evinced little interest in saving the built environment. Given the country's history to that point, this is not surprising.

The European colonists inherited little in the way of historic artifacts to preserve. The truly old remains were not theirs. Indian ruins were either obliterated (like the people themselves), or set aside (again like their creators) on reservations, as trophies of conquest or reminders of a barbarism now happily overcome. Each advance into the continent set transcendence of history more firmly at the heart of the national culture.

The European migrants were ambivalent about their own past. While they honored Old World roots, they emphasized New World beginnings. The American Revolution enhanced this ambivalence. On the one hand, the rebels, staunch republicans and good Protestants, took a historic view of their position; they considered themselves inheritors of a millenia-long struggle against aristocratic, monarchical, and priestly rule. But when the new republic had been established, most politicians, businesspersons, and academicians exhuberantly dismissed the past. Their youthful society would shed outworn European customs and perhaps break free of the burdens of history altogether.[1]

Certainly the new nation's ruling classes felt little need to base their legitimacy on an appeal to antiquity, as European monarchs and aristocrats did. Quite the reverse. Northern merchants and industrialists proclaimed their self-made status and promoted the idea that all Americans were free to escape the past: If ordinary people believed they were not shackled to an inherited place, and could, in time, rise economically and socially, they would have no need to challenge those currently in authority. Even the southern slave planters, who adopted Walter Scott flourishes, claimed they were "natural" aristocrats rather than descendents of a distinguished lineage—an intelligent strategy, as few of their pedigrees would have withstood close scrutiny.

As a corollary, the American elite had little class interest in preserving history's residue. When remains of the past hindered the present accumulation of profit, they were routinely dispatched to the dustbin of history. Such tributes as were due republican forerunners could be made conveniently compatible with the imperatives of progress. New buildings could evoke old forms—Grecian banks and Roman railroad stations allowed a future-oriented culture to pay its respects to an honored tradition.[2]

The majority of the population may have had quite different attitudes toward preserving the past. Most seventeenth and eighteenth century European immigrants were displaced peasants and artisans who envisioned America as a great commons where they might reconstruct social relations demolished by the rise of European capitalism. They resisted the emerging market culture and considered land less a commodity than a homesite. Urban artisans—staunch upholders of a revolutionary republican tradition—similarly held out against dehistoricizing tendencies. Slowly, during the nineteenth century, this would change as the communal restraints and legal safeguards that had braked the emergence of American capitalism crumbled. Some small farmers would be displaced through the workings of the speculative and mortgage markets, driven west, and disconnected from traditional roots. Others, seduced into the new order by rising land values, would plunge with gusto into real estate speculation, imbibing its attendant disregard for tradition. And artisanal workplaces and communities would be repeatedly torn apart or relocated to suit the demands of capitalist development. Both defeat and opportunity, and the continuing arrival of immigrant newcomers with minimal historical connections to their new locations, eventually would produce a working-class variant of upper-class ahistoricism.

But for those who presided over the country's economy during most of its early history, "progress" took precedence over preservation. As a New

Yorker remarked in 1825, "We delight in the promised sunshine of the future, and leave to those who are conscious that they have passed their grand climacteric to console themselves with the splendors of the past."[3]

Preservation Pioneers

Between the 1880s and the 1940s four groups began to protest casual demolition of the past.

The first was composed of descendants of the merchants and textile magnates of antebellum New England. By the end of the nineteenth century, these patricians found their inherited political and cultural authority ebbing away to plutocrats above and immigrants below. To restore their position the Brahmins assumed custodianship of the American inheritance. Banding together in geneological and historical societies, they underlined their pedigree by preserving its tangible remains, saving threatened properties by passing the hat among members of their class. In the course of these crusades, a genteel sensibility crystallized that condemned the unrestrained working of the market—a sensibility the easier to sustain because, like the European aristocrats with whom they identified, the Brahmins were living off an earlier generation's accumulation.[4]

Brahmins also engaged in preservation activities in the West. After the Civil War, pacification drives broke the back of armed Native American resistance, and the Plains Indians, like so many before them, were put on reservations. Hard on the army's heels came America's first anthropologists and archaeologists, many from the northeastern patriciate, intent on exploring the artifacts of Indian cultures. They found, to their dismay, that stockmen and prospectors had preceded them and were busily looting ruins and gravesites to meet the demands of a booming market in Indian antiquities. Using methods preservationists had worked out in the East, the anthropologists bought up historic relics and transferred them to public ownership, thus fencing them off from the market. Frederick Putnam of Harvard's Peabody Museum, for example, raised funds from preservation-oriented Bostonians, purchased the Great Serpent Mound, and deeded it to the state of Ohio.[5]

But the threatened areas were so vast that the preservationists soon concluded that only Congress could protect the past from the present. In 1906, they obtained passage of the Antiquities Act. The law gave the president authority to set aside public lands as national monuments, to levy criminal fines for excavating or destroying ruins, and to grant permits to scientific and educational institutions for field work. In 1916 management of federally owned "historic properties" was centralized in the National Park Service, within the Department of the Interior.[6]

The second group of 1880–1940 preservationists were descendants of the antebellum planter class living in the backwater river and seaport towns of the Old South, some still wealthy, others reduced to genteel poverty. Like the New England Brahmins, they were preoccupied with the past, dreaming

nostalgically of the golden days when their ancestors had been undisputed masters of the region.[7]

In the 1920s the aristocracy woke abruptly to find itself under assault. The grillwork and paneling of old southern homes had become fashionable. (The demand for Southiana, like that of the earlier craze for Indian relics, may have been fueled by Hollywood's national circulation of local images, first of the Wild West, then of the Old South.) Northern connoisseurs and avaricious museum directors flocked south to cannibalize gentry estates. Oil companies wanted to set up gas pumps in the middle of southern towns to meet the needs of the new automobile era. Southerners organized to beat back these new Yankee invasions.[8]

Charleston led the way. In the 1920s the Society for the Preservation of Old Dwelling Houses, composed of "society" women from the old battery district, fought to ward off Standard Oil filling stations, but steadily lost ground. Then, as the Brahmin anthropologists had done in the case of western lands, they turned to the state for support. In 1931 the women, supported by alarmed civic leaders, got a city ordinance passed establishing the Old and Historic Charleston District. A board of architectural review was given authority to approve all changes to historic buildings in the area.[9]

Thus was born the first "historic district" through an innovative use of zoning, in itself a newly popular exercise of governmental authority. Zoning had emerged in the 1900–20 period as a way of confronting the obstacles private ownership of property presented to profitable urban investment. City zoning began by blocking uses of the land that could "ruin" a neighborhood; in New York, Fifth Avenue stores got industrial sweatshops zoned out. Initially frowned upon because it restricted property rights, zoning was accepted once it became clear that by promoting stability, it enhanced property values. In the decade after 1910, zoning underwrote the creation of exclusive upper-class residential suburbs and villa districts, as insurance companies and banks flocked to invest in planned and safeguarded communities. Charleston's law essentially zoned by building age, rather than by building type.[10]

The historic district device was soon copied, particularly in the South. In New Orleans, for instance, local business groups, architects, civic leaders, and property owners set out to save the Vieux Carré—the historic French Quarter. They got a constitutional amendment passed by voters in 1936, empowering the city to create the Vieux Carré Commission, which it did the next year. In 1939 a court ruling established the commission's authority to place restraints on private property holders' rights to demolish historic buildings.[11]

The third preservation-minded group was a handful of multimillionaire industrialists, including Henry Ford and John D. Rockefeller Jr. Though their products were helping dismantle the old society, they turned to saving parts of it from devastation. Restorations such as Rockefeller's Williamsburg and Ford's Greenfield Village became popular enterprises among the corporate rich in the 1920s.

The superwealthy, I have argued elsewhere, sought partly to celebrate their newly won preeminence, and partly to construct a retrospective lineage for themselves by buying their way into the American past. Preservation also afforded a way of carving out a distinctive cultural position within the larger capitalist class. Monopolists had little love for the competitive scramble of the marketplace. Some of these millionaires were still involved in direct capitalist accumulation; others, like Rockefeller Jr., were second generation, but all could afford to turn up their noses at imperatives that still ruled regular businessmen. The grand restorations simultaneously demonstrated their disdain for the market and their capacity to transcend it.[12]

A fourth body of nouveaux preservationists came from the professional and managerial strata, a group that assumed a critical role in American life in the 1880–1920 period. Summoned into being by corporations and governmental bureaucracies, professionals developed an independent culture of efficiency with a distaste for the market at its core. Appalled by chaos, congestion, contagion, and class strife, some repudiated capitalism. Most, however, worked within the system to overcome antiquated and irrational practices that blocked the efficient accumulation of capital. This concern led some of them, by a variety of indirect routes, to historic preservation.[13]

In the 1890s some architects, landscape architects, and engineers tried to rationalize and discipline U.S. cities by beautifying them—reorganizing them around a matrix of broad avenues and monumental neoclassical buildings. The White City at the Columbian Exposition of 1893 embodied their hope that the authority of antiquity could restrain the anarchy of modern America. They soon learned that pseudo-historic architecture alone could not generate a desirable social order.[14]

Increasingly, many of the new professionals sought state intervention to halt or regulate various anarchic business practices. After the turn of the century, ministers, engineers, doctors, lawyers, and architects set out to ameliorate the worst offenses. Land use was a key concern. On the national level, they worked to put western land and water management into professional and "scientific" hands. This dovetailed nicely with Brahmin archeologists' wishes to regulate access to Indian relics, and contributed to the passage of the 1906 Antiquities Act. At the municipal level, the planning fraternity was instrumental in fashioning zoning legislation, which the southern gentry adapted to preservation ends.

Slowly, alongside the corps of ladies (and some gentlemen) who had been the backbone of preservation efforts, a body of (almost invariably) male historic preservation professionals grew up. Restorationists (Rockefeller, in particular) hired architects and engineers to renovate or reconstruct old buildings. Southern gentility worked with businessmen and lawyers to forge preservation law.

It was not until the 1930s, however, when the federal government began to involve itself in preservation, that these professionals developed a semi-independent operating base. In the early thirties, the National Park Service took on professionally trained historians to do public interpretations at historic parks and battlefield sites, and hired twelve hundred unemployed architects to survey and record all "historic" buildings in the United States for the Historic American Building Survey (HABS). The Works Progress Administration hired archeologists to excavate and record sites about to be flooded by such massive river damming programs as the Tennessee Valley Authority, and set historians to work on Federal Writers' Project programs. And between 1934 and 1941, the Civilian Conservation Corps undertook restoration projects that employed hundreds of historians and historical technicians.[15]

In 1935 came the most dramatic New Deal entry into the preservation field. The Historic Sites Act authorized the Department of the Interior, acting through the National Park Service, to acquire property, preserve and operate privately owned historic or archeological sites, construct museums, develop educational programs, and place commemorative tablets. Almost overnight a massive federal presence had been authorized, and the National Park Service swiftly established a Branch of Historic Sites and Buildings to carry out the mandate. This Branch of History, as it was informally known, hired a cohort of historians, who began planning a massive educational program using historic sites to illustrate major themes in U.S. history.[16]

The National Park Service was never able to institute a general plan for heritage preservation. It was limited by the Historic Sites Act, which reflected the approach of the traditional preservation community, particularly those responsible for Colonial Williamsburg. (A Rockefeller lawyer drafted the bill eventually adopted by Congress.) The Park Service historians did not have the power to acquire endangered property through the exercise of eminent domain. Nor could they halt the extensive demolition work undertaken by the New Deal itself, through its slum clearance and roadway construction programs. Indeed, in St. Louis, the National Park Service was forced to serve as an unwilling sponsor for the Jefferson National Expansion Memorial—an urban-renewal-project-cum-real-estate-scam that destroyed a historic riverside area in the name of honoring the frontier past.[17]

Still, the publicly funded programs expanded the preservation movement and broadened the meaning of "historic" from what the upper classes had meant by it. The HABS project, for instance, recorded buildings with no connection to famous white persons but with important meanings for local communities, and the WPA state guidebooks, commemorative markers, and collections of local lore reflected a populist conception of public history. This tendency of the rapidly growing number of state professionals, once freed from dependence on private sector employers, to move leftward was arrested by the termination of the New Deal and the outbreak of war. Federal historical programs were slashed and converted to caretaker operations or purveyors of patriotic agitprop. But the experience left its mark on the veterans of the 1930s—people who would form the cadre of postwar preservation programs.

Between the 1880s and the 1940s—in many ways the heyday of American industrial capitalism—a constituency emerged that questioned the prevailing dismissal of the past. Northern old money, southern patricians, the creme of the monopoly capitalist stratum, and new professionals in and out of government: All developed a distaste for unrestrained capitalism. Historic preservation became an emblem of that distaste: Historic artifacts were not to be subjected to market considerations (partly because they were more valuable to these groups as symbols of legitimacy).[18]

But if preservationists rejected conventional cultural codes they did not succeed in overturning them. Quite the opposite: "Modernist" sensibilities emerged in architecture, fashion, and the fine arts. Twenties intellectuals reveled in the accelerated tempo of time, the rupture of traditions, the liberating break with conservative constraints, and the exhilaration of commodity abundance. Functionalists stripped away and cast off nineteenth-century Victorian clutter, but with the gewgaws went much of that culture's historical concreteness. And the new culture of consumption, spurred by the advertising industry, substituted novelty for memory as a cultural imperative.[19]

In such a culture, the best preservationists could do was declare a few sites to be historic "reservations"—off limits to developers. The larger culture tolerated these parenthesized places—New England homes, antebellum planter residences, historic battlefields, colonial reconstructions, and Indian "homelands"—partly because there were so few of them, and partly because they were so utterly irrelevant to the onrushing flow of events.

New Recruits

Nevertheless, by the mid 1940s, preservationists were pleased with their limited gains. Moreover the war had diminished the threat to the built environment by curtailing building programs. Still, preservationists looked to the postwar period with foreboding. They were right to have worried.[20]

After victory, a flood of federal money poured into urban renewal, suburban development, and highway construction. A government-fostered "growth coalition" of real estate developers, urban planners, city Democrats, suburban Republicans, bankers, construction workers, quasipublic "authorities" and corporate-dominated planning bodies ripped up slums and "blighted" areas, replacing them with the corporate command and control centers the new multinational economy required. The middle class left happily (or was squeezed out) and motored to the new suburbs on the new highways.[21]

The impact on the historic environment was devastating. Roads were rammed through city centers, urban renewal demolished vast downtown tracts, and by 1966 fully one half of the twelve thousand properties recorded by HABS thirty years earlier had been torn down. The growth coalition seemed to revel in leveling the past. It was the Age of Robert Moses. Theorists of capitalist civilization cheered, applauding the system's willingness to destroy the old in the interest of innovation and productivity.[22]

The growth coalition's activities between 1945 and 1966 galvanized the various preservation constituencies. It drew them together, forced them to pool resources and expertise, and eventually led them to broaden their social base in order to resist the onslaught on the past. In a sense the bulldozer battalions created the modern preservation movement.

In 1947, responding to the quickening pace of development, preservationists organized the National Council for Historic Sites and Buildings to plot strategy. The meetings included geneological society leaders, amateur and professional historians, architects, archeologists, engineers, and civic planners, but were dominated by National Park Service professionals and Williamsburg people. Financing was provided by the Mellon banking family. The council drew up plans for a National Trust that would propagandize for historical preservation. As did the English National Trust, the new body would also assume title to historic properties whose owners could no longer keep them up and operate them as museums.[23]

Congress obligingly created the National Trust in 1949. The Lilly Foundation and the duPonts chipped in to support the new organization, but the Mellons remained the real underwriters: in 1957, they gave the trust a $2.5 million endowment.[24]

The trust acquired and managed some historic properties; got the Historic

American Building Survey revived in 1957; and, with Colonial Williamsburg, worked to "professionalize" historic site interpretation. The period thus saw the strengthening of one of the major constituency groups of the movement, the professional public historians created in the 1920s and 1930s by private organizations and the federal government.[25]

What the National Trust did not do was make much headway against the 1950s' juggernaut of progress. It succeeded only in supporting the creation of more reservations and establishing itself as the organizational voice—albeit a weak one—of historic preservation. Facing overwhelming odds, the trust was further hampered by its narrow base in a thin sliver of the upper classes.[26]

In the 1960s, wider support for historic preservation began to emerge, rooted largely in the growth of resistance to urban renewal. Some opposition came from working-class neighborhoods resisting demolition, though in this period their efforts were usually in vain. A much stronger counterforce was generated by inner-city middle class constituencies. In 1961, for example, Jane Jacobs, an editor of *Architectural Forum*, organized successful opposition to an urban renewal project in New York's West Greenwich Village.[27]

Jacobs, along with Herbert Gans, Edward Hall, and Ada Louise Huxtable, argued that destroying old buildings destroyed the fabric of healthy urban communities. The bleak postwar high-rise structures were inhuman: Their spatial arrangements shattered social networks and their bland environmental and temporal homogeneity denied the need for spatial diversity and historical connectedness. Both the suburbs and the projects undermined peoples' personal and social identities (this was the period of popularity for Eriksonian theories about identity crises). One supporter argued that the continuing demolition of traditional historical neighborhoods and landmarks constituted a "national emergency" because "individuals feel both more secure and more purposeful when they recognize that they exist as part of an historical continuum."[28]

These concerns dovetailed nicely with the Cold War fears of the Kennedy and Johnson administrations that destruction of the past might engender a national identity crisis, which the nation could ill afford. National Trust leaders played to this concern, and warned of "a future in which America found itself without roots, without a sense of identity, with nothing to lose." The marriage of the concern over personal and national identity was reflected in Jack Kennedy's discourses on national purpose and Jackie Kennedy's restoration of the White House and celebration of its historical value in television tours.[29]

Black urban rioting soon gave power and force to these arguments. The 1964 Harlem eruption, soon dwarfed by those in Watts (1965) and Detroit (1967), had many roots, but prominent among them was the assault of the urban renewal and highway construction programs on the already tattered fabric of inner-city life.[30]

To critiques of social scientists and protests in the streets were added the concerns of some big city mayors who—as much as they liked downtown construction—began to fear the consequences of steady population loss and the consequent erosion of the middle-class urban tax base.

While these diverse opponents began to erode the growth coalition's prestige—planners rethought their theories about urban renewal, Robert Moses began his slide from power, and historic districts spread—the developers were being undercut from a different direction. The development of mass tourism in the 1950s and 1960s—buoyed by the new roadways and the general prosperity—made it appear there was money to be made by preserving the past.

There had been hints of this notion before. The conversion of historic houses into shrines had often been touched with the promotional. Preservationists, understandably enough, had appealed to entrepreneurial self-interest when soliciting donations. And Ford and Rockefeller had opened up hotels to house the growing number of visitors to their restorations. But these harbingers were nothing compared to the postwar tourist boom.[31]

In 1964, 94.5 million people drove their thirty-four million automobiles over 130 billion miles on their vacations and spent more than twenty billion dollars as they went. Many of those millions motored to historic sites. Colonial Williamsburg's paid attendance went from 166,000 in 1947 to nearly 710,000 in 1967, and the increase was not unusual. Old Sturbridge went from less than 12,000 to over 520,000 in the same period, and Greenfield Village passed the 1,000,000 mark in 1960. Between 1960 and 1962, attendance at all historic sites in Massachusetts went up 50 percent.[32]

The phenomenon transcended the big name sites. In 1960 New York State's Joint Legislative Committee on Preservation and Restoration of Historic Sites reported that "Tourism has become big business. . . . And historic sites more and more are luring the tourist." In 1964, twenty-nine states listed tourism as one of their three largest industries. As Jonathan Daniels proclaimed, "History has become a cash crop as eagerly tended as the hope for industrial plants."[33]

Even the historic districts—originally conceived as residential enclaves—proved to be wildly profitable draws. A 1964 study done for the New Orleans Chamber of Commerce found that the French Quarter brought in more money than anything except the port itself. Tourism had made New Orleans one of the top four convention cities, influenced national and regional corporation decisions to locate there, and accounted for much of the extraordinary strength of the city's retail, hotel, and office market. The study set a dollar value of $150 million on New Orleans' historic architecture.[34]

As the evidence mounted up, historic preservation began to appeal to enterprising local boosters and small businessowners began to rethink the demolition/development approach. Beginning in 1959, for example, a young investment banker, Leopold Adler II, presided over a sharp change of direction in Savannah's preservation community. Working with a successful suburban developer, Historic Savannah employed a revolving fund (basically a line of credit from now sympathetic banks) to purchase, restore, and re-sell old buildings with restrictive covenants attached. They worked out public relations themes and highway signs, developed historic house museums, tour routes, brochures, visitors' centers, restaurants and motels that carried through historic themes. It worked. Construction, real estate activity (with attendant commissions and profits), land values, tourist revenues, bank deposits, the restaurant business, and retail sales all soared. *Fortune* magazine was impressed: "Anachronism can be made to pay off in urban civilization."[35]

Preservation Law

By the mid-1960s, then, the original core of genteel preservationists had been joined by potentially powerful allies: Middle class professionals resisting wholesale destruction of old but viable communities and local businessowners sniffing profit in the past. But these groups held quite different perspectives. Traditionalists wanted to save old buildings for their use-value as homes, communities, and symbols. Entrepreneurs were less interested in meaning than marketability. How were these enemies to coalesce?

A clue to cooperation emerged from contemporary objections to historic museums. The proper way to preserve the past, critics were suggesting, was to integrate it with the present. "Preservation," Ada Louise Huxtable argued, "is the job of finding ways to keep those original buildings that provide the city's character and continuity and of incorporating them into its living mainstream"—not placing them in "sterile isolation."[36]

Thus was born the doctrine of "adaptive reuse." Historic buildings should not be mummified, but recycled. The exterior shell should be kept and the interior devoted to some profitable usage. To these preservationists, unlike the DAR-types, the original "aura," the building's connection to specific people and events, was unimportant. They shifted their emphasis from meaning to ambience.

"Adaptive reuse" declared an end to antagonism between preservation and development. Traditionalists could save and reuse instead of isolate and venerate; (re)developers could incorporate the old into the new. Together they could take on the bulldozer developers and their allies in the federal bureaucracy. "Adaptive reuse" was thus a progressive philosophy in its original context but, by justifying putting "a new building in the old shell" as being a "modern solution that still manages to evoke the past," Huxtable and her colleagues were on the road to legitimating the developers she had been battling so long.[37]

The immediate question, however, was how to forge an effective political program, a problem addressed in 1965 by a blue-ribbon commission assembled by the National Trust and Colonial Williamsburg. The group issued a manifesto—"With Heritage So Rich"—condemning unrestrained growth as a danger to national identity: "A nation can be a victim of amnesia. It can lose the memories of what it was, and thereby lose the sense of what it is or wants to be." Adaptive reuse was proclaimed the solution: "Let us save what we have around us that is good, not for exhibition, not for 'education,' but for practical use as places to live in and to work in." The federal government was declared the proper agency to accomplish these ends.[38]

A whirlwind legislative campaign followed, orchestrated by National Trust Chairman Gordon Gray, a powerful man with entree into the highest Congressional circles through his R.J. Reynolds family connections and high-level service under Truman, Kennedy, and Johnson.[39]

In response to this campaign, Congress passed the National Historic Preservation Act, which wrote virtually every National Trust recommendation into law, a wholesale victory for the "adaptive reuse" approach. The law established a National Register of Historic Places, which was to list all sites, buildings, structures, and objects found by professionals to have been "significant" in American history, architecture, archeology, or culture. It also authorized matching grants to states to further local preservation projects; required each state to develop coherent plans to preserve its historic legacy and to appoint a state historic preservation officer to coordinate the program; and put the National Trust on the federal payroll. Finally, and crucially, the act created the Advisory Council on Historic Preservation, which all federal agencies were required to consult before demolishing properties listed on the National Register. The Advisory Council did not have authority to halt other federal bureaucracies, but the prior review process did slow the hitherto smooth workings of the highway and urban renewal machines.[40]

Two other 1966 acts rounded out the victory. The Department of Transportation Act blocked destruction of historic properties by five major agencies unless they could prove there was "no feasible and prudent alternative," and even then they were required to "minimize harm." The Demonstration Cities Act—a major reaction against urban renewal—enjoined Housing and Urban Development to "preserve and restore areas, sites, and structures of historic or architectural value" and authorized grants of two-thirds the cost of surveys of such sites.[41]

The growth coalition did not roll over and play dead with the passage of the Historic Preservation Act of 1966. For a time (1966–72) Secretary Weaver at HUD slowed the bulldozing and increased rehabilitation (by 1972 it had tripled the 1955–65 rate). But soon the Model Cities program—under fierce pressure—backed away from social and environmental planning, aid to the poor, and citizen involvement. Selling out to the growth interests, the program became a public works bonanza for medium-sized cities.[42]

Then Nixon and Ford scrapped or consolidated many of the 1950s and 1960s programs (Urban Renewal, Model Cities) in the 1974 Housing and Community Development Act. The act was supposed to eliminate urban slums, and it required low and moderate income populations be included in the planning process and benefit from the programs. But under the New Federalism, local governments were to be given Community Development Block Grants to subsidize private development projects and to do as they pleased with the money, so local power elites sent the money flowing to convention centers, office buildings, shopping malls, and the like. This process accelerated with the 1977 institution of the Urban Development Action Grant (UDAG) program, which provided, as urban renewal had, federal money for land acquisition, site clearance, and infrastructure improvements. Responsibility for complying with federal environmental legislation was transferred to local government hands and once again hotels and convention centers began to replace historic structures. Despite the preservationists' victories, it remained open season on the cities.[43]

Faced with these ongoing challenges, and responding to the climate of the late 1960s and early 1970s, the preservation movement expanded to include a burgeoning new urban gentry and militantly populist neighborhood conservationists (who drew energy from the black, womens', ecology, anti-corporate, and antiwar movements). By the mid-1970s, the strengthened preservation coalition scored a succession of legislative and judicial triumphs against their bulldozer enemies.

New Frontiers

In the late 1960s and early 1970s, as corporate and financial headquarters flourished in city centers, demand for white collar professional, managerial and technical workers rose significantly (twenty-five percent between 1960–70). Most commuted to the central business districts from the suburbs, but many others—especially those who had come to the city as youths to study or work—sought housing near their work. This stay-in-the-city trend also was fed by demographic and cultural upheavals of the times: Smaller and more numerous households (widows living alone, kids leaving home earlier, couples marrying later and divorcing more often, women working outside the home). The baby-boom singles and working couples either did not care for the child-centered suburbs or found that housing and commuting costs priced them out of the suburban market. These young professionals and managers formed the core of a new urban gentry.[44]

What attracted them to the sections of the city they chose, apart from location and price, was a neighborhood's "historic character." Perhaps their sensibilities had been shaped by rebellion against the rootless suburbs in which they grew up and a desire to live in communities with an authentic and aged heritage. The "urban homesteaders" researched their homesite's past, got caught up in the excitement of restoration work, and lovingly defended the built environment against developers.[45] But in their attentiveness to their new neighborhood's older past some gentry ignored its recent history—most crucially, how they themselves had displaced former residents.

Realtors and developers insulated many from such realities, buying up houses, evicting tenants, rehabbing, and reselling at fat markups to wealthier buyers. Surviving old residents were flushed out at the next stage as tax assessments went up, fancy shops arrived, the old infrastructure crumbled, and it became too expensive or too alienating to hang on. And if they stubbornly did remain, local governments would enforce long unused codes and condemn old housing for investors waiting in the wings. If need be, thugs and arsonists would finish the job. The end result might be an exquisite "golden ghetto," restored to a pristine moment in time, stripped (as Williamsburg had been) of all traces of those who had inhabited it in the intervening years.[46]

If some gentry were blind to displacement, others knew perfectly well what they were doing. They wanted temporally scarce commodities because they knew their value would rise. The existing community was a hindrance: It undermined the "historic" ambience that would make the investment pay off.[47]

Other gentry, still, responded neither with naivete nor calculating ruthlessness, but with moral righteousness: They were not destroying impoverished communities with long established folkways and roots, but were wiping out "blight" and crime. The head of Spring Garden Civic Association, noting that Hispanics were being driven out of that gentrifying Philadelphia neighborhood, was pleased: "When all else fails, try capitalism. It works. . . . The private market is changing the neighborhood, and it's changing it in an appropriate way." Others cultivated an imperial attitude; seeing themselves as beleaguered islands of civility, the new gentry sought to expand their territory. One New Orleans proponent of transforming the multiethnic Irish Channel community admitted: "Renters are being displaced. It is sad, but the only hope for the neighborhood."[48]

Living in historic areas became a badge of class distinction. They were expensive and, given their scarcity, exclusive in a way even the fanciest suburbs could not be. Proprietorship of the past once again became a vehicle of legitimation—an echo of the DAR era—although it did not require ancestral connections *and* it afforded a source of accumulation at the same time.

The ultimate gentry objective was to have their neighborhood designated as an historic district. District status roped off an area and forbade demolition or unapproved alterations within it. Like suburban zoning, the districts attempted to freeze time and the accumulation process at a moment favorable to the gentry. "Historic" status would protect them both from the slovenly poor and crude developers, yet not unduly restrict their right of private property: Individual historic buildings remained salable commodities.

In 1955 only twenty cities had historic district commissions. By 1966 there were 100, by 1976 there were 492, in all fifty states; by 1982 there would be 900.[49]

At first—following Williamsburg and the Brahmins—only the eighteenth century would do. But given the increase in demand, soon there were not enough eighteenth century remains to go around. The historic charm and values of the nineteenth century were accordingly discovered. After the Victorian craze had run its course, 1920s art deco—previously scorned—was reevaluated and found desirable. The expanding definition of "historic" opened new terrain to speculative assaults and ensuing displacement.[50]

Ironically, those who refused to rein in the market fell victim to it themselves. In New Orleans' French Quarter, for example, rents and prices did not stop climbing after the poor were gone. Upper-middle-class whites soon found themselves priced out of the historic district as "unassuming little houses were converted into spiffy pads for the very rich." In New York, those squeezed out of Manhattan were forced, willy-nilly, into becoming the agents of gentrifying new areas in Brooklyn. The spread of the "brownstoners" often had a negative impact on preexisting communities, but at the same time widened the territory controlled by those with the resources and the commitment to fight the wrecking crews.[51]

The second set of 1960s recruits to the preservation movement were working and lower middle class people—largely white ethnics—who set out to save their neighborhoods from demolition. Their goal (similar to that of the original Charlestonians, though at a different class level) was to preserve not simply historic buildings but historic communities. Adopting the tactics of the civil rights and antiwar movements, grass roots organizations sat in, picketed, petitioned, and began to slow the bulldozers. The Chicano community of Tucson, Arizona, for example, learned in 1971 that a planned freeway would destroy their barrio. They were particularly incensed that the projected route ran right through El Tiradito (the Wishing Shrine), the symbolic, spiritual, and historical center of the neighborhood. They marched on the state highway department, circulated petitions, worked with local architects, historians, journalists, and churches, turned the freeway into a major political issue, and won. Even when they were not able to stop projects, community fury made developers increasingly wary and raised the costs of doing business.[52]

These neighborhood groups linked up to form support networks such as National People's Action and the National Association of Neighborhoods. These groups in turn demanded and got reforms such as the anti-redlining laws—the Home Mortgage Disclosure Act (1975) and the Community Reinvestment Act (1977). In 1977 the Carter administration responded to their growing political muscle by creating the National Commission on Neighborhoods. The commission recommended establishing neighborhood cooperatives; attacked growth-industry-related banks, state legislatures, and municipal unions; asked for an end to federal support for suburbs; and called for federal development money, winning, in 1978, a ten billion dollar community investment fund to finance, purchase, and rehabilitate three hundred thousand units of housing.[53]

The neighborhood conservationists were a complex lot. At times they were classic populists, beating off the attempts of speculators, developers, bankers, and state bureaucrats to commodify their neighborhoods. They were strongly commited to the traditional. They contested the homogenization of their culture, and stood for particularity, originality, and irreplaceability against the monolithic uniformity of corporate architecture that had blotted out neighborhood distinctiveness. They often supported microhistory movements and underwrote local museums, oral history programs, community pageants, grass roots bicentennial celebrations, and ethnic revivals. The local historians reminded many neighborhoods that they had once been independent municipalities. This fostered local pride, and sometimes, though not inevitably, led to the community's seeking historic district status; some actually refused a historic designation.

On the other hand, many of the neighborhood conservationist groups were fearful, defensive, parochial, and racist. Many—especially those created in the aftermath of the black riots—sought to keep "traditional" (white) values intact by beating back black inroads, including public housing and school busing. Ethnic roots could be celebrated in a chauvinist and exclusive way.[54]

In the seventies, the established preservation movement reached out to this new constituency by broadening its definition of "historic." In 1974 the American Institute of Planners called on the movement to "preserve the unique pasts of all groups." By 1976 the Advisory Council reported that

> No longer does the term "historic district" necessarily mean cobblestones, arching oaks, and serene federal-period houses. It may now also designate a working class area of rehabilitated houses and corner bars that reflect both an epoch of local history and an ethnic or cultural strain that has figured prominently in community development.

Broadening the definition of what was "historic" from famous sites to entire working-class areas expanded communities' available defenses against developers by offering them existing legislative protections.[55]

A third, quite special set of conservationists were those, chiefly blacks, who set out to preserve their neighborhoods from historic preservationists. In 1970 the president of Capitol East Community Organization denounced restorationists as "scavengers [who have] come in and squeezed out our people." His group placed red placards in storefronts and home windows which stated: Capitol East Is Our Community and We Will Fight to Stay. CECO also passed out leaflets which read:

> Niggers, wake up! Do you realize that blacks used to live in Georgetown and were pushed out? They were asleep! Do you see blacks being removed daily from Capitol Hill? Brothers, you are sleeping! They are starting to push blacks out again! Everytime you see an expensively restored house it means another black man is out. Wake up![56]

In Kansas City, Joe Louis Mattox, founder of the Birdland Historic Preservation Society, agreed: "It is not the time for blacks, the faithful, to turn over the keys to the cities to those who ran off and left their heritage." Carl Holman, president of the National Urban Coalition, asserted in 1978: "You're going to start seeing some very rough clashes when these same blacks and browns who could not live in other folk's neighborhoods find they cannot stay in their own."[57]

In the 1970s blacks occasionally blocked foundation or government support for gentrification or engaged in rehabilitation programs of their own. But there was seldom overwhelming support for preservation in black communities. Many were ill disposed to preserving places indelibly connected with white supremacy and/or poverty. It was one thing to restore some historic sites, like Weeksville in Brooklyn, that black people had constructed and controlled; quite another to be reminded about the bad old days. Blacks preferred, where feasible, to move into new and modern buildings in the cities or suburbs.[58]

Traditional preservationists had a lot of trouble establishing an alliance with black constituencies, even apart from black reluctance. Partly this was because, in their bones, "historic" meant beautiful, and many sites of poor peoples' housing or worship were not pretty. Another problem was that such strategies as preservationists had developed for dealing with the problem did not work well. Protecting a black area by making it into an historic district might destroy it. Jackson Ward, in Richmond, Virginia, was an old nineteenth-century free black community. In 1976 it was placed on the National Register to protect it from land developers and highway builders. This set off a boom among real estate speculators and affluent young whites attracted to its certified "historic" character. In other situations, it proved difficult to get National Register designations for securely black neighborhoods, such as Houston's Fourth Ward or Austin's Robertson Hill, if local developers wanted the land for urban renewal projects.[59]

At their best intentioned, preservationists could not grapple fundamentally with displacement because they accepted the framework of a marketplace of privately-owned property. Their response to the threatened destruction of buildings or communities boiled down to preemptive buying. But when the potential buyers were poor, or lacked the political power to command state funds, failure was guaranteed: The communities would pass to those who commanded stronger purchasing power.

Back in 1964, Arthur Ziegler noted that Pittsburgh preservation was devastating the poor. He founded the Pittsburgh History and Landmarks Foundation "to involve them in the restoration activity rather than dislocating them." But Ziegler's minimal successes depended on spillover Mellon money ("in Pittsburgh we were blessed with private foundations that invested in our proposals"), and worked only in areas where liberal gentry wanted to retain a multiracial character. Foundations and the government refused to support antidisplacement programs in all-black areas.[60]

Similarly, Lee Adler left the Historic Savannah Foundation in 1967 because it was displacing the poor. He set up the Savannah Landmark Rehabilitation Project (SLRP) with the laudable goal of buying half the houses in a gentrifying black area, restoring them (using minority contractors, neighborhood Comprehensive Training and Employment Act [CETA] workers, local capital, and federal money), and then subsidizing the original tenants with federal funds. After two years of work SLRP had saved just two dozen units; later, the supporting federal programs were eliminated. The mistake was believing they could achieve real power through the marketplace. "The one consistent method that does not fail and produces tangible results," Adler said, "is that of buying and selling properties. So, the name of the game is real estate." Thinking themselves hard-nosed, they were in fact fatally naive victims of the utopian capitalist fantasy that profit motives can be harnessed for the public good.[61]

Still, the established preservation movement did acknowledge the situation of preservation-displacees and tried to respond to the problem. They sponsored conferences, wrote books, and launched programs like the Inner City Venture Fund, which aimed at preserving the historic resources of minorities, native Americans, and ethnic populations.[62]

Triumphs

In the sixties and seventies, then, the movement reached out to and gathered strength from new constituencies. In 1966 there had been twenty-five hundred preservation groups; in 1976 there were six thousand. Moreover, the cultural and political tide seemed to be running in the preservationists' direction. Everywhere, a new sensibility rejected unrestrained "progress," "growth," and "newness." Urban renewal was intellectually and culturally discredited in the planning community. In 1974 Robert Caro wrote a biography excoriating Moses and won a Pulitzer Prize for it the next year. Management of scarce resources was the order of the day during the energy crisis. Conservationists, environmentalists, and historic preservationists (considered as a species of temporal ecologists) fashioned an emerging alliance under the banner of "heritage preservation."[63]

The new allies were crucial, because despite the temper of the times and the 1966 laws, the growth coalition's offensive continued. The Housing and Urban Development office, for instance, routinely ignored advisory council comments and tore down historic areas at local developers' behest. So the National Trust returned to the cloakrooms and corridors of official Washington seeking an expanded federal role.

First, the National Trust sent many of its best people into the bureaucracy to battle for adherence to established legislation. Preservationists in the Park Service's Office of Archeology and Historic Preservation struggled, in the late sixties, to save immediately endangered sites. They were hampered by minimal funding, and checked by experienced fighters in other agencies. Blocked in the bureaucracy, they went back to Congress and helped win the Environmental Protection Act of 1969, which strengthened their hand. In 1971, they got President Nixon to issue Executive Order 11593, which required recalcitrant agencies to conduct inventories of historic properties in their domains and to "exercise caution" about demolishing them.[64]

These efforts slowed, but failed to halt, the momentum of destruction. A visit by National Trust and advisory council experts to Western Europe, Japan, and the Soviet Union, where preservation efforts were far more advanced, convinced them they needed stronger legal authority. In 1974 they set up a lobbying group—Preservation Action—and launched a new legislative drive. They redeployed old legitimation arguments, given new edge by a decade of protest and upheaval. They also tested new arguments, praising the greater energy efficiency of old housing stock and the employment possibilities of labor-intensive rehabilitation projects. Finally, they drew upon their allies in the neighborhood conservation movement, a source of considerable political strength. In the history-conscious bicentennial year, Congress gave them two crucial pieces of legislation.[65]

One, the National Historic Preservation Fund Act, expanded their power within the bureaucracy to hinder or prevent other federal agencies from demolishing "historic properties." The Advisory Council on Historic Preservation was given rulemaking authority, upgrading its recommendations from guidelines to laws. It also declared that properties the council deemed "eligible" for the National Register were entitled to the same legal protections as those already on it. The Act also added financial muscle: It authorized a 700 percent increase in funding, and 70–30 matching grant funds to states for preservation planning.[66]

The second law—the Historic Structures Tax Act—opened up a new front on one of the key terrains of the federal government, the tax code. It mandated tax disincentives for anyone who demolished historic buildings. It also authorized tax benefits (quick write-offs) for anyone who rehabilitated historic properties and used them for income producing purposes. This law went a long way toward eliminating the biases against preservation embedded in the tax codes.[67]

While the National Trust had been engineering a massive expansion of preservationist power in the federal government, states and cities had been energetic in passing historic district legislation. The resultant body of law and regulation—while not as powerful as similar state provisions in the Soviet Union or Western Europe—nevertheless constituted a remarkable assertion of government control over the private land market. It was inevitable that such constraints would come under legal counterattack.[68]

The constitutional basis for preservation law was the so-called "police power"—the right of the state to enforce regulations that constrained private property owners without having to pay them compensation—because such regulation was for the "public good." This was a shaky position. Since 1909, the Supreme Court had deemed only health and safety matters sufficient justifications for police power intervention. Mere "aesthetic" considerations were not. Preservationists had been unwilling to deploy the far more powerful constitutional basis of "eminent domain"—the unquestioned right of the state to take private property in return for just compensation—because they knew full well that U.S. landed capital would vigorously fight such state impairment of its prerogatives. Besides, having the state buy each and every endangered building would be murderously expensive and require a gigantic bureaucracy to run.[69]

In the 1960s and 1970s pro-preservation lawyers fought for a breakthrough in police power jurisprudence. The National Trust sponsored the first National Conference on Historic Preservation Law in May 1971. In legal briefs and scholarly articles they sought a formula that might reconcile a heightened concern with aesthetics (historic continuity was placed under this rubric) and traditional owners' rights. But this was difficult to do. Consequently, in the course of confronting the contradiction between private and public desires, some preservationists argued that a completely new view of property rights was needed, one that recognized social needs as paramount, and curtailed rights of private ownership that had been traditional for centuries. And the statutes, ordinances, court decisions, and administrative procedures effected in the seventies inched their way toward that position.[70]

A critical step forward came in 1978. Ten years earlier, the Penn Central Railroad had announced plans to build a two-million-square-foot office building on top of a historic landmark they owned—New York City's Grand Central Station. New York sued to block the project. Penn Central argued that the historic district law, because it prevented them from exploiting the developmental possibilities of their property to the fullest, constituted a "taking" of property that, under the Fourteenth Amendment, required they be paid "just compensation." The Supreme Court ruled, 6–3, that Penn Central's position was "simply untenable." They noted that the corporation was already getting a "reasonable return" on its property; that the law allowed it to transfer the unused development rights on its airspace to another property; and found that a law "providing services, standards, controls, and incentives that will encourage preservation by private owners and users" to be clearly constitutional. To find otherwise, Justice Brennan noted, "would of course invalidate not just New York City's law, but all comparable landmark legislation in the nation." While hardly adopting the proto-socialist arguments advanced by some preservation lawyers, when measured against the legal situation fifty or one hundred years earlier, it was a startling restriction on the rights of private property and the freedom of the marketplace.[71]

Everybody's Doin' It

The preservationist alliance's triumph coincided with the collapse—and conversion—of its traditional enemy. In the mid-seventies, a world-wide recession knocked the wind out of the growth movement and brought development to a dramatic halt. As boosters and builders suddenly confronted an "age of limits," a sea change in their attitudes toward historic preservation got underway.[72]

The recession bit immediately into housing construction. Rising mortgage rates lowered demand, high interest rates made new construction more costly, and the federal government imposed a public housing moratorium. Housing starts plummeted. In 1976, for the first time, more Americans repurchased old than bought new homes. By 1982 85 percent of American families had been priced out of the housing market, just at the time the baby boomers were trying to enter it.[73]

This set off a preservation surge. People who could not afford to move began to fix up what they had. At the same time, it became more profitable than ever to rehabilitate old buildings and gentrify them. As a 1980 study confirmed, real estate values in historic districts soared. Savannah's had risen 276 percent in the previous ten years, while the average for the rest of the city had been only 184 percent. Banks that had once redlined inner city areas now leaped to finance them. By 1977, residential property rehabilitation was estimated at thirty-two billion dollars—38 percent of all construction.[74]

Rehabilitation money also began flowing to the casualties of the previous generation. Main Streets attracted funding in their attempt to combat the malls, undertaking facade renovations, and trading on their old-time ambience.[75]

There were even bigger capital flows into providing services to the residents, office workers, tourists, and regional middle-class shoppers who had been drawn to the central business districts. One particularly lucrative enterprise was the historic market movement. Developers like James Rouse, finding the suburbs saturated with malls, now parlayed historic designations into funding magnets from federal, state, city, and private sources. San Francisco's Ghirardelli Square had pioneered in 1964; it was followed by Denver's Larimer Square, Seattle's Pioneer Square, Atlanta's Underground, St. Louis' Laclede's Landing, and equivalents in Annapolis, Louisville, Boston, and Pittsburgh. They paid off handsomely; one businessman enthused that the markets "demonstrated conclusively that preservation and business are compatible." "We have seen the past," he said, "and we see that it works."[76]

More dramatically still, whole towns whose economy had been demolished by long term capital flight and/or the recession, decided to exploit the tourist potential inherent in their history. Relics of former stages of economic development were recycled by private developers blocked from growth projects. They turned industrial plant to service sector uses: Factories became boutiques, breweries became museums, warehouses became restaurants and condos, iron furnaces became offices, mining towns became ski resorts. Lowell, Massachusetts, capitalizing on its nineteenth-century industrial "character," attracted $350,000 from banks, $2 million from a bond issue, and $26 million in local, state, and federal commitments.[77]

The financial rewards engendered a wonderfully expedient development of historical interest. Seneca Falls, New York, a declining manufacturing community, had paid virtually no attention to its local women's rights legacy. With its rediscovery by feminists and historians, and Congressional establishment of a Women's Rights Historic National Park, local businesses poured money into remodeling the downtown district, even designing statues of feminist heroines. As a village trustee noted, the enthusiastic merchants "don't give a hoot" about feminism, but "they see the money opportunity. I mean, if you've got Old Faithful in your town, you are in favor of geysers."[78]

The preservation boom stimulated a demand for more professionals. Williamsburg and Cooperstown had long been running training seminars; now the universities entered the field. James Marston Fitch started the first graduate course in the preservation of historic architecture at Columbia in 1964. By 1975 ninety architecture schools in the United States and Canada offered either degrees in preservation or preservation-related programs and courses. Some of these graduates joined the ranks of the cadre of preservation professionals called into being by the new federal legislation. Some worked directly for the Department of Interior, the Advisory Council, or the staff of the many agencies who were trying to cope with new regulations; others labored throughout the country as state historic preservation officers. Others worked, as employees or consultants, for communities and developers, helping them do the bureaucratic paperwork required to qualify for federal funding.[79]

Finally, in the altered conditions of the 1970s, even the behemoths of business moved toward a preservation stance. From the 1920s until the mid-1960s, U.S. corporations had routinely torn down old plants and built anew, despite steadily rising construction costs, because costs of capital had declined enough to offset them. By the 1970s expensive capital generated rethinking. It became apparent that converting old office or factory space was 30–40 percent cheaper than constructing from scratch; that rehabbing took less time because work could continue during the winter; that it was less disruptive of business operations; that it reduced land costs; and that it avoided environmental impact statements, local building code hassles, and battles with preservationists. Given the new culture of retrenchment, preservation even afforded good publicity and advertising outlets.[80]

Banks, oil companies, insurance corporations, and heavy manufacturing firms—often using special development subsidiaries—began recycling their own buildings or buying up old plants for adaptive reuse. Between 1970 and 1977, rehabilitation of nonresidential buildings increased from 3.5 percent to 25 percent of the construction market, representing approximately twenty billion dollars worth of construction. By 1982 the estimated value of commercial rehabilitation reached $51.6 billion.[81]

The 1976 tax laws speeded the process. Developers now sought the designation of buildings or areas as historic sites because that entitled them to tax benefits. National Register listings went from 13,538 to 24,347. In four years, twenty-five hundred projects qualified, valued at $1.2 billion. Urban Development Action Grant money began flowing to preservation projects—by 1980, 39 percent of the total allotments. Increasingly, federal dollars would underwrite a historic core (as at Lowell), and developers would benefit from the boost in property values around its periphery.[82]

Diehard developers did an about-face. Businessowners had long viewed preservation as a constraint on their right to maximize returns on their property, and the movement's anticommercial tone had only exacerbated their suspicions of it. Preservation had been grudgingly supported as a prop to legitimacy, but this uncongenial task had been left to genteel elites, patrician women, and superrich dabblers. And even then most businesspersons—believing accumulation itself to be capital's best legitimation—feared preservation would inhibit the cornucopia of commodities. Now, however, preservation was useful not simply in legitimating capital but accumulating it, and business embraced it with enthusiasm. As one mortgage banker explained:

> Historic preservation is in many ways a sophisticated type of real estate development. . . . The stereotype of the local ladies club attempting to save some old building is long out of date. . . . It is possible to identify several *billion* dollars of historic preservation projects in the portfolios of financial institutions in this country.[83]

For its part, the preservationists eagerly welcomed their new allies into the fold. A National Trust vice president rejoiced that the movement had

> learned to shift from aesthetic appeals to bottom-line shrewdness. . . . After the decades of saving presidents' birthplaces and war heroes' headquarters, the preservation movement has leap-frogged into alliances with environmentalists, developers, and merchandisers.[84]

For a short period in the depressed late seventies, then, it seemed as if *everybody* liked historic preservation. People flocked to join the National Trust. Individual membership went from 30,000 in 1970 to 160,000 in 1980. Major corporations such as Alcoa, American Iron and Steel, CBS, Chemical Bank, Exxon, Ford, IBM, Time, and Xerox signed on as National Trust Corporate Associates—by 1979, over one hundred in all.[85]

The coffers and political clout of the National Trust swelled accordingly. Its staff went from forty-seven to over two hundred, and it provided services to all the members of its now wildly contradictory constituency—grants to local neighborhood conservationists and poor tenants threatened with displacement, educational programs and conferences for preservation professionals, vocational training for restorationist technicians, legal information to developers, private owners, towns, and corporations. The trust dealt with its internal contradictions by fudging or ignoring them. And why not? It worked. The barbarians had been beaten.[86]

Backlash

In the eighties, the barbarians struck back.

Proctor & Gamble landed one of the earliest blows. In 1980 the company was infuriated at the impending involuntary designation of its corporate headquarters as an historic landmark. Aware that—given the Penn Central decision—once the designation was announced its hands would be tied, it muscled its way onto the floor of Congress. Representative Joseph McDade (R-Pa.) attached to pending legislation an amendment requiring an owner's consent before industrial facilities could be put on the National Register. National Trust lobbyists, hitherto so successful, found to their dismay that they were utterly unable to roll back this "ominous" provision. Indeed, Congress went on to institute owner-consent provisions for all register designations and repealed the disincentives provision of the 1976 Tax Act.[87]

At the same time, the judicial victories came under attack. The Supreme Court had stated explicitly in the Penn Central decision that the question of what "historic" meant would remain subject to judicial review. In August 1980 a federal judge in Virginia reversed the Interior Department's 1974 designation of fourteen thousand acres in the state as a rural "national historic district"; the court even barred the government from accepting gifts from Virginia landowners of "scenic easements" by which they bound themselves not to alter the architecture or landscape. The court thus upheld a strip mine developer (behind whom lay W. R. Grace and Company, the chemical conglomerate) who argued that the "historic" designation was improper. As a local preservationist pointed out, "this decision, if it stands, will bastardize retroactively every historic landmark designation in the country. Not one of them is now safe from challenge."[88]

Another dramatic indication of the shifting temper of the times came on 4 December 1981 when Detroit police removed armed members of the Poletown Neighborhood Council from the Church of the Immaculate Conception, ending four years of resistance by community residents in the courts and the streets to the planned demolition of their homes. General Motors had agreed to build a plant that would provide six thousand desperately needed jobs within Detroit city limits if the city would seize and raze 450 acres of a mixed Polish and black working-class neighborhood. The residents proposed alternatives that would allow factory and community to coexist, but GM was not interested. The unions, city administration, and courts backed the corporation. Demolition proceeded, leveling 1,500 homes, 150 businesses, 16 churches, and a hospital.[89]

General Motor's heavyfooted intervention signaled a reversal of attitudes. The takeover was as much a macho attempt to reassert corporate prerogatives as it was motivated by a simple search for profitability in hard times. Most of the cleared land was to be used for parking lots; vertical parking could have avoided much demolition. GM's decision not to swerve or compromise recalled Robert Moses' hauteur. Pro-GM spokespeople denounced preservationist attempts to save Poletown. Detroit's director of planning insisted that a "community whose heyday has passed may glory in the past. . . . But a group attempting to better its condition needs to focus on the future." She undoubtedly found significant support in the black community when she argued that Detroit could not afford to "dwell excessively on the memories of its former white community or else it will not give living expression to . . . its present population, which is over 50 percent black."[90]

These straws in the wind accurately forecast the coming of the Reagan administration hurricane. The right wing considered historic preservation—like rent control, environmental protection, occupational health and safety regulation, and laws against usury—an intolerable constraint on private accumulation. Moreover preservation, to these throwbacks to the old accumulative order, was a cultural and political danger. No fools, they had sniffed out the antimarket logic in the emerging body of administrative rules and legal decisions. Now creative destruction's time had come round again, and they set out enthusiastically to reverse every gain the movement had made since 1966.

For openers, Interior Secretary James Watt called for "zerobudgeting" the entire historic preservation program: He asked Congress to eliminate all funding for the National Trust and the state historic preservation organizations. Other Reaganites fanned out to undermine the preservationists' position in the bureaucracy. Their agenda, as summed up in the January 1984 report of the Grace Commission (headed by the same Peter Grace involved in the lawsuit discussed above) was to wipe out the Advisory Council's ability to halt other federal agencies from destroying historic properties; to repeal the section of the Highway Act reining in the Department of Transportation; to remove constraints on the Interior Department's ability to undertake strip mining; to end restrictions on what could be done with Community Development Block Grant (CDBG) funds. The administration also proposed establishing enterprise zones in U.S. cities (modeled on Hong Kong and Taiwanese practices) which would suspend all controls on entrepreneurial freedom of action: Condo-men would be free to bulldoze as they pleased.[91]

On the other hand, Reagan's 1981 tax laws actually enhanced benefits for preservation. The law provided a 25 percent investment tax credit for approved rehabilitation of certified historic structures: Renovators could subtract one of every four dollars spent on preservation work directly from their federal income taxes. Watt explained that the Trust's "historic mission of working with the private sector is logical and appropriate to this administration's philosophy." What he meant was that Reaganism would dismantle any constraints on capital, but had no objection to providing handouts to banks, developers, landlords, and construction firms. If economic forces in the eighties favored preservation over bulldozing, that was fine with Watt.[92]

Preservation and Development

The response of the preservation movement to the Reagan offensive was to scurry toward its real estate right and away from its populist left. Preservationists largely abandoned any attempts to build a mass base, wrote off displacees, and hitched their wagon to their traditional worst enemies. The National Trust, in particular, cast its lot with capital. It hired as its new president, Michael Ainslie, a businessman in management, marketing, and real estate development, who announced his intention to adopt "more financial-and real estate-oriented approaches." The coordinator of Preservation Action, Nellie Longsworth, enthused that "rehabilitation and preservation have finally made it into a larger arena and we can take pride in the results that are produced by private investment." There were side offerings to the displaced—the Inner City Ventures Fund made limited funds available to non-profit neighborhood self-help groups to acquire housing in historic districts for low income and minority residents—but concern over displacement and the neighborhoods dwindled dramatically. Environmentalism and ecology were out, entrepreneurialism was in. The editor of the National Trust's magazine, *Historic Preservation,* laid it on the bottom line: "Making a profit makes preservation possible. . . . If an entrepreneur doesn't have a fighting chance to end up with a profit, it's going to be good-bye old building."[93]

On the face of things, tacking to the right worked brilliantly. Appeals to Congress for support on grounds that preservation made money for developers and provided jobs paid off. Here was a constituency that had the clout to withstand the neo-conservative offensive. In every year of Reagan's first administration, Congress overrode zerobudgeting and reinstated preservation funding, albeit with serious cuts. The enterprise zone proposal passed the Senate three times, but was thrice beaten back by the House, and dropped in the 1984 tax proposals. And Congress overruled a direct attempt to slash Advisory Council authority. The preservation position did erode—through countless administrative and budgetary decisions—but far less than Reagan and Watt had intended.

And the strategy saved buildings. Major real estate syndicators who might have torn down old structures now rushed to certify them as "historic," thus qualifying for the tax breaks of the 1981 act. As one certification official noted, "We're seeing a new type of clientele—bankers, lawyers, developers. . . ." In 1980, $346 million of rehabilitation projects had been approved for tax breaks; by 1983, $2.2 billion worth had passed historic muster. By the end of fiscal 1984, a total of $7.8 billion had gone into 9,000 historic rehab projects which had generated 310,000 jobs, $5.5 billion in new earnings, and $19.5 billion in increased retail sales. Historic preservation had become big business and big business could hold Reaganism at bay.[94]

But the preservation community, seemingly triumphant, was in fact in an extremely dangerous position, having grabbed a wolf-in-sheep's-clothing by the tail. Their strategy ignored the fact that capital had no commitment to preservation other than as a convenient cover for quick returns in hard times. "Historic preservation" was for them a device to transfer state benefits to private developers and give the handouts a "conservative" patina. As Paul Goldberger noted, "developers now routinely use preservation rhetoric for their own ends without adopting its values, and their ends are often antithetical to the preservationists."[95]

One of the many consequences of the rightward tilt was a continuing decline in the traditional preservationist concern with authentic symbolic meanings. Seldom, now, did the adaptively reused artifacts illuminate the roots of the present, set in motion mythic reverberations, or expand contemporary historical consciousness. Although the DAR and the Rockefellers had distorted the past, at least they had been concerned with meanings; the contemporary crowd was into surfaces, styles, and the historic as stage setting.

A droll example of this was the emergence of facadism (also known as facadectomy and facadomy). In this form of Potemkin preservation, developers tore down an old building but preserved its streetfront wall. This they affixed, like a historic veneer, to a high rise condo or hotel. It was, someone said, like preserving polar bears in the form of rugs. The preservation community began to split over this burlesque—interestingly, along the lines of its original formation. In Charleston, where it all started, UDAG money helped a developer plop an office complex (including a 430 room hotel, a 500 car garage, and 64,000 feet of retail space) right in the heart of the 1931 historic district. This was considered acceptable to the Historic Charleston Foundation (descendants of the business joiners) because it was fronted by the preserved facade of the row of old buildings it replaced. But the twenty-seven-hundred-member Preservation Society, with its roots in the 1920s movement, denounced this as an outrage, and sued—unsuccessfully—to halt it.[96]

More alarmingly, it soon appeared that while the Reaganites would assist preservation projects if profitable, they had no compunction whatever about reverting to old-style bulldozing when that was the path to profitability. In 1981, for instance, UDAG gave $21.5 million to build a hotel in New York City's Times Square (and the city added another $100 million in tax abatements). Standing in the way were four old Broadway theaters; one was on the National Register, another was eligible. Watt muscled the Advisory Council into approving their demolition.[97]

Worse was to come. In November 1984, to the preservation strategists' shock and dismay, Reagan's Treasury Department issued a tax "simplification" plan that called for the total repeal of tax incentives for historic rehabilitation. The move was not specifically aimed at the preservationists. Rather, Pentagon voraciousness dictated massive cutbacks in domestic spending, and neo-conservatives wanted to dismantle a host of tax-code-supported social policies. Some in the administration even regretted the likely impact on a program that stimulated private investment. But sacrifices were in order and repeal seemed likely to pass in some form or other. Repeal would send a wrecking ball swinging toward a now brittle preservation edifice, made susceptible to shattering due to an excessive dependence on tax policy and fair-weather friends.

Where Next?

Preservationists may survive this current assault, but what of the future? In considerable measure that depends on larger trends in the economy. If interest rates drop, oil prices come down, and the economy recovers, capitalists will drop their new found preservation sentiments in a flash. Facadism, Reaganism, and the Poletown putch are only indicators of a larger truth: Preservation's allies in the big business world have no principled concern for preservation. Banks and development corporations have only the thinnest sense of being members of communities whose histories merit recalling. They see their country not as a society, but an economy—a grid of opportunities—and their actions are dictated by the probabilities of profit. In an economic revival, preservationists, deserted by the right, would find few allies on the left. Indeed, the movement's inability or unwillingness to confront displacement and its lack of ties to the labor movement leave it wide open to attack by a revitalized growth coalition that appeals for black and working-class support in the name of housing and job development against "limousine liberal" preservationists.

It is also possible that the economy will not recover, but continue to lurch in and out of recessions. In the presence of continuing high interest rates, and the absence of reindustrialization or a housing boom, real estate and corporate capital will probably continue to accept historic preservation as the best bargain available. But if the current approach to preservation is maintained, it will simply accelerate the paired processes of gentrification and displacement. In that event, older American cities will proceed down the European road. In the last generation, almost every major city in Europe, and hundreds of smaller ones, has had its historic center preserved and its social relations transformed by a new urban enclosure movement. One by one, working-class areas have been invaded by the new gentry and had their former inhabitants resettled in high rises on the city outskirts. Now only the wealthy and the corporations can afford to reside in the historic centers of Paris, Rome, or Amsterdam.[98]

Unless something is done, U.S. cities will go the same route. Displacement is the order of the day all over the country. The process is startlingly clear in New York City where the future may well see a gentry invasion of Harlem. Manhattan may become a preserve for corporate offices, small shoppes, theaters, adaptively reused historic markets (South Street Seaport is a harbinger), hotels, and gentry housing—with blacks, Hispanics and poor whites packed off to the periphery. In a still grimmer vision, American cities will be heavily patrolled and well-armed "historic" ghettos, defending themselves against beggars, muggers, and squatters; the past itself will have become a hated emblem of class domination.[99]

But is there an alternative? Perhaps, but it will require a massive reversal of direction by the organized preservation community. Recall its trajectory to date. For its first century, preservationism remained an upper-class movement intent on blocking free market demolition of old buildings, either through preemptive purchase or state intervention. The genteel and the wealthy were motivated partly by aesthetic concerns and partly by a desire to enhance their own legitimacy through an association with hallowed symbolic artifacts. Between the 1940s and early 1960s, to gain additional support in their losing battle with developers, they allied with middle-class professionals and small businesses who were also threatened by the march of Progress. This required a shift in strategy—from parenthesizing to adaptive reuse. At the time this seemed a reasonable compromise, indeed a progressive step forward. Huxtable was convinced that putting "a new building in the old shell" was a "modern solution that still manages to evoke the past." This belief was sustainable for a time, but in retrospect, we can see that adaptive reuse, by pulling back from the older antimarket critique, facilitated the process of gentrification. There was nothing inherently wrong with adaptive use except that in practice it meant that only those with market power got to use and enjoy old buildings.[100]

In the late sixties and early seventies the movement expanded again. It increased its base in middle-class gentry neighborhoods, worked with businesspersons attracted by the profitability of the past, and also reached out to working-class neighborhood conservationists and anticorporate environmentalists. The tensions between history as heritage and history as commodity grew sharper, but the overarching imperative of combating the growth coalition kept the contradictory coalition together.

In the early eighties, with growth proponents weakened by recession and a reactionary administration in power, the temptation was understandably great to shift to a reliance on preservation through the market, suitably guided by tax policy. Buildings and communities were saved if they had pecuniary possibilities, gentrification's impact on the poor was benignly overlooked, and the movement's already attenuated concern with historic meaning was weakened to the vanishing point. After a century of sensitivity to the menace of an unrestricted marketplace, the preservationist leadership now convinced itself that the pursuit of profit could be harnessed to serve social needs.[101]

This was, I believe, a reversible error. Historic preservation can survive without corporate backing, but only if it rebuilds its shrunken political base. The history of the movement suggests that preservationists' natural (if not always comfortable) allies are environmentalists, tenants organizations, civil rights groups, neighborhood conservationists, unions, public housing activists, and others working for large-scale social change. For historic preservation, like these others, is a reform movement: It goes against the grain of the dominant culture.

To strike up such a connection, however, would require preservationists to be more aware of and more committed to overcoming the negative effects of the preservation process. Preservationists might establish their sensitivity to the concerns of potential allies by admitting that historic continuity, while an important human need, must be balanced against other human needs, such as that of the present generation for housing. To gain the support of potential colleagues, preservationists might back policies that guaranteed affordable housing for all citizens, even if such policies alienated bankers, developers, and some of the gentry, such as one irate couple who wrote recently: "Housing of the poor never was and should not be an objective of the preservation movement. If we are not housing the poor adequately, our social programs are to blame, not the preservationist, and definitely not those who have made a personal commitment to rescuing the past from obliteration." This may be true, but if the movement is to garner widespread support it will have to demonstrate its commitment to changing those blameworthy social programs.[102]

It might do this by making historic preservation part of an overall land-use package that included rent subsidies, nonmarket allocation of credit (replacing private mortgages with direct government grants and low interest loans), support for nonprofit community-based developers and neighborhood organizers, rehabilitation programs for current tenants with controlled rents or full relocation, city investments in vacant or blighted buildings, tax reassessments, and the abolition of tax shelters for speculators. The experience of popular coalitions in Hartford, Cleveland, Berkeley, and Santa Monica during the seventies suggests local taxing mechanisms and regulations can successfully control developers, bankers, realtors, and speculators in the short run. But ultimately the goal might have to be the abandonment of the current government-subsidized "free market" housing system and its replacement with a system that guarantees decent housing to all citizens as a social right.

Preservationists have argued that we must treat city centers like valuable artifacts. But without addressing the pressures that make it difficult or impossible to do so, the chances of success are not high. I am suggesting that if we enhance popular control over the production and distribution of goods, including housing, if we provide shelter for those who need it and make resources available to those who want to fix up their own neighborhoods, people would likely be more than willing to honor collective memories. Only when citizens are not confronted with the choice of a preserved past or a squalid present can preservationism have a secure future.[103]

In a revived coalition, it could be the special role of architects, historians, Park Service professionals,local history amateurs, neighborhood activists and historic house enthusiasts, to forge a preservationism that negates the ahistorical, uncritical, and self-centered sensibility of much contemporary culture; that saves the material remains of the past in a way that illuminates the course of American history; that uses historic artifacts to provide more than just sterile ambience and a sense of cozy continuity; that severs the connection between preservation and class privilege, thus avoiding the looming fate of the American city; and raises for popular consideration the possibility that ultimately the only way to prevent the private appropriation, perversion, and destruction of our common heritage is to overhaul the social system that threatens it.[104]

Notes

This essay first appeared in *Presenting the Past*, edited by Susan Porter Benson, Steve Brier and Roy Rosenzweig (Philadelphia: Temple University Press, 1986). I have left it intact, and addressed developments of the succeeding decade in the next chapter, "Preservation Revisited."

1. David Lowenthal, "The Place of the Past in the American Landscape," *Geographies of the Mind: Essays in Historical Geosophy*, ed. David Lowenthal and Martyn J. Bowden (New York, 1976), 89–117; Lowenthal, "The American Way of History," *Columbia University Forum* 9, no. 3 (summer 1966).
2. On historicist architectural allusions see Paul Goldberger, *The Skyscraper* (New York, 1981), 39, 44, 53.
3. Cadwallader Colden, *Memoir, at the Celebration of the Completion of the New York Canals*, cited in Lowenthal, "The Place of the Past," 93.
4. On the Brahmins, see "Visiting the Past" in this volume; and Barbara Miller Solomon, *Ancestors and Immigrants: A Changing New England Tradition* (New York, 1956).

   For a comparison to the emergence of a bourgeois preservation lobby in England, see Michael Bommes and Patrick Wright, " 'Charms of residence': the Public and the Past," *Making Histories: Studies in History Writing and Politics*, ed. Richard Johnson et al., (Minneapolis, 1982), 273–5.
5. Thomas F. King, Patricia Parker Hickman, and Gary Berg, *Anthropology in Historic Preservation: Caring for Culture's Clutter* (New York, 1977), 10–19.
6. King, Hickman, and Berg, *Anthropology in Historic Preservation*, 10–19; Oscar Gray, "The Response of Federal Legislation to Historic Preservation, *Law and Contemporary Problems* 36, no. 3 (summer 1971), 312; Ronald F. Lee, *The Antiquities Act of 1906* (Washington, 1970).
7. Charles B. Hosmer Jr., *Presence of the Past: A History of the Preservation Movement in the United States Before Williamsburg* (New York, 1965), 306–12; Charles B. Hosmer Jr., *Preservation Comes of Age: From Williamsburg to the National Trust, 1926–1949* (Charlottesville, 1981), 232–34; Patrick Gerster and Nicholas Cords, eds., *Myth and Southern History* (Chicago, 1974).
8. Hosmer, *Preservation Comes of Age*, 234–6; Edward D. Campbell, *The Celluloid South: Hollywood and the Southern Myth* (Knoxville, 1981).
9. Nathan Weinberg, *Preservation in American Towns and Cities* (Boulder, Colo., 1979), 39; Hosmer, *Preservation Comes of Age*, 232–74.
10. M. Christine Boyer, *Dreaming the Rational City: The Myth of American City Planning* (Cambridge, Mass., 1983).
11. Hosmer, *Preservation Comes of Age*, 290–306; Jacob H. Morrison, *Historic Preservation Law* (Washington, 1965), 12, 157–58.

    In San Antonio, a 1921 flood led consulting engineers from Boston to propose paving over the San Antonio River. In response, local affluent and well-connected women founded the San Antonio Conservation Society, and in 1924 convinced the city the river was an asset (with the aid of a puppet show about preservation as a "goose that laid golden eggs"): John Pastier, "After the Alamo," *Historic Preservation*, 35, no. 6 (May–June, 1983), 40–7.

12. On this movement, see "Visiting the Past," in this volume, 9–15.
13. On professionals, see Magali Sarfatti Larson, *The Rise of Professionalism* (Berkeley 1977); Boyer, *Dreaming the Rational City*; Pat Walker, ed., *Between Labor and Capital* (Boston, 1979).
14. Boyer, *Dreaming the Rational City*, 46–56.
15. King, Hickman, and Berg, *Anthropology*, 22–4; Wolf Von Eckardt, "Federal Follies: The Mismanaging of Historic Preservation," *Historic Preservation* [hereinafter cited as *HP*] (January–February 1980), 2; Weinberg, *Preservation* 24; Hosmer, *Preservation Comes of Age*, 509–62.
16. On the 1935 act: King, Hickman, and Berg, *Anthropology*, 23, 202–4; Ronald F. Lee, "The Preservation of Historic and Architectural Monuments in the United States," *National Council for Historic Sites and Buildings Newsletter* 1, no. 4 (December 1949), 2; Hosmer, *Preservation Comes of Age*, 562–76. On Branch of History: *ibid.*, 580–99.
17. Hosmer, *Preservation Comes of Age*, 626–49.
18. For European parallels, see Eric Hobsbawm and Terence Ranger, eds., *The Invention of Tradition* (Cambridge, England, 1983).
19. On 1920s "modernist" tendencies of capitalist development, see Susan Buck-Morss, "Benjamin's Passagen-Werk: Redeeming Mass Culture for the Revolution," *New German Critique* 29 (fall 1984), 211–40; Richard Wightman Fox and T.J. Jackson Lears, eds., *The Culture of Consumption* (New York, 1983).
20. See the prescient talk by Ronald F. Lee, chief historian of the National Park Service, "The Effect of Postwar Conditions on the Preservation of Historic Sites and Buildings," cited in Hosmer, *Preservation Comes of Age*, 818.
21. On growth coalition: John H. Mollenkopf, "The Postwar Politics of Urban Development," *Marxism and the Metropolis*, ed. William K. Tabb and Larry Sawyers (New York, 1978), 117–51; Alan Wolfe, *America's Impasse: The Rise and Fall of the Politics of Growth* (New York, 1981), 83, 96. On popularity of suburbanization see Mark I. Gelfand, *A Nation of Cities: The Federal Government and Urban America, 1933–1965* (New York, 1975), 149–50, 155, 217–18, 350–1.
22. Martin Anderson, *The Federal Bulldozer: A Critical Analysis of Urban Renewal, 1949–1962* (Cambridge, Massachusetts, 1964), 54, 65; Charles Abrams, *The City is the Frontier* (New York, 1965), 133; Wolfe, *America's Impasse*, 94–96; Weinberg, *Preservation*, 30. On the prestige of the new, the impact of planned obsolescence on popular taste, and general reflections on the emergence of a facsimile culture, see James Marston Fitch, *Historic Preservation: Curatorial Management of the Built World* (New York, 1982).

23. See Hosmer, *Preservation Comes of Age*, 809–65; David Finley, *History of the National Trust for Historic Preservation, 1947–63* (Washington, D.C., 1965). For differences over the line such propagandizing should take, see NCHSB *Quarterly Report*, 1, no. 1 (March 1949), 1–6.
24. Elizabeth D. Mulloy, *The History of the National Trust for Historic Preservation, 1963–1973* (Washington, D.C., 1976), 11–13, 26–27. (The council stayed in existence until 1953 when it merged with the trust.)
25. To Ronald F. Lee, chief historian of the National Park Service and secretary of the National Council, "professionalization" meant getting away from the kinds of "local lore and legendary anecdotes purveyed by commercial guides." Interpretation, he thought, should be done "by trained historians and museum curators in a manner commensurate with the dignity and significance of the nation's historical heritage." [Lee, "Preservation," 8–9]. In this period Colonial Williamsburg joined the National Park Service and the American University to put on seminars in the preservation and interpretation of historic sites and buildings; Cooperstown inaugurated a similar seminar in American history and culture. [Lee, "Preservation," 7–8].
26. Additional historic zoning districts were created in this period. On Georgetown's construction by local bankers, lawyers, architects, and diplomats interested not in saving homesteads but investment in planned redevelopment, see NCHSB *Quarterly Report*, 2 (1950), 91; Edward F. Gerber, "Historic Georgetown, Inc.: The Economics Involved in Preservation," *Urban Land* 34, no. 7 (July–August 1975), 14–26. Society Hill, Capital Hill, and Historic Annapolis soon followed: Mulloy, *National Trust*, 12; Gelfand, *Nation of Cities*, 185.
27. On Jacobs: Weinberg, *Preservation*, 30; Abrams, *The City is the Frontier*. Mollenkopf notes there were major community protests in the 1960s in Boston, Cambridge, and San Francisco: "Postwar Politics of Urban Development," 141.
28. Quotation is from Joyce Brothers, in *HP* 17, no. 3 (May–June 1965), 113–14. On this critical group generally, a good introduction is Peirce F. Lewis, "The Future of the Past: Our Clouded Vision of Historic Preservation," *Pioneer America* 7, no. 2 (July 1975), 1–20. See also Jane Jacobs, *The Death and Life of Great American Cities* (New York, 1961); Herbert Gans, *The Urban Villagers* (New York, 1962); Ada Louise Huxtable *Will They Ever Finish Bruckner Boulevard?* (New York, 1970).
29. Mulloy, *National Trust*, xi.
30. Alan Wolfe (*America's Impasse*) sees the poor taking to the streets starting in 1964, in a rage at urban renewal, highway construction, and the rise of the medical industrial complex. Mollenkopf notes that virtually all riot areas were sites of major renewal efforts, notably in Newark. "Postwar Politics," 142–3. See also Gelfand, *Nation of Cities*, 215; Bernard J. Frieden and Marshall Kaplan, *The Politics of Neglect: Urban Aid from Model Cities to Revenue Sharing* (Cambridge, Mass., 1975), 33.
31. Hosmer, *Presence of the Past*, 262, 268, 293; Laurence Vail Coleman,

Historic House Museums (Washington, 1933), 23; Warren James Belasco, *Americans on the Road: From Autocamp to Motel, 1910–1945* (Cambridge, Mass., 1979).

32. Tony P. Wren, "The Tourist Industry and Promotional Publications," *HP* 16, no. 3 (1964), 111–13; William T. Alderson and Shirley Payne Low, *Interpretation of Historic Sites* (Nashville, 1976), 22.

33. New York State: Morrison, *Preservation Law*, 54. For 1964 figures see Wren, "Tourist Industry," 112. Daniels: Jonathan Daniels, *Life is a Local Story* (Nashville, Tennessee, 1964), quoted in Wren, "Tourist Industry," 111; Walter Muir Whitehill, *Independent Historical Societies* (Boston, 1962), 461.
34. Wren, "Tourist Industry," 113–14. This was a widespread phenomenon. For discussions of Santa Barbara, Annapolis, Newport, Natchez, and a variety of western towns, see Whitehill, *Independent Historical Societies*, 551 and his chapter on "Mammon and Monuments"; "Annapolis," *American Preservation* [hereafter cited as *AP*] 1, no. 1 (October–November 1977), 27; Hosmer, *Preservation Comes of Age*, 359, 371.
35. On Savannah see Leopold Adler II, "Preservation as Profitable Real Estate in Savannah," in National Trust for Historic Preservation, *Economic Benefits of Preserving Old Buildings*, (Washington, D.C., 1975), 143–7; see also *AP* 2, no. 3 (February–March 1979), 11–24; Weinberg, *Preservation*, 95–107.

    San Antonio businessowners also saw the light. About to embark on a new round of development, they changed course and spent hundreds of thousands to landscape parkways and restore Spanish missions. As a spokesman reported, San Antonio was "beginning to recognize that to destroy those things that set it apart from other cities is to kill the goose that laid the golden egg." On San Antonio: Wren, "Tourist Industry," 114.

    To these big city converts were added hosts of small town Main Street shopkeepers, driven to the wall by competition from the highway linked malls: Anderson, *Federal Bulldozer*, 68; Gelfand, *Nation of Cities*, 195, 338–9, 361.
36. Ada Louise Huxtable, "Lively Original Versus Dead Copy," *New York Times* (9 May 1965), reprinted in Huxtable, *Bruckner Boulevard*, 211–12. See also Lowenthal, "American Way of History," 27.
37. Huxtable, *Kicked a Building Lately?* (New York, 1976), 234.
38. Sidney Hyman, "Empire for Liberty," *With Heritage So Rich*, ed. Albert Rains et al. (New York, 1966), 1; Whitehill, "The Right of Cities to be Beautiful," in Rains, *Heritage*, 55; Gelfand, *Nation of Cities*, 187, 192, 318.
39. John Greenya, "The Quiet Power of Gordon Gray," *Historic Preservation* 35, no. 5 (September–October 1983), 26–9.
40. The text of the act can be found in King, Hickman, and Berg, *Anthropology*, 205. See also Mulloy, *National Trust*, 68–85; Robert R. Garvey and Terry Brust Morton, *The U.S. Government in Historic Preservation:*

A *Brief History of the 1966 Historic Preservation Act and Others* (Washington, 1975).

41. Heywood T. Sanders, "Urban Renewal and the Revitalized City: A Reconsideration of Recent History," *Urban Revitalization*, ed. Donald B. Rosenthal (Sage, 1980), 103–26; Gelfand, *Nation of Cities*, 361–67, 374; Frieden and Kaplan, *Politics of Neglect*, 33–4.
42. Wolfe, *America's Impasse*, 103–5; Gelfand, *Nation of Cities*, 361, 374.
43. Bernard J. Frieden and Arthur P. Solomon, *The Nation's Housing: 1975–1985* (Cambridge, Mass. 1977); Frieden and Kaplan, *Politics of Neglect*, 267; Raymond A. Rosenfeld, "Who Benefits and Who Decides: The Uses of Community Development Block Grants" in Rosenthal, *Urban Revitalization*, 211–35; John Ross, "Impacts of Urban Aid," in Rosenthal, *Urban Revitalization;* Advisory Committee on Historic Preservation, *Report to the President and Congress* (1980), 20–22; Phyllis Myers, "Urban Enterprise Zones: UDAG Revisited? " *HP* 33, no. 6 (12 November 1981).
44. Phillip L. Clay, *Neighborhood Renewal: Middle-Class Resettlement and Incumbent Upgrading in American Neighborhoods* (Lexington, Mass., 1979), 3–15, 20; Mollenkopf, "Postwar Politics," 128; James Henry Johnson Jr., *Incumbent Upgrading and Gentrification in the Inner City: A Case Study of Neighborhood Revitalization Activities in Eastown, Grand Rapids*. Ph. D. dissertation (Michigan State University, 1980), 23.
45. Johnson, "Incumbent Upgrading," 24. For my speculations about how the popularity of the old was generated by the sterility of the new, see Wallace, "Visiting the Past," in this volume 25–26.
46. Chester Hartman, Dennis Keating, and Richard LeGates, *Displacement: How to Fight It* (Berkeley, Cal., 1982), 1–25.
47. Advisory Council on Historic Preservation, *Report to the President and the Congress of the United States (1979)* (Washington, D.C., 1980) [hereinafter cited as ACHP, *Report for 1979*], 1–3. In 1979, a redeveloper sued the Historic Alexandria Foundation (Virginia) for refusing to give him historical plaques for his houses because real estate agents told him they added ten thousand dollars to each property. *Ibid.*
48. Amy Singer, "When Worlds Collide," *HP* 36, no. 4 (August 1984), 39; Jason Berry, "The 'Upgrading' of New Orleans," *The Nation* (23 September 1978), 271. For similar gentry imperialism in East Capital Hill, see Rohrbach, "Poignant Dilemma," 4–7; in Savannah, "Savannah," *AP* 2, no. 3 (February–March 1979), 22.
49. Johnson, *HP* 32, no. 6, 33; ACHP *Report for 1982*, 39. By 1981 New York City's Landmarks Preservation Commission had designated forty-one historic districts. Five were in Harlem, but most roped off gentry quarters like Gramercy Park, Brooklyn Heights, Greenwich Village, and the Upper East Side. The Commission regulated 15,000 buildings, 2 percent of city's housing stock. *New York Times* (20 September 1981), 56.
50. Myers and Binder, *Neighborhood Conservation; New York Times* (20

September 1981), 56; *HP* 1, no. 3 (February–March 1978), 71.

51. Lewis, "Future of the Past," 18.
52. America the Beautiful Fund, *Old Glory: A Pictorial Report on the Grass Roots History Movement and the First Hometown History Primer* (New York, 1973), 37–9. This book details dozens of other local stories, but this remains another area badly in need of further research. Episodes worth exploring include New Haven's Wooster Square, Baltimore's Fells Point, and New York's SOHO. On developer wariness see National Trust, *Economic Benefits*, 76.
53. On the National Peoples Action see *AP* 1, no. 1 (October–November 1977), 26. A study by the New World Foundation found two thousand neighborhood self-help groups active; *AP* (May–June 1980), 7–8. On the National Commission on Neighborhoods see *AP* (April–May 1978), 4–5 and "James Barry, "The National Commission on Neighborhoods: The Politics of Urban Revitalization," *Urban Revitalization*, 165–87. On the fund see *AP* (August–September 1978), 5. On antiredlining see Richard Hula, "Housing, Lending Institutions and Public Policy," *Urban Revitalization*, 77–99; William K. Tabb, *The Long Default: New York City and the Urban Fiscal Crisis* (New York, 1982), 96–97.
54. David Morris and Karl Hess, *Neighborhood Power: The New Localism* (Beacon 1975); Phyllis Myers and Gordon Binder, *Neighborhood Conservation: Lessons from Three Cities* (Washington Conservation Foundation, 1977). Restrictive covenants had been one of the oldest devices for "preserving" property values; it had always been considered acceptable to block the free market on racist grounds.
55. On the AIA statement: Lachlan F. Blair and John A. Quinn, eds., *Historic Preservation: Setting, Legislation, and Techniques* (Urbana, Illinois, 1977), 13. On the traditional movement's reaching out to neighborhoods: Advisory Council on Historic Preservation, *The National Historic Preservation Program Today* (Washington, D.C., 1976), 3. In 1977 James Biddle, president of the National Trust, called neighborhood conservation a major issue for preservationists. *AP* 1, no. 2 (February–March 1978), 3, 71; *AP* 2, no. 1 (October–November 1978), 76–7; *New York Times* (March 2, 1980), viii, 1, no. 1; Arthur P. Ziegler Jr., *Historic Preservation in Inner City Areas: A Manual of Practice* (Pittsburgh, 1971), 8, 17–18; Peter Thomas Rohrback, "The Poignant Dilemma of Spontaneous Restoration," *HP* 22, no. 4 (October–December 1970), 4–10; *Wall Street Journal* (6 February 1961); "Savannah," *AP* 2, no. 3 (February–March 1979), 22; Paul J. Goldberger, "The Dangers in Preservation Success," National Trust, *Economic Benefits*, 159–60.
56. Rohrback, "Poignant Dilemma," 7.
57. Rohrbach, "Poignant Dilemma," 7; Joe Louis Mattox, "Ghetto or Gold Mine—Hold On to that Old House," *AP* 1, no. 3 (February–March 1978), 3; *AP* 1, no. 3 (February–March 1978), 71.
58. Weinberg, *Preservation*, 110; Biliana Cicin-Sain, "The Costs and Bene-

fits of Neighborhood Revitalization," in *Urban Revitalization;* Andrea Kirsten Mullen, "Preservation in the Black Community: A Growing Commitment," *HP* 34, no. 1 (January–February 1982), 39–43; "Weeksville Rediscovered and Restored," *Metropolis: The Architecture and Design Magazine of New York* (July/August 1984).

59. Raymond P. Rhinehart, "Preservation's Best Interests," *Preservation News* 16, no. 10 (October 1976), 5; Andrea Kirsten Mullen, "A Black Preservationist Speaks Out," *HP* 35, no. 6 (November–December 1983), 12–13.
60. Ziegler, *Historic Preservation,* v. On the black community's refusal to let whites in, and the consequent capital boycott, see Weinberg, *Preservation,* 109–10.
61. "Savannah Landmark: A New Type of Landlord," *AP* 2, no. 3 (February–March 1979), 16–17; George McMillan, "Staying Home in Savannah," *HP* 32, no. 3 (March–April 1980); Adler, "Preservation as Profitable Real Estate," 143–7, 190; Michael D. Newsom, "Blacks and Historic Preservation," *Law and Contemporary Problems* 36 (1971), 423–31.
62. *AP* (May–June 1980), 3; Hartman, *Displacement,* 164.
63. ACHP, *Report for 1980,* 9; Frank Stella, *New Profits from Old Buildings* (New York, 1979), 2. Preservation journals for mass audiences were also launched in this period: ACHP, *Report for 1980,* 10.
64. Gordon Gray, Trust President, quipped: "I only regret that I have but one staff to give to my country.": *AP* 2, no. 1 (October–November 1978), 50. On new legislation, see King, Hickman, and Berg, *Anthropology,* 41–63; Mulloy, *National Trust,* 94–108.
65. *A Report by the US Historic Preservation Team of the US-USSR Joint Working Group on the Enhancement of the Urban Environment, May 25–June 14, 1974* (Washington, DC, 1975), 8–15; ACHP, *National Historic Preservation,* 59–62, 79–97. On lobbyists and PA see *HP* 34, no. 1; Jane Holtz Kay, "The National Trust," *AP*, 2, no. 1 (October–November 1978), 74; *AP,* 1, no. 1 (October–November 1977), 8; *Preservation Action Alert* [hereafter cited as *PAA*] 1, no. 1 (January 1976), 1; Steve Weinberg, "Lobbying Congress . . . The Inside Story," *Historic Preservation* 34, no. 1 (January–February 1982), 17–18. The Advisory Council claimed that "the most vital energy resource for this country is its sense of purpose. That sense of purpose, of national identity and destiny, is nourished by symbols from our past, reminders of our unique experiences and goals." ACHP, *National Historic Preservation,* 1. See also Mulloy, *National Trust,* xv.
66. Nellie L. Longsworth, "After 200 Years—What?" *Historic Preservation: Setting, Legislation and Techniques,* ed. Lachlan F. Blair and John A. Quinn, (Urbana, Illinois, 1977). The expanded council included all cabinet members except Labor. 1980 Amendments required federal agencies to minimize harm to landmarks to the "maximum extent possible.": ACHP, *Report for 1982.*

Preserving the Past: Historic Preservation in the United States

67. On Tax Act, see Longsworth, "After 200 Years," 4; *Tax Incentives for Historic Preservation*, ed. Gregory E. Andrews (Washington, 1980); *PAA* 1, no. 4 (October 1976), 3.
68. Frank B. Gilbert, "Assessing the Grand Central Decision," *HP* 32, no. 5 (September–October 1980), 39; England: Graham Ashworth, "Contemporary Developments in British Preservation Law and Practice," *Law and Contemporary Problems*, 36, no. 3 (summer 1971), 348–61.
69. Morrison, *Preservation Law*, 20–1.
70. Morrison, *Preservation Law*, ix; Joseph L. Sax, "Takings, Private Property and Public Rights," *Yale Law Journal* 81 (1971), 149–86; Malcolm Baldwin, "Historic Preservation in the Context of Environmental Law: Mutual Interest in Amenity," *Law and Contemporary Problems* 36, no. 3 (summer 1971), 432–41; "Aesthetic Zoning: Preservation of Historic Areas," *Fordham Law Review* 29 (1961), 729–40; Ellen L. Kettler and Bernard D. Reams Jr., *Historic Preservation Law: An Annotated Bibliography* (Washington, D.C., 1976), iii.
71. Gilbert, "Assessing Grand Central," 38–9; Frank Greve, "David Bonderman, Esq., Preservation's Unsentimental Hero," *Historic Preservation* 35, no. 1 (January–February 1983). Cf. Ada Louis Huxtable's comments in *New York Times* (9 July 1978), II, 21:1.

    It should be kept in mind that the districts the decision upheld were for the most part elite enclaves. It is interesting to speculate on whether or not the simultaneous legal affirmation of suburban zoning, environmental and aesthetic regulation, and historic preservation, do not represent the efforts and interests of upper-middle-class stratum who in mid to late sixties developed a cultural resistance to unrestrained growth—which was now increasingly associated with lower class expansion. For analogous thoughts on the suburban desire to protect investment ["Bang the bell, Jack, I'm on board."] through exclusionary zoning, see Bernard J. Frieden, *The Environmental Protection Hustle*, (Cambridge, Mass., 1979); Roger Alcaly and David M. Mermelstein, eds., *The Fiscal Crisis of American Cities* (New York, 1977), 63, 73; Mollenkopf, "Postwar Politics," 125.
72. ACHP, *Report for 1979*, 2; Biliana Cicin-Sain, "The Costs and Benefits of Neighborhood Revitalization," in *Urban Revitalization*. Note that to the degree that the careless culture of planned obsolence was a function of cheap energy, which in turn was related to American imperial power, liberation and nationalist movements in the Third World helped force a reconstruction of American preservation consciousness.
73. Bernard J. Frieden and Arthur P. Solomon, *The Nation's Housing: 1975–1985* (Cambridge, Mass., 1977); ACHP, *Report for 1980*, 15; ACHP, *Report for 1982*; Clay, *Neighborhood Renewal*, 15. On 1976, see ACHP, *Report for 1979*, 2.
74. Booz, Allen, Hamilton study: *New York Times* (2 March 1980), VIII, 1:1. Rehabilitation to 38 percent: Parker, "Preservation Can Make a Profit," 23;

75. Jonathan Walters, "Main Street Turns the Corner," *HP* 33, no. 6 (November–December 1981), 36–45.
76. Robert Campbell, "Lure of the Marketplace: Real-Life Theater," *HP* 32, no. 1 (January–February 1980), 46–8; Arthur M. Skolnik, "A History of Pioneer Square," in National Trust, *Economic Benefits*, 15–19; Clay, *Neighborhood Renewal*, 12–13; ACHP, *Report for 1982*.
77. Jonathan Walters and Sace Davis, "The Boom in Born-Again Buildings," *HP* 36, no. 4 (August 1984), 18–19; Terrence Maitland, "Corporate Takeovers," *HP* (September–October 1981), 42–48; Paul Edward Parker Jr., "Preservation Can Make a Profit," *HP* (September–October 1979), 22–3. On Lowell see Ron LaBrecque, "New Industry for Mill City, USA," *HP* (July–August 1980), 32–9. On Providence, Savannah, and New York see *New York Times* (7 April 1980); "Savannah," 11–25; Roberta Brandes Gratz and Peter Freiberg, "Has Success Spoiled SOHO," *HP* 32, no. 5 (September–October 190), 9–15.
78. *New York Times* (13 August 1981).
79. Mulloy, *National Trust*, 173; Kay Holmes, "Learning About the Real World," *HP* (July–August 1980), 2–3; Marsha Glenn, "Academic Programs in Historic Preservation: An Up-to-Date Survey of the Field," *Journal of the Society of Architectural Historians* 35, no. 4 (December 1976), 265; King, Hickman, and Berg, *Anthropology* 43; National Trust for Historic Preservation, *Annual Report, 1976–1977* (Washington, D.C., 1977), 14–15. See the *National Council of Preservation Education Newsletter* for ongoing projects of preservation programs.
80. Frank Stella, *New Profits from Old Buildings: Private Enterprise Approaches to Making Preservation Pay* (New York, 1979) [an authoritative study commissioned by the corporate elite], 3–21 and *passim;* Charles N. Tseckares, "Adaptive Office Space in Old Buildings," National Trust, *Economic Benefits*, 76; Parker, "Preservation Can Make a Profit," 22–3.
81. Stella, *New Profits*, 2; Parker, "Preservation Can Make a Profit," 23; ACHP, *Report for 1982*.
82. *Preservation News* [hereinafter cited as *PN*] November 1981; *PN* April 1981; Curry, "Finding Shelter," 27–31; "Preservation Movement Comes of Age," *New York Times* (14 October 1979), VIII, 1:1 and (7 October 1979).
83. John Sower, "Financing and Developing Large Commercial Preservation Projects," National Trust, *Economic Benefits*, 133; National Association of Building Owners and Managers 1980 report, "Renaissance in Office Buildings" (How to Convert Old Office Buildings into Luxury Apartments): ACHP, *Report for 1980*, 12.
84. Robertson E. Collins, Foreword to Weinberg, *Preservation*, xi–xii.
85. National Trust for Historic Preservation, *Annual Report 1975–1976* (Washington, D.C., 1976), 1; National Trust, *Annual Report 1976–1977*, 10, 13, 19, 38; ACHP, *Report for 1980*, 9. Only two union organizations signed on, the AFL-CIO and the International Union of Bricklayers and Allied Craftsmen: *ibid*.

86. National Trust, *Annual Report 1976–1977*, 19.
87. *PAA* 5, no. 1 (January 1980); Leonard Curry, "Finding Shelter in Old Buildings," *HP* (March–April 1980), 30; *PAA* 3, no. 5, 4, no. 2, 5, no. 2. There were deregulation moves afoot at the state level, too. For anti-preservationist arguments in Waterbury, Connecticut ["Waterbury is not a historic city. It is a city for surviving."] see Elise Vider, "The City that Said 'No'," *HP* 32, no. 5 (September–October 1980), 52. In New York, Saint Bartholomew's Church, blocked from constructing a high-rise, led a move in the Legislature to overturn landmarks legislation on grounds it violated First Amendment freedom of religion rights. [*New York Times* (31 January 1984).]
88. *New York Times* (12, 13 August 1980).
89. Jeanie Wylie, "A Neighborhood Dies So GM Can Live," *The Village Voice* 26, no. 28 (July 8–14, 1981), 1; "Corporate Domain," *The Nation* (4 April 1981), 389; Richard Hodas, "Neighborhood and Factory Could Exist," *HP* 33, no. 1 (January–February 1981); Hartman, *Displacement*, 147–9. A film, *Poletown Lives!* is available from Information Factory, 3512 Courville, Detroit, MI 48224.
90. Corinne L. Gilb, "Detroit Must Move Forward," *HP* 33, no. 1 (January–February 1981), 47–9.
91. *Preservation Action Alert*, *Historic Preservation*, and *Preservation News* for 1981–1985; Steve Weinberg, "Super List," *Historic Preservation* 34, no. 4 (July–August 1982), 10–17; Phyllis Myers, "Urban Enterprise Zones: UDAG Revisited?," *HP* 33, no. 6 (12 November 1981), 12; *New York Times* (24 September 1983).
92. Weinberg, "Lobbying Congress," 19–25; *PN* (June 1981); *HP* 37, no. 3 (June 1985), 4.
93. PAA, (August 1983), 8; *PN* May 1981.
94. Lee A. Daniels, "New Tax Breaks Spurring Preservation," *New York Times* (23 May 1982), 8, 1; Jonathan Walters and Sace Davis, "The Boom in Born-Again Buildings," *Historic Preservation* 36, no. 4 (August 1984), 18–19; *Preservation News* (January 1984), 3; Andre Shashaty, "The Deal Makers," *Historic Preservation* 35, no. 3 (May–June 1983), 14; *Preservation News* (March 1985), 1.
95. Goldberger, "The Dangers in Preservation Success," 159–61. For similar warnings about the current coziness see Peter Brink, "A Bottom Line?" *AP* 1, no. 2 (December–January 1977–1978) and Peirce Lewis ["We can hardly complain of barbarism if we deliberately lie down with barbarians"], "Future of the Past," 16.
96. Carl Abbott, "The Facadism Fad: Is it Preservation?" *Historic Preservation* 36, no. 5 (October 1984), 42–7. The vogue for "postmodern" architecture, which amounts to putting historicist flourishes on the facades of new structures, bears interesting resemblences to facadism proper.
97. On hotel see *PN*, January and September 1981; *New York Times* (12 February 1982).

98. Giuseppe Campos Venuti, "The Conservation of the Architectural Heritage as a Means of Stimulating and Diversifying Economic Activity at the Regional and Local Levels," *Council of Europe Symposium No.* 6 (Strasbourg, 1978).
99. On a particularly brutal displacement of one thousand blacks and Puerto Ricans in Hartford, Connecticut, in 1981, by Aetna Life, see *PN*, September 1981. For the estimate that 2.5 million Americans are forced to move from homes and neighborhoods from all causes each year (the official government figure is 1.4 million involuntarily displaced) see Hartman, *Displacement*, 3, 5.
100. Huxtable, *Kicked a Building Lately?* 234.
101. John Kenneth Galbraith warned that "Preservationists must never be beguiled by the notion that we can rely on natural economic forces or that we can rely on the market. If we do, a large number of important art objects, artifacts and buildings will be sacrificed. The reason is that the market works on a short-time dimension, and the people who respond to the market are different from those who ultimately gain from conservation or preservation." "Preservationists Will Reap What They Sow . . . Eventually," *HP* 32, no. 5 (September–October 1980), 29.

    See the conclusion of Bommes and Wright, based on the English experience, that maintains capitalist property relations can only be preserved if they are reproduced through new accumulative cycles, which in turn necessitates the constant transformation of social relations in accordance with the needs of capital. The ensuing widespread change and actual demolition leads to conflict with the preservation lobby. Bommes and Wright, " 'Charms of Residence'," 275.
102. Philip Langdon, "Plain Talk About Displacement," *HP* 32, no. 2 (March–April 1980).
103. On a larger land use package see the summary of Planners Network ideas in Peter Dreier, "Dreams and Nightmares: The Housing Crisis," *The Nation* (21–28 August 1982).
104. The most imaginative preservation efforts in the world have been undertaken in Bologna, where sociocultural engineering aims at preserving both people and places. See Campos Venuti, "The Conservation of the Architectural Heritage"; Fitch, *Historic Preservation*, 40–41, 67.

Preservation

Revisited

(Reprinted with special permission of King Features Syndicate.)

In the 1980s historic preservation was big business. The movement's center of gravity had swung from its populist left to its real estate right. The strategy of saving old buildings and communities by relying on the marketplace—suitably guided by tax policy—seemed brilliantly successful. The 1981 rehabilitation tax credits were channeling billions into adaptive reuse.[1] Then, two blows dramatically reshaped the preservation landscape.

The first jolt came in 1986 when an improbable coalition of Republican conservatives and Democratic liberals drastically altered the tax code, sewing up many of the loopholes wealthy investors had used to shelter income and avoid paying taxes. Rehabilitation credits—the mainstay of the preservationist-developer alliance—proved a collateral casualty. The reformers had not been gunning for preservationists, particularly. Indeed, they left the credit for renovating certified historic buildings in place, albeit reduced from 25 percent to 20 percent. But the new rules barred wealthy investors from offsetting profits garnered in their primary "active" businesses, with losses from investments in which they were but "passive" partners. In addition, an annual limit of seven thousand dollars was slapped on the amount of rehab tax credits permitted most people, and upper bracket taxpayers were forbidden to use them at all.[2]

The evisceration of tax breaks came just as the crash of 1987, the ensuing recession, and the savings and loan crisis were chilling overheated real estate markets to near torpidity. Developer interest in historic rehabilitation nosedived. In 1984 the Interior Department had received 3,214 applications for certification; by 1989 requests had dropped to 994; and by 1993 annual investment generated by the tax credit program was down by 75 percent from its mid-eighties high.[3]

Property versus Preservation

The second shock came with the emergence of the self-styled "property rights" movement. This lupine initiative garbed in libertarian sheep's clothing sought to strike down any government regulations that impeded owners from maximizing returns on their holdings. The aggrieved Propertied included a variety of constituencies—landowners, real estate developers, loggers, miners, corporate farmers—all united behind a claim that their Fifth Amendment rights were being trampled by Big Government. Their intellectual guru was Richard Epstein of the University of Chicago Law School, who argued (in his 1985 book *Takings: Property Rights and the Power of Eminent Domain*) that whenever government rules hindered an owner from developing property to its highest and best use, this constituted a "taking" that entitled the owner to reimbursement. As Epstein read the Fifth Amendment—"nor shall private property be taken for public use without just compensation"—takings embraced not just a conventional exercise of eminent domain like seizing land for a highway, but any government imposed constraint whatever, be it an environmental law, labor code, building permit or zoning regulation.[4]

This reactionary doctrine leapt backwards over decades of legislation and centuries of judicial decisions—all granting government the right to block owners from using their property to injure others, while not requiring owners be compensated for loss of illegal profits. The theory harkened back to Blackstone's vision of property as affording an owner "sole and despotic dominion . . . in total exclusion of the right of any other individual in the universe." It talked only of rights, not responsibilities; only of taking, not of giving. Vociferous in demanding reimbursement for owners harmed by government action, the doctrine was silent about giving back unearned windfalls accrued from public policy (as when construction of a highway interchange boosted the value of adjacent property).[5]

Not surprisingly, the property rights doctrine quickly picked up support from those motivated by simple greed or driven by competitive pressures—primarily corporations intent on strip mining, clear cutting, overgrazing, polluting, and sidestepping erosion control. But it also attracted more populist supporters from the ranks of smaller property holders enmeshed in complex and rigidly bureaucratic procedures that were sometimes overzealously enforced.[6]

Preservation Revisited

With Republican appointees rapidly filling up the nation's courts, the Propertied jettisoned objections to judicial activism and fought for decisions enshrining property rights doctrine, winning some partial victories.[7] Most simply decreed that property owners denied all reasonable use or return might be entitled to monetary damages. Thus in *Lucas v. South Carolina Coastal Council* (1992), the Supreme Court ruled that a developer prevented by dune protection measures from building homes on his beachfront property was entitled to compensation—i.e., payment for obeying the law. The decision acknowledged this was an "extraordinary circumstance" as no productive use was permitted, thus rendering the property basically worthless. A June 1994 ruling (*Dolan v. City of Tigard*) represented a stronger move in a prodevelopment direction. By a 5–4 vote, the Court shifted the burden of proof for demonstrating environmental harm to local governments. This reversed the old rule that landowners had to prove a land-use regulation would remove substantially all economic value from their property before it could be considered a taking, and was hailed by advocates as a breakthrough.[8]

While the big legal battalions concentrated on the high-stakes environmental issues, smaller artillery units set their sights on the corpus of historic preservation law. The primary target was the 1978 Penn Central decision. The Supreme Court had ruled that New York City's landmark ordinance, which denied a property owner the right to maximum profit from his holding, did not impose an unconstitutional taking requiring monetary compensation, so long as he or she retained a reasonable economic use of the property. It affirmed, in other words, that rights incident to property ownership were not absolute but subject to reasonable regulation for the benefit of the larger community.[9]

Attacks on this ruling did not fare well. The closest the Propertied came to a breakthrough was a July 1991 decision by Pennsylvania's Supreme Court. In declaring that owners of a landmarked art deco movie palace should be allowed to demolish its interior, the court effectively struck down Philadelphia's historic preservation ordinance. If other states had followed suit, it would have been a mortal blow. Yet none did. Instead, in 1994, after a forceful effort by the National Trust's Legal Defense Fund, the maverick court reversed itself and returned to the corral.[10]

In beating their retreat, the Pennsylvania judges had, no doubt, taken note of the U.S. Supreme Court's refusal to renege on Penn Central, even in the face of novel lines of attack. In 1986 Saint Bartholomew's Church had filed suit against New York City and its Landmarks Preservation Commission, protesting rejection of a plan to hoist a forty-seven-story office tower on its site. Saint Bartholomew's argued that New York's landmarks law not only violated its Fifth Amendment property rights, but its First Amendment rights to freedom of religion as well. But in March 1991 the Supreme Court refused to review a 1990 federal appeals court ruling against the church. Subsequent decisions quashed similar challenges in other states.[11]

Yet despite these successes, the ultimate outcome remained bound up with the broader and far-from-resolved takings issue. If the Court were to shift its standard from "reasonable" to "highest and best" use, and decide that government must compensate owners for any and all lost or unrealized value due to a regulatory burden, the entire body of preservation law might well topple.[12]

Contract on Preservation

As they battled in the courts, the Propertied opened up a second front in the political arena. High on their hit list was historic district legislation.

By 1991 more than six thousand local governments had passed ordinances permitting municipalities to restrict destruction or alteration of buildings without approval from a reviewing commission.[13] Though politicians, businessowners, and homeowners had long supported this species of land use regulation—from which tax revenues, profits, and enhanced property values flowed—recent disaffections had rendered it newly vulnerable. Developers had once supported and even initiated National Register district designations, the better to secure tax credit eligibility; after 1986 they were more likely to oppose them. Opposition to preservation restrictions gained ground among smaller property owners. Some homeowners found landmark decisions arbitrary and onerous. The costs of "authentic" rehabilitation and "proper" maintenance seemed irksomely to outweigh the benefits.[14] The larger political climate also favored preservation's critics. With talk show hosts railing against "political correctness," it was easier to characterize landmark commissioners as commissars.[15] By the 1990s, moreover, many properties whose historicity was widely accepted had already been designated. Newer choices were often claimed to be less worthy—especially if they hindered capital investment, or (under prevailing aesthetic canons) did not "look" like landmarks.[16]

In this atmosphere, some historic districts got voted out of existence, others reduced, and others end-runned.[17] In April 1992, pushed by developers, Virginia passed a law that allowed property owners to veto designation of historic properties listed in the Virginia Landmarks Register.[18] In March 1995 the Illinois Legislature began considering a proposal to exempt all private property from the State Agency Historic Resources Preservation Act.[19] But they were scooped in June by Oregon, which became the first state to declare that "a local government shall allow a property owner to refuse to consent to any form of historic property designation." The legislation applied to property already designated, and to National Register as well as locally-listed structures.[20]

The Propertied also lashed out at preservationists in the federal bureaucracy. In 1988, at the suggestion of Attorney General Ed Meese (and his youthful Epstein-devotee advisors), President Reagan had issued an executive order reversing recent practice. Instead of forcing (for instance) the Transportation Department to take heed of activities that might adversely affect historic artifacts, the new ruling required a lengthy analysis of all federal actions that might "substantially affect" the value or use of private property.[21]

In 1989 Interior Secretary Donald Hodel used this executive takings order to justify denying National Historic Landmark status to a property once owned by John Jay. In 1992 Hodel's successor, Manuel Lujan Jr., withdrew the fourteen thousand acre Brandy Station Civil War Battlefield from a list of sites judged eligible for inclusion in the National Register, thus aiding a developer intent on constructing an industrial park in the site.[22] And after the developer's lobbyists bussed in elderly farmers wearing Protect Our Property Rights buttons, the Virginia Legislature also repealed the state's historic designation of Brandy Station, even though it was for educational purposes only and without regulatory effect.[23]

Opponents of federal preservation programs won other piecemeal victories, as in the case of the Resolution Trust Corporation (RTC). Established in 1989 to liquidate foreclosed properties that the government had inherited during the savings and loan crisis—a portfolio of properties which included hundreds of historically significant structures—the RTC was specifically exempted from compliance with section 106 of the National Historic Preservation Act.[24]

Attempts were made to cripple the National Trust itself, but these, at first, were beaten back handily. A house proposal to delete the trust's entire fiscal year 1994 appropriation failed by 315–11.[25] But although federal funding increased under Bush and Clinton, the absolute sums remained paltry, and many state offices had to slash staff just as the return of the bulldozer mentality augured an increase in responsibilities.[26]

In 1990, moreover, a congressional movement inaugurated a major push to write Reagan's executive takings order directly into federal law. In 1993 Senator Robert Dole tried—and failed—to enact a Private Property Rights Act. It would have required agencies to "assess" what impact their regulations might have on property owners, in essence imposing an obstructive but not insuperable bureaucratic hurdle for preservationists.[27] Then Newt Gingrich's Contract With America proposed a much tougher law. It sought to require the government to financially "compensate" property owners for any federal regulation that reduced the value of even a section of their holdings by as little as 10 percent. Aggrieved property owners had only to drop in the nearest mailbox a demand for payment to the agency concerned, and within six months it would have to comply. Federal land management authorities would be forced either to pay polluters billions of dollars not to pollute, or, far more likely, forego enforcing the regulations. Many advocates cheerfully admitted that their immediate ambition was to gut the Clean Water Act and Endangered Species Act, and their longer term goal was to rollback most regulatory law—environmental protection, rent control, banking and labor laws, health and safety rules, and the entire corpus of New Deal welfare legislation.[28]

The triumph of right wing Republicans in the 1994 congressional elections brought these proponents of the Propertied to power. In March 1995 the House of Representatives approved a version of this legislation and sent it to the Senate. There Dole, now majority leader and a presidential aspirant, abandoned his relatively moderate "assessment" approach and signed on to the full-blown "compensation" bill demanded by his hard-right rival Phil Gramm. The resulting Omnibus Property Rights Act was a truly lunatic piece of legislation. Under its sweeping definitions of property and government action, were the Fed to change interest rates, and stock prices go down, the government would have to reimburse the stockholders for their loss. Clinton administration officials estimated that once unscrupulous law firms began bringing ever more imaginative claims against the government, the price tag on the House version of the property rights bill would probably run to twenty-eight billion dollars within seven years, with the cost of the Senate bill incalculably higher. The president threatened a veto, and the outcome of this particular round remained uncertain, but the issue had, seemingly irreversibly, been placed on the national agenda.[29]

The news on the historic preservation front was even grimmer. The House decreed a two year "glide path" to extinction for the National Trust—cutting half its budget for the forthcoming year, and the other half the next. Counterpressure in the Senate produced a five year extermination plan, with only a 20 percent cut budgeted for fiscal year 1996; but, when the September 1995 Conference Committee adopted the House version, zero-budgeting of the trust, a goal of preservation opponents since the Reagan era, appeared on the verge of attainment.

Sober Second Thoughts

These dramatically changed conditions prompted serious retrospection among preservationists about the development-based strategies of the 1980s. It now seemed to some that preoccupation with the "how to" of saving buildings had obscured "why" it was they were being preserved. They also observed that facadism had at times diminished a building's worth as an historical artifact; that big commercial restorations had not necessarily rejuvenated adjacent neighborhoods; that some projects galvanized by tax credits and easy money from deregulated savings and loans institutions had been poorly thought out, and, strapped with debt, had tumbled into foreclosure; and that some developers extracted sizeable profits from rehabbing only until the tax credits had run out, at which point they dumped their properties. Above all, preservationists found that developers had proved to be fair-weather allies, in favor of restoration so long as it generated the highest rate of return, and against it once they sniffed greater profits in demolition and new construction.[30]

Many preservationists nevertheless fondly recalled the years of flowing billions. Recounting the undoubted benefits that the preservation boom had brought to builders, manufacturers, publishers, architects, interior designers, and merchandisers, they argued strongly that restoration of the tax credits would provide greater profits for a greater number than the property rights approach. But despite some support in Congress, the effort got nowhere. The cautious Clinton, in whom many had placed high hopes, failed to put restoration on his legislative agenda.[31]

Others who continued to urge the compatibility of preservation and profitability stressed the economic benefits of heritage tourism. They cited Arthur Frommer's dictum that "tourism simply doesn't go to a city that has lost its soul." The National Trust launched a tourism initiative to help areas focus on indigenous elements that might distinguish them from their competitors. Preservationists presented the benefits of heritage tourism as being an argument against property rights theorists: Owners of historic properties should not be allowed to jeopardize wider profitability by a short-sighted pursuit of personal gain.[32] This weapon, however, was capable of cutting those who wielded it. If historic structures were to be saved on narrow market grounds—because they enhanced tourist revenues—there seemed no logical or moral basis for resisting the Propertied if they could demonstrate that higher profits could be generated by demolition, followed by construction of, say, a new sports complex.

Despite this nostalgia for the go-go years, the combination of lost tax credits and the property rights offensive pushed preservationists towards embracing new strategies and reviving older ones. It became clear they would have to broaden their base of support to survive the unpropitious years ahead.

In 1991, the National Trust adopted a new mission statement. It pledged to "foster an appreciation of the diverse character and meaning of our American cultural heritage and to preserve and revitalize the livability of our communities by leading the nation in saving America's historic environments."[33] This manifesto embraced three distinct but overlapping claims: Preservation could promote multicultural comity, help revive wounded inner cities, and partner the ecological movement. Each merits a brief examination.

Expanding the Past

Having long contended that old buildings served as anchors of collective identity, preservationists now suggested that saving historic structures in poor urban neighborhoods might reweave shredded social fabrics, regenerate civic discourse, aid "multicultural adaptation", and "combat some of the divisions that exist in our society."[34]

Many acknowledged this would require changing preservation practice—crucially, by prying open the definition of what was "historic." A broader range of physical remains would have to be salvaged, even if they lacked aesthetic distinction or historic "significance" as traditionally defined, in order to represent a wider variety of pasts.[35] Helping variegated cultural communities preserve what was of historic value to *them*—rendering their histories visible—would diminish their need to withdraw into cultural enclaves of their own, and render them more willing to "share in the civic discourse".[36] Embracing cultural diversity in the past would nourish cosmopolitanism in the present.

Not everyone in the movement accepted this approach. Some resisted abandoning traditional architectural and historical criteria—rather as conservatives contested analogous efforts by universities and museums to expand the scholarly canon or diversify public history offerings. Others worried that preserved vernacular buildings might simply be used to fabricate an idealized multicultural past, especially if the movement continued to shy away from unflattering memory markers—sites of conflict or exploitation.[37] Some wondered if minority sites would not get treated in the conventional way, as relics to be restored to their original condition, instead of being interpreted as palimpsests which revealed change over time.[38] Minority preservationists agreed that saving indigenous structures might help revitalize and stabilize communities by instilling neighborhood pride. But they also suggested that poor people living in hand-me-down slum buildings would continue to favor the new over the old, especially if preservation continued to be associated with gentrification.[39]

Beyond these reservations loomed the fact that, coming from a still overwhelmingly white middle-class movement, an identity-oriented approach could seem naive, patronizing, and grossly inadequate as a response to urban misery. The 1980s shift from populism to real estate had rendered preservationists vulnerable to skeptics. Might they not just be using a fashionable multiculturalism—and fears of urban disorder—to legitimate (and fund) their troubled movement?[40]

Preservation Revisited

Heritage and Housing

Preservationists insisted they were concerned with more than the well-being of buildings. Their second initiative called for the economic revitaliza-

tion of cities—a new, improved, people-centered, urban renewal program. Rehabilitating the vast urban storehouse of abandoned old buildings would provide decent shelter—not, this time, for outside gentry, but for the existing residents, the ill-housed, and the homeless—while creating jobs for city citizens. National Trust President Richard Moe pledged to demonstrate the "connection between preservation and livable communities. . . ."[41]

Some proponents of this approach (including Moe) were still intent on winning restoration of the tax credits, and they pointed proudly to boom-era rehab work as evidence of what preservation could do for cities. But that track record afforded little evidence of prowess at housing the poor. The tax incentives may, as claimed, have spurred twelve billion dollars of private investment into historic buildings between 1976 and 1990, but most of the money had flowed to offices, hotels, convention centers, and festival marketplaces. And of the roughly 110,000 housing units that were rehabbed using historic rehabilitation tax credits, low and moderate income families could afford fewer than 14,000 of them—a mere 1,000 units a year.[42]

The bottom-line problem was that tax credits had applied only to income-producing renovations, and poor people could not afford market rates of return. The distress of inner cities increased in the 1980s and the contrast between slum areas and (often adjacent) exclusive historic enclaves grew ever more apparent and abrasive.[43] Arguably, tax credit based preservation had been part of the problem, not part of the solution.

So 1990s-era preservationists, even those wistful about 1980s-era programs, pressed ahead with new departures (which in some cases meant reviving old approaches of the 1960s and 1970s). They urged passage of low income housing tax credits. They advocated job training programs in renovation. They proposed transferring city-owned vacant buildings to people needing homes, rehabilitating abandoned historic structures as senior citizen housing, granting rehab tax credits to actual home owners (not just landlords or speculative developers), and relying on community groups and neighborhood groups to purchase and manage restorations as a guarantee against gentrification.[44]

Some of these proposals were put in practice, notably in Pittsburgh, home of activist Stanley Lowe. In the 1970s Lowe had believed that preservation worked against the city's African American community. When Arthur Ziegler of the History and Landmarks Foundation tried to save buildings in his Manchester community, Lowe helped fight him off, preferring to tear down old brick row houses and build the kind of tract houses suburban whites favored. By 1983 he had changed his mind; he joined Ziegler's operation and helped save Manchester from further demolition.

Lowe's primary goal was not preservation—though he supported it—but neighborhood growth and improvement. In 1988, aided by grants from old Pittsburgh family foundations (Mellon, Scaife, Heinz), he helped found the Pittsburgh Community Reinvestment Group (PCRG), an alliance of twenty-two community development organizations. The organization began making use of the 1977 Community Reinvestment Act (CRA), which required lending institutions to make loans to qualified borrowers, of all income levels, in the neighborhoods from which deposits originate. Lowe's group analyzed the bank records of local lending institutions and found poor CRA compliance rates, notably a high rejection rate of black applicants as compared to whites. The PCRG filed protests, brought busloads of demonstrators to recalcitrant banks, got the mayor and school board to withdraw millions from holdout lenders, and generated reams of publicity.

Such militancy, backed by CRA muscle, secured substantial neighborhood reinvestment programs. Over six hundred million dollars in bank commitments flowed into historic rehabs, home mortgages at below-market rates, loans to small local businesses, and a restored old mansion for senior citizens—none of which exposed the banks to high risk of default. Preservation may not have been Lowe's first order of business, but it was certainly an indirect beneficiary.[45]

Other innovative projects flowered.

- A movement called Youth-Build reclaimed old structures for low-income residents, using the labor power of sixteen to twenty-four year olds (some of them former gang members) who, in their year of service, learned the fundamentals of a construction trade, and earned credits for a high school equivalency diploma.[46]
- The Savannah Landmark Rehabilitation Project worked with the NAACP, local ministers, bankers, and city officials to transform Victorian houses into apartments for people with low and moderate incomes.[47]
- A Boston group redeveloped one hundred lodging house rooms for homeless people.[48]
- The Washington, DC organization, Samaritan Inns, raised $2.2 million from local businesses to renovate a building whose eighty apartments were rented at rates based on tenants' ability to pay. Thirty other nonprofit groups in the capital city generated another seven hundred homes and apartments at below-market rates.[49]
- The New York Landmarks Conservancy, in 1982, created a revolving fund, the New York City Historic Properties Fund, capitalized

with proceeds from the redevelopment of the Federal Archives Building in Greenwich Village. Over the next decade it distributed four million dollars in below-market-rate loans (along with technical assistance) to low- and middle-income neighborhoods whose property owners had limited access to other sources of funding.[50]

The total amount of housing produced, while not enormous, was substantial enough to demonstrate that historic preservation and affordable housing were not inherently antithetical goals.[51]

Ironically, given their battles with Saint Bartholomew's and other would-be ecclesiastical developers, preservationists intent on urban revitalization also set out to help rescue endangered inner-city churches. Often the only institutions left in a collapsing neighborhood, these churches served as community centers of the last resort—hosting head start, aids, youth, day care, and meals programs. But as their own buildings aged and deteriorated, the dwindling, often impoverished congregations found it hard to get secular philanthropists, foundations, corporations, banks, or local governments to help keep them standing.

The New York Landmarks Conservancy's Sacred Sites Program, established in 1985, went on to provide over one million dollars in matching grants for maintenance and restoration of religious buildings in the city and state; it also helped more than three hundred congregations with technical services and workshops. In 1989 Partners for Sacred Places was established in Philadelphia to extend such efforts on a nationwide basis.[52] In Chicago, the National Trust's Midwest regional office launched the Inspired Partnerships program, with financial aid from the Lilly Endowment. Offering help on a non-profit, non-denominational basis, it provided inspection reports, energy audits, training in maintenance repair, help in selecting contractors, and fund raising.[53] In Charlotte, North Carolina, preservationists joined with the black community to reroute a planned street around a local church, and then raised funds to make it an Afro-American Cultural Center.[54]

Eco-preservation

Historic preservation's third strategic departure was to enlist in the environmental army, aligning itself alongside groups fighting against air and water pollution, and for the preservation of open spaces and endangered species.[55]

Such an alliance had been difficult in the 1980s, when preservationists had cast their lot with developers—ecologists' mortal enemies.[56] Now a linkup with such powerful protectors seemed not only feasible but necessary. It did not escape the National Trust's notice that while its own ranks hovered around two hundred thousand, the leading environmental organizations could muster several million members between them.[57] These battalions, and the tremendous public support for their cause, had given environmentalists enviable influence in policy making councils.

Such an alliance was as logical as it was opportune. As preservationists now began to proclaim, there was a substantial congruence in the two movements' philosophies.

"We used to say that historic preservation is real estate," announced one authoritative manifesto. "Now we are saying that preservation is land use and stewardship."[58] The key text for new sermons was Jefferson's: "The earth belongs in usufruct to the living." The historic built environment was part of the common cultural heritage, the national patrimony: Historic buildings, like natural resources, should be held in trust for future generations.[59]

Such a philosophy provided an ethical purchase point for resisting assaults by the "property rights" crowd—and indeed for taking the offensive against them. The "owners" of cultural treasures were trustees and fiduciaries, not absolute overlords. They were no more free to auction off parts of the public's cultural domain than they were entitled to do as they pleased with wetlands or the habitats of endangered species.[60]

If the environmentalists' doctrine of "stewardship" inspired enthusiasm and emulation, so did their notions of "sustainable use" and "land use management." These precepts called for preemptive preservation. Rather than erecting legal fences around historic patches, preservationists should take part in designing the land use controls that set the terms of development in cities and regions—thus ensuring new growth was compatible with the historic (and natural) landscape. "Tomorrow," said real-estate developer John F. W. Rogers, "preservation will largely be about managing change."[61]

Again, such concepts got preservationists off defense, onto offense. Cutting through property rights pleas about getting government off their backs, sustainable use advocates noted that government subsidies had allowed development to run amuck. Governments had built roads and laid sewers out to edge city subdivisions; subsidized auto transport; allowed home mortgage deductions; and imposed mandatory separation of land uses. All these subsidies had senselessly re-created on the periphery institutions and infrastructure that existed in the centers, breeding the twin evils of ecologically unsound growth and inner-city devastation.[62] Managed growth preservationists rejected the promethean imperative, and hoped (admittedly late in the day) to halt further exploitation of finite cultural and natural resources. They cast the recycling of historic structures as an ecologically superior alternative to supporting suburban sprawl.[63]

If environmentalism sustained an expansive vision, it also provided cover for a cautious retreat. Many preservationists saw in the notion of Conservation Zones an alternative to historic districts, a sort of historic district lite. These territories—which might be organized around environmental or visual features, as well as historic or architectural ones—established broad land use guidelines. They regulated construction, demolition, and alterations to existing buildings. But the controls were less invasive, they dispensed with cumbersome architectural review processes, they demanded less onerous standards for maintaining historical authenticity. Many cities—Philadelphia, San Francisco, Roanoke, Annapolis, Atlanta, Boston, Dallas and Phoenix among them—found them appropriate where "the neighborhood does not require, or the politics do not support, historic districts."[64]

Conservation districts, moreover, like the even larger heritage areas (a.k.a. heritage parks or heritage corridors), allowed preservationists to break with their building-by-building focus and think of saving historic terrains on a wholesale rather than retail basis. Heritage areas were usually regional landscapes organized around a notable large-scale feature—a river, a canal, a railroad, or a system of hills. As they embraced a wide range of natural and cultural artifacts, so they were supported by a broad constellation of politically potent beneficiaries. Entities like the Illinois and Michigan Canal National Heritage Corridor and the Blackstone River Valley National Heritage Corridor won the consolidated backing of history buffs, recreation enthusiasts, wildlife groups, prairie grass conservationists, tourist promoters, economic developers, and enough congresspeople to win federal designation.[65] It remains to be seen if these coalitions might serve as nuclei for the kinds of regional planning efforts needed to cope with the disastrous impact of deindustrialization on vast sections of the American landscape.

If preservationists dined heartily at the environmentalists' table, they also contributed to the common feast. When the battle over Disney's America broke out, National Trust President Moe wheeled his troops into the fray, declaring the new Battle of Manassas to be "one of the most significant preservation issues to come along in many years." They were well positioned to lend weight to the argument that the Disney development would do more just than the usual damage to the countryside—strip malls, air pollution, and the like. It would destroy as well a historic ambience rooted in the Piedmont's dense agglomeration of historic towns and battlefields. Although the sanctification of battlefields had its problematic aspects—particularly for preservationists trying to transcend their "George Washington slept here" origins—the ability of hallowed ground to keep marketeers at bay undeniably contributed to the larger victory.[66] Moe was right to say: "We can at least be grateful that Disney's plans have brought historians, conservationists, and preservationists together in a unified front that, I hope, will set a precedent for the future."[67]

Will preservation's latest shift of emphasis prove permanent? It is impossible to say. Shifts in the larger economy, or alterations in the tax codes, could send the movement back toward development country. So far, after all, much of the bold new thinking remains just that, a matter of talk and planning. The preservation coalition, moreover, is hardly a unified entity. Those in the market-based heritage-tourism wing have different and to some degree conflicting agendas from those who favor multi-cultural, inner city, or ecological approaches. (Tourists who motor to Kykuit are unlikely to take a trip to Pittsburgh's Manchester.) Others who continue to focus on the day-to-day issues of saving threatened sites, running historic districts, developing curriculum programs, and nurturing local identity, may be uncomfortable with new initiatives. It remains to be seen what percentage of the National Trust's remaining monetary and political resources (as distinct from rhetorical emphasis) will be committed to various alternative strategies.

But as the movement ponders its future, it might be worth noting that in the years 1987–1994, when preservationists experimented with new approaches in the post-tax-credit and property rights era, the National Trust's membership rose from 197,000 to 250,000. If keeping company with environmentalists and urban activists draws in vital new recruits, then the organizations dedicated to salvaging America's past will play a bigger role in shaping America's future.[68]

Notes

This essay was written specifically for this book, as an update to the previous chapter, "Preserving the Past: Historic Preservation in the United States."

My thanks for invaluable advice and counsel go to Peg Breen, Paul Spencer Byard, Page Cowley, James Marston Fitch, Linda Gillies, John Halpern, Dorothy Marie Miner, Kellis Parker, and lastly to Daniel Bluestone, whose insights and information were of such caliber and quantity I would list him as coauthor, were it not for my desire to render him blameless for remaining errors of fact or infelicities of interpretation.

1. See the preceeding chapter in this volume ("Preserving the Past: A History of Historic Preservation in the United States"), 178–221.
2. See Jeffrey H. Birnbaum and Alan S. Murray, *Showdown at Gucci Gulch: Lawmakers, Lobbyists, and the Unlikely Triumph of Tax Reform* (New York: 1987); Margaret Opsata, "How Pros Play the Rehab Game," *Historic Preservation* (May/June 1987), 34; Thomas J. Colin, "What Next for a Troubled Industry?," *Historic Preservation* (May/June 1988), 32–5.
3. In 1986 St. Louis had finished 129 tax credit assisted projects; in 1993 it completed but 16. Kim Keister, "Comeback On Hold," *Historic Preservation* (July/August 1993), 57. On the post-reform fallout see Madeline Cirillo Archer, "Where We Stand: Preservation Issues in the 1990s," *Public Historian* 13, no. 4 (fall 1991), 27–8; "Rehab Takes a Fall," *His-*

toric Preservation* (September/October 1990), 51; *Historic Preservation News* (September 1991), 4; *ibid.* (May 1992), 8; *ibid.* (January 1993), 8.

Not all developers bailed out. Although investors able to risk $50,000 to $100,000 departed the scene, major syndication firms like Boston Bay Capital, Dover Historic Properties, and Historic Landmarks turned to smaller players, bundling investments in units as low as $3,000. These larger entities stuck to bigger, less risky projects, and were unlikely to undertake projects in marginal neighborhoods. Colin, "What Next for a Troubled Industry?" 32–5.

The rehabilitation industry, moreover, had developed a momentum of its own. So long as costs of new construction remained high, and recession kept potential profits low, it seemed likely that substantial amounts of restoration work would continue. But even the most optimistic agreed that "economic subsidies and incentives will remain essential to help direct market forces toward preservation solutions," and it was precisely those supports that were evaporating. Sally G. Oldham, "The Business of Preservation is Bullish and Diverse," *Historic Preservation Forum* (winter 1990), 14–19.

4. David Helvarg, "Legal Assault on the Environment," *The Nation* (30 January 1995), 126; Peter Overby, "The Politics of Mine-ing," *Common Cause Magazine* (summer 1994), 10.
5. Overby, "The Politics of Mine-ing," 13. Donovan D. Rypkema noted that in claiming any decline in value resulting from public land-use limitation entitled an owner to compensation, property rights advocates were in effect demanding a floor be set under the risk of real estate ownership. But no such guarantee applied to other investments, as when the value of Lockheed bonds sank after the government chose McDonnell Douglas to build a new bomber. Nor did advocates ever suggest an "offsetting ceiling limiting the enhanced value generated from the same source." "Property Rights/Property Values: The Economic Misunderstandings of the Property-Rights Movement," *Historic Preservation Forum* (July/August 1993), 26. See also Adam Diamant, "Government Takings? What About Givings?" *Christian Science Monitor* (24 February 1995), 18, no. 1.
6. Eric T. Freyfogle, "Owning the Wolf: Green Politics: Property Rights, Ecology Rights," *Dissent* (fall 1994), 481–3; Overby, "The Politics of Mine-ing," 10–13; Jonathan H. Adler, "Takings Cause," *National Review* (19 December 1994), 36.
7. Again the goal was a restoration of the nineteenth-century status quo, when activist judges shaped property law to foster economic growth, allowing factories to spew smoke without incurring liability to neighbors. Freyfogle, "Owning the Wolf," 484; Morton J. Horwitz, *The Transformation of American Law* (Cambridge, Mass., 1977).
8. Richard J. Roddewig, "Historic Preservation and the Constitution," *Historic Preservation Forum* (July/August 1993), 13–15; Freyfogle, "Owning the Wolf," 484; Adler, "Takings Cause," 35; Overby, "The Politics of Mine-ing," 10.

9. David A. Doheny, "Property Rights and Historic Preservation," *Historic Preservation Forum* (July/August 1993), 8.
10. *Historic Preservation News* (February/March 1994), 6. The Pennsylvania court's initial ruling was an effort at elevating Justice Renquist's dissent in the *Penn Central* case to dominant status; its reconsidered position, sustaining the basic concept of designation (even while finding that the Pennsylvania law did not authorize designation of interiors), marked its readherence to the majority position in *Penn Central*.
11. *Historic Preservation News* (October 1990), 1; *ibid.* (April 1991), 1–2; Thomas Sweeney, "Our Biggest Challenge?" *Historic Preservation News* (May 1992), 12; Richard J. Roddewig, "Historic Preservation and the Constitution," *Historic Preservation Forum* (July/August 1993), 19–20; Joseph L. Sax, "Property Rights and Public Benefits," *Past Meets Future: Saving America's Historic Environments*, ed. Antoinette J. Lee, (Washington D.C. 1993), 137–43.
12. Overby, "The Politics of Mine-ing," 12.
13. Archer, "Where We Stand," 29.
14. Even a staunch preservationist like Arthur Ziegler thought the federal and state bureaucracies interpreted preservation too literally. In assuming that original designers had wrought perfection, they tended to block perfectly reasonable adaptive restorations. Arthur P. Ziegler, "The Early Years," in *Past Meets Future*, 63. Exacting design or materials requirements, it should be noted, were far more characteristic of federal programs which handed out grants or tax credits. Local regulatory bodies, like historic district commissions, generally sought only "appropriate" restoration, a less burdensome standard, and despite some celebrated complaints, they retained widespread support.
15. *Historic Preservation News* (February 1992), 4; H. Grant Dehart, "The Future of the Preservation Movement," *Historic Preservation Forum* (September/October 1991), 6.
16. In fact, many of the newly selected sites and districts passed muster even by the most exacting criteria. Given preservation's uneven development, many structures with traditional associative and architectural pedigrees remained (and remain) unlandmarked. Some areas had established commissions belatedly, others had adopted a cautious step-by-step approach.
17. Archer, "Where We Stand," 32; Michael A. Tomlan, "Preservation Practice Comes of Age," in *Past Meets Future*, 79.
18. Thomas A. Lewis, "Property Rights and Human Rights," *Historic Preservation Forum* (July/August 1993), 50–51.
19. William Presecky, "Preservation Law is Facing a Challenge," *Chicago Tribune* (6 March 1995), 1:5.
20. Alicia Rodgriguez, "The Right to Refuse," *Historic Preservation* (May/June 1995), 17–18.
21. President Clinton left this executive order in place. Overby, "The Politics of Mine-ing," 10.

22. *Historic Preservation News* (November 1992), 10–11.
23. Sweeney, "Our Biggest Challenge," 12–13; Doheny, "Property Rights and Historic Preservation," 9; Lewis, "Property Rights and Human Rights," 50–51.
24. Joshua J. Bloom, "The Banking Crisis and Cultural Resources: The Role of RTC and FDIC in Liquidating Historic Properties," *Historic Preservation Forum*, (fall 1994), 4.
25. *Historic Preservation News* (October/November 1993), 10.
26. In fiscal year 1991 $28.71 million went to the state historic preservation offices, $5.77 million to the National Trust, and $2.2 million to the advisory council. In FY94, the appropriated sums were $31 million, $7 million, and $2.959 million respectively. *Historic Preservation News*, (December 1990), 1; *ibid.* (October 1991), 5; *ibid.* (May 1992), 5; *ibid.* (December 1992), 7; *ibid.* (February/March 1994), 5.
27. Some thirty state legislatures considered—and six states actually adopted—similar legislation between 1991–3. *Historic Preservation Forum*, (July/August 1993), 8. The Farm Bureau, the National Association of Realtors, Cattlemen's Association and the mining industry have been particularly active in promoting these state initiatives. After Arizona passed a takings law in 1992, environmentalist opponents collected 71,000 signatures to put it to a referendum. Despite being outspent by development forces 2–1, a strong grass roots effort in support of strong environmental protection won 60 percent of the vote. Helvarg, "Legal Assault on the Environment," 128.
28. Helvarg, "Legal Assault on the Environment," 128.

    This campaign is driven not only by crude self-interest, but by the righteous zealotry of true belief. The propertied concur firmly with Joseph Schumpeter's description of capitalism as a force for "creative destruction." They deem demolition of constraints on profit-making to be inherently progressive, assuming as they do that pursuit of private vice leads to public virtue, through the grace of Adam Smith, our Lord. Gingrich really believes that government bureaucrats and elite professionals are a sclerotic force, choking off development—as indeed they can be at times. It is all the more important for preservationists to be remember that such prometheanism appeals to Americans, and to guard against bureaucratic excesses that might lend credibility to critics.
29. *New York Times* (3 March 1995), A19; *ibid.* (4 March 1995), A1.

    In October 1994 the House nearly accepted the addition of amendments to a bill aimed at creating "heritage areas." Proposed by Rep. Billy Tauzin (D-La.), point man for the property rights movement, they would have made compliance with local zoning laws voluntary, and required compensation for landowners deprived of any income from any use of their land. Bruce Babbitt, "Forging the Link Between Past and Present," *Historic Preservation Forum* (winter 1995), 4–6; John

McQuaid, "Tauzin Nips House's Heels on Property Rights," *Times-Picayune* (6 October 1994), 3:1.

See Dick Thompson, "Congressional Chain-saw Massacre: G.O.P.'s Environmental Policy," *Time* (27 February 1995), 58–60; Harvey Wasserman, "Green Alert: Anti-Environmental Proposals Embedded in the Contract with America," *The Nation* (6 February 1995), 153.

30. Daniel Bluestone has noted that although preservation's "claim to public support lies in large part in its ability to spatialize history, making the past more palpable, more memorable," buildings, landscapes, and districts do not speak for themselves. Because their historical meaning is gathered "through prior education and experience or through current interpretation," preservation "needs to examine more critically the perspective and content of the historical narratives it preserves and promotes." Daniel Bluestone, "Preservation and Renewal in Post-World War II Chicago," *Journal of Architectural Education* (May 1994), 210.

On facadism see Samuel Y. Harris, "Alternative Use as a Preservation Strategy," *Historic Preservation Forum* (September/October 1993), 17–20; Archer, "Where We Stand," 26–8; William Murtagh, *Keeping Time: The History and Theory of Preservation in America* (New York, 1988), 167–70.

St. Louis's Union Station reopened in 1985 as a hotel and shopping mall, after the most costly ever rehabilitation of an historic building in the United States. Although it did become a bustling destination, expectations that it would spark a wider renaissance went unfulfilled. Keister, "Comeback On Hold," 52–3.

On rehabbing and tax credits see Fred H. Copeman et al., "Tax Reform Aftermath: What's New in Preservation Financing," *Preservation Forum*, (spring 1990), 20; Dehart, "Future of the Preservation Movement," 6.

31. Oldham, "Business of Preservation," 14–19. See Thomas J. Kuber's contribution to "Tax Reform Aftermath: What's New in Preservation Financing?" *Preservation Forum* (spring 1990), 23; *Historic Preservation News* (July/August 1993), 7.

32. Cherl Hargrove, "Building Partnerships through Heritage Tourism," *Historic Preservation Forum* (July/August 1991), 29; Richard Moe, "President's Note," *Historic Preservation* (July/August 1994), 6. The feisty Frommer favored tougher measures. "We need to challenge the view of business that the marketplace alone must determine the fate of American cities," he added, calling for "a more confrontational approach to real estate developers." He sought government intervention to save whole districts, lest "advocates of unrealistic and so-called libertarian theories destroy, in effect, our American cities." See Frommer, "Historic Preservation and Tourism," *Historic Preservation Forum* (fall 1988), 10–12.

33. Jane Brown Gillette, "A Retrospective," *Historic Preservation* (March/April 1994), 52.
34. Henry G. Cisneros, "Bridging America's Visions," in *Past Meets Future*, 89.
35. Archer, "Where We Stand," 37–9; Dehart, "Future of the Preservation Movement," 6.

    Bluestone notes that saving buildings can privilege; and make more memorable, the particular historical narratives that those remains illustrate. Conversely, when preservationists devalue, ignore, and acquiesce in the destruction of other buildings—usually vernacular structures—their absence reinforces the privileged narrative by making it harder for alternative histories to be rendered palpable. Bluestone, "Preservation and Renewal in Post-World War II Chicago," 210.

    For an exemplary project that successfully rescued and/or interpreted buildings associated with the history of workers, women, and people of color in Los Angeles—that used "the power of place to nurture social memory"—see Dolores Hayden, "The Power of Place: Urban Landscapes as People's History," *Historic Preservation Forum* (winter 1995), 10–17.
36. Kenneth B. Smith, "Caring for our Communities," in *Past Meets Future*, 102–3, in response to Arthur Schlesinger Jr.'s argument (in *The Disuniting of America*) that "multiculturalism threatens the ideal that binds America."
37. Antoinette J. Lee, "Cultural Diversity in Historic Preservation," *Historic Preservation Forum* (July/August 1992), 28–41.

    Peter H. Brink and H. Grant Dehart noted that changing demographics, with minorities becoming the majority, would alter what the nation valued and sought to preserve. They argued that historic preservation could help interlink diverse cultures, citing an assertion that "When people's lives and stories are valued, they will join in the whole." Brink and Dehart, "Findings and Recommendations," in *Past Meets Future*, 17.

    The movement took steps to expand its own diversity, establishing a scholarship program for minorities that helped change the cultural composition of the annual conference. Gillette, "A Retrospective," 52; W. Brown Morton III, "Forging New Values in Uncommon Times," in *Past Meets Future*, 38.
38. Mitchell Schwarzer, "Historic Character and the Representation of Cultural Diversity," *Historic Preservation Forum* (November/December 1993), 42–9.
39. Thomas Fisher, "Roundtable: Preservation in Minority Communities," *Progressive Architecture* (May 1992), 156–8. See also "African American Heritage is Focus of Symposia," *Historic Preservation News* (August/September 1994), 10–11.
40. In some cases it seemed preservationists had adopted the new emphasis only after deciding that local residents had become as great a threat to historic properties as bulldozers. The Los Angeles riots jolted the five-

thousand-member Los Angeles Conservancy (LAC)—hitherto an ally of developers—into rethinking its relation to area residents. During the upheaval, the group had concentrated on winning dispatch of a police detail to save an art deco structure occupied by I. Magnin. But afterwards, seeking to overcome their isolation from the community (and to forestall future outbreaks), the LAC got local school children involved in the work of rehabilitation and contacted the Central American Refugee Center to set up workshops on the neighborhood's cultural heritage. See Andrea Oppenheimer Dean, "Sifting through the Ruins," *Historic Preservation* (September/October 1992), 48–54.

41. Thomas W. Sweeney, "Promote Preservation's Role in Revitalizing Communities," *Historic Preservation News* (June 1993), 6; Richard Moe, "President's Note," *Historic Preservation* (March/April 1993), 6.
42. Moe urged reestablishment of the rehabilitation tax credits as a major incentive for "urban revitalization." He pointed out that since 1980 the Main Street program had generated over $2.9 billion in physical improvements, and produced 20,839 new businesses and over 64,000 new jobs. Richard Moe, "President's Note," *Historic Preservation* (January/February 1993), 6; Moe, "President's Note," *Historic Preservation* (July/August 1994), 6. For more on the economic benefits of preservation—including job creation, infrastructure maintenance, and tax base enhancement—see Donovan D. Rypkema, "Economics and Historic Preservation," *Historic Preservation Forum* (winter 1995), 39–45. Opsata, "How Pros Play the Rehab Game," 34; Richard D. Wagner, "Urban Downtown Revitalization and Historic Preservation," *Historic Preservation Forum* (September/October 1993), 53; Thomas J. Colin, "A Historic Anniversary," *Historic Preservation* (May/June 1986), 25. On the effects of tax credit on the poor see "Rehab Takes a Fall," 51. Cf. Colin, "What Next for a Troubled Industry?," 32–5, who estimates 16,000. The National Trust's highly touted Inner City Venture Fund had managed to rehabilitate only 400 or so buildings by 1994, providing perhaps 1,700 units of affordable housing. Moe, "President's Note," *Historic Preservation* (May/June 1994), 6.
43. Thomas W. Sweeney, "Preservation: A Record of Economic and Social Achievements," *Historic Preservation News* (January 1993), 8; Archer, "Where We Stand," 33–4.
44. Archer, "Where We Stand," 36–40; Keister, "Comeback On Hold," 56–7; Harry Schwartz, "A Federal Historic Rehabilitation Tax Credit for Home Ownership," *Historic Preservation News*, (October/November 1994), 12; Sweeney, "Preservation: A Record of Economic and Social Achievements," 8; *Historic Preservation News* (February 1991), 4.

    The National Trust set up a Community Partners for Revitalization program to develop pilot projects that could demonstrate the effectiveness of various strategies. Moe, "Presidents Note," *Historic Preservation* (May/June 1994), 6.
45. Stanley A. Lowe, Walter C. Kidney, and John Metzger, "The Pittsburgh

Experience," *Historic Preservation Forum*, (May/June 1991), 26–33. Stanley Lowe, "Creating Livable Communities in Pittsburgh," *Historic Preservation Forum*, (January/February 1994), 28–35. Roberta Brandes Gratz, "The Preservationist," *Town & Country* (April 1994), 93.

Not surprisingly in the current climate, the Community Reinvestment Act is itself under siege. Republicans have announced initiatives to weaken or gut the law. See Kim Nauer, "Turning the Tables," *City Limits* (February 1995), 18–23.

46. After working successfully in Boston, St. Louis, San Francisco and eleven other locations, a confederation of these locally managed and financed programs pushed for and secured a setaside for $17.5–40 million in the Housing and Community Development Act of 1992. Allen Freeman. "We Need Love, We Need Support, We Need Attention . . . ," *Historic Preservation* (May/June 1993), 29.

    Commerce Department data showed that spending one million dollars on rehabilitating an older building created five more construction jobs and three more permanent jobs than an equal amount spent on new construction. *Historic Preservation* (July/August 1994), 6.
47. Chris Warner, "Lee Adler Finds a Way," *Historic Preservation* (May/June 1988), 64. See also Cisneros, "Bridging America's Visions," in *Past Meets Future*, 85–91.
48. *Historic Preservation News* (March/April 1993), 6.
49. *Historic Preservation News* (February 1991), 4.
50. New York Landmarks Conservancy, *New York City Historic Properties Fund;* New York Landmarks Conservancy, *Newsletter* (fall 1994).
51. Melinda J. Matthews, "Affordable Housing and Historic Preservation," *Historic Preservation Forum* (May/June 1992), 6–11. Harlem-based preservationist Michael Adams noted that landmarks laws were one of the few mechanisms that gave people in minority communities a way to hold owners of properties accountable for maintaining them. "Roundtable: Preservation in Minority Communities," 156–8. Others linked up the revitalization and identity arguments, suggesting that characterless public housing did not improve peoples lives. Sweeney, "Preservation: A Record of Economic and Social Achievements," 8.
52. New York Landmarks Conservancy, *Sacred Sites Program;* Tomlan, "Preservation Practice Comes of Age," 79.
53. Andrea Oppenheimer Dean, "Inspired Partners," *Historic Preservation* (May/June 1994), 28. See also: *Historic Preservation News*, (April 1991), 8.
54. Harvey Gantt, "Reassessing our Agenda," *Historic Preservation Forum* (January/February 1993), 10. See also the work of the New Mexico Community Foundation in aiding the restoration of adobe churches. Thomas J. Lueck, "The Struggle to Preserve Old Churches," *New York Times* (18 March 1990).
55. Tersh Boasberg, "A New Paradigm for Preservation," in *Past Meets Fu-*

ture, 150; William J. Murtagh, "Janus Never Sleeps," in *Past Meets Future*, 56; *Historic Preservation News* (February 1992), 4.

56. Tomlan, "Preservation Practice Comes of Age," in *Past Meets Future*, 77.
57. T. Allan Comp, "Learning from Heritage Development," *Historic Preservation Forum* (November/December 1991), 6.
58. Brink and Dehart, "Findings and Recommendations," in *Past Meets Future*, 18.
59. Dehart, "Future of the Preservation Movement," 6; Morton, "Forging New Values in Uncommon Times," 38.
60. Morton, "Forging New Values in Uncommon Times," 40; Dehart, "The Future of the Preservation Movement," 6.
61. Wagner, "Urban Downtown Revitalization and Historic Preservation," *Historic Preservation Forum* (September/October 1993), 53; Brink and Dehart, "Findings and Recommendations," in *Past Meets Future*, 19; Boasberg, "A New Paradigm for Preservation," in *Past Meets Future*, 146.

    Preservation needed to change its relation with government as the environmentalists had, and go from being outsiders to being participants in the elective or bureaucratic bodies that established policy. Archer, "Where We Stand," 34–5; Rogers quoted in Brink and Dehart, "Findings and Recommendations," in *Past Meets Future*, 18.

    Folding preservation into planning can be problematic if carried too far. Planning commissions deal in broad brush strokes, with massed buildings, not specific structures. Empowered watchdog organizations, backed by alert constituencies, are probably still the safest bet for keeping wreckers at bay.
62. Neal R. Peirce, "The Age of the Citistate," *Historic Preservation Forum* (January/February 1994), 19–27.
63. Boasberg, "A New Paradigm for Preservation," in *Past Meets Future*, 150.
64. Deborah Marquis Kelly and Jennifer Goodman, "Conservation Districts as an Alternative to Historic Districts," *Historic Preservation Forum* (September/October 1993), 6–14; Brink and Dehart, "Findings and Recommendations," in *Past Meets Future*, 19; Boasberg, "A New Paradigm for Preservation," in *Past Meets Future*, 147.
65. Shelley Mastran, "Introduction: Heritage Partnership," *Historic Preservation Forum* (July/August 1994), 4–5; Comp, "Learning from Heritage Development," *Historic Preservation Forum* (November/December 1991), 6–11; Archer, "Where We Stand," 29–31, 34–6.
66. *Historic Preservation News* (August/September 1994), 20–21. See the "Disney's America" chapter in this volume, 165-166.
67. Richard Moe, quoted in *Organization of American Historians Newsletter*, 22, no. 3 (August 1994), 9.

    Local and community public historians also have a role to play in mobilizing the political energy to defend threatened historic sites and districts. By fostering popular memories, historical scholarship, community oral history, and innovative design projects for public spaces can strengthen the constitutency for preservation. See Dolores Hayden, *The Power of Place: Urban Landscapes as Public History* (Cambridge, Mass.; 1995).

68. Indeed, the besieged national environmental groups will no doubt welcome an infusion of grass roots energy. Since the advent of the Clinton administration, several major organizations, including the National Audubon Society, the Sierra Club, and the Wilderness Society, have suffered substantial drops in income and membership, in part because they diverted energy from grassroots organizing to palavering with the powerful. Daniel Weiss of the Sierra Club believes that "we perhaps spent too much time talking to people in the White House and not enough time talking to people who live next to toxic waste dumps." Overby, "The Politics of Mine-ing," 13. See Nancy Shute, "Capitol Shakeup," *The Amicus Journal* (winter 1995), 24–5.

Section IV

Ronald Reagan and the Politics of History

Ronald Reagan as George Custer and Errol Flynn as Jeb Stuart, in *The Santa Fe Trail* (1940). (© 1940 Turner Entertainment Co. All Rights Reserved.)

One of the first things Ronald Reagan did upon entering the White House was to purge the presidential portraits. Down from the place of honor in the Cabinet Room came Thomas Jefferson and up went Calvin Coolidge. It clearly indicated the impending neoconservative attempt to return the country to the golden days of the Dollar Decade, before the New Deal and Great Society were even gleams in secular humanist eyes. But to a historian, the purge signalled something else, the arrival in power of an administration that intended to wage symbolic war on the terrain of history.

Reagan and his colleagues set out both to claim historical pedigree for contemporary right-wing policies and to reconstruct an edifice of historical explanation that was largely dismantled, by professional historians and popular protest, in the 1960s and 1970s. Several of his forays into the past received national, even worldwide attention. But the degree to which interventions around historical interpretation became central to his presidency has been perhaps insufficiently appreciated.

Reagan and his intellectual adjutants engaged in a number of skirmishes in this respect. For example, Reaganites wheeled out some of their biggest rhetorical artillery in an attempt to destroy the "Vietnam syndrome," that annoying cluster of public memories impeding their filibustering in Central America. To reverse widely held negative assessments of America's Vietnam endeavor, they insisted the war was a legitimate, indeed "noble" effort to bar communist expansion; they made stab-in-the-back pronouncements about the media's and the antiwar movement's responsibility for the war's failure;

did end runs around the prevailing antipathy by trying to smuggle a blurred Vietnam experience into the pantheon of popularly-accepted American wars; and baldly rewrote Southeast Asian history. Reagan, for example, claimed that before French colonization, North and South Vietnam were two separate countries; that it was Ho Chi Minh who refused to participate in the elections mandated by the 1954 Geneva Conference; that unarmed American advisers in South Vietnam were attacked with "pipe bombs"; and that in reaction Kennedy authorized sending a division of Marines. Each of these statements was totally untrue. Taken together they produced a false narrative that transformed America's intervention into a virtuous response to communist wickedness. This, in turn, contributed to his larger project of restoring America's Galahad self-image—badly tarnished by the hellish realities of the Indochina war and the exposure, by a generation of historians, of some of the darker aspects of the American past—and helped resurrect the imperial culture that sped us along the road to Vietnam in the first place.

At Bitburg, Reagan recast the history of yet another military conflict, World War II, again trying to alter or bury memories that hindered right-wing geopolitical initiatives. At first he straightforwardly argued against "reawakening the memories" of the Holocaust "because we now find ourselves allies and friends of the countries that we once fought against. . . ." Seeking to obliterate an inconvenient but obdurate legacy, he asserted: "I don't think we ought to focus on the past. I want to focus on the future. I want to put that history behind me." (Perhaps the president thought this an attainable goal because of his belief that "the German people have very few alive that even remember the war, and certainly none of them who were adults and participating in any way.") When it became clear that induced amnesia was politically unfeasible, he assayed a reinterpretation of Nazism, reducing that complex historical phenomenon to "one man's totalitarian dictatorship." It was this analysis exempting all Germans but Hitler from responsibility for the war that facilitated his infamous proposition that the Waffen SS entombed at Bitburg "were victims, just as surely as the victims in the concentration camps."

Reagan also sought to legitimate his obsession with overthrowing the Sandinistas by justification-through-historical analogy, calling the contras—that collection of hireling thugs and hit men prowling the borders of Nicaragua—the "moral equivalent" of the "founding fathers." Supporting this canard on the generation of 1776 required overlooking the contras' Somocista heritage, their butchery of civilians, their drug-running proclivities, and their complete reliance on outside funding (which, if we must indulge in historical analogies, made them the modern-day equivalent not of George Washington's troops but of the Hessians, George III's hired gunslingers). The larger insistence that the Nicaraguan Revolution was the brain child of

Soviet imperialists required obliviousness to the long history of U.S. interventions in Central America: American Marines stormed ashore in Nicaragua before the Bolshevik Revolution had transpired.

On the domestic front, Reagan and the neoconservatives, in order to legitimate turning the American clock back to 1920, propagated a pseudohistorical analysis of the rise of the federal government. The right wing's assault on state power—or, more precisely, on those aspects of it which they did not like—rested on the bogus proposition that Big Government grew and grew in response to demands by blacks, welfare chiselers, do- gooders and federal bureaucrats, and then sat, like a fat dragon, on the backs of beleaguered corporations, squashing entrepreneurial initiative, until its victims prevailed on "Sir Ronald" to drive it away. Purveying such a line helped immeasurably in garnering political support for budget cuts and tax reforms that favored the rich. But making this interpretation plausible required eliding a variety of facts: That the surge of big government in the 1930s was part of a desperate attempt to save a collapsed capitalism from its own failures; that Washington's growth in the 1940s was due first to the war, and then to the establishment of a postwar military apparatus which was cheered on by the defense contractors and multinational corporations whose interests abroad it helped support; that the ballooning of the federal government in the 1950s and 1960s was, in large measure, a corporate-applauded use of public resources to underwrite private profitability (highway construction made auto company dividends possible) or to stave off challenges to the stability of the system by ameliorating the damage, to people and the environment, created by its workings.

Elsewhere on the home front, Reagan stood guard at the gate of the traditional American pantheon of heroes, barring unwanted intruders. He supported Jesse Helms's campaign to block Martin Luther King's birthday from being made a national holiday, on the grounds that King might yet be proved a Communist. Making a hero of King, it was feared, would put a crimp in right-wing efforts to dismantle the fruits of the civil rights movement, and give comfort to the political constituency—American blacks—who were Reagan's most committed enemies.

Reagan also seized upon the occasion of the 1986 ceremonies rededicating the Statue of Liberty to distort the history of the "immigrant experience," less to legitimatize a particular policy than to undergird a general ideology.

To summarize, the administration launched an aggressive and broad-based attack on prevailing understandings of the past. Now it might be argued that this was an unexceptionable, indeed perfectly legitimate project. There is, after all, no such thing as a single historical "truth." All history is a human production—a deliberate selection, ordering and evaluation of past events, experiences, and processes. Consequently, there have always been and will always be great differences amongst those who issue and defend competing constructions of the past. My generation of professional historians had overturned much of the established wisdom of the 1940s and 1950s, and Reagan—quite deliberately—set out to overturn us.

Back in 1970, in a speech entitled "Ours is Not a Sick Society," Reagan blamed student unrest on intellectuals who misled them: "I have news for [the students]—in a thousand social science courses, they have been taught 'the way it is *not*'." He told the American Bar Association in 1983 "One of my dreams is to help Americans rise above pessimism by renewing their belief in themselves." This enterprise had a specifically historical dimension: "Our cause," he said, "must be to rediscover, reassert, and reapply America's spiritual heritage to our national affairs." Such blemishes as mar that heritage were inconsequential: "Whatever sad episodes exist in our past, any objective observer must hold a positive view of American history, a history that has been the story of hopes fulfilled and dreams made into reality."

In 1981 Reagan addressed the Notre Dame graduating class:

> Now, I know that this period of your life, you have been and are critically looking at the mores and customs of the past and questioning their value. Every generation does that. May I suggest, don't discard the time-tested values upon which civilization was built simply because they're old. More important, don't let today's doom criers and cynics persuade that the best is past, that from here on it's all downhill. . . . My hope today is that in the years to come and come it shall—when it's your time explain to another generation the meaning of the past and thereby hold out to them the promise of their future, that you'll recall the truths and traditions of which we've spoken. It is these truths and traditions that define our civilization and make up our national heritage. And now, they're yours to protect and pass on.

The sleight of hand here is that what Reagan laid out for us was "the truth." Apart from the disturbingly dogmatic quality of the assertion (Reagan presented himself as sole possessor of the truth rather than more modestly claiming that his interpretation of events better encompassed the available evidence), the problem here is that, as we have noted, Reagan's historical pronouncements (like many of his statements about current affairs) were riddled with inaccuracies and falsehoods. He consistently refused to be bound by the historical profession's cardinal rule—you can not make up facts to suit your theories. No self-respecting historian, of whatever political persuasion, would have published the steady stream of untruths that Reagan did, and if she or he did, they would have been summarily drummed out of the profession.

Indeed a small industry emerged that was devoted to chronicling the president's misstatements about contemporary and historical events. Within it, a heated debate sprang up about how to interpret the Reagan "reign of error." Some thought he misspoke on details but got the essentials right. Others thought him an ignorant but genial fool. A third group saw him as a conscious, habitual liar. Journalist Christopher Hitchens, for instance, derided the image of Reagan as "a hapless blooper merchant" and insisted that his presidency "has been a sort of experiment in the limits of mendacity, made even more objectionable by its presentation as a 'wing-and-a-prayer' inspired amateurism." But the debate's choices between deceit, ignorance, and excessive enthusiasm were too restrictive.

To be sure, Reagan lied. He had been doing so for a long time. Back in 1937, when Reagan was exploring a movie career and an agent asked about his experience, he responded by markedly embellishing the reality, reasoning, he tells us in his autobiography, that "a little lying in a good cause wouldn't hurt." (A phrase that could neatly have served as the credo of the Irangate operation.) But even Hitchens wondered if at least some of the roots of Reagan's mendacity did not run below the threshold of purposive consciousness. He recalled the president's preposterous 1983 assertion, to Israeli Prime Minister Yitzak Shamir, that he (a Hollywood warrior) had actually assisted in the liberation of the Nazi death camps. In 1984 Reagan repeated the claim—to Simon Wiesenthal, no less. Hitchens argued that this "is an insult to the victims whose moral credit he is trying to appropriate. It is an insult to those who did risk their lives. And it is a lie. In fact, given the certainty of detection, it almost counts as a pathological lie." Now it is true that Reagan's mind repeatedly slipped between remembering things the way they were and the way he would have liked them to be. But this is, after all, a common enough failing, and only if carried to extremes is it evidence of a psychotic inability to distinguish reality from fantasy. But the deeper problem with Hitchen's perspective was not that it was wrong, rather that it rooted the problem too narrowly in Reagan's personal psyche.

It is more profitable to take the flagrantly cavalier quality of Reagan's rhetoric as being a clue that he was operating outside the domain of history and thus was not subject to the canons of scholarship. The president, I think, repeatedly sidled over the border—at times hard to discern but nevertheless very real—between history and myth. The historical disinformation he retailed with such conviction can better be understood as an attempt not to produce revisionist history, but to perpetuate (or resuscitate) a structure of myths.[1]

Myth, more readily than history, forgives the subordination of facts to the higher end of value creation. There is, admittedly, a great deal of romanticized, sentimentalized, and sycophantic history about, but the ideal of the profession insists on a continual dialectical interaction between theoretical practice and empirical reality. The Reagan approach soared happily above the messy, complex, poignant, painful, and contingent ground of history into a stratosphere of idealized fantasies, and did so without remorse or fear of contradiction.

If the Reagan approach was mythic, it had less in common with, say, Greek tragedians, than with such contemporary American mythmasters as the "imagineers" of Disney World. Their approach, as summarized by one of their ranks, is instructive: "What we create is a 'Disney Realism,' sort of utopian in nature, where we carefully program out all the negative, unwanted elements and program in the positive elements." Sure "Main Street" (a supposed recreation of the town where Walt grew up) isn't the way it *really* was. Rather: "This is what the real Main Street should have been like."[2] Compare this with the procedures of those who managed Reagan's political advertising. In the 1984 presidential campaign, Assistant White House Chief of Staff Richard Darman issued a revealing memo on rhetorical strategy: "Paint Ronald Reagan," he ordered speechwriters, "as the personification of all that is right with or heroized by America. Leave Mondale in a position where an attack on Reagan is tantamount to an attack on America's idealized image of itself—where a vote against Reagan is in some subliminal sense, a vote against mythic 'AMERICA'."

This elimination of inconvenient memories, this retrospective tidying up of the past, was not considered to be tampering with the truth, but rather bringing out deeper truths. Indeed, the mythmaking process exempted its producers from the problem of error. Concern for factual truth became a superficial, surface matter—"the hobgoblin of little minds," to borrow Emerson's phrase—to be subordinated to the presentation of spiritual essences. Reagan spewed out "factoids," which may have been right or wrong, but all of them, like iron filings in a magnetic field, arranged themselves in the same direction; he never made an error that underwrote a pro-Soviet or prowelfare state reading of history. But the teflon presidency endured as long as it did, not only because Americans considered getting names and dates wrong to be eminently excusable, but because people (quite properly) did not judge myths by the standards of history.

Another reason Reagan's speech was more akin to myth than history is that it embodied nonlinear, noncausal ways of understanding the relationship between past and present. Mythmakers, like historians, discern patterns in the past and present them to their audiences to help them locate themselves and establish meaning and value in their lives. But they do so by positing immanent metahistorical teleologies. The past becomes merely the record of the working out of an innate or divine design. This renders the historical project immaterial. It becomes superfluous to analyze the passage of time in order to illuminate its legacy—the matrix of constraints and possibilities that human beings constructed and bequeathed to the present, the matrix within which present actors must work. One resorts to the past only to remember, through rites, rituals, and mythic replays, the moral messages there inscribed.

This approach to time is widespread, characteristic of many of the cultures anthropologists track. Its practitioners, ensconced within an enchanted circle of tradition, find the work of the historian irrelevant. They prefer to collapse time, to focus on founding myths, to reject historicity altogether. Their temporal needs are met by symbolically reenacting historical scenarios. They seek not to recollect but to reactualize, not to gain perspective on the past but to fuse past and present, not to temporalize present actors but to identify with former ones. The point of the past is to provide "evidence" for the truth of one or another metahistorical myth. In Reagan's case, "history" becomes the cosmic record of the eternal conflict between good and evil, of which America's struggle with godless communism is merely the latest encounter. As Paul Erickson notes in his illuminating analysis of Reagan's 1964 speech nominating Barry Goldwater for president, the symbolic strategy transformed the crusade for the Republicans into an epoch battle on the order of the exodus of the Jews from Egypt, Christ's sacrifice on the cross, and the battle of Concord Bridge.

In fact, a good deal of Reagan's rhetoric dwelt on peculiarly American foundation myths. At the ceremony preceding the reillumination of the Statue of Liberty, Reagan spoke of John Winthrop (the first governor of Massachusetts Bay), who, in 1630, just before landing in the New World, told a little group of "Quakers [*sic*] on the tiny deck of the Arabella [*sic*]" that "the eyes of all the world were upon them . . . [and] they must be a light unto the the nations of all the world—a shining city upon a hill." Reagan went on, "Call it mysticism if you will, I have always believed there was some divine providence that placed this great land here between the two great oceans, to be found by a special kind of people from every corner of the world." The descendants of these special people had a global mission: "Our work can never be truly done until every man, woman, and child shares in our gift, in our hope, and stands with us in the light of liberty." "We," he concluded, "are the keepers of the flame of liberty. We hold it high tonight for the world to see, a beacon of hope, a light unto the nations."

Reagan's use of Winthrop illustrates how foundation myths can be put to dangerous ends. Precisely because they are not situated in a specific historical context but rather are abstract emblems or exemplary tales, they may be detached from their actual moorings and redeployed to almost any purpose.

Take Reagan's misuse of Winthrop's shipboard sermon, "A Model of Christian Charity." By deleting the original context he stripped the Puritan project of its truly radical dimension. The "city upon a hill" was an enterprise of revolutionary exiles—Cromwell himself had considered coming to Massachusetts—intended as an alternative to corrupt England. Those who did not flee to Massachusetts chopped off the king's head, and many Puritans went back to join the rebel forces. The imagery Reagan featured once had *radical* substance.[3] But Reagan put the mythicized discourse to profoundly antirevolutionary uses. It required a mood-wrenching effort to break free of the spell woven by a trained actor at the height of his powers. And to remember that the man calling on Americans, "for love of liberty," to "champion, even in times of peril, the cause of human freedom in far-off lands," was, in fact, rallying support for Jonas Savimbi, Augusto Pinochet, Somoza's legatees, and beleaguered Boers trying to stem a planet-wide assault on apartheid. It was the same with his assertion that the Contras were "moral equivalents" of the founding fathers. By ritually equating a symbolic wellspring of the American experience (the Revolution) with contemporary right-wing enterprises, he aimed to forge an indissoluble spiritual link—to foster an identification—between the founding fathers, contemporary Americans, and assorted reactionaries around the planet. The mind set he sought to create was a mystic communion impervious to contradiction by facts. Reagan's genius was his ability to construct bastions of a mythic imagination that were impregnable to merely cognitive assaults. Only when he shattered the foundation symbology of his own presidency did he become vulnerable to the legions of reason.

Irangate sent Reagan's popularity into a tailspin. Why, after being impervious to the truth for so long, was he suddenly rendered vulnerable? It was not, after all, the first time he had been caught preaching one thing and practicing another. Many in Reagan's nationwide audience had been quite prepared to overlook his discrepancies, to accept that his task was to proclaim virtue, but not necessarily to embody it. But there was one symbolic construction that required special care and attention, for it was the foundation image of his own presidency—Ron Reagan: The man who hung tough with the Ayatollah. When, through compassion, or foolhardiness, or incompetence, he presided over the dealings that stretched the disjunction between rhetoric and reality too far, he (as it were) snapped his own symbolic spell and was dragged from the enchanted rhetorical sphere he had constructed. But what is important, and what remains to be explained, is his long and brilliant run.

Hollywood and History

So far I have suggested that Reagan was able to comfortably (and therefore convincingly) make statements dramatically at variance with widely known facts because they were nestled in a supportive context of myth which validated them for believers. But this still leaves two aspects of the matter in need of clarification. How did he come by his mythology? And how was he able to prevail upon large numbers of the American people to share it with him? A partial answer to both questions requires a brief exploration of the relationship between the form and content of Reagan's myths and the subculture of which he was so largely a product—that of Hollywood.

The impact on the president of his years in tinsel town has not gone unnoticed, but a few comments on the cinematic roots of Reagan's sensibility seem warranted here. Some of these are obvious. Reagan spent much of his adult life in a relatively insular world; as even right-wing supporters like Paul Weyrich admit, "his Hollywood background has sometimes prevented him from being sensitive enough to the realities that are out there." Then again, the process of filmmaking is a model for would-be mythmakers: In the world of filmic make-believe, happy endings could be—were often required to be—manufactured at will. Good actors (and even second rate ones) routinely worked themselves into believing their scriptwriters' scenarios. Snippets of celluloid could be abstracted from their original context and redeployed to suit an editor's purpose. And scenes that did not work well could be left on the cutting room floor.

More interesting, perhaps, is the impact on Reagan of the *content* of particular films, or types of films. Many people noted Reagan's general reliance on the movies for his images of reality. On one occasion, the president told a White House audience of Jews on Holocaust Day that, unlike right-wing extremists who claimed the Holocaust was an invention, he knew it had happened because he had seen movies of it. Jules Feiffer suggested, with tongue only partly in cheek, that had he not, "he might today be calling it the Holocaust theory, as suspicious of the Holocaust as he is of evolution." Feiffer went farther, suggesting that "if Ronald Reagan in his Warner Brothers days had been cast in a movie about Charles Darwin, today he would believe in evolution."

Now this is overstated, of course, but it does seem that Reagan's immersion in The World that Hollywood Built—an imaginative construct that includes a historical dimension—was a major source of the mythic iconography he carried around in his political unconscious. Michael Rogin argues that Reagan "found out who he was by whom he played on film"; that he engaged in an active merger of his on and off screen identities (becoming producer and script writer where originally he was only an actor); and that the resulting (con)fusion between life and film produced "Ronald Reagan."

It is also the case that Reagan's first, most impressionable, and most successful years in Hollywood came at a moment—the tail end of the 1930s and very beginning of the 1940s—when the industry, with World War II looming, had begun constructing a mythic past that was worth fighting for. In those years, the backlots worked overtime churning out nostalgic movies about times that never existed except in the imagination of movie moguls and screenwriters. In 1939–1940 alone the major studios issued a barrage of "history" films that conjured up—or, better, collectively constructed—a "spirit of America past," including, among many others: *Gone With the Wind*, *Drums Along the Mohawk*, *Young Mr. Lincoln*, *Abraham Lincoln in Illinois*, *Union Pacific*, *Stagecoach*, *Young Tom Edison*, *Edison the Man*, *The Howards of Virginia*, *Stanley and Livingston*, *The Real Glory*, *The Story of Alexander Graham Bell*, *Dodge City*, *Let Freedom Ring*, *Mr. Smith Goes to Washington*, *The Fighting 69th*, *Little Old New York*, *Northwest Passage*, *Dark Command*, *The Oklahoma Kid*, *Lillian Russell*, *Brigham Young-Frontiersman*, *Kit Carson*, *Geronimo*, *The Return of Frank James*, and *Land of Liberty* (Hollywood's contribution to the World's Fair).

Reagan's own foray into the genre was a portrayal of George Armstrong Custer in *The Santa Fe Trail*. (This 1940 epic was sandwiched between the two films that made the most impact on Reagan, *Knute Rockne—All American* [1940] and *Kings Row* [1942].) The plot revolved around the largely imaginary activities in the 1850s of a clatch of soon-to-be-famous army officers, including Errol Flynn as Jeb Stuart, who tangle with John Brown, played by Raymond Massey as a crackpot villain, a manipulative outside-agitator of slaves, who are not interested in freedom. The film was such a mishmash of fact and forgery that Bosley Crowther was moved to write in his *New York Times* review that: "For any one who has the slightest regard for the spirit—not to mention the facts—of American history, it will prove exceedingly annoying."

Not all the films of this period evoked precisely the same past, but there is a good deal of overlap in their characterization of U.S. history. This uniformity of perspective is partly explained by noting that Hollywood's search for a usable past was part of a much larger cultural phenomenon of the 1930s, which Warren Susman has characterized as an attempt to define the meaning of The American Way of Life, a process initiated by the shattering experience of the Depression and accelerated by the rapidly darkening world situation. Hollywood studios (like many American intellectuals) turned away from the estrangement and cynical debunking of the 1920s and the radicalism of the early 1930s to a nationalistic celebration of America and its institutions as superior to those of European barbarism. And the bedrock of America was the People. The People (as opposed to the proletariat) were

the common folk, the nation's repository of goodness, and they included almost everyone except economic and political elitists (evil bankers and party bosses). The discovery and celebration of the American People was a widespread phenomenon: museums featured folk art exhibits, folk music had a resurgence, WPA murals and guidebooks focused on the folk, populist history and historical novels had a heyday. Even the Communist Party, then in its popular front period, featured the slogan: Communism is Twentieth-century Americanism. (In 1937, when the DAR somehow failed to commemorate the anniversary of Paul Revere's ride, a New York City chapter of the Young Communist League hired a man to dress up in colonial garb and ride down Wall Street on horseback carrying a sign proclaiming: The DAR forgets, but the YCL remembers!)

The high priests of the cult of the People were the moviemakers, and the movie houses were its (well attended) temples: In 1938 there were over eighty-million movie admissions a week in U.S. theaters (a number equal to 65 percent of the entire population). Cinema houses prefaced their programs with—literally—flag waving ceremonies on stage and the singing of the national anthem. Will Hays, Hollywood's spokesperson, endorsed films "which discussed the values of our present day democracy and emphasized the traditions that have made this country great." In 1939, of the 574 feature films Hollywood produced, 481 were in some way celebrations of American life.

The search for America also involved a search for America's cultural roots. In Hollywood the vehicle for this was the historical movie, especially the western, a genre which experienced a dramatic revival in 1939. Through these films—about the American Revolution, frontier individualism, wagon trains menaced by red hordes and saved by the cavalry, gracious planters, rugged industrial entrepreneurs, and the triumph of civilization over savagery and a threatening environment—ran characteristic themes of optimism, patriotism, and democracy. And populism: Critiques of self-serving and greedy businessmen continued to appeal to audiences in the late 1930s.

The history films—particularly those by the masters of the period, John Ford and Frank Capra—also conveyed a strong sense that while Americans in the past had at times been manipulated or dominated by figures of evil, they had always been aroused (usually by a figure like Lincoln or Jefferson Deeds, who had risen from the ranks of the people itself) to fight on to ultimate triumph. Many of these films were hugely successful (with left film critics and filmmakers as well as popular audiences) because of their strong evocation of a democratic spirit. But despite the surface radicalism of this message, they were, as Charles Maland notes, ultimately conservative in their assertion that to succeed, Americans needed only to apply traditional wisdom and values to contemporary problems. Capra's Grandpa Vanderhof (in *You Can't Take it With You*) denounces "ismania": "Communism, fascism, voodooism. Everybody's got an ism these days." What Americans needed was to "know something about Americans: John Paul Jones, Patrick Henry, Samuel Adams, Washington, Jefferson, Monroe, Lincoln, Grant, Lee, Edison, Twain. When things got tough for those boys they didn't go around looking for isms." American values had their wellspring, the history films argued, in the small town cultures (eastern, western, or southern) of the eighteenth and nineteenth centuries.

The problem is that the historical portraits were more fancy than fact, both in their particulars—*Young Mr. Lincoln* was strewn with fabrications—and in the general portrait that emerged. The films celebrated farmers, but were unwilling to recall the reality of farm movements; lionized workers, but sidestepped the historical reality of capital-labor struggles; sentimentalized the old South, but finessed discussing slavery. These were historical utopias—immensely appealing, but often about as real as Disney's Main Street. This did not bother the filmmakers. In *The Man Who Shot Liberty Valance* (1962), John Ford has a young reporter ask Senator Ransom Stoddard (Jimmy Stewart) if a purportedly factual event from the past might not be a legend, and Stoddard replies: "When the fact becomes legend, print the legend." For Ford, as it would be for Reagan, truth was beside the point, which was to affirm that the American Way of Life had deep roots in the American experience. The movies were moral fictions placed in historical settings.

More problematic than the mythological character of movie history was the inadequacy of the myth to problems at hand. The films eschewed presentations of the political, economic, and social contexts within which their protagonists operated—backgrounds which could have been made as dramatic and exciting for audiences as real history in fact is—and instead opted for the flat and easy moralizing of melodramas. History became a matter of good men vanquishing evildoers. Characters were cardboard creatures of allegory, supposed manifestations of aspects of timeless human nature, not agents rooted in a particular moment of contingency. The strengths of the American democratic tradition were, for all the flag waving, made less rather than more accessible. The films used national symbols as incantations; goosebump raising scenes sought to summon up the almost magical powers believed inherent in the Liberty Bell or the Lincoln Memorial. (During the war, troops would be brought to Colonial Williamsburg for inspiration.) While such rallying efforts may have boosted morale, they were poor devices for grappling with reality. Neighborliness and the Golden Rule were not up to defeating the Depression or the Nazis any more than volunteerism is a satisfactory substitute for government—despite Reagan's advocacy of it, which he supported by citing speeches read by Gary Cooper playing Jefferson Deeds! Indeed, when Capra began pushing his analysis deeper, in *Meet John Doe*, he foundered; it would not be Capra and Ford but Chaplin and Wells who would produce films that confronted the real crises of the times.

These cinematic constructs, moreover, could be pernicious as well as misleading. Take the classic movie approach to the "winning of the West." It depicted an expansion of civilization by populist sodbusters and sheepherders who triumphed over savage Indians, evil cattle "barons," and anarchic outlaws. A central mythic image was the wagon train drawn up in a defensive circle against hordes of screaming redskins until rescued by the Seventh Cavalry. This iconography (borrowed from D.W. Griffith's *The Birth of a Nation*, which depicted a band of whites holed up in a cabin and surrounded by hordes of screaming blacks until rescued by the Ku Klux Klan) not only inverted the reality of the historical and moral relations between whites and Indians, but once it was widely accepted, it provided a latent set of images and values that could be detached from their original context and deployed to lend an aura of self-righteousness to other foreign policies. The most notorious case in our lifetime was Vietnam.

The interplay between history and cinema mythology could get incredibly complicated. Lyndon Johnson once told his National Security Council: "Hell, Viet Nam is just like the Alamo." Commander William Travis had drawn a line in the dust telling those who would stay and die not to cross it, and LBJ (who insisted on telling young soldiers, falsely, that his great, great-grandfather had died at the Alamo) equated retreating in Vietnam with crossing that line. Perhaps Johnson's convictions were reinforced by a 1960 movie, *The Alamo*, starring John Wayne as Davy Crockett (he also produced and directed it). Wayne's gungho version became, for many, the official interpretation of the nineteenth-century realities. This was the more understandable because, at the time, in the Alamo itself, there hung a mural commemorating the battle which substituted the faces of the Hollywood actors for those of the original heroes. The person presented to millions of tourists as Davy Crockett was John Wayne. (Only later, under the impact of the new social history, did the Alamo feel compelled to send the mural to the mothballs.)

Reagan, I believe, was drawn deeply to such a version of American history, and he retained both its mythic content and its casual disregard for the relevance of historical truth. It is also likely that Reagan was influenced by the revisionist quality of the post-1939 process. He lived through and participated in a successful overcoming of the more radical mid-thirties filmic rendition of America's past and present. This, I suspect, provided a model for his own later crusade in the 1970s and 1980s to reverse the representations generated in the radical 1960s.[4]

Reagan projected an axiomatic certainty about things that were untrue not because he had a weak or impoverished historical sensibility, but because he had none at all. Like many in traditional societies, he lived not in a world of historicity, but in a world of eternal contemporaneity. The founding myths of society were timeless truths, to be reenacted through ritual and ceremony. What was peculiarly American about him is that the sacred texts were only occasionally those of ancient tales or scriptures. When Reagan spoke about the importance of tradition and how much the past matters, as a good conservative supposedly should, his temporal reference point was not the sprawling, messy, contradictory reality of the last few centuries in America, but rather "Hollywood history," an artifact of mass cultural production, created in the late 1930s, and refashioned in the crucible of hot and cold wars.

Historical Revanchism

This excursion to movieland may help explain why Reagan believed what he said, but it still leaves us with the problem of how he convinced others. During the 1960s and 1970s many Americans, spurred on by the antiwar, civil rights, feminist, native American and gay movements, experienced a major disillusionment. People drew sharper lines between fact and fiction, and extricated themselves from Hollywood's perspective of the past. Even Hollywood responded to the times: Compare *Roots* with *Gone with the Wind*. Much of this reflection was done by participants in the political projects of the day, and much by professional historians (myself included) who were involved in or sympathetic to those projects. This is not to say that historians had finally learned a timeless truth, or that we were not capable of romanticizing or sentimentalizing slaves, women, Indians, and working people. Still, I believe our analyses were more adequate to the facts of American history than those that had been promulgated by apologists for the status quo. We were capable of embracing (indeed our political sympathies required us to embrace) the stories of a far wider variety of social groups than had ever before been considered by historians. And by shedding a narrow nationalism and developing more global and ecumenical perspectives, we helped undermine the chauvinisms that had facilitated America's disastrous involvement in Vietnam.

Then, with the collapse of the long postwar boom and the loss in Vietnam, there was a clamor, especially on the part of those who had never been happy about the demythification process in the first place, to jettison the new history and return either to older historical formulations or to myth, in a process Paul Erickson has called an "orgy of re-illusionment." From Reagan's perspective, of course, it was a return to sanity. As he said to West Point students in 1981, "I'm happy to tell you that the people of America have recovered from what can only be called a temporary aberration. There is a spiritual revival going on in this country, a hunger on the part of the people to once again be proud of America."

What, then, was the appeal of Reagan's rhetorical cultural revanchism? Let me be very clear that, for all my focus here on ideologies and symbol systems, a host of very material attractions drew particular Americans to Reaganism like hogs to the trough—attractions Mike Davis has laid out in his *Prisoners of the American Dream*. The fact is that some Americans gladly jettisoned history and embraced myth because, consciously or unconsciously, doing so supported their relatively privileged position. Ignorance, after all, can be based on a desire not to know. Latin Americans have a saying: "North Americans never remember, and we never forget." In some cases, therefore, amnesia was the tribute that memory paid to expediency.

But what of the many whose interests might, arguably, have better been served by a continuing confrontation with history? There are a variety of reasons that might help account for their disaffection. For one thing, the practice of history is not comforting. It is, rather, profoundly subversive. Yosef Yerushlami (in *Zakhor: Jewish History and Jewish Memory*) notes the purpose of history is not to bind up severed memories, but to create a new kind of recollection. "With unprecedented energy it continually re-creates an ever more detailed past whose shapes and textures memory does not recognize. But that is not all. The historian does not simply come to replenish the gaps of memory. He constantly challenges even those memories that have survived intact. . . . All these features cut against the grain of collective memory which . . . is drastically selective. Certain memories live on; the rest are winnowed out, repressed, or simply discarded by a process of natural selection which the historian, uninvited, disturbs and reverses." Ultimately people will accept such strong medicine only if they have faith in the power of reason to enlighten their world. In times when reason seems ill equipped to the task, myth becomes the more appealing alternative.

Secondly, Reagan's approach was in some ways congruent with what I have taken to calling America's historicidal culture—one that systematically undercuts our ability to situate ourselves in time. For a host of reasons dealt with in the Introduction to this book, Americans tend to assume the past is dead and have trouble recognizing that the present grew out of and now rests upon the past. In such a climate the flowers of myth can grow luxuriantly.

Other explanations can be attributed to the president's particular skills. Recall our discussion of the Hollywood roots of Reagan's own convictions: He was, after all, not the only person so influenced. The poet John Clellon

Holmes has written that "the experience of movie going in the thirties and early forties . . . gave us all a fantasy life in common, from which we are still dragging up the images that obsess us." That fantasy life, moreover, was passed along to succeeding generations who were not original communicants. The impact of the old films, to be sure, got diluted with time; younger viewers saw them in rerun houses or on television, detached from the cultural and social atmosphere that surrounded them as the country drifted into war. But they lurked, nevertheless, in our collective celluloid unconscious. The sacred texts—and Capra and Ford were at the center of late thirties Hollywood in a way that Wells and Chaplin were not—remained available for reinvocation by fervent evangelical cinematic fundamentalists. Reagan, by his very ability to relive with conviction, to reenact, to reproject that original movie sensibility became the high priest who could perform rites and rituals that moved our filmic soul.

Another (similarly quasitheological) explanation dwells on his ability, when the nation's self-confidence about domestic and foreign affairs was shaken, to lead a revival in America's civil religion. Reagan's core text was that Americans remained the chosen people of God, his agents on earth to create the good society. Breathing new life into the American Dream, which Erickson calls the "confused but nevertheless potent set of convictions and visions that translates history into mythology," Reagan threw out a psychic life-preserver to people who felt themselves adrift.

And Reagan offered more: His was an activist vision. Reagan made his audiences into leading characters in a grand drama, and he derided those who promoted a historical analysis that led to passive paralysis: Mondale, Reagan claimed in 1984, thinks "America is the victim, flinching under the blows of history." This insistence that Americans were agents not subjects was popular with people who felt themselves powerless. And history, after all, is not a prima facie tool of power. A sense of history tells us nothing (nor should it) about what to do in the present. And because historical awareness cannot provide guidelines for the future (although it is an indispensable precondition to coming up with viable ways forward), while myth comes complete with a vision of a new (or, more often, restored) social order, history can be less attractive to people in urgent need of solutions.

Remembrance and Resistance

So Ronald Reagan had a lot going for him as spokesman for a right-wing revanchist movement. His own experiences in the mass culture industry provided a superb background for the tasks of political leadership he assumed. What does this suggest about the post-Reagan era? It is unlikely that the right will soon produce such an apposite champion—consider the patent insincerity of George Bush or the perfervid floridity of Pat Robertson—for Reagan was overwhelmingly the product of a particular historical moment. But the mythologizing project he initiated is too valuable for the right to abandon. What lessons can be drawn from this review about best to how to deal with its future manifestations?

First, it is important to keep in mind that for all the acquiescence to Reagan, there was a great deal of resistance to the neoconservatives around the issues of history, myth, and memory. Popular recollections—"living" memories—proved remarkably tenacious: Reagan was unable to significantly alter the public's negative view of the Vietnam War, and an overwhelming majority of the country rejected military adventurism in Central America (citing the former debacle as their reason). Reagan was forced to abandon Jesse Helms on the Martin Luther King holiday issue. And his attempt to put Nazism behind us succeeded only in stirring up major controversy, demonstrating, as Jurgen Habermas has written, that "a collective regression cannot be staged by administrative fiat alone." How is this to be explained?

Part of the answer is that the mythmasters lost when they met resistance from organized groups devoted to remembering the historical record. In the case of Bitburg, for example, Reagan ran afoul of the Jews, a people well aware that social, like individual memory, is often fickle and fleeting; that collective memory cannot be counted on after one or two generations; and that the protection and cultivation of memory must be an ongoing process—institutionalized, embedded in ritual and ceremony. Yad Vashem, the Heroes and Martyrs Memorial Authority, was established in Jerusalem by Israeli parliamentary law in 1953 expressly to commemorate the Holocaust, to institutionalize the perpetual activity of remembrance. In America, the U.S. Holocaust Memorial Council has launched a series of formal Holocaust education programs, and a number of museums and memorials have been constructed in recent years. These activities in turn aided the ability of American Jews to protest, with some measure of success, the Bitburgian flight from history.

This record of resistance suggests a way to counter future remythification programs. We need a politics of "organized remembrance." We need to develop strategies to restore and sustain a collective memory. We need to make a persuasive case that history can be more useful to people than myth. We must convince them that while myth may comfort at first it will eventually make matters worse—ruled by myth, we misdiagnose our problems and hamper our search for solutions—whereas history, which may disconcert us in the beginning, will be instructive in the end. Such a campaign must explain, not guilt-monger. It must have some humility about its inherent limitations. And it must engage the feelings as well as the minds of its auditors: As Yerushalmi well puts it; "Those who are alienated from the past cannot be drawn to it by explanation alone; they require evocation as well."

An oppositional movement should remember that there is a host of media through which America's sense of history can be strengthened, ranging from Hollywood movies, to television docudramas, to the official memorials that serve as public memory markers, to the history museums (the institutions perhaps most explicitly devoted to nourishing a historical sensibility and acting as trustees of the public memory). Some of these cultural agencies have begun in recent decades to move away from the kind of mythologizing that characterized them previously. They should be encouraged to more actively defend the historical approach and to connect past and present.

To be sure, if public historical institutions do bring their analyses down to the present, as opposed to cutting them off at some safely distant point in the past, they will run the risk of becoming politically "controversial," but this is exactly what they should be in this time of highly political assault on the historical method itself. Now, for example, is the time to tackle the problem of Vietnam. The upcoming generation knows almost nothing of the reality of that dreadful war, and hence is vulnerable—especially through movies and television—to just the kind of ideological rollback the right wants to achieve. We should move now to strengthen popular memories, through massive oral history projects (that recapture on video, audiotape, and the printed page the experiences of those who fought in and against the war), through films, through museum shows, through television specials, through memorials (of which the one in Washington is a splendid example precisely because its terrible specificity leaves little room for the mythologizing impulse), through public rituals and commemorations, and through small group retellings (in classrooms and living rooms), to ensure that the "Vietnam syndrome" enjoys a long and hearty life.

More generally the goal should be to equip ourselves with a historical purchase point from which we can better grasp the current public policy choices that confront us. History will not (like myth) tell us which way to go: That depends on who we are and what we want. The future will be decided not by the past, but by the outcome of contention in the present between people with different visions of what they want the future to be. Understanding how the present emerged from the past maximizes our capacity (whoever we are) for effective action in present—no more, but no less. History can be a major support for democracy. To ignore its potential contributions is to impoverish, even imperil ourselves.

Notes

This appeared in *Tikkun* 2, no. 1 (1987), and I have left it intact.

1. I want to emphasize that none of this is to suggest that all right-wing interpretations of the past are inherently mythic (which would be a thinly disguised way of asserting that my brand of history is true and those with

which I disagree are false). At this moment, conservative professional historians are locked in confrontation with the critical scholarship of the last generation. But they have had much tougher sledding than Reagan had. Precisely because they are historians, they must engage in real intellectual combat and must develop plausible revisionist counterperspectives and support them with evidence. Reagan, on the other hand, simply jumped over the mass of recent historical studies and landed back amidst the old verities.

2. It is interesting that both Disney and Reagan fudged their *own* history, bathing fairly wretched childhood experiences in a Norman Rockwell glow. Disney's father was an itinerant failure, given to exploiting and beating his kids until, one by one, they ran off; Reagan's early years were shadowed by his father's alcoholism, unemployment, and constant relocation, years that got gauzed over in his official recollections.
3. In Massachusetts, however, Puritan gentlemen and ministers brooked no challenges to their own rule, which makes Reagan's characteristically sloppy error about the Quakers interesting. In fact, Winthrop's audience on the Arbella were not Quakers. Winthrop loathed the various superradical sects that sprang up during the English Revolution, among whom were the Levellers, the Diggers, the Ranters, the Antinomians, the Fifth Monarchists, and . . . the Quakers, and did his best to ban them from Massachusetts (in an early form of immigration restriction). When Quakers did make their way into Massachusetts Bay, decades later, it is notorious that the Massachusetts authorities subjected them to whipping, ear cropping, branding, and judicial murder. Winthrop is no doubt writhing furiously in his grave at Reagan's confusing him with his archenemies. It is typical of Reagan as historian that he was either blissfully unaware of this or could have cared less.

   The point here is not that Reagan made mistakes (though he was notorious for remembering things in a way that suited his needs). The point, rather, is that Reagan was not purveying history, for which truth is of the essence, but perpetuating myth, which plays by different rules.
4. Still another available model for Reagan (in content and process) was the newsreels of the day. Henry Luce's *March of Time* (1935–51) and its imitators (especially Hearst's *News of the Day*) were famous for using film clips that may have had nothing to do with the events under discussion, but which evoked desired responses in the audiences. Luce baldly admitted the newsreels could best be characterized as "fakery in allegiance to truth."

The Battle of the Enola Gay

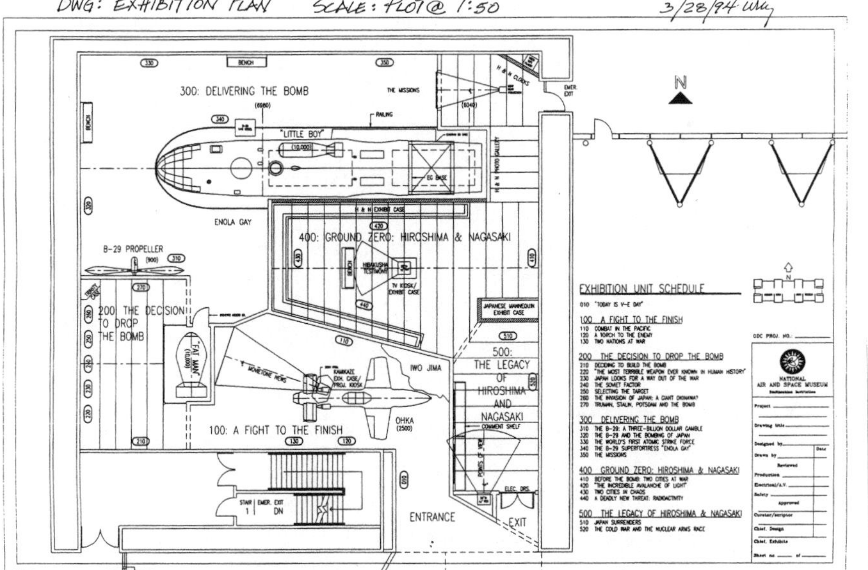

Blueprint for planned National Air and Space Museum exhibition, "Crossroads: The End of World War II, The Atomic Bomb, and The Origins of the Cold War." (Courtesy, National Air and Space Museum.)

When the *Enola Gay* went on display in June 1995, visitors to the Smithsonian's National Air and Space Museum (NASM) found a truncated airplane: Only fifty-six feet of fuselage could be squeezed into the building. But more than wings were missing. So was the exhibition that got sheared away after a campaign of vilification arguably without precedent in the annals of American museology.

In the summer of 1994, reports flaming through the mass media had denounced the impending show as a monstrous attempt to recast the history of World War II. A typical description, by *The Washington Post*'s Eugene Meyer, called it "an antinuke morality play in which Americans were portrayed as ruthless racists hellbent on revenge for Pearl Harbor, with the Japanese as innocent, even noble victims fighting to defend their unique culture from 'Western imperialism.'" Editorials blasted "antiAmerican" curators and warned that "revisionists" had hijacked the museum to promulgate politically correct (PC) history.

Air force veterans responded angrily. Here they were, amidst the festivities marking the fiftieth anniversary of the Normandy landings, ready to take their turn in the sequence of celebrations. Instead, said the media, youthful visitors to the Smithsonian would soon find their grandparents reviled as racists and war criminals.

These assertions were based on a misconstruction of NASM intentions, and a profound misrepresentation of what the curators actually wrote. Few of the angry vets ever read the proposed scripts—not unreasonably, given that each of the eventual five was over five hundred pages long and none was easily available. Neither had many of the pundits, most of whom cribbed their analysis from a series of articles by John T. Correll, editor of *AIR FORCE Magazine*.

My review of the scripts and their fate suggests that most of Correll's charges were unwarranted, some outrageously so. I do not claim that NASM officials were fault free. There were indeed problems with their first draft—though mostly these were errors of omission rather than commission—and their handling of the crisis once it blew up left much to be desired. But by no means did they deserve the abuse heaped upon them.

More than individual reputations are at stake here. The scrapping of the *Enola Gay* exhibition raises troubling questions about the future of public historical discourse in the United States. The successful campaign to muzzle the Smithsonian was a battle fought on the history front of America's ongoing culture war. This essay seeks to understand the event and to set it in its larger context.

First Draft

The initial script of "Crossroads: The End of World War II, The Atomic Bomb, and The Origins of the Cold War" (12 January 1994) had five parts, one per gallery, each consisting of proposed label copy and suggested artifacts.

The first section ("A Fight to the Finish") dealt primarily with the final year of the war. The introductory segment asserted Japan's culpability for the sequence of events that led to the bomb. Recapitulating Japan's 1930s expansionism ("marked by naked aggression and extreme brutality"), it sketched the course of the war from Pearl Harbor on, mentioning Japanese atrocities, use of slave labor, racist attitudes, and maltreatment of prisoners of war ("often starved, beaten, and tortured.") It then—in a space dominated by a kamikaze aircraft looming overhead—zeroed in on the fierce Japanese resistance at Iwo Jima and Okinawa, finding in it "a terrible warning of what could be expected in the future."

The section did include two shortly to be infamous sentences: "For most Americans, this war was fundamentally different than the one waged against Germany and Italy—it was a war of vengeance. For most Japanese, it was a war to defend their unique culture against Western imperialism."

These were not great sentences—not wrong, in context, but easily misrepresented. Americans *were* in a fury in 1945—and why *shouldn't* they have been, given Pearl Harbor, four years of ferocious war, and recently declassified accounts of the Bataan death march? Many were calling for revenge, some even for extermination. But this is not to say—nor did the script—that the war, or the bomb, were only motivated by vengeance.

Nor was it wrong to observe that the Japanese believed unconditional surrender would mean the end of the emperor system and the collapse of their culture. Or that many Japanese—then and to this day—represented their racist exploitation of other Asians as a shield against western imperialism. The script did not ratify this self-perception, it demonstrated it, as crucial to understanding the tenacity of Japanese resistance.

But opponents wrenched the sentences out of context and used them to stoke outrage. Even after they were swiftly dropped, and the Smithsonian had explicitly and indignantly denied the construction put upon them, critics trotted them out again and again, in the absence of any other sentences that would so well serve their purpose.

Correll also argued that this section did not represent the history of Japanese aggression graphically enough to offset the emotional impact of later material on the effects of the bombing. Counting the number of photographs of suffering Americans and finding it lower than the number depicting suffering Japanese, he charged that a victimology thesis lay embedded in the structure of the exhibition.

He was partly right about the effect, totally wrong about the intention. There was no plot to delete evidence of Japanese wickedness in order to manipulate visitors into finding Americans immoral. Any exhibition focused on the *Enola Gay* and its bombing run would, almost by definition, depict more Japanese than American casualties.

But curators did face a museological conundrum. Ground Zero artifacts and images, no matter how few their number, pack a wallop. So does the *Enola Gay*. Together they could overshadow almost anything in a merely introductory section. Designers at first resisted a "balance of corpses" approach—giving, for example, equal space to the slaughter at Nanking, where more died than at Hiroshima and Nagasaki—in part because they rejected the vengeance thesis that they were accused of promulgating. It was the critics, after all, who insisted that Hiroshima was justified not because of prior Japanese outrages—although they had to be fed into the moral equation—but as a military action taken to expeditiously end the war Japan had started.

The curators, moreover, were assuming that most visitors already knew something about Pearl Harbor and the war in the Pacific—subjects treated extensively in an adjacent NASM gallery. This was a mistake. For most young Americans, those events are as distant as the Punic Wars. The museum admitted its mistake. In succeeding drafts the curators would expand the initial section, adding dramatic material on Japanese outrages (though none would tackle the history of American expansionism in Asia, nor would any critic remark on this oversight). Finally the staff would design a four-thousand-square-foot prefatory exhibition on the war in the Pacific. Tellingly, the addition of this contextual material would fail to assuage the critics.

Correll's passion for context stopped short when it came to the second section, an analysis, housed in one of the smaller galleries, of "The Decision to Drop the Bomb." Here the objection was to problematizing something deemed utterly unproblematic. Truman dropped the bomb to shorten the war and save lives, period. Raising questions about that decision, from the vantage point of "hindsight," was infuriating and illegitimate.

But questions were raised at the time, and by the nation's preeminent civilian and military leaders. The endgame of World War II raised tactical and strategic issues of great political, moral, and military complexity. The script reviewed some debates that arose among participants at the time, and later between historians, explicitly labeling them as "Controversies." Why did these explorations create such an uproar?

One firestorm erupted over a hypothetical question: if the United States had had to invade Japan to end the war, how many Americans would have died? The conventional popular wisdom on this subject is that perhaps half a million would have fallen. But this was a postwar judgement. In 1947, former Secretary of War Henry Stimson, intent on rebutting Hiroshima critics like John Hersey, claimed there would have been over one million American *casualties*. Truman later claimed one half million *lives* were at risk, a figure that Churchill doubled.

The exhibit draft, for all that it was accused of employing hindsight, relied instead on wartime estimates by MacArthur, Marshall, and various joint chiefs of staff planning committees, rather than using after-the-fact figures that even the American Legion admitted were "incredibly high." It concluded that it "appears likely that postwar estimates of a half million American deaths were too high, but many tens of thousands of dead were a real possibility."

This enraged the critics. They claimed NASM had pruned the figure to render the bomb-drop immoral, as if only a gigantic quantity of saved lives could offset the enormous number of civilians actually killed. There is, one would hope, some statistic that might generate moral misgivings. Would saving one-thousand American soldiers—one hundred—ten—justify killing one-hundred-thousand civilians? But the script never raised such a question, never challenged the position that if an invasion had been the only alternative, the savings in lives would have justified the bombings.

The tougher question—which the script did ask—is whether or not an invasion was necessary in the first place. Huge numbers of veterans believed that it was inevitable, and that dropping the bomb therefore saved their lives, and the lives of many Japanese as well. But were they right? The exhibit script offended some by recalling that powerful wartime figures believed it was possible to end the war with neither nuclear bombings *nor* an invasion.

Leading military men insisted that the combination of blockade and conventional bombing had brought Japan to its knees. Top navy admirals "believed that its blockade could force Japan to quit the war, while many army air forces' generals thought firebombing could force surrender by itself or in conjunction with the blockade." The script also cited the U.S. Strategic Bombing Survey, conducted after the surrender, which said the war would "certainly" have ended before the end of 1945, probably before 1 November.

Label copy also took note of direct military opposition to nuclear weapons. The show quoted a statement made in 1950 by Admiral William D. Leahy, Truman's chief of staff, in which he denounced the bombing as adopting "ethical standards common to barbarians in the dark ages," but added cautiously that "1945 documents only suggest that he was skeptical that the atomic bomb would ever work." It mentioned General Eisenhower's claims in 1948 (and later) that he had opposed its use in conversations with Truman at Potsdam in 1945, but suggested that "corroborating evidence for these assertions is weak."[1] The script did not, however, engage the contemporary and postwar reservations of American airmen such as Henry H. ["Hap"] Arnold, the commanding general of the U.S. Army Air Forces, or Generals Carl Spaatz and Curtis LeMay.[2]

One "Historical Controversy" panel asked: "Would the War Have Ended Sooner if the United States Had Guaranteed the Emperor's Position?" The text noted some scholars believe this. More to the point, Acting Secretary of State (and former ambassador to Japan) Joseph Grew, Navy Secretary James Forrestal, Assistant Secretary for War John McCloy, General Douglas MacArthur, Admiral Leahy, Winston Churchill, and Herbert Hoover were among the many who thought that modifying the unconditional surrender formula to allow retention of the emperor would strengthen the peace faction, aid in winning and effectuating an early surrender, and facilitate the postwar occupation. Truman rejected this advice—though in the end, after the bombs were dropped, Hirohito was allowed to retain his throne.

Some historians say Truman (counseled by Secretary of State James Byrnes) feared that modification would provoke vehement popular and congressional protest. Some even argue that by waiting until the A-bombs were ready in August, the U.S. high command may have muffed an opportunity to end the war in June, thus costing American lives. The script, however, said no such thing. It stated instead that while "it is possible that there was a lost opportunity to end the war without either atomic bombings or an invasion of Japan," these alternatives were "more obvious in hindsight than they were at the time." Citing the counterargument—that it took the shock of the bombs (and Russian intervention) to "give Hirohito a face-saving way to force a surrender on his hard-liners"—and noting the impossibility of proving either case, the text concluded that this particular debate "will remain forever controversial."

Another question was asked: Did Truman drop the bombs primarily to forestall Soviet creation of an Asian sphere of influence, and gain diplomatic leverage in the already emerging Cold War? There are historians who argue this. The show did not. It said explicitly that "most scholars have rejected this argument, because they believe that Truman and his advisers saw the bomb first and foremost as a way to shorten the war." Concern about the Russians only "provided one more reason for Truman not to halt the dropping of the bomb."

Was dropping atom bombs on cities a violation of rules of war? There were strictures against attacking civilian populations; democracies had denounced fascists for violating these rules in Barcelona, Guernica, London, and China; and reservations about bombing civilians were raised by Eisenhower, Leahy, and Marshall. But the show argued that for most Americans, the earlier moral constraints against killing civilians had already crumbled in the course of a savage war, and that most key decision makers "did not see [nuclear attacks] as being drastically different than conventional strategic bombing. . . ."

Was dropping the bomb racist? In Europe the U.S. Army Air Forces stuck to precision attacks on military targets—or at least professed to—as late as the Dresden firebombing, when Marshall and Stimson publicly disavowed any policy of "terror bombing on civilian populations." Days later General LeMay napalmed Tokyo, launching an incendiary campaign that killed more civilians in five months than the Allies had in five years of bombing Germany. Some historians have argued that anti-Asian racism helps explain the difference in approach.

The script, however, did not even raise the issue. It did note that most Americans considered their European enemies to be good people misled by evil leaders, while viewing Japanese as "treacherous and inhuman." The text traced this disparity in attitude to contemporary horror at Japanese atrocities and to longstanding anti-Asian racism. (The script also underscored *Japanese* racism, observing that "Allied people and leaders were pictured as inhuman demons, lice, insects, and vermin," and that "propaganda made frequent reference to the 'Jewish' nature of the Allied cause.") Nevertheless, the proposed label copy insisted that nuclear weapons would have been used against Germans had they been ready in time, thereby denying the charge of racial motivation.

Should there have been a warning or a demonstration? The script mentioned the objections raised by scientists and officials like McCloy and Undersecretary of the Navy Ralph Bard. (It did not, oddly, mention the reservations expressed by General Marshall. In May 1945 Marshall said the bomb should be dropped only on a "straight military objective such as a large military installation," and then, if necessary, on a manufacturing center, but only after civilians had been warned so they could flee.) The text also laid out the "valid concerns that a warning could endanger Allied servicemen and that a demonstration might be ineffective or a failure"—objections on which Truman relied. And it emphasized that Hiroshima at that time was still a military target—all too readily, in the opinion of some historians.

The important thing to note about this part of the exhibition is that, overall, it adequately and appropriately provided visitors with a sense of the complexities of the bombing decision and the controversies surrounding it. It is possible to quarrel with this or that formulation. The information could have been presented in greater depth, and more dramatically, perhaps by using videotapes of historians and participants. Some of the label copy could have been, and almost certainly would have been, formulated more cogently. It was, after all, a first draft; few writers would want their initial efforts subjected to such fierce and public scrutiny. But given those attacks, what is striking is the text's conformity with the findings of responsible scholarship, its moderate and balanced stance on the issues, and the fact that, in essence, it supported Truman's decision.

The third section, "The World's First Atomic Strike Force," was planned for the cavernous arena where the giant plane was to be housed. Here the exhibition script presented the pilots' story "extensively and with respect," as Correll admitted on one occasion. Indeed the show emphasized the bravery and sacrifices of those who fought. But neither Correll nor anyone else ever again remarked on this vast mass of material, which so starkly contradicted claims that the NASM dishonored veterans. Nor was there ever any discussion of the fifteen-minute videotape the museum put together with crew members from the two bombers, a commemorative component that veterans who saw it loved.

Critics seized instead on the fourth section, "Cities at War," which looked at Hiroshima and Nagasaki's role in the Japanese military effort, and then depicted the nuclear devastation wrought upon them. Here visitors were to have moved into a somber space of giant blowups, powerful objects, and taped reminiscences of survivors. Correll decried not only the number but the nature of the artifacts included—a lunchbox containing "carbonized remains of sweet green peas and polished rice," a fused rosary. But the stubborn facts are that high school girls were out in force on 6 August clearing rubble at what became Ground Zero, and that Nagasaki was the center of the Catholic community in Japan. It is possible that a more understated display may have been more effective, and aroused less ire, though opponents disliked even its later, toned-down version.

Was the museum, as charged, angling for America to "apologize for its use of the atomic bomb to end World War II?" asked NASM's then-director Dr. Martin Harwit? "Of course not! Should we show compassion for those who perished on the ground? As human beings, I believe we must."

The analysis of bomb damage, moreover, was intended to educate, not manipulate. Information about the split-second annihilation caused by the blast, the way the seventy-two hundred-degree fahrenheit heat vaporized people, and the short and long-term effects of radiation, made clear the error of contemporary assumptions that nuclear bombs were merely bigger versions of conventional ones. Some critics argued there was no need for NASM to rehearse such gruesome information as it was already widely known. Alas, the latest Gallup Poll found that one in four Americans do not even know an atomic bomb was dropped on Japan, much less what impact it had when it exploded.

In the last gallery, a coda on "The Legacy of Hiroshima and Nagasaki" spoke to this educational vacuum. It treated the bombings as not simply the end of World War II but as "symbols of the arrival of the nuclear age, and as a glimpse of the realities of nuclear war." Although the exhibit could hardly do more than gesture at the complex history of the Cold War in the space allotted, it did at least raise some important issues.

It offered an all-too-brief survey of the postwar nuclear arms race. It noted the invention of hydrogen bombs, a thousand times more powerful than their atomic predecessors. It mentioned the buildup of world stockpiles to seventy-thousand warheads by the mid-1980s. It sketched the emergence of antinuclear movements concerned about atomic-test fallout and radioactive wastes. It discussed the end of the Cold War and the signing of arms control agreements. And it referred to the continuing dangers of nuclear proliferation and atomic terrorism. Its concluding panel stated: "Some feel that the only solution is to ban all nuclear weapons. Others think that this idea is unrealistic and that nuclear deterrence—at a much lower level—is the only way that major wars can be prevented."

Offense and Defense

The draft composed on 12 January was discussed by a group of scholarly advisers on 7 February 1994.[3] Most had suggestions for improvement but almost everyone was basically laudatory. Dr. Richard Hallion, the Air Force Historian, called it "a great script." He joined with his military historian colleague Herman Wolk in pronouncing it "a most impressive piece of work, comprehensive and dramatic, obviously based upon a great deal of sound research, primary and secondary," in need only of a "bit of 'tweaking.'"

The Air Force Association (AFA) thought differently. During the previous summer and fall, Harwit, with admirable if incautious openness, had actively solicited the group's involvement. Though he received a strongly negative response to a July 1993 concept treatment, Harwit nevertheless sent along the January 1994 draft script for review. The AFA, breaching confidentiality, leaked it to media and veterans groups, accompanied by a slashing Correll critique in the April 1994 issue of *AIR FORCE Magazine*—a sneak attack that set the terms and tone of the ensuing debate. (Hallion now also became a vigorous critic, the "great script" of February becoming "an outright failure" by April.)

Over the following months inaccurate and malicious accusations tumbled forth in a variety of forums. The *Washington Times* said Truman's reasoning for using the bomb "was dismissed by the curators in favor of a theory that he ordered the bomb dropped to impress Soviet leader Josef Stalin." The *Wall Street Journal* said scriptwriters "disdain any belief that the decision to drop the bomb could have been inspired by something other than racism or blood-lust." Picking up on Correll's claim that kamikaze pilots were treated "with near-mystical reverence," the *Journal* decried the "oozing romanticism with which the *Enola* show's writers describe the kamikaze pilots." The curators had supposedly called them "youths, their bodies overflowing with life," a charge reporter Ken Ringle repeated the next day in *The Washington Post*. But the quoted text was in fact an excerpt from a pilot's journal, included to give viewers "insight into [the kamikaze's] suicidal fanaticism, which many Americans would otherwise find incomprehensible."

Washington Times columnist R. Emmett Tyrrell, Jr. called the museum staff a bunch of "politically correct pinheads." Had one million Americans died invading Japan, Tyrrell added, "surely that would have left some of the present pinheads . . . fatherless or even, oh bliss, unborn."

Lance Morrow, writing in *Time*, found the script "way left of the mark." It managed to "portray the Japanese as more or less innocent victims of American beastliness and lust for revenge." "A revisionist travesty," the text "seemed an act of something worse than ignorance; it had the ring of a perverse generational upsidedownspeak and Oedipal lese majeste worthy of a fraud like Oliver Stone."

Increasingly, critics charged anti-Americanism. When Harwit asked if veterans really suspected the National Air and Space Museum was "an unpatriotic institution," Correll replied: "The blunt answer is yes."

The AFA editor began probing the Smithsonian staff's backgrounds. Director Harwit had a suspicious resumé. He had been born in Czechoslovakia and raised in Istanbul, Correll noted, before coming to the United States in 1946. Harwit had, to be sure, joined the U.S. Army in 1955–7, but he had been "influenced" by his work on nuclear weapons tests at Eniwetok and

Bikini. This experience had led him to assert that "I think anybody who has ever seen a hydrogen bomb go off at fairly close range knows that you don't ever want to see that used on people."

As for the curators, Correll pointed out that "none of them [were] veterans of military service," that one (Tom Crouch) planned a lecture at the "Japanese Cultural and Community Center of Northern California," and that another (Michael Neufeld) was of Canadian origin.

Ringle of *The Washington Post* observed that the said Canadian had spent his undergraduate years at the University of Calgary from 1970–4, "when Americans were fleeing to Canada to escape the Vietnam War." Ringle contrasted Neufeld with an elderly American prisoner-of-war (POW), who during an interview came "close to tears" wondering if the curator was not suggesting "that the thousands of Japanese killed by those bombs were somehow worth more than the thousands of American prisoners in Japan?"

Pundits hammered at the curators' deficient patriotism. Jeff Jacoby of the *Boston Globe* claimed the script was "anti-American." Jonathan Yardley in *The Washington Post* called it as "a philippic not merely against war but against the United States," a piece of "anti-American propaganda."

The American Legion, too, said the script inferred "that America was somehow in the wrong and her loyal airmen somehow criminal . . ." One disgruntled veteran, noting that the Japanese "have bought most of Hawaii and lots of the United States," added: "Let's hope they have not bought the Smithsonian."

Congressmen picked up the un-American refrain. Sam Johnson (R-Texas), an Air Force fighter pilot for twenty-seven years and a POW in Vietnam for seven, denounced the scripts as "a blatant betrayal of American history." Peter Blute (R-Massachusetts) fired off a letter to Smithsonian Secretary Robert McCormick Adams, cosigned by twenty-three colleagues, condemning the proposed exhibit as "biased" and "anti-American."

Unprepared for such a barrage, Smithsonian officials scrambled to placate their opponents. Distancing himself somewhat from his curators, Harwit told his staff that "a second reading shows that we do have a lack of balance and that much of the criticism that has been levied against us is understandable." He called for revisions to accommodate legitimate concerns.

The staff of NASM issued a second version on 31 May—now renamed "The Last Act: The Atomic Bomb and the End of World War II"—and then a third on 31 August. Each expanded the treatment of earlier Japanese aggression. Each cut out some of the objects and language deemed objectionable. Each was greeted by renewed demands for additional changes.

Congresspeople escalated their involvement. Senator Nancy Kassebaum (R-Kansas) was already on record as insisting that "we should not interpret the dropping of the bomb as we look at it today," but rather "put it in the context of the time" (as if the script had not run into trouble for doing precisely that). On 19 September she introduced a Sense of the Senate Resolution. It declared that even with the latest changes the script was "revisionist and offensive." The Senate enjoined the NASM to avoid "impugning the

memory of those who gave their lives for freedom" (though even Correll had admitted it treated the veterans "with respect").

Senator Slade Gorton (R-Washington) laid out even more explicitly the kind of historical interpretation the government might deem acceptable. He attached to the Interior Department's appropriations bill a provision that Congress "expects" the *Enola Gay* exhibit to "properly and respectfully recognize the significant contribution to the early termination of World War II and the saving of both American and Japanese lives."

On 21 September, the day Gorton's injunction was adopted, Smithsonian officials sat down for their first marathon negotiating session with the American Legion. The Institution had turned to the nation's premiere veterans' group, using the good offices of Smithsonian Undersecretary Constance Newman, thinking perhaps that if it could be persuaded to sign off on a script, further assaults might be forestalled.

For a time the strategy seemed to be working. "This exhibit is taking a more balanced direction," said a Legion spokesman. "It's not a propaganda piece by any means." But to obtain this support museum representatives had to submit to a line-by-line script review—"they drafted pages while we talked," boasted a Legion spokesman—and to accept extensive transformations. High-ranking Smithsonian officials believed they were responding to valid concerns raised by an important focus group, addressing issues of style not substance, and grouping caveats (but not eliminating them) in order to emphasize the main line. But the scripts that emerged from this process—a fourth on 3 October, and a fifth and final one on 26 October—had been shorn of nuance and controversy.

The last version evoked Japanese bushido ideals ("Die but never surrender") to justify asserting that invasion "casualties conceivably could have risen to as many as a million (including up to a quarter of a million deaths)." This estimate, museum spokesmen conceded, was not based on any new evidence but was an "extrapolation" from Okinawa casualties. The treatment of alternatives to invasion, debates over unconditional surrender, questions about Nagasaki, the reservations of high ranking military and civilian figures like Leahy, Eisenhower, and even Truman himself—all were now drastically reduced, or deleted altogether. Further Ground Zero images and artifacts—especially those depicting women, children and religious objects—were jettisoned; only a single picture of a corpse remained. The last section dealing with nuclear proliferation was scrapped.

The exhibition, originally an effort to understand the *Enola Gay*'s mission, had become an effort to justify it. As the script now summarized the story: "Japan, although weakened, was not willing to surrender. The atomic bomb offered a way to change that. A bloody invasion loomed if atomic bombs did not force Japan to surrender. . . . For Truman, even the lowest of the estimates was abhorrent. To prevent an invasion he feared would become 'an Okinawa from one end of Japan to the other,' and to try and save as many American lives as possible, Truman chose to use the atomic bomb."

The last words were given to six veterans who had written NASM during the controversy. Four of the six cited letters endorsed the script's thesis. "I honestly feel," wrote one, "that millions of lives, both American and Japanese, were saved by that one crew on that one airplane!" "Americans, in my estimation, should make no apologies for strategic firebombing or dropping the atomic bomb," said another. "It took that to win the war!"

So thoroughgoing and one-sided were the changes that they amounted to a recantation. As the outgoing national commander of the Legion reported to his troops: "We went face to face with the Smithsonian officials, and they blinked."

Now it was the scholarly community's turn to protest. The Organization of American Historians' (OAH) executive committee wrote the Smithsonian's board of regents on 19 September urging them "to support the National Air and Space Museum staff." On 22 October it condemned "threats by members of Congress to penalize the Smithsonian Institution." The OAH also deplored "the removal of historical documents and revisions of interpretations of history for reasons outside the professional procedures and criteria by which museum exhibitions are created."

On 16 November a group of forty-eight "historians and scholars" charged a "transparent attempt at historical cleansing." They protested the excision of documents, the removal of artifacts, the whiteing out of contemporary and historical debates, and the alteration of interpretations in the absence of new evidence. Though "we yield to no one in our desire to honor the American soldiers who risked their lives during World War II to defeat Japanese militarism," the historians said, the deletion of so many "irrevocable facts" had reduced the exhibit "to mere propaganda, thus becoming an affront to those who gave their lives for freedom."

Peace groups, too, objected. The Fellowship of Reconciliation, Physicians for Social Responsibility, Pax Christi USA and others declared that pressure from military and veterans groups had "compromised the integrity of the exhibit." Activists met with NASM officials on 15 December 1994 to decry "political censorship." They demanded the exhibit state that why the bomb was dropped and whether it had been necessary to end the war "are matters of vigorous scholarly and public debate on which Americans do legitimately disagree."

Amid all this uproar, the organized museum community remained noticeably silent.

Endgame

The focal point of these charges and countercharges was the newly arrived Smithsonian secretary, I. Michael Heyman. Before his official installation on 19 September 1994, the former chancellor of the University of California at Berkeley had opposed AFA-inspired pressure on NASM. Writing in August for the October issue of *Smithsonian* Magazine, the incoming secretary urged resisting those who "want the exhibition to be devoted solely to the justifications for dropping the bomb (with omissions of its effects)." Curators, he insisted, were educators not propagandists.

After his installation, Heyman tried to use the outcry from the scholars and peace groups to carve out a middle ground position. "The Institution is now being criticized from both ends of the spectrum—from those who consider the exhibition as a 'revisionist' product critical of the United States to those who accuse us of staging an exhibition which glorifies the decision of the United States to use atomic weapons. . . . This indicates to me that we are probably squarely in the middle, which, as a national institution, is not a bad place to be."

But the AFA was not interested in compromise, it wanted unconditional surrender. The revision of 26 October, Correll admitted, had corrected many of "the worst offenses," removed most "anti-American speculation," and attained "parity" in casualty photos. No matter: it was still not "an acceptable salvage job." It continued to ask questions, "to doubt, probe, and hint." "I don't think there should be doubts about whether that policy [of unconditional surrender] is right," Correll declared, in effect setting himself above most of the nation's wartime leaders. It was, he concluded, "no longer enough to clean up this exhibition script." Now it was "imperative" that Smithsonian officials go after the curators who had "produced such a biased, unbalanced, anti-American script in the first place."

The American Legion, however, remained a stumbling block. In October Director of Internal Affairs Hubert R. Dagley II had rejected narrow views of the controversy that denounced the show only as "an unflattering portrayal of one branch of the armed forces" or "an indictment of strategic bombing." The Legion expressed what it considered more high-minded concerns—the exhibit's "potential to undermine not only our people's faith in their forefathers, but also their confidence in a revered and respected American institution"—the Smithsonian. Although it rejected an outright endorsement, it did not condemn the script it had helped produce.

But the Legion came under attack from media-inflamed veterans for being "more liberal" and "not as combative" as the AFA. By January, the group was backing away from neutrality, claiming the fifth script had not gone far enough, and hinting that without additional changes it would shift over to opposition. Indeed, on 4 January, National Commander William M. Detweiler made an in-house recommendation to call for cancellation.

Changes were forthcoming, but not ones the Legion was looking for. In mid-November, a delegation of historians led by advisory committee member Barton Bernstein had met with Harwit. They presented him with documentary evidence falsifying the 26 October draft's claim that, in the crucial meeting on 18 June 1945, Truman had been given an estimate of 250,000 casualties for the invasion of Kyushu. They cited Admiral Leahy's diary entry, written that evening, which stated that "General Marshall is of the opinion that such an effort will not cost us in casualties more than 63,000 of the 190,000 combatant troops."

On 9 January 1995, Harwit—his scholarly integrity on the line—proposed to the Legion a change in this volatile subject. He submitted two pages of new label copy. They did not, as was widely reported, accept 63,000 as an "official" figure; the historians all agreed such numbers were speculative. But the new text did drop the 250,000 figure, along with equally ungrounded claims that American casualties "conceivably could have risen to as many as one million (including up to a quarter of a million deaths)." The revised text continued, however, to underscore Truman's awareness that Japan had "some two million troops defending the home islands"; his fear of "an Okinawa from one end of Japan to the other"; the likelihood that many additional Allied and Asian lives would have been lost; and the fact that for Truman, "even the lowest of the casualty estimates was unacceptable." It concluded, as before, that "to save as many lives as possible, he chose to use the atomic bomb."

This may have been more accurate but it made the Legion leadership's already shaky position completely untenable. On 19 January, seizing the opportunity Harwit had naively handed them, they called for the show's cancellation. In a public letter to President Clinton, they charged the Smithsonian with including "highly debatable information which calls into question the morality and motives of President Truman's decision to end World War II quickly and decisively by using the atomic bomb."

Five days later, on 24 January eighty-one congresspeople sent a letter to Secretary Heyman demanding Harwit's ouster for his "continuing defiance and disregard for needed improvements to the exhibit."

Opposition opinion now crystallized around a suggestion of General Paul

Tibbets, the man who had named the *Enola Gay* (after his mother) and piloted it over Hiroshima. Early in the debate, Tibbets, unhappy that many were "second-guessing the decision to use the atomic weapons," had issued a soldierly injunction: "To them, I would say, "Stop!" The plane, Tibbets declared, needed only an eleven word label: "'This airplane was the first one to drop an atomic bomb.' You don't need any other explanation." Tibbets wanted no questions, no controversies, no account of bombs bursting in air.

Facing special hearings in the House and Senate, threats to the Smithsonian's budget (77 percent of which came from the federal government), and a loss of confidence among corporate contributors on whom he was counting to fund a planned 150th anniversary celebration in 1996, Secretary Heyman called it quits. On 30 January 1995, adopting Tibbet's position, he scrapped the exhibition in favor of "a display, permitting the *Enola Gay* and its crew to speak for themselves."

Stakeholders

Heyman argued this was the wrong show in the wrong place at the wrong time. The NASM had "made a basic error in attempting to couple an historical treatment of the use of atomic weapons with the fiftieth anniversary commemoration of the end of the war." The veterans "were not looking for analysis," he said, "and, frankly, we did not give enough thought to the intense feelings such an analysis would evoke." The implication was that curators should have waited a few years, or even a decade, until the old soldiers had faded away.

It is a plausible position. Some veterans certainly saw Air and Space more as shrine than museum. Aviator groups—convinced the Smithsonian had barred the B-29 out of embarrassment—had been fighting for years to get it restored and displayed, to validate their wartime sacrifices. It was Harwit, ironically, who came to their defense. Convinced they deserved a commemoration he pushed to have the restoration ready for the fiftieth anniversary. Some vets no doubt felt betrayed to learn the NASM intended to raise any questions whatever about the plane's mission, even those asked by their wartime commanding officers. As did Tibbets, they wanted the *Enola Gay* presented pristinely, like the *Spirit of St. Louis*, not juxtaposed with evidence of the damage it had wrought, even if that damage was declared justifiable.

So perhaps it was foolhardy to make the attempt. Perhaps, once the distress became apparent, the NASM should have folded its hand immediately, avoiding the drawn-out and damaging saga that followed. But there are problems with such a seemingly politic perspective.

First, while historian Edward Linenthal is right to remark that fiftieth anniversaries "intensify arguments over any form of remembrance" because they "are the last time when you have massive groups of veterans or survivors who are able to put their imprint on the event," the mere passage of time does little to dull the edge of controversy. Recall the brouhaha that exploded over "The West as America" show—a treatment of century-old events—and the impassioned debates that broke out over Columbus' enterprise on the *five-hundreth* anniversary of his first voyage.

Second, the postponement strategy is condescending to the veterans. Many protestors were not acting out of "feelings"—in contrast to the museum's "analysis"—but from a belief that the show was advancing an analysis with which they disagreed. Many were simply out to achieve the "balance" or "context" that the mass media assured them was atrociously absent. If the museum had aggressively presented them with accurate information about the first script—and certainly the last one—many might have been won to the Smithsonian's side in support of a full-rigged exhibition. Witness the posting on a WWII e-mail network from a veteran and former exhibition critic: "I have reviewed the most recent script (number 5) and it is a considerable improvement over its predecessors and in fact I am not unhappy about it."

This raises, in turn, the third and largest problem. Heyman has faulted his curators for paying insufficient attention to the Smithsonian's "stakeholders." Apart from the fact that NASM worked with veterans all along—in the end so closely that they may have abdicated their curatorial responsibilities—the comment suggests the secretary has not sufficiently confronted the dilemmas museums face these days.

In recent years curators have reached out to communities they wish to represent and address, seeking to involve them in the process of exhibit production. Excellent in theory, this has proved difficult in practice. In the case of immigrants, blacks, workers, women, and Native Americans, it turns out to be no simple matter to discover who exactly "the community" is. Or who gets to speak for that community. Or what to do when some groups contest the right of other groups to serve as spokespeople. Or how to respond to claims that, e.g., only Latinos can/should speak for Latinos. Or how to rebut a group that denies a museum's right to say anything at all about it without prior approval. Or what to do when an exhibit offers a variety of perspectives on a controversial issue, only to be met with a dogmatic insistence that only one of the perspectives is true, that the very notion of debate is "relativistic" and illegitimate.

The problems are no less complex when dealing with atomic bombs. Why are WWII veterans the significant "stakeholders" here? Are not the World War II and the postwar proliferation of nuclear arms issues of transcendent national importance and of concern to all American citizens?

And even if veterans are the "relevant public," which veterans are we talking about? There have been a variety of military actors in this drama; the press and Smithsonian alike too easily conflated them. There is no question that old soldiers gave the anti-NASM protest its moral legitimacy and political clout. But they were not the only combatants in this struggle. Part of the NASM's problem, I think, is that it never quite realized who and what it was up against.

The Battle for Air and Space

John Correll introduced NASM curators to his constituency; let me introduce his constituency to the wider world. The Air Force Association has been presented throughout this affair as a veterans organization. Even Harwit described it as "a nonprofit organization for current and former members of the U.S. Air Force." But a perusal of the ads in Correll's *AIR FORCE Magazine* (AFM) makes instantly clear that it is a good deal more than that. In marked contrast to the American Legion's journal, where the wares on sale include hearing aids, power mowers, Florida retirement homes, and talking memo-minders, the AFM's pages are festooned with glossy advertisements for sleek warplanes produced by various of the Air Force Association's 199 Industrial Associates (whose ranks include Boeing, du Pont, Martin Marietta, Northrop Grumman, Rockwell, and Lockheed, which hawks its F-16 to Correll's readers for only "a $20 million price tag.")

The AFA, in fact, is the air wing of what Dwight Eisenhower called the military-industrial complex. It was founded in 1946 at the instigation of Hap Arnold (with Jimmy Doolittle as first president). Arnold, hyperattentive to public relations, set up the AFA to lobby for creation of an independent air force, to fight postwar budget cutbacks, and to "keep our country vigorously aroused to the urgent importance of airpower." It has been the semiofficial lobbying arm of the United States Air Force ever since.

In succeeding decades the AFA institutionalized relations with the defense industry by sponsoring mammoth expositions of military hardware (known to critics as the "arms bazaar"); opposed Kennedy's test-ban treaty; denounced Johnson's refusal to unleash airpower in Vietnam (a Correll predecessor deplored America's renunciation "of the use of even the smallest of nuclear weapons"); battled the peace movement; railed against the "anti-military, anti-industry" atmosphere of the 1970s; and warned about the dangers associated with a "relaxation of tensions, and an end to the cold war."

But the Cold War ended, as did the glory days of the Reagan buildup, and the AFA turned to fighting the cutbacks in military budgets "demanded by the liberal community." During the period Correll was assaulting the Air and Space Museum, his magazine featured articles like "Another Year, Another Cut," "Boom and Bust in Fighter Procurement," "This Isn't the Bottom Yet," "More Base Closures Coming Up," and "The Case for Airpower Modernization." When not urging Congress "to shift the burden of the cuts to entitlement spending—and thus spare defense," AFM writers were warding off attacks from the Army ("They need money," said Correll, "and they are ready to take a bite out of the Air Force to get it") or making preemptive strikes on the Navy.

In an era of imperiled budgets and reduced political clout—a function, Correll believed, of the diminishing percentage of veterans in the country and Congress—the AFA was more than ever concerned with image. "Attitude surveys show waning desire among young people to join the military," Correll noted, a decline he attributed in part to negative portrayals by the news media and entertainment industry.

Whether one thinks well or ill of the AFA's positions, it should come as no surprise to find it paying meticulous attention to how the premiere achievement of American airpower—arguably the one instance in which strategic bombing, not an army invasion or a navy blockade, triumphantly ended a major war—would be treated at the most popular museum in the world.

The AFA's relationship with the NASM, moreover, was consanguineous. Hap Arnold, who fathered the AFA in 1946, begat the NASM the very same year. Arnold wanted to give aviation a history and extend the wartime interest in aeronautics into the next generation. The general saved large numbers of his war birds from being converted to scrap metal, and he lobbied Congress for a museum. To bolster his case, Arnold sought and received supporting petitions from 267 museum boosters, many of them representatives of such aviation firms as Northrop, Lockheed, Douglas, McDonnell, Sperry, Sikorsky and Republic, the same constituency from which AFA would draw its Industrial Associates. One witness stressed that a museum could win thousands of future voters to the cause of aviation, voters who in turn would influence their congressman "to develop aviation, both civil and military, in the years to come."

In the decades after Congress established the National Air Museum (expanded to embrace Space in 1966), relations with the AFA were cordial and fraternal. In 1949, for instance, the National Air Museum cooperated with the Air Force Association in putting on the National Air Fair, the country's largest air show to date. It was at this event that the *Enola Gay*, flown in by Colonel Tibbets from storage in Arizona, was officially presented to the Smithsonian.

When the museum's drive for a building on the mall got stalled during the Vietnam War, it was reignited by Senator Barry Goldwater, board chairman of the AFA's Aerospace Education Foundation and soon-to-be recipient of its highest honor, the H.H. Arnold Award. Goldwater declared the NASM "a cause that is right" and "a cause that deserves a fight." A properly housed museum that presented a "patriot's history" would, he argued, inspire the nation's "air and space minded" young people. Interestingly, Goldwater did not think the *Enola Gay* should be included in that story. "What we are interested in here are the truly historic aircraft," he explained to a congressional committee. "I wouldn't consider the one that dropped the bomb on Japan as belonging to that category."

After the new building opened in 1976, the NASM blossomed. Its world-class collection of airplanes (like Lindbergh's *Spirit of St. Louis*) accumulated over decades by the indefatigable Paul Garber, along with the awesome lunar landers, moon rocks, and missiles assembled during the triumphal era of space flight, helped attract enormous crowds. The NASM became the most massively visited museum in the world, welcoming in recent years over eight million people a year.

But NASM went beyond simply amassing aircraft. It was one of the first museums anywhere to seriously examine the evolution of aviation and astronautic technology. Like most museums of science and industry, however, NASM kept its focus on the hardware, adopting an evolutionary approach that assumed technological development was inherently progressive. It was, as former director (and former astronaut) Michael Collins said, "a cheery and friendly place," marked by a "spirit of optimism." Another former director, Walter Boyne, a career Air Force officer, prolific historian, and AFA member, kept the institution on the same path.

Relatively little attention was paid to the social consequences of flight, particularly military flight. The WWI and WWII galleries remained little more than cabinets of aero-curiosities. The collections of planes and mementoes, the heroic murals, the minishrines (fashioned from personal effects and reminiscences) to AFA deities Hap Arnold and Jimmy Doolittle—none of these grappled with the fundamental purpose of war, the infliction of damage on the enemy.

This did not trouble the museum's corporate sponsors or military donors or the Air Force Association. The institution was largely run by ex-military personnel; it featured gleaming civilian and military aircraft (most of them emblazoned with corporate logos and/or service insignia); it trumpeted aviation's very real technological accomplishments while ensuring that seldom was heard a discouraging word. The NASM promoted just the kind of public image that Arnold, Goldwater, and the AFA had always intended to foster.

NASM did not lack for critics, however. A 1979 *White Paper on Science Museums* suggested that its decontextualization of artifacts and its cozy compliance with the promotional demands of corporate donors made it "basically a temple to the glories of aviation and the inventiveness of the aerospace industry." Later commentators concurred in calling it "a giant advertisement for air and space technology." And by the late 1980s the Smithsonian Council agreed that it was no longer "intellectually or morally acceptable to present science simply as an ennobling exploration of the unknown," or technology merely as "problem solving beneficial to the human race."

In 1987 Cornell astrophysicist Martin Harwit was chosen over an air force general to be the new NASM director. Harwit set out to demonstrate the social impact of aviation and space technology—the ways it transformed daily life "both for the good and the bad." This applied to the military sphere, too. "No longer is it sufficient to display sleek fighters," he said, while making no mention of the "misery of war."

The NASM continued to do traditional kinds of AFA-friendly programming. It put on a commemorative program for the fiftieth anniversary of Jimmy Doolittle's raid over Tokyo. It mounted an exhibit (curated by Neufeld, the suspect Canadian) that honored the P-47 Thunderbolt, delighting the two-thousand-member association of its former pilots. Harwit also supported Richard Hallion (later a vigorous critic of the *Enola Gay* scripts) in creating a laudatory show on airpower in the Gulf War.

But Harwit also authorized new departures. NASM treatment of military hardware had heretofore invariably skirted its lethal purposes, even in the case of Nazi weaponry. Label copy for the museum's V-2 rocket emphasized its progressive role in the history of technology. In 1990, however, the V-2 was given new panels which recounted its use as an indiscriminate instrument of murder (they included the NASM's first-ever image of a corpse); noted it was built by concentration camp prisoners, thousands of whom perished in the process; demonstrated how scientists like Wernher Von Braun avoided grappling with the ethical implications of their work; and provided superior technical detail about rocketry. Press reaction was startled but positive. One reviewer hailed the new "truth in labeling" as "striking in comparison to the fairy tale it has replaced. . . ."

Another novel exhibition deployed an American Pershing II missile side-by-side with a Soviet SS-20 as the twin foci of an examination of arms control agreements. This, too, garnered only positive reports.

Next, in 1991, the institution replaced its old World War I gallery—whose artifacts had fallen prey to insect infestation—with a rich and imaginative show. It began with popular culture images depicting the war as a series of romantic duels between "knights of the air"—pulp magazine accounts, a compilation of clips from Hollywood films, and Snoopy and his flying doghouse ("Curse you, Red Baron"). The origin of these images—which resonate to this day—was traced to wartime newspapers, businesspersons, and government propagandists who seized on the courage and daring of individual aces to portray aerial combat as a chivalric adventure. But the careful analyses that followed made clear the grim and unglamorous realities of fighter pilot life and death. Powerful dioramas of trench warfare and discussions of particular battles also demonstrated the important but secondary role of wartime air power, and dramatic displays of Germany's air attacks on London illustrated the birth of civilian bombing.

Again, reaction in the mainstream press was overwhelmingly favorable. Hank Burchard of *The Washington Post* was astonished to find such "rank heresy" in an institution "that has from the beginning served as the central shrine of the military-industrial complex." Though he complained that the exhibition still soft-pedaled the realities of aerial combat, which was "more akin to assassination than to jousting," he concluded: "But hey, a museum largely run by pilots can hardly be expected to badmouth them, and anyway this is a quibble compared with the quantum leap forward into historicity that this exhibition represents."

Finally, a direct precursor of the *Enola Gay* show—a five-minute videotape on the restoration process, which included powerful images of bomb damage—attracted considerable visitor attention and no negative commentary whatever. To key NASM staff it seemed that these plaudits and silences had cleared the way for the *Enola Gay*. Despite the continuing trepidation of some within the institution, they swept ahead with plans for the exhibition.

From the perspective of the AFA these new initiatives must have seemed like serpents wriggling their way into the Garden of Eden. Certainly Correll's April 1994 AFM critique of the *Enola Gay* included a retroactive blast at the World War I exhibition—that "strident attack on airpower"—as having been a harbinger of what followed. Everything about it appalled him. The curators' notion that "dangerous myths have been foisted on the world by zealots and romantics." The criticism of the "cult of air power," with the sainted Billy Mitchell among the designated offenders. The "theories" quoted in the exhibit's companion book about military airpower having the potential for "scientific murder" (Correll apparently forgetting for the moment that the offending phrase was actually Eddie Rickenbacker's, the most famous of all U.S. aces, who reminded Americans that "fighting in the air is not a sport. It is scientific murder.") The way the show emphasized "the horrors of World War I" (as opposed to its upbeat dimensions?). And above all, the fact that it "takes a hostile view of airpower in that conflict," to the point where "the military airplane is characterized as an instrument of death."

To his credit, Correll published in the June 1994 AFM a strong rejoinder from Richard H. Kohn, former chief of air force history for the U.S. Air

Force. The NASM, Kohn argued, had in recent years succeeded "in broadening the scope and value of its exhibits by presenting thoughtful, balanced history rather than mere celebration of flight and space travel." The World War I exhibit, he said, was "not at all hostile to airpower. It presents the war realistically and explains aviation's role in it." It was Correll, not the curators, who favored a "political use of the museum: to downplay war's reality and to glorify military aviation." Such a bias, Kohn insisted, "would not be in keeping with the museum's or the Smithsonian's mission and would embarrass the Air Force community, which, having experienced the history, would want it presented truthfully—with strength, balance, sensitivity, and integrity."

Correll was having none of it. He believed, borrowing the words of a fellow editor, that "a new order is perverting the museum's original purpose from restoring and displaying aviation and space artifacts to presenting gratuitous social commentary on the uses to which they have been put." People come to NASM to see old aircraft, Correll claimed. "They are not interested in counterculture morality pageants put on by academic activists." It was precisely because curatorial "interests and attitudes have shifted" that the *Enola Gay* exhibit had gone wrong. It was imperative that the Smithsonian's "keepers and overseers take a strong hand and stop this slide" and get the museum back on track.

Here, I think, one can see the structural faultlines that underlay the surface struggle over texts. How the *Enola Gay* was to be interpreted was important in its own right. How to interpret the meaning of Hiroshima was of vital significance both to the AFA and to NASM; indeed the plane itself had been entwined in the institutional lives of both organizations since their inception. But the curators' exhibition plans for the *Enola Gay* were also seen as the latest in a series of museological departures that taken together signaled AFA leaders that "their" institution was being taken away from them.

They were determined to get it back. The wrestling match over control of the interpretation was emblematic of the struggle for control of the institution. The AFA, less interested in improving the scripts than in axing its opponents, adopted a policy of taking no prisoners. Convinced the curators were subverting the museum, it was but a short step to accusing them of subverting the Republic.

In the supercharged atmosphere surrounding the fiftieth anniversary of Hiroshima, Correll's charges easily touched off a museological conflagration. But to understand why it developed into a national incident we need to examine the larger context. For the battle of the *Enola Gay* was only one of several engagements that broke out that summer, all along the "History Front" of a wider Culture War.

Historical Correctness

In his 1993 book, *See, I Told You So,* Rush Limbaugh warned his fellow conservatives that "we have lost control of our major cultural institutions. Liberalism long ago captured the arts, the press, the entertainment industry, the universities, the schools, the libraries, the foundations, etc."

"This was no accident," he explained, noting that "in the early 1900s, an obscure Italian communist by the name of Antonio Gramsci theorized that it would take a 'long march through the institutions' before socialism and relativism would be victorious." If these key institutions could be captured, "cultural values would be changed, traditional morals would be broken down, and the stage would be set for the political and economic power of the West to fall."

In the last twenty-five years, Limbaugh continued, "a relatively small, angry group of anti-American radicals"—the "sixties gang"—finally succeeded in executing Gramsci's master plan. Seizing the commanding heights of the cultural economy, they became "firmly entrenched in all of the key cultural institutions that are so influential in setting the agenda and establishing the rules of debate in a free society." From these redoubts they denigrated American values, policed the nation's thought and speech, promoted victimization theories, exalted women and people of color over white males, and pushed a divisive multiculturalism. At the same time their allies in the welfare and regulatory bureaucracies were busy squashing entrepreneurial initiative.

Of particular concern were those who "bullied their way into power positions in academia." These professors immediately set about demolishing traditional history, the sort which "was once routinely learned by every schoolchild in America." They promulgated instead "a primitive type of historical revisionism." The essential revisionist message—the core of the "indoctrination taking place today in American academia"—consisted of several propositions: "Our country is inherently evil. The whole idea of America is corrupt. The history of this nation is strewn with examples of oppression and genocide. The story of the United States is cultural imperialism—how a bunch of repressed white men imposed their will and values on peaceful indigenous people, black slaves from Africa, and women."

Up and down this new "politically correct" canon Rush roamed, succoring casualties of the onslaught. Poor Christopher Columbus, accused of wiping out savages (who were in any event "violent and brutal"), was the victim of a hoax perpetrated by the sixties gang, who routinely "ascribe fictitious misdeeds to people not alive to defend themselves." The Pilgrims and Puritans, another trashed group, are "vilified today as witch-burners and portrayed as simpletons" in order to cover up the importance of religion in "shaping our history and our nation's character." The early pioneers had single-handedly "tamed a wilderness"—"nothing was handed to them"—but now their antigovernment vision and self-reliant accomplishments were being "turned upside down" in order to justify the reign of Big Government.

A full response to such falsehoods would take us too far afield, but let me briefly attend to the last two. Despite Limbaugh's portrait of the state of religious studies, scores—hundreds—of scholars have over the past thirty years produced a superb and respectful body of work on religion in American life; one could fill a small library with volumes on the seventeenth century alone. As for Limbaugh's sturdy pioneers, they were among the first to demand—and receive—governmental aid in the form of land grants, roads, canals, railroads, and armies. This quasisocialism passed to their twentieth-century descendants, who vigorously sought agricultural subsidies, military contracts, and the giant irrigation and electrification projects that built up sunbelt/gunbelt states with tax dollars drained from their frostbelt cousins.

But pointing out Rush's errors—a cottage industry these days—is somewhat beside the point. Myths can not be refuted by facts. And Limbaugh was out to launch a crusade, not an academic conference. "As we saw during the 1980s," he told his troops, "we can elect good people to high office and still lose ground in this Culture War. And, as we saw in 1992, the more ground we lose in the Culture War, the harder it is to win electoral victories. What we need to do is fight to reclaim and redeem our cultural institutions with all the intensity and enthusiasm that we use to fight to redeem our political institutions."

Happily a field marshal had appeared with exactly the credentials needed to wage such a war. Newton Leroy Gingrich had long since proven himself a master of the political arts, having battled his way to a leadership role in the House of Representatives. He was also an ex-professor of history, and eager to intervene in the battle against Revisionism. In 1993 Gingrich began beaming a twenty-hour college course called "Renewing American Civilization" to more than 130 classrooms across the country, and the ten million subscribers to National Empowerment Television.

Central to the course was an analysis of U.S. history, not a subject in which Gingrich had been rigorously trained. Although he had taken some courses in American history at Tulane, his major was in modern European, and, at the behest of his adviser, he wrote his 1971 Ph.D. dissertation on "Belgian Education Policy in the Congo, 1945–60." During his professorial years at West Georgia College (1970–1978) he spent only four years in the history department—teaching mainly western civilization and European subjects—before moving over to the geography department and launching an environmental studies program. Most of his time at West Georgia was given over to repeated runs for Congress, leaving little time for scholarly research. Indeed by 1975, having published nothing whatsoever, he realized he had no chance of getting tenure and abandoned the notion of applying for it. Had he not been elected to Congress he would have been out of a job. Yet Gingrich brushed aside questions about his expertise. "I'm not credentialed as a bureaucratic academic," he noted waspishly, "I haven't written 22 books that are meaningless."

In his 1994 lectures, especially one given 12 February on "The Lessons of American History," and in speeches and interviews throughout the year, Gingrich asserted the existence of an "American exceptionalism," which he believed was rooted in distinctive "American values." These included individualism, "the religious and social tenets of puritanism," the centrality of private property, freedom from government control, and the availability of opportunity (which left Americans "prepared to countenance very substantial economic inequalities"). He admitted past contradictions between profession and practice—slavery, male-only suffrage—but seemed to believe these had been overcome not by organized struggles, but by an ineluctable rippling out of the ideals themselves. Unlike his competent dissertation, or his 1984 *Window of Opportunity*, which advanced an ersatz-Marxist thesis about a contradiction between America's forces of production (a computer-driven information revolution) and its social relations of production (a putatively anti-technological welfare state and culture), Gingrich's more recent teaching conveyed little sense of agency, little awareness of how history happens.

Gingrich, in fact, said remarkably little about U.S. history, and a fair amount of what he did say was wrong. There was little sustained encounter with actual historians, though he occasionally waved books at his class (Daniel Boorstin's volumes were favorite wands), and he was fascinated by Gordon Wood's suggestion that conservative Republicans should claim descent from Jefferson, not Hamilton. He did urge students to read biographies, but as sources of inspiration or for tips on problem solving. (He himself claimed to have been fortified during his repeated defeats in Georgia politics by reading lives of Lincoln, and accounts of Churchill's tribulations had buoyed him up while struggling single-handedly to unseat Speaker Jim Wright.) As had his hero Ronald Reagan, Gingrich reached back to late 1930s and early 1940s movies for his version of American history, citing *Boys' Town* on orphanages, or *Abe Lincoln in Illinois* on the great railsplitter—though he also embraced more contemporary sources, such as Hollywood's recent version of *The Last of the Mohicans*.

Gingrich invoked classic American myths, the truth (or more often falsity) of which was of little concern compared to their serviceability as moral fables. The point of studying the past was not to discover how things changed but to ransack it for role models. Newt's was a "McGuffeyite history-of-America-by-edifying-anecdote," as Gary Wills has noted.[4]

Gingrich's idealized U.S. past was also a static one. For centuries, nothing much happened. Then, in the 1960s, things lurched into sudden downward motion. From 1607 to 1965, as he put it in his somewhat discombobulated manner, "there is a core pattern to American history. Here's how we did it until the Great Society messed everything up: don't work, don't eat; your salvation is spiritual; the government by definition can't save you; governments are into maintenance and all good reforms are into transformation." Then, abruptly in the sixties, "the whole system began decaying." Why? Because the United States got beguiled by irresponsible, "self-indulgent, aristocratic values." And these led, apparently overnight, to the welfare state, drug use, hippies, multipartner sex, and the pregnant poor. "From 1965 to 1994"—an epoch that would seem to embrace the Age of Reagan as well as the Age of Johnson—"we did strange and weird things as a country."

The culprits were the same ones Limbaugh had fingered—counterculture elitists who despised traditional values. From the 1770s to the mid-1960s, there had been "an explicit long-term commitment to creating character," crucially by studying history. But secular left-wingers could not "afford to teach history because it would destroy the core vision of a hedonistic, existentialist America in which there is no past and there is no future, so you might as well let the bureaucrats decide." For Gingrich, properly taught history was a form of ideological inoculation; without it, we "get drowned in European socialist ideas, and we get drowned in oriental ideas of mandarin hierarchy." Once the booster shots stopped coming, the country swiftly succumbed to a host of moral maladies.

The solution was clear. It was time to return to "teaching the truth about American history, teaching about the founding fathers and how this country came to be the most extraordinary civilization in history." We should get back to Victorian basics, burnish up the old fables. "We spent a generation in the counterculture laughing at McGuffey Readers and laughing at Parson Weems's vision of Washington." Cherry tree and little hatchet, redivivus.

In truth, Gingrichian history bore little relation to America's complex and sprawling saga. What he had crafted, rather, was a secularized sacred narrative that flowed from an Edenic past through a fall from grace in the sinful sixties into a degenerate present, and on, hopefully, to future redemption through a return to prelapsarian values.

Republican Revanche

Redemption drew nigh in the summer and fall of 1994, as the insurgent "conservative" movement spearheaded by Limbaugh and Gingrich drove towards capturing Congress. It was at just this moment that the *Enola Gay* first appeared on Republican radar screens, courtesy of the Air Force Association. It proved an irresistible target.

Out on the hustings right-wing candidates had been happily beating up on the monstrously powerful thought police and bureaucrats, whose un-American values and policies they blamed for the country's disorder and decay, as well as the declining fortunes of white male voters. Along came an exhibition in which, allegedly, arrogant PC curators accused white males (aged veterans, no less) of being racist aggressors. Better still, it supposedly cast the Japanese as victims, rather than as transgressors to be held accountable for their immoral actions. In exactly the same way, the politically correct crowd had claimed victimhood status for blacks, women, and assorted welfare layabouts, who were in fact responsible for their own condition.

The show thus afforded yet another opportunity for shifting (white male) electoral attention away from the Republicans' corporate sponsors, who were assiduously dismantling the nation's industrial economy, downsizing vast numbers of (white male) middle managers and (white male) factory workers into the ranks of the un- and under-employed.

Conservative commentators picked up and amplified Correll's critique. The exhibit script provided clear evidence (according to right-wing columnist John Leo) that "the familiar ideology of campus political correctness" had been "imported whole into our national museum structure." Critics were quick to point out that this was not the Smithsonian's first transgression. Back in 1991 the National Museum of American Art's "The West as America" had critiqued the pioneer saga celebrated by Limbaugh-Gingrich-ism, touching off an uproar. Writing in the *Wall Street Journal,* Matthew C. Hoffman of the Competitive Enterprise Institute suggested that, over the previous several years, there had been "a gradual change in the Smithsonian's character." Little by little "a portion of the national heritage it represents has been lost to a campaign of ideological revisionism." It was now in the hands of "academics unable to view American history as anything other than a woeful catalog of crimes and aggressions against the helpless peoples of the earth."

Republican congressmen—like Sam Johnson (Texas), Tom Lewis (Florida), and Peter Blute (Massachusetts)—feasted on the issue all summer and fall of 1994. In August, for instance, Lewis opined on behalf five other congressmen and himself that the museum's "job is to tell history, not rewrite it." Republican senators were also active. Slade Gorton won passage of his injunctive legislation. Nancy Kassebaum cast her directive resolution in such a fashion that with the election less than two months away, no Democrats, not even liberal ones, were prepared to vote against it. More disturbingly, no one, right or left, took issue with the assumption underlying such initiatives—that the federal government had the right to mandate historical interpretations.

Standards Bearer

On 20 October, just as the fifth and final *Enola Gay* script was emerging from the latest round of revisions, the history wars escalated once again. Lynne Cheney, former head of the National Endowment for the Humanities (NEH), launched a preemptive strike in the *Wall Street Journal* against the *National Standards for United States History*, due to be issued five days later. Several years in the making, and funded in 1992 by the NEH while Cheney was still director, the document was intended as a voluntary guide for teachers. Astonishingly ambitious, it offered broad analytical themes, over twenty-six hundred specific classroom exercises, and suggestions for encouraging historical thinking. Over six thousand teachers, administrators, scholars, parents, and business leaders were involved in the drafting process, which was marked by wide-ranging open debates, and the involvement of thirty-five advisory organizations, including the Organization of American Historians, the Organization of History Teachers, the American Historical Association, the National Education Association, and the American Association of School Librarians.

No matter. In her *Wall Street Journal* piece, and in subsequent articles and interviews, Cheney chanted the standard mantra: An inner core group—gripped by a "great hatred for traditional history," and intent on "pursuing the revisionist agenda"—had, "in the name of political correctness," made sure that a "whole lot of basic history" did not appear. She proved this to her satisfaction by adopting Correll's pseudostatistical method. "Counting how many times different subjects are mentioned in the document yields telling results," she wrote ominously. Traditional heroes were underrepresented, women and minorities mentioned too often; references to (black female) Harriet Tubman cropped up more often than to (white male) Ulysses S. Grant. In addition, the *Standards* lacked "a tone of affirmation," directed attention to social conflict, and invited debate not celebration. Predictably, she concluded her initial blast with a call for battle against the all-powerful "academic establishment."

Cheney's analysis bordered on the disinformational. The *Standards* were not a textbook, a dictionary of biography, or a compendium of important facts, much less a pantheon or catechism. Counting white faces and listing a few famous absentees was therefore disingenuous: The issues and events that the document urged exploring patently required reference to the supposedly spurned generals and presidents. In addition, bean counters more scrupulous than Cheney discovered not only that the vast majority of cited individuals were in fact white males, but that the two most-often-mentioned of the genus were Richard Nixon and Ronald Reagan.

Cheney's real objections—assuming they were motivated by more than mere personal ambition and political calculation—seemed to be to the paradigmatic shift the *Standards* represented. In its pages the American past was not a simple saga of remarkable men doing remarkable deeds. Those deeds were included—despite Cheney's charges, for example, the Constitution was treated extensively—but so, too, were less laudatory dimensions of the historical record. Slavery was examined, not to denigrate the American past, but to understand it. And the *Standards*, like much contemporary scholarship, embraced the experience of ordinary people—as heroes of their own lives and as collective actors on the world-historical stage.

Some fellow conservatives—notably Diane Ravitch—were also critical of the *Standards* but balked at Cheney's demand that they be scrapped. Especially given the *Standards*' drafters expressed willingness to respond to substantive objections, such as complaints that monetarist theories explaining the Great Depression were slighted, or that a few dozen (out of twenty-six hundred) classroom exercises could arguably be described as shepherding students to preselected conclusions.

But most of the crew that copied Correll now echoed Cheney. Though few in numbers—far fewer than the multitudes that had fashioned the *Standards*— their command of media megaphones allowed them to manufacture another uproar. Rush Limbaugh weighed in four days after Cheney's initial intervention. With his usual insouciant disregard for facts, he informed his radio audience that the "insidious document" had been "worked on in secret." In truth, the drafts had been hammered into shape in countless sessions of democratic discussion embracing enormous numbers of participants, including twenty-three days of formal (tape recorded) meetings, and hundreds of copies had been dispatched to all who requested them. Limbaugh pronounced it "an intellectually dishonest, politically correct version of American history" that ought to be "flushed down the toilet." With tedious predictability, columnist Charles Krauthammer called it "a classic of political correctness." The *Wall Street Journal* bundled letters on the subject under the headline: History Thieves. And John Leo o'er-hastily objected to the elevation of one Ebenezer McIntosh, a "brawling street lout of the 1760s," to the heroic stature of a Sam Adams; unfortunately for Leo, McIntosh turned out to be an important leader of the Stamp Act Demonstrations in Boston. Not for three weeks did a major national news story—in the *New York Times*—do much more than parrot Cheney's charges, and by then, the election was over.

Victory in November did not stem the Republican assault on revisionists. Indeed, their accession to political power shaped the *Enola Gay* endgame. Speaker-to-be Gingrich made clear that efforts to enact the Contract with America—a package of proposed legislation meant to dismantle much of the regulatory and welfare state and ladle out breaks to business—would be accompanied by a campaign to "renew American Civilization." In a postelection interview he said that the new Republican leadership intended to improve the country's moral climate, especially by "teaching the truth about American history." Before the month was out Gingrich had called for eliminating the NEH, in part because it had sponsored the history standards, which he pronounced "destructive for American Civilization."

Almost immediately upon taking office, Gingrich, acting (he said) "as speaker, who is a Ph.D. in history," chose a new historian of the House of Representatives. Christina Jeffrey, not an historian at all, but an associate professor of political science at Kennesaw State University who had helped him launch his course, was given the task of helping "in reestablishing the legitimacy of history." "History" received a setback that January when Gingrich abruptly fired Jeffrey. As it transpired, in a 1986 evaluation of an educational program that included an examination of the Holocaust, Jeffrey had argued that: "The program gives no evidence of balance or objectivity. The Nazi point of view, however unpopular, is still a point of view and is not presented, nor is that of the Ku Klux Klan." Moreover, she had characterized the since widely adopted program as embodying a "re-education method" that "Hitler and Goebbels used to propagandize the German people," a method later "perfected by Chairman Mao," and which was "now being foisted on American children under the guise of 'understanding history.'"

With this misstep, initiative passed momentarily to the Senate. On 18 January, Senators Robert Dole and Slade Gorton won passage (by 99–1) of a nonbinding Sense of the Senate Resolution. It urged that the present history standards not be certified by the federal government, and that funds for any future ones go only to those which "have a decent respect for the contributions of Western civilization, and United States history, ideas and institutions, to the increase of freedom and prosperity throughout the world." Democrats, noting that leaders of the *Standards* project had already met with critics six days earlier, argued against the resolution, but agreed to support it, if made nonbinding.

A week later, House members returned to the fray. On 24 January sixty-eight Republicans (including House Majority Leader and Gingrich ally Dick Armey) and thirteen Democrats demanded Martin Harwit's ouster. Representative Blute elaborated: "We think there are some very troubling questions in regard to the Smithsonian, not just with this *Enola Gay* exhibit but over the past 10 years or so, getting into areas of revisionist history and political correctness. There are a lot of questions that need to be answered."

On the 26 January, critics began tying the two issues together. Columnist George Will claimed "the Smithsonian Institution, like the history standards" was "besotted with the cranky anti-Americanism of the campuses. . . ." Lynne Cheney, in guileful congressional testimony, seized on one of the twenty-six hundred teaching examples to argue that fifth or sixth graders who learned about the end of World War II from the proposed history standards would know only that the United States had devastated Hiroshima, but nothing of Japanese aggression. In fact the standards called explicitly for analysis of the "German, Italian, and Japanese drives for empire in the 1930s"; and a suggested teaching activity for seventh and eighth graders was to construct a time line that included the "Japanese seizure of Manchuria in 1931."

Also on 26 January Speaker Gingrich also named Representative Sam Johnson—the ardent *Enola Gay* show critic who had alerted him to the issue—to the Smithsonian's board of regents. The following day Gingrich announced he had found "a certain political correctness seeping in and distorting and prejudicing the Smithsonian's exhibits," and declared the museum should not be "a plaything for left-wing ideologies."[5]

Four days later Heyman scuttled the *Enola Gay* exhibit.[6] Now in full retreat, he also announced "postponement" for at least five years of a planned exhibit on air power in Vietnam; suggested that critics of "political correctness" in recent interpretive exhibits had a point; and promised the regents he would review and, where necessary, rectify current exhibits that board members believed reflected "revisionist history." Heyman refused to fire Harwit, but then long-time Smithsonian critic Senator Ted Stevens (R-Alaska) announced he would go ahead in mid-May 1995 with previously threatened hearings on the philosophical underpinnings of the exhibit. On 2 May Harwit resigned. The continuing controversy, he said, had convinced him "that nothing less than my stepping down from the directorship will satisfy the Museum's critics." Regent Sam Johnson immediately made clear that Harwit's departure was not enough, that only a full scale purge of "revisionists" would do.

The actual exhibition opened on 28 June 1995. It proved even more of a retreat than had been anticipated. Heyman claimed it simply reported "the facts," but it was heavily larded with AFA-style interpretation. The label copy declared that "the use of the bombs led to the immediate surrender of Japan and made unnecessary the planned invasion of the Japanese home islands. Such an invasion, especially if undertaken for both main islands, would have led to very heavy casualties among American and Allied troops and Japanese civilians and military. It was thought highly unlikely that Japan, while in a very weakened military condition, would have surrendered unconditionally without such an invasion." This, of course, finessed a host of issues, among them the role of the Soviet declaration of war (utterly unmentioned here), the question of whether a *conditional* surrender might not have ended the war with neither invasion *nor* bombing, and the considered judgement of many wartime leaders that the Japanese might well have surrendered before the earliest possible invasion.

Nor, apart from a twenty-second video snippet showing bomb effects (which may or may not have included an almost subliminal image of a corpse), and label copy saying that the two bombs "caused tens of thousands of deaths" (by most accounts, a gross understatement), was there any confrontation with the destruction of Hiroshima and Nagasaki. "I really decided to leave it more to the imagination," Heyman said at a 27 June news conference.

The "aircraft speaks for itself in this exhibit," the secretary added, and indeed NASM scattered additional pieces of the giant plane throughout the embarrassingly bare galleries, trying to fill them up with mammoth chunks of metal. But, in fact, it is the *Enola Gay*'s pilot and crew who speak on its behalf, in a sixteen-minute concluding video presentation. It is certainly appropriate to include the crew's reminiscences as part of the story. But why should their ringing retroactive justification of their mission (and that of their colleagues over Nagasaki) be privileged, and the troubled postwar reflections of men like Eisenhower, Leahy, and even Truman himself be proscribed? It is as if the plane that dropped the atomic bomb were an artifact akin to a kettle or a wedding dress, which required only some donor-provided information about its original usage.[7]

Fallout

What are the larger meanings, and likely consequences, of the battle over the *Enola Gay*? The victors have suggested their own answers to these questions. Newt Gingrich told the National Governors' Association, "The *Enola Gay* fight was a fight, in effect, over the reassertion by most Americans that they're sick and tired of being told by some cultural elite that they ought to be ashamed of their country." The editorial page of the *Wall Street Journal*, that GHQ of reaction, proclaimed it a triumph for the public, which had successfully "stuck its snoot inside the sanctums tended lo these many years by the historians."

This is faux-populist hogwash. In truth, this generation of historians and curators has thrown open the historical tent flaps, and embraced the experience of a far broader range of Americans than had ever before been represented in museums. Just as opinion polls belie right-wing claims that public broadcasting is an elite-only enterprise, so too the vast number of citizens flocking to public historical presentations (far more than attend professional sports events) contradict claims that historians are out of touch with the larger culture.

The people packing into history museums, local historical societies, preserved historic places and National Park Service sites are drawn in part by the novel presence of their forebears' voices and stories. Not only women and people of color are now depicted extensively but vast numbers of white males as well—the farmers and miners, sailors and steelworkers, clerks and professionals who had never before been deemed of sufficient stature to warrant inclusion in the marble mausoleums stuffed with the portraits and possessions of "historically correct" statesmen and entrepreneurs. At long last the American past is as crowded, diverse, contentious, and fascinating as is the American present.

Conservative cant about liberating the masses from political correctness is more than merely misleading. The only "PC" displayed in the *Enola Gay* affair was the prior censorship that shut down the real exhibition and barred people from judging it for themselves. It was bad enough watching the show get throttled; it is insufferable to hear the censors whine about their powerlessness. If this Orwellian recasting of suppression as liberation is not rejected, if the right is allowed to frame the issue this way, the Smithsonian's humbling may herald further repression.

There are two ways so-called conservatives might try to expunge the scholarship they detest, or at least keep it bottled up inside the academy.

One is to gut governmental funding. Just as Republican Congresspeople have invited business lobbyists to the legislative drafting tables, the abolition of NEH and the National Endowment of the Arts and National Public Radio and Corporation for Public Broadcasting will make public history programming, like access to the airwaves, dependent on corporate funders. This will further narrow the range of acceptable historical presentations (few such enterprises will care to be identified with controversial issues), or lead to puff pieces like the histories of transport, energy, and food that Disney "imagineers" crafted for General Motors, Exxon, and Kraft at EPCOT.[8]

But for all the new elite's libertarian professions about reducing the power of big government, they seem drawn to authoritarian solutions. In the case of the Air and Space Museum, congresspeople laid down an official historical "line" and demanded the firing of curators who did not toe it. Gingrich himself believes our ailing culture can be cured through state intervention, "first of all by the people appointed to the Smithsonian board." Regent Sam Johnson—Newt's first cultural commissar—agrees completely that "this Congress has an opportunity to change the face of America," and makes clear that his goal is "to get patriotism back into the Smithsonian."

Suppression follows all too logically from such premises. If traitors have seized the nation's cultural bastions, it is essential to root them out. The *Wall Street Journal* professes amazement that "the history profession pushed its 'new history' this far without challenge," and seeks to terminate the enterprise forthwith. Historians "fear that one set of assumptions is simply going to be imposed by fiat in place of their own," the *Journal* notes. "That would be unfortunate, we guess. But we do not plan to feel very sorry for these academics. . . ."

The new expurgators are busily scrutinizing the "history textbooks, curricula and museum displays" that John Leo believes have become "carriers of the broad assault against American and Western culture." An outfit calling itself the American Textbook Council damned Paul Boyer's update of Merle Curti's classic history survey for, among other things, pointing out the achievements of environmentalists. John Leo blasted the same study using the now time-dishonored technique of counting up biographical references and declaring white male faces insufficiently in evidence. Lynne Cheney censured a textbook by Gary Nash, former president of the Organization of American Historians and codirector of the history standards project, for dwelling on McCarthyism and Watergate, and being "gloomier than the story of the United States ought to be."

Even that nemesis of gloom, the Walt Disney Company, got its corporate wrist slapped by the new censorians. When Disney's America, the proposed history theme park, announced it would "not take a Pollyanna view" of the American past and would even evoke the experience of slavery, conservative apparatchik William Kristol warned: "If you're going to have a schlocky version of American history, it should at least be a schlocky, patriotic and heroic version," rather than something "politically correct," making "suitable bows to all oppressed groups."

Though the new nabobs have so far restricted themselves to a relatively niggling negativism, we should not underestimate how fast and how far things could slide. Although the United States has never had a state ministry of culture to dictate historical "lines," we have had plenty of private vigilantes patrolling our cultural institutions to ensure they promoted "patriotic" perspectives. In 1925 the American Legion declared that history textbooks "must inspire the children with patriotism" and "speak chiefly of success"; and the organization expended considerable energy during subsequent decades—especially in the 1950s—demanding that intellectuals it deemed un-American be muzzled or fired.

There are disturbing signs that this rough beast has been waked again. *Air Classics*, a popular magazine for aviation buffs, has been inspired by the November 1994 elections—which proved "Americans are taking control of their government . . . and their institutions"—to set the Smithsonian in its gun sights. It aims to "oust the revisionists who want to forever change history in favor of the enemy," and to establish a permanent committee to "constantly monitor the NASM, and similar institutions to stop a repeat of their nearly successful treachery."[9]

Such assaults, even if restricted to the rhetorical, can lead to museological self-censorship. The NASM has already put off its Vietnam exhibition, and across the mall, at the National Museum of American History, curators worry openly that fallout from the *Enola Gay* affair will contaminate future exhibitions. "Once it's known that Air and Space sat down to a line-by-line review of the script with the American Legion," said one, "Who's next? The Christian Coalition."

Yet it will not do to overstate the degree of danger. Serious obstacles confront those who would revive a full-rigged McCarthyism. For one thing the Cold War is over. The absence of an external communist menace makes it harder to demonize internal opponents. Indeed, the thawing of controls on the practice of history in Russia and Eastern Europe provides an embarrassing counterpoint to newfound U.S. government interest in policing the past. The same issue of the *New York Times* that reported four score congresspeople had called for the firing of "defiant" curators also reported that Polish historians "have suddenly begun to savor the new-found freedom to examine and write about their country's history as they see it. . . ." Further loosening of ideological bonds abroad will hinder their imposition at home.

In the case of the *Enola Gay*, Japan served as an acceptable substitute for the Evil Empire. Attacks on the exhibition gained strength and plausibility from Japan's egregious approach to its past. Americans (and Asians) had been rightfully indignant at the cabinet ministers, educators, and curators who for decades downplayed or denied Japan's record of aggression, in sharp contrast to Germany's willingness to apologize for the criminal activities of its fascist state. The Hiroshima Peace Memorial Museum presented its city and country solely as martyrs and victims, as if the war had begun the day the bomb was dropped. This allowed critics to charge that National Air and Space—which was to have borrowed artifacts from the Hiroshima Museum—shared (or had been ensnared by) its lenders' politics.[10]

But those politics had begun to change. Under pressure from internal critics, particularly socialist and pacifist groups, Japan had taken significant steps toward accepting responsibility for launching the war and committing atrocities. Historians like Professor Yoshiaki Yoshimi, by irrefutably proving that Korean "comfort women" had been forced to service the Imperial Army, prodded the government into reversing its denial of responsibility. Leading intellectuals and politicians (including the Socialist Prime Minister Tomiichi Murayama) called for a Parliamentary apology to the Asian countries Japan invaded. Although this met with vehement opposition from a coalition of conservative parties, bureaucrats and business leaders, a 1994 poll found the Japanese people believed 4 to 1 that their country had not adequately compensated the citizens of conquered nations.[11]

In Hiroshima itself, recently elected Mayor Takashi Hiraoka argued "that when we think about the bomb, we should think about the war, too." Overcoming opposition from groups like the Great Japan Patriots Party, he won installation of new exhibitry in June 1994, just as the *Enola Gay* affair was heating up, which described in detail the city's role in the war effort.[12]

This makes the Smithsonian's cancellation particularly ironic, with the Americans (under pressure from the right) refusing to reflect on the past just as the Japanese (under pressure from the left) were beginning to confront it. Ironic and unfortunate, in that closing down a public historical enterprise that transcended narrow nationalist interpretations muffed an opportunity to bind up old war wounds and reconcile former enemies. Still, if Japan continues along this "revisionist" path, it will be harder for American xenophobes to replicate a triumph which, in any event, was rooted in singular circumstances. And while Japan may be a tough competitor, it is a capitalist competitor, and an ally to boot: It will not be as easy to (as it were) "yellow-bait" intellectuals as it once was to "red-bait" them.

Critics of mainstream academic and public historians face a different kind of problem: You can not fight something with nothing. It is clear what the new censorians do not like—though Gingrich affixes his "counterculture" and "socialist" labels so indiscriminately that his Enemies List lacks the nice precision of Nixon's. What is not so clear is what they would put in place of the historical edifice they seek to tear down.

Most insist history should be heroic. "I think our kids need heroes," says Lynne Cheney. "I think that they need models of greatness to help them aspire." But apart from the fact that the only heroes the right deems worthy are those already enshrined in the traditional pantheon—the Harriet Tubmans in our past do not seem to cut the mustard—trumpeting great deeds is not much of a substitute for serious analysis of the nation's historical development.[13]

Nor is "patriotic" history, not that it is clear exactly what this means. From Matthew Hoffman's wistful recollection in the *Wall Street Journal* of the days when the Smithsonian stuck to "unapologetic celebration," it would appear that they long for unqualified boosterism. Now it is completely appropriate to insist that hard-won American accomplishments, like the steady expansion of democratic and constitutional government, be fully recounted in any full-scale historical reckoning. As indeed they are in the works of current practitioners; despite conservative canards, the *History Standards* pay them rich tribute. But does "patriotism" require striking from the public record all instances where practice fails to live up to preachment? Is their slogan, "Triumphs sí, tragedies no?" Are we to return to the see-no-evil days when Colonial Williamsburg, Inc., could present its eighteenth-century town without mentioning that over 50 percent of its residents were slaves? I suspect most Americans want their historians to pursue the truth, not generate feel-good fantasies. As Secretary Heyman said when he was still resisting closure, it is not the Smithsonian's job "simply to offer a romantic portrait of the nation's past; Hollywood and Disney do that quite well."

What academics have going for them, despite the cartoon characterizations their opponents bruit about, is the immense body of scholarly work they have put together over the past generation. It will be difficult (though not impossible) for opponents to vault over it and sport about in fields of mid-nineteenth century pieties. Nor will the museums that have so successfully quarried this mine of information and analysis be easily driven back to decontextualized displays of the material culture of a privileged few.

If future *Enola Gay* debacles are to be avoided, however, museums will have to be smarter and tougher than they have ever been before. If the National Air and Space Museum can be faulted for anything, it is underestimating the tenacity and tactics of its likely opponents, and not realizing it had *enemies*. "We've been extremely outclassed," admitted NASM spokesman Mike Fetters in September 1994. "Had we known how intense the AFA's efforts would be, we'd have moved a bit more promptly and aggressively to get our information distributed to veterans, the media, and Congress."

The way to forestall such disasters is not to retreat into controversy-free blandness; given the current climate, that is probably impossible anyway. Museum planners should instead routinely think through a show's potential political impact. They should identify groups that might be affected by, or have a particular interest in, an exhibition. Once identified, the institution should seek out and, where feasible, engage these groups in authentic dialogue.

Museums, including NASM, have done a lot of this in recent years. But it has been relatively easy so far. Curators have mostly been building bridges to sympathetic constituencies—women, African Americans, Native Americans, and white working-class ethnic communities that shared the goal of making museums more diverse and democratic.

In the future political impact assessments will have to identify potentially harsher critics as well. If a projected exhibition on the history of urban crime intends to flag handgun availability as a problem, it would be wise to anticipate National Rifle Association objections. If designers of a show on the history of public health plan to call attention to preventable lung cancer, they had best be prepared for the wrath of the tobacco industry. Treatments of prostitution, pollution, civil rights, birth control, political corruption, homosexuality, welfare, urban planning, historic preservation, deindustrialization, foreign relations—almost anything, in truth, that tries to set contemporary issues in historical perspective—can be expected to outrage some part of the populace, somewhere along the political spectrum. Should such critics be declared "stakeholders" and given an automatic veto? I think not. There are better alternatives available, options whose feasibility have been tested in practice, options which can enhance rather than foreclose discussion.

One approach is to clearly label a given show as embodying the point-of-view of the curators. It would be presented as the analogue of an op-ed piece, or a column, rather than a news story. The authors-curators could be clearly introduced up front, with pictures and bios. They could lay out, in videotaped prefaces, what they are seeking to accomplish. This would undercut the notion that exhibitions are the products of omniscient and invisible narrators. It would also allow curatorial convictions to be distinguished from those of the institution, as is done routinely on television in disclaimers that state that the views presented are not necessarily those of the broadcaster. At the end of the exhibit, moreover, both critics and visitors could be given the opportunity of commenting on the presentation, using media formats ranging from simple three-by-five cards tacked on a wall to video-taped snippets playing on monitors.

Another strategy would be to incorporate differing perspectives into the exhibition itself. Museums should not duck debate but welcome it. Fascinating shows could be fashioned by pitting alternative perspectives one against the another: creationists versus evolutionists, developers versus preservationists, advocates versus opponents of affirmative action.

In most cases proponents will settle for being participants in a conversation. But what happens if they will not? What happens if the NRA insists that all references to gun control as a desirable response to urban crime be deleted? What happens if fundamentalists object to having their divinely sanctioned beliefs paired with those of secular-humanist Darwinians? What to do when the Air Force Association denounces the very notion of laying out differing perspectives on the Hiroshima bombing as being inherently unpatriotic? How to respond when the very idea of presenting controversies is rejected as controversial?

Here, I think, it is essential for individual institutions to be able to refer to standards of professional rights and responsibilities, fashioned by the museological community at large. These should be akin to but not identical with standards of academic freedom in that they would apply to institutions, not individuals. A public historical organization might be expected to make use of up-to-date scholarship, follow appropriate rules for gathering evidence in its own research, provide ways for critics and visitors to respond to exhibitions, fairly present a range of opinions on controversial issues, and offer over time a reasonable variety of political perspectives. If museums adhered to such procedures, they would be guaranteed the right to mount whatever exhibitions they chose to, free from political interference.

The standards should state the principles that underlie such a call for relative autonomy, and justify its value to the larger society. Curators are educators of a special kind. They have particular responsibilities to listen to their communities. But they also have valuable skills and information to contribute to that community and a responsibility to pursue the truth. If they carry out their civic and professional obligations in a responsible manner, it is in the best interest of that larger community that they be protected from intimidation.

If and when drafters get around to hammering out principles defending freedom of historical enquiry, they might consider four sentences from a *New York Times* editorial of 30 January 1995, responding to attacks on the Smithsonian. "To reduce the complexities or painful ambiguities of the issue to slogans or historical shorthand is wrong. . . . To let politicians and groups with a particular interest frame the discussion and determine the conclusion is worse. . . . The real betrayal of American tradition would be to insist on a single version of history or to make it the property of the state or any group. . . . Historians and museums of history need to be insulated from any attempt to make history conform to a narrow ideological or political interest."

The existence of such a public historical charter might well bolster the position of beleaguered institutions. But then again, it might not. Paper rights are one thing, power realities another. What could a museum do if it played by the rules and still came under attack?

In part it would have to take responsibility for its own self-defense. It should have analyzed in advance who an exhibit's potential allies and enemies were likely to be, and thought through a contingency plan for enlisting the former and fending off the latter. Such a blueprint should include an agenda for action, right on down to identifying the media experts and friendly politicians who could be enlisted at short notice to help explain the institution's position to press and public alike.

But isolated institutions can do only so much. There must be a commitment by the larger museum community to help out. An attack on one museum's freedom of expression should be seen as an attack on all. Most Americans believe museums are dedicated to the pursuit and display of truth. They enjoy a rare reputation among our cultural and political establishments, and any capitulation to political or commercial pressures tarnishes that image. If one institution yields to noisy minorities, or even perceived majorities, the hard-won credibility of all museums will quickly unravel, for who can sustain confidence in institutions whose exhibitions have been purchased or imposed?

In the event of future *Enola Gays*, professional bodies should launch their own investigations. If such inquiries find that an institution has operated in compliance with generally accepted standards, and been subjected to unwarranted harassment, then the entire community should speak out vigorously on its behalf. The museum world should also forge alliances with other cultural institutions—like public libraries, schools, universities, e-mail networks, and publishers of print and electronic media—who now routinely come under fire. Jane Alexander, head of the National Endowment for the Arts, has set a splendid example by traveling to all fifty states and mobilizing grass roots arts groups. If, as I believe, museums have developed and retain a substantial reservoir of popular support, they might consider mobilizing their constituents in defense of freedom of expression.

If all this fails, and we are faced with more shuttered galleries, we may have to consider borrowing methods other dissidents have found useful. The Air and Space story did not end with the opening of the amputated exhibit. An alliance of scholars, curators and peace activists engaged in demonstrations, teach-ins, and a counter-exhibition, a sort of *musée de refusé*. If the shutdown galvanizes the public historical community into further and concerted action, then perhaps the battle of the *Enola Gay*, which now seems a setback, may prove in the end to have been a victory.

Notes

This essay was originally undertaken in late 1994, at the behest of *Museum News*, and, shortly thereafter, *Museums Journal* (its English counterpart). Once I discovered the dimensions of the affair I decided to write it up as a chapter for this book. Although it grew too large for either magazine, both have printed excerpts from it, and the *Radical Historians' Newsletter* reproduced virtually the entire piece.

My thanks to those who agreed to be interviewed: Barton J. Bernstein, Kai Bird, Tom Crouch, Stanley Goldberg, Richard Hallion, Martin Harwit, Akira Iriye, Robert Lifton, Arthur Molella, Gary Nash, Michael Neufeld, Michael Sherry, Martin Sherwin, Barbara Clark Smith, and several former colleagues of Professor Gingrich at West Georgia College.

Thanks also to Mike Fetters of NASM, who was endlessly helpful, and Steve Aubin of the Air Force Association, who provided useful information.

Thanks, too, to readers of earlier drafts: Barton Bernstein, Kai Bird, Eric Foner, Frances Goldin, I. Michael Heyman, Michael Kammen, Richard Kohn, Harry Magdoff, Jane Milliken, and Jon Wiener. But especially to Ted Burrows, Hope Cooke, Edward T. Linenthal, Martin Sherwin, and Alfred Young, whose criticisms and encouragements were of the highest caliber and are deeply appreciated.

1. Leahy's judgement in 1950 was: "It is my opinion that the use of this barbarous weapon at Hiroshima and Nagasaki was of no material success in our war against Japan," as "the Japanese were already defeated and ready to surrender because of the effective sea blockade and the success-

ful bombing with conventional weapons." Eisenhower asserted in 1963 that Japan "was seeking some way to surrender with a minimum loss of 'face' " and that "it wasn't necessary to hit them with that awful thing."

2. Arnold, Spaatz, and LeMay opposed dropping the atomic bomb except as part of an invasion. Arnold pressed these views as late as the Potsdam Conference in late July 1945, but in the end deferred to General Marshall. After the war, Arnold said that "atomic bomb or no atomic bomb, the Japanese were already on the verge of collapse," and LeMay believed that "even without the atomic bomb and the Russian entry into the war, Japan would have surrendered in two weeks." Some think these judgements stemmed from fear that superbombs would torpedo the generals' dreams of a postwar independent air force with seventy wings and thousands of fliers.
3. The group included: Barton J. Bernstein of Stanford, a student of nuclear policy; Stanley Goldberg, a scholar studying General Groves and his Manhattan Project; Akira Iriye of Harvard, a historian of Japanese American relations; Richard Rhodes, author of *The Making of the Atomic Bomb;* Martin Sherwin, Dartmouth historian and author of *A World Destroyed: The Atomic Bomb and the Grand Alliance;* Victor Bond, a medical doctor at Brookhaven National Laboratory; Edward T. Linenthal, student of American attitudes to war memorials; Dr. Richard Hallion, Air Force Historian; and, contrary to claims that curators consulted no one with actual wartime experience, Edwin Bearss, chief historian of National Park Service, a decorated Marine veteran, present at Pearl Harbor, wounded at Guadalcanal, and a strong supporter of the script. This group met only once, although they were also consulted, over succeeding months, on a seriatim basis.
4. Newt's immobilized past stands in stark contrast to his vision of a flexible future. He seems oblivious to the contradiction, perhaps because he thinks he needs a fixed base from which to launch his "third wave" revolution. But this is to deprive himself of the historical tools that might help him understand (and shape) the way a society moves from one era to another.
5. It is hard to imagine that if Newt had ever actually stepped foot in the National Air and Space Museum he would not have been pleased with the WWI exhibition his allies so detested. Gingrich claims as a transformational defining moment his visit, at age 15, to the Verdun battlefield. There he peered through the windows of an ossuary containing the bones of one-hundred-thousand unidentified bodies. "I can still feel the sense of horror and reality which overcame me then," he wrote in his 1984 book *Window of Opportunity*. "It is the driving force which pushed me into history and politics and molded my life." The WWI exhibition features a giant photograph of the Verdun ossuary. Pity he is intent on denying others even an echo of the experience he found so moving and instructive.

6. President Clinton, whose past and present relations with the military left him in no position to challenge the decision, observed with his usual caution that while "academic freedom" was an issue here, he "nonetheless felt that some of the concerns expressed by veterans groups and others had merit."
7. Not surprisingly, after previewing the exhibition on 21 June Tibbets wrote Heyman he was "pleased and proud" of it. It simply presented the "basic facts," he argued preposterously, without any "attempt to persuade anyone about anything." This happy outcome, Tibbets added, "demonstrates the merits and the positive influences of management"—whose firm hand was again in evidence on opening day, when twenty-one demonstrators with the *Enola Gay* Action Coalition were hauled away by a U.S. Park Police SWAT team.
8. Newt's a trailblazer here, too. Of the wealthy donors who picked up the six-hundred-thousand dollars first year costs of his "Renewing American Civilization" lectures, those contributing over $25,000 were "invited to participate in the course development process"—giving a new twist to the notion of a "free market in ideas."
9. In June 1995 the Bradbury Science Museum in Los Alamos mounted an exhibition on the atomic bomb prepared by a Santa Fe peace group. In featuring photos of ground devastation it infuriated veterans and former Manhattan Project workers. Not having seen the exhibit, I can not comment on its interpretive perspective. But it is a chilling sign of NASM fallout that Harold Agnew, former director of the Los Alamos National Laboratory (which owns the museum), wrote a veterans' group that if the show was not changed, staff members' jobs might be at risk. "We got rid of the Smithsonian curator over the *Enola Gay* fiasco," he said. "Hopefully the Bradbury staff will understand."
10. "They are bending over backwards it looks like to accommodate the Japanese," said Sam Johnson. Ironically, curator Tom Crouch was on record as being "really bothered, angered, by the way that the Japanese find it so difficult to put wartime issues in real context. Their view is to portray themselves as victims." Crouch, however, saw parallels in this country. "As I listen to the folks who criticize this [exhibit], I hear something similar to that. There's real discomfort about looking at destruction on the ground. . . . I hear critics saying, 'Don't tell part of the story.' They want to stop the story when the bomb leaves the bomb bay."
11. A "Japan Committee to Appeal for World Peace '95," composed of scholars and cultural workers, called for an "apology and compensation for damages to the Asian peoples whom we victimized," and urged the Japanese government and Diet to "clearly articulate the government's self-reflection on Japan's responsibility for past colonial rule as well as the Asia-Pacific War. . . ."

   The political establishment teetered back and forth on this issue.

Prime Minister Murayama went to Beijing in spring 1995 and said: "I recognize anew that Japan's actions, including aggression and colonial rule, at one time in our history caused unbearable suffering and sorrow for many people in your country and other Asian neighbors." He also wrote a scroll: "I face up to history."

The Japanese nationalist right did not. Shigeto Nagano, justice minister and former chief of staff of the army, insisted in May 1995 that the massacre of hundreds of thousands of Chinese at Nanking in 1937 was a "fabrication," and he reaffirmed that Japan, in invading Asian countries, had been "liberating" them from Western colonial powers.

On 12 May 1995, however, a Tokyo High Court ruling of the previous October was affirmed, thus sanctioning Japanese historian Saburo Ienaga's thirty-one year struggle against the Education Ministry for whitewashing schoolbook accounts of the massacre. The court also revoked the Ministry's theretofore accepted right to determine historical "truth."

On 6 June 1995, the right-wing Liberal Democratic Party forced a compromise on the Parliamentary apology front. A resolution carried the lower house expressing remorse for causing "unbearable pain to people abroad, particularly in Asian countries." But the wording was ambiguous enough to allow for varying interpretations (thus "hansei" could mean "remorse," or merely "reflection"). The upper house refused even to consider such a resolution.

A week later, on 14 June, the government responded by establishing a fund to provide medical and social welfare assistance to former comfort women. Although it fell short of what some of the women had demanded, it was accompanied by a statement of remorse and apology.

Finally, Prime Minister Murayama, on 15 August, during fiftieth anniversary commemorations of the war's end, made the most explicit declaration yet. Noting the damage and suffering caused by Japan he said: "I regard, in a spirit of humility, these irrefutable facts of history, and express here once again my feelings of deep remorse and state my heartfelt apology." "Our task," he added, "is to convey to the younger generations the horrors of war, so that we never repeat the errors in our history."

12. Similarly, Tokyo's Metropolitan Edo-Tokyo Museum mounted a major exhibition for the March 1995 fiftieth anniversary of the city's being firebombed. Though retaining a focus on domestic suffering, it included information on 1930s and 1940s militarism. (Video clips showed Japanese bombers attacking Chongquing.)
13. More irony: A small industry has sprung up in Japan that caters to youth "searching for heroes in an uncertain world," by producing books, comics, and computer games (like Commander's Decision) that rewrite World War II history in Japan's favor, granting it retroactive victory, while omitting all mention of wartime atrocities.

Bibliographical Notes

The basic texts are the five exhibition label scripts. The first was: National Air and Space Museum, "The Crossroads: the End of World War II, the Atomic Bomb, and the Origins of the Cold War," 12 January 1994. All subsequent versions were entitled "The Last Act: The Atomic Bomb and the End of World War II," and were issued on 31 May 1994, 31 August 1994, 3 October 1994, 26 October 1994. For Harwit's proposed changes to the last draft, see label copy: "Invasion of Japan—At What Cost," 3 January 1995. See also NASM, "Exhibition Planning Document," July 1993. For a published version of the initial script see *Judgment at the Smithsonian*, edited by Philip Nobile (New York, 1995).

For Correll's corpus see John T. Correll, "War Stories at Air and Space," *AIR FORCE Magazine*, April 1994; *idem.*, "The Decision That Launched the *Enola Gay*," *ibid.*, April 1994; *idem.*, "The Smithsonian Plan for the *Enola Gay*: A Report on the Revisions," *AFA Update*, 28 June 1994; *idem.*, "Museum Promises to Change *Enola Gay* Exhibition," *ibid.*, October 1994; *idem.*, "The Three Doctors and the *Enola Gay*," *ibid.*, November 1994; *idem.*, "Airplanes in the Mist," *ibid.*, December 1994; *idem.*, "Air and Space Museum Hit by Academic Backlash," *ibid.*, January 1995.

For media critics of the exhibition see Hugh Sidey, "War and Remembrance," *Time*, 23 May 1994; Jeff Jacoby, "Smithsonian Drops a Bomb in World War II Exhibit," *Boston Globe*, 16 August 1994; Charles Krauthammer, "World War II, Revised, Or, How We Bombed Japan out of Racism and Spite," *The Washington Post*, 19 August 1994; "War and the Smithsonian" *Wall Street Journal*, 29 August 1994; Lance Morrow, "Hiroshima and the Time Machine," *Time*, 19 September 1994; Ken Ringle, "At Ground Zero: Two Views of History Collide Over Smithsonian A-Bomb Exhibit," *The Washington Post*, 26 September 1994; Jonathan Yardley, "Dropping a Bomb of an Idea," *The Washington Post*, 10 October 1994; John Leo, The National Museums of PC," *U.S. News & World Report*, 10 October 1994; *idem.* "The PC Attack on Heroism: National Air and Space Museum Exhibit on World War I Pilots," *U.S. News & World Report*, 31 October 1994; Eugene L. Meyer, "Revisionism, Revised," *Bulletin of the Atomic Scientists* 50, no. 6 (12 November 1994); Robert P. Newman, "What New Consensus," *The Washington Post*, 30 November 1994; Editorial, "The Smithsonian Changes Course," *The Washington Post*, 1 February 1995; *Air Classics* (April 1995).

Just as this manuscript headed off for production, a splendid and devastating analysis of press treatment of the affair arrived. See Tony Capaccio and Uday Mohan, "Missing the Target," *American Journalism Review* (July/August 1995), 19–26.

For Richard Hallion's laudatory comments and moderate suggestions for revision, penned before he became a leading critic, see Richard Hallion and Herman Wolk, "Comments on Script, 'The Crossroads' . . . ," February 1994.

For the American Legion's position see Brian D. Smith, "Rewriting *Enola Gay*'s History," *The American Legion* 137, no. 5 (November 1994); Hubert R. Dagley II, "We're Making Sure that Smithsonian Corrects *Enola Gay* Exhibit," *Washington Times*, 14 October 1994; Julie A. Rhoad, "The Proposed *Enola Gay* Exhibit, Is It an Accurate Portrayal of History?" *American Legion Auxiliary NATIONAL NEWS* (January–February 1995).

See also Statement Offered by Brigadier General Paul W. Tibbets at the Airmen Memorial Museum, 8 June 1994.

For the history of National Air and Space Museum see Establishment of a National Air Museum, *Hearings before the Committee on the Library*, House of Representatives, 79th Congress, Second Session on H.R. 5144, To Establish a National Air Museum, 13 February 1946; U.S. Congress, House, Subcommittee on Library and Memorials, Committee on House Administration, *Smithsonian Institution: General Background*, 91st Cong., 2d session, 21 July 1970; Howard Learner, *White Paper on Science Museums* (Washington, D.C., 1979); Michal McMahon, "The Romance of Technological Progress: A Critical Review of the National Air and Space Museum," *Technology and Culture* (1981); Walter J. Boyne, *The Aircraft Treasures of Silver Hill* (New York, 1982); Samuel A. Batzli, "From Heroes to Hiroshima: The National Air and Space Museum Adjusts Its Point of View," *Technology and Culture* (1990); Arthur P. Molella, "The Museum That Might Have Been: The Smithsonian's National Museum of Engineering and Industry," *Technology and Culture* (1991); C. D. B. Bryan, *The National Air and Space Museum*, second edition (New York, 1992).

On the World War I show, see the NASM publication, Dominick A. Pisano et al., *Legend, Memory and the Great War in the Air* (Washington, D.C., 1992). For commentary see Michael Killan, "Grounded in Reality: Exhibition finds the Mythic WWI Ace was a Flight of Fancy," *Chicago Tribune*, 26 November 1991; Edwards Park, "Around the Mall and Beyond," *Smithsonian* (December 1991); Hank Burchard, "Plane Truths During WWI," *The Washington Post*, 22 November 1991.

See also Daniel S Greenberg, "Smithsonian Space Museum Exhibits Add Truth to Labeling," *Houston Post*, 4 December 1990; "Notes and Comment: SS-20 Missile at National Air and Space Museum," *New Yorker*, 13 August 1990.

For statements from the museum staff see Robert McCormick Adams, "A Smithsonian Artifact for 39 Years, the *Enola Gay* is Still a Long Way from Being Put on Permanent Exhibition," *Smithsonian* (July 1988); *idem.* to Martin Harwit, 17 July 1993; Michael Kernan, "Smithsonian Secretary Robert McCormick Adams Looks to New Horizons," *Smithsonian* (September 1994).

Martin Harwit, "Comments on Crossroads," [Internal Memorandum], 16

April 1994; "Harwit Responds," *AIR FORCE Magazine* (May 1994); *idem.*, "The *Enola Gay:* A Nation's, and a Museum's, Dilemma," *The Washington Post*, 7 August 1994; *idem.*, "*Enola Gay* and a Nation's Memories," *Air & Space* (August/September 1994).

I. Michael Heyman, "Smithsonian Perspectives," *Smithsonian* (October 1994); *idem.*, "Letter to the Editor," *U.S. News and World Report*, 31 October 1994; *idem.*, Transcript of Remarks at National Press Club Luncheon, 23 February 1995.

Tom Crouch to Martin Harwit, "A Response to the Secretary," [Internal Memorandum], 21 July 1993.

For the official history of the AFA, see James H. Straubel, *Crusade for Airpower: The Story of the Air Force Association* (Washington, D.C., 1982).

On the wider History War see George F. Will, "The Real State of the Union," *The Washington Post*, 26 January 1995; "The Trend of History," *Wall Street Journal*, 31 January 1995; Matthew C. Hoffman, "Politics Come to the Smithsonian," *Wall Street Journal*, 24 June 1994; Rush Limbaugh, *See, I Told You So* (New York, 1993).

On Gingrich: Newt Gingrich, with David Drake and Marianne Gingrich, *Window of Opportunity: A Blueprint for the Future* (New York, 1984); "Lessons of American History," *Renewing American Civilization*, Cassette number 6, 12 February 1994; Fred Barnes, "Revenge of the Squares: Newt Gingrich and Pals Rewrite the '60s," *New Republic*, 13 March 1995; Dale Russakoff, "He Knew What He Wanted," *The Washington Post*, 18 December 1994; Dale Russakoff and Dan Balz, "After Political Victory, a Personal Revolution," *The Washington Post*, 19 December 1994; Dan Balz and Charles R. Babcock, "Gingrich, Allies Made Waves and Impression," *The Washington Post*, 20 December 1994; Garry Wills, "The Visionary," *New York Review of Books*, 23 March 1995; Elliot Krieger, "Gingrich Embraces Vision of Brown Professor," *Providence Journal-Bulletin*, April 16, 1995.

On Jeffrey see *New York Times*, 8 January, 10 January 1994; "Christina Jeffrey Responds," *The Washington Post*, 24 January 1995; Jeffrey, "Playing Politics with History," *Wall Street Journal*, 28 March 1995.

On the proposed history standards: National Center for History in the Schools, *National Standards for United States History* (Los Angeles, 1994); Lynne V. Cheney, "The End of History," *Wall Street Journal*, 20 October 1994; Gary B. Nash, "National Standards in U.S. History: A Note from the President," *Organization of American Historians Newsletter* (November 1994); Carol Gluck, "History According to Whom?" *New York Times*, 19 November 1994; Jon Wiener, "History Lesson," *The New Republic*, 2 January 1995; Page Putnam Miller, "History Standards Under Attack in Senate," *National Coordinating Committee for the Promotion of History Update*, 18 January 1995; Frank Rich, "Eating Her Offspring," *New York Times*, 26 January 1995; Todd Gitlin, "History Standards," *New York Observer*, 30 January 1995; John Leo, "History Standards are Bunk," *U.S. News and World Report*, 6 February 1995;

"Maligning the History Standards," *New York Times*, 13 February 1995; Frank Rich, "Cheney Dumbs Down," *ibid.*, 26 February 1995; Lynne Cheney, "Mocking America at U.S. Expense," *New York Times*, 10 May 1995; Diane Ravitch, "Revise, but Don't Abandon, the History Standards, *Chronicle of Higher Education*, 17 February 1995.

For chronologies and reports of the controversy see John R. Dichtl, "A Chronology of the Smithsonian's 'Last Act'," *Organization of American Historians Newsletter* (November 1994); John Kifner, "Hiroshima: Controversy that Refuses to Die," *New York Times*, 31 January 1995; Arnita Jones and Page Miller, "*Enola Gay* Controversy Continues," *Organization of American Historians Newsletter* (February 1995); "A Museum in Crisis," *U.S. News and World Report*, 13 February 1995.

For critical commentary, start with the works of Edward T. Linenthal, an original Advisory Board member and public history scholar: "Historical Cleansing at the National Air and Space Museum: The *Enola Gay* Controversy," unpublished paper, December 1994; Edward T. Linenthal, "Can Museums Achieve a Balance Between Memory and History?" *The Chronicle of Higher Education*, 10 February 1995; Edward T. Linenthal, "Reflections on the *Enola Gay* Controversy at the National Air and Space Museum," in *History Wars: The Enola Gay and Other Battles for the American Past*, edited by Tom Engelhardt and Edward T. Linenthal (New York, 1996).

For other important assessments, see Stanley Goldberg, "An Exhibit is Not a Book—It's Not a Movie Either," unpublished paper, 1994 (Goldberg, also an advisor, resigned in protest over NASM's later script revisions); Gar Alperovitz, "Questioning Hiroshima," *Boston Globe*, 20 August 1994; "The Smithsonian and the Bomb," *New York Times*, 5 September 1994; Kai Bird, "The Curators Cave In," *New York Times*, 9 October 1994; Karen J. Winkler, "Who Owns History?" *The Chronicle of Higher Education*, 20 January 1995; Barton Bernstein, "Hiroshima Rewritten," *New York Times*, 31 January 1995; Joel Achenbach, "The Pablum Museum," *The Washington Post*, 1 February 1995; Kai Bird, "Silencing History" *The Nation*, 20 February 1995; Lonnie G. Bunch, "Fighting the Good Fight: Museums in an Age of Uncertainty," *Museum News* (March/April 1995).

Tony Capaccio contributed a nice piece of investigative journalism in " 'Truman' Author Errs on Japan Invasion Casualty Memo," *Defense Week*, 11 October 1994. When pressed for contemporary evidence of high casualty estimates, AFA spokesman Steve Aubin turned to Air Force Historian Hallion, who turned to David McCullough's *Truman*. McCullough cited a memo of 4 June 1945, written by General Thomas Handy of Marshall's staff, saying five-hundred-thousand to one million lives would be saved, "which shows that figures of such magnitude were then in use at the highest level." But the document did not say that (as journalist Philip Nobile has pointed out). Handy had been asked by Secretary Stimson to comment on a paper from a then unnamed economist (in fact Herbert Hoover). Hoover used those figures; Handy dismissed them as "entirely too high." McCullough, in a 24 September 1994 letter to *Defense Week* acknowledged: "I made a mistake and I regret it. . . ." McCullough went on to say, quite properly, that the rightness or wrongness of the decision should not be argued or justified on the basis of such figures, though critics of the show had indeed been arguing in this vein. When informed of McCullough's error, Hallion said: "That's news to me . . . OK. That takes care of that one." None of this ever made the mainstream press.

For histories of the bombing and the air war start with the excellent summary by J. Samuel Walker, "The Decision to Use the Bomb: A Historiographical Update," *Diplomatic History* 14 (1990), 97–114.

Martin J. Sherwin, *A World Destroyed: The Atomic Bomb and the Grand Alliance* (New York, 1975); Ronald Schaffer, *Wings of Judgment: American Bombing in World War II* (New York, 1985); Ronald H. Spector, *Eagle Against the Sun: The American War with Japan* (New York, 1985); Gar Alperovitz, *Atomic Diplomacy: Hiroshima and Potsdam* (New York, 1985); John W. Dower, *War without Mercy: Race and Power in the Pacific War* (New York, 1986); Michael Sherry, *The Rise of American Air Power: The Creation of Armageddon* (New Haven, 1987); Leon V. Sigal, *Fighting to a Finish: The Politics of War Termination in the United States and Japan, 1945* (Ithaca, N.Y., 1988); John Ray Skates, *The Invasion of Japan: Alternative to the Bomb* (Columbia, S.C., 1994); Stewart L. Udall, *The Myths of August: A Personal Exploration of Our Tragic Cold War Affair with the Atom* (New York, 1994); Barton J. Bernstein, "The Atomic Bombings Reconsidered," *Foreign Affairs* 74, no. 1 (January/February 1995).

For the scholarship on the numbers issue, see Rufus E. Miles Jr., "Hiroshima: The Strange Myth of Half a Million American Lives Saved," *International Security* 10 (fall 1985), 121–40; Barton J. Bernstein, "A Postwar Myth: 500,000 Lives Saved," *Bulletin of the Atomic Scientists* 42 (June/July 1986), 38–40; Barton J. Bernstein, "Seizing the Contested Terrain of Early Nuclear History: Stimson, Conant, and their Allies Explain the Decision to Use the Atomic Bomb," *Diplomatic History* 17 (winter 1993), 35–72; James G. Hershberg, *James B. Conant: Harvard to Hiroshima and the Making of the Nuclear Age* (New York, 1993); Peter Maslowski, "Truman, the Bomb, and the Numbers Game," *MHQ: The Quarterly Journal of Military History* 7, no. 3 (spring 1995), 103–7. The Maslowski piece is in *A Special Issue: The End of the War with Japan*, which contains many other relevant articles, notably Haruko Taya Cook, "The Myth of the Saipan Suicides," which suggests the notion of a kamikaze nation that would fight suicidally to the bitter end was wildly overdrawn.

On American's skimpy knowledge of Hiroshima: Bob Herbert, "A Nation of Nitwits," *New York Times*, 1 March 1995.

On the way Japan handles its past see Ian Buruma, *The Wages of Guilt:*

Memories of War in Germany and Japan (New York, 1994); Herbert P. Bix, "How Japan and Germany Remember Their Military Pasts," *Christian Science Monitor*, 27 July 1994.

For recent developments see David E. Sanger, "Hiroshima Takes Fresh Look at Why Bomb Fell," *International Herald Tribune*, 5 August 1994; Nicholas D. Kristof, "Stoically, Japan Looks Back on the Flames of War," *New York Times*, 9 March 1995; T.R. Reid, "Japan Revising Past Role: More Aggressor, Less Victim," *The Washington Post*, 11 March 1995; Stephen Kinzer, "Confronting the Past, Germans Now Don't Flinch," *New York Times*, 1 May 1995; Nicholas D. Kristof, "Japan Expresses Regret of a Sort for the War," *New York Times*, 7 June 1995; Nicholas D. Kristof, "Japan to Pay Women Forced into Brothels," *New York Times*, 15 June 1995; Kenzaburo Oe, "Denying History Disables Japan," *New York Times*, 2 July 1995; David E. Sanger, "Coloring History Our Way," *New York Times*, 2 July 1995; Sheryl WuDunn, "Murayama Apology Stills Some Critics, But Debate Isn't Over," *International Herald Tribune*, 16 August 1995.

On the exhibition as opened see Paul W. Tibbets to I. Michael Heyman, 21 June 1995; Joel Achenbach, "*Enola Gay* Exhibit: Plane and Simple," *The Washington Post*, 28 June 1995; Lonnae O'Neal Parker, "*Enola Gay* Exhibit Opens to Protest, Mixed Reviews," *The Washington Post*, 28 June 1995; "Opening Statement of Smithsonian Secretary I. Michael Heyman," [Smithsonian Institution Press Release, 27 June 1995]; "*Enola Gay* Display opens at Smithsonian's National Air and Space Museum" [Smithsonian Institution Press Release, 28 June 1995].

On Los Alamos Museum show see *The New Mexican*, 6 June 1995.

On Polish historians "new-found freedom": *New York Times*, 25 January 1995.

On cultural vigilantism in (and over) the past see James W. Loewen, *Lies My Teacher Told Me* (New York, 1995); Ellen Schrecker, *No Ivory Tower: McCarthyism and the Universities* (New York, 1986).

I found two electronic bulletin boards extremely useful. The MUSEUM-L list (reachable at this address: LISTSERV@UNMVMA.UNM.EDU) allowed me to listen in to the interesting debate over the exhibition among museum professionals. And the WWII-L list (LISTSERV@UBVM.CC.BUFFALO.EDU) put me in touch with an extensive community of World War II veterans and buffs. (Mike Fetters of National Air and Space's Office of Public Affairs joined the list at one point, engaging critics in ongoing conversation, down in the electronic trenches). These discussion groups, like many others, archive their exchanges, and I was able to retrieve material from those months when conversations were most energetic.